Cosmic Sage

IMAOKA Shin'ichirō: Prophet of Free Religion

George M. Williams

Kindle Edition
Uniquest Publishing
2019

All proceeds will go for the support of Indigenous Hawaiian education, culture and religion at Marae Ha‘a Koa, Wai‘anae, O‘ahu, Hawai‘i

Table of Contents

Dr. IMAOKA Shin'ichirō at 105, century-old sage and prophet

Preface

"Preface. But please read it."
--quotation of Martti Larni

As IMAOKA[1] Shin'ichirō turned one hundred, his influence increased even as his life remained a mystery. He was a mirror for others to see their best and highest selves. Living as "egoless" as possible, he lived an unusual type of spirituality. His image in the mirror was less his than of the highest ideal of those who admired him. Yet, he was there.

The reason for this Preface arises from the attempt to write about a person whose spiritual practice of "egolessness" left few specifics concerning his moral and religious journey. Each chapter of IMAOKA's 106 year-long life must devise a way of finding him in those whom he assisted, in the causes or tasks that he undertook, and in the "graduations" from the "schools of life" in which he learned.

Cosmic Sage attempts to weave together IMAOKA Shin'ichirō's life story. His century-long activities and accomplishments touch upon so many topics that a reader may feel taxed to maintain interest in all of them. Those who knew him during the last 40 years of his life – for he outlived those who knew him earlier – described him with their religious ideals. Thus,

1. The family name will be written in "ALL CAPS" for Japanese individuals except as used in quotations. Honorifics such as *sensei* or *san* will be used rarely (an academic practice), except in this introductory chapter. Titles of individuals will only be used for clarity or in quotations. I hope that you, as the reader, will accept this as not being disrespectful.

IMAOKA sensei was all these: a Bodhisattva-Kami-Christian-Unitarian-sage – the Emerson of Japan. Each of these religious perspectives or evaluations saw him as their highest conception of humanity: Buddhist, Shinto, Christian, or religious radical.

Such ecumenical projections may have a basis in how he had developed. Our purpose is to find what can be learned from IMAOKA's life in the shadows of others – his activities, service, causes, life crises, values, and the thoughts found in his essays. Perhaps together these will give some insight into his moral and spiritual evolution.

Each chapter must devise a way of finding him in this backstage evidence. His essays were never put together in extended studies or elaborated systematically. Thus, his philosophy is found less in his words than in what he chose to do – as pastor, translator, educator, and crusader for interfaith understanding and cooperation.

Religious terminology is usually loaded, privileged and often prejudicial. English words like *liberal*[2] and *conservative* now have 21st century meanings. Care needs to be taken in seeing their usage in the volatile cultural period in which IMAOKA lived. The idea of "freedom" was foreign, and *jiyū* was used to convey this alien concept. *Jiyū* translated both *free* and *liberal*. *Jiyū* also encompassed all that was progressive and scientific. And politically, the word pointed to a vision of a new and modern Japan. *Jiyū* was as contradictory and radical then in Japanese as it is a cliché in English now.

IMAOKA's attention to language could merit him being compared to Emerson. Yet, time has changed the key words he used: in English, *freedom* and *religion* and in Japanese, *jiyū* and *shūkyō*. When these words entered everyday usage in the Meiji era, they were foreign and very difficult to understand. Yet, both of these

---

2. Italicized words and phrases may signal vocabulary that is special, privileged or weighted. *Freedom* is such a word-concept for IMAOKA.

words became his central concern. How could they be experienced? What were their components? Could there be freedom in religion? Each chapter of his life will unfold aspects of freedom that affected his religious journey. From his Confucian teachers he looked for an exact meaning that was true to the reality of freedom (*jiyū*). From Buddhism, especially Zen, a mixture of rational and mystical knowing would see freedom or liberation as if it were a *koan* to be experienced but not verbalized.

IMAOKA would not be guilty of simple, binary thinking (right-wrong, good-bad, true-false). He was certainly guilty of paradoxes, word-play and multiple ways of knowing. He was both a rational and a mystic. And, mystic's words and concepts often point beyond simple meanings. Freedom and religion are central in each chapter of his life.

This Preface suggests some practical strategies in reading the range of topics that span a century of his remarkable life. There are a Glossary of key terms and personalities and Timelines to help. One might read each chapter sequentially as a historical biography of one of Japan's important religious leaders. The same approach will work for the reader who is interested in a spiritual biography, learning about the religious journey of an exemplar of Japanese religion – with conversions, existential crises, moral development of character and wisdom. Appendix B summarizes some relevant studies and insights. Treasures are hidden in the footnotes for those who appreciate documentation.

Readers interested in topics of religious studies will find IMAOKA Shin'ichirō's encounters with all three Japanese religions (Buddhism, Shinto and Christianity), plus Japanese Confucianism. And that encounter is not shallow, as he worked with and was one of the influencers of an age of major cultural transition. For other readers, it is the topic of Japanese cultural transition itself, beginning in the Meiji era, that will provide insight into one of the most influential groups of the period. Collectively, the word invented for them was *yuniterian* – Japanese Unitarians, New Buddhists, liberal Shintoists, religious progressives and radicals. The chapters of Section III contain an account of their gathering at Unity Hall of the American Unitarian Mission. Their thirty-year history has gone unwritten.[3]

Readers who are wanting to know more about international interfaith dialogue and cooperation in Japan will find a wealth of information in the chapters of Section IV. IMAOKA's involvement and leadership has been honored but with little detail – again, because of his very Japanese style of leading from the shadows and out of the limelight. That is where Japanese look for true leadership. He enabled others who became better known to Westerners: Founder NIWANO Nikkyo of Risshō Kōseikai, Guji YAMAMOTO Yukitaka of Tsubaki Grand Shrine and more.

Something quite modern will be seen in IMAOKA's religious identities, maintaining multiple perspectives as a Christian, Buddhist, Shintoist, mystic, and non-theist without mixing them. The reader will come to her or his own conclusion as to whether IMAOKA did this coherently. Or more precisely, whether or not the author has presented IMAOKA Shin'ichirō coherently.

While others in the *yuniterian* movement focused on economic equity and political freedom, IMAOKA thought that the essence of freedom was religious. How he came to this view and what that entailed is one problematic of this study.

Finally, studies of religious personalities have sought exemplars of spiritual integration and possibility. Carl Jung professed that his quest failed. He did not find an example of an integral personality even in India. Appendix B looks at these studies

---

3. A companion work by Prof. Michel Mohr, *Buddhism, Unitarianism and the Meiji Competition for Universality* (Harvard, 2014) is the only other study in English to touch upon the history of the American Unitarian Mission in Japan.

and theories in relation to IMAOKA.

So, proceed by finding a path that focuses on the topics that most interest you. Hopefully, an exemplar of a liberating faith will emerge and something of his message of *jiyū shūkyō* (free religion) will illumine your understanding of his vision of becoming a true human being.

Acknowledgements

There are so many to thank: IMAOKA sensei's family, especially his daughter-in-law, Emi-san; Risshō Kōseikai and Tsubaki Grand Shrine whose projects brought me to Japan several times a year with opportunities to be with IMAOKA sensei; Alan Seaburg who asked me to evaluate materials that turned out to be from the Japan Unitarian Mission of which IMAOKA was its last executive secretary; members of Collegium and friends worldwide who encouraged my research, principal of whom was Richard Boeke; Michel Mohr without whose guidance in the Meiji Era this book would not have been completed; my sister, Linda Youngs, and granddaughter, Cassidy Williams, who were proof readers; and all my teachers whose ideas have affected my understanding of life. Lastly, I wish to thank my wife, Zizi, who stuck by me and put up with a decade of my becoming a hermit for the task of finishing this book.

And as IMAOKA sensei would always say with a chuckle: "Please criticize my mistakes." That is, those of the author.

SECTION ONE: AN INTRODUCTION

Chapter 1

Such a Responsibility

> Coincidentally, I was born in the year (1881) before Emerson died in 1882. Also, I followed in his footsteps at Harvard, and since he was a Unitarian and my great teacher of free religion, I feel a great responsibility in accepting his spiritual legacy.
>
> – IMAOKA[4] Shin'ichirō

Thirty years have passed since the death of Dr. IMAOKA Shin'ichirō (b. September 16, 1881 – d. April 11, 1988), the apostle of Free Religion in Japan. He was all but forgotten in the West when I first met him. Then he was rediscovered by the Japanese nation at his one hundredth birthday – and is being remembered again. His message and life were never fully comprehended. His writings, filled with paradoxes and contradictions, may not be easily understood, but, for me, meeting him in person was a transformative experience. His life was a puzzle – each piece relating to the next in a new and unique way.

I found evidence of this unusual sage at the end of my first sabbatical in 1979. I was searching for living exemplars of the Asian religious traditions, about which I taught in a state university. My

[4] Again, the family name will be in "ALL CAPS" for all Japanese individuals except as used in quotations. Honorifics such as *sensei* or *san* will be used rarely (an academic practice), except in this introductory chapter. Titles of individuals will only be used for clarity or in quotations. I hope that you, as the reader, will accept this as not being disrespectful.

goal in the classroom was to suspend the "truth question" about whether or not Hinduism, Buddhism, Daoism, Confucianism or Shinto were *true*. Of course, they are existentially true for those who lived their wisdom. I sought to meet individuals who had realized their traditions' truths in their own lives. I met and interviewed wonderful human beings, some narrow and dogmatic in their views, others open and models of courage in facing life's challenges. Yet, finding "liberal religious leaders" in Asia had been a dream with little success. And in Japan, I had missed such an exemplary religious figure to whom my notes pointed. He had "infected" two quite conservative religious traditions with a strand of "liberal religion." One was Nichiren Buddhism, and the other was Shrine Shinto.

IMAOKA Shin'ichirō was an enigma. Those who knew him said he was "great and important," but there were few specifics. On my first visit to Japan, friends there said that IMAOKA was a 99 year-old Christian, quite ill and grieving from his wife's recent death, thus unavailable for me to meet him. Besides, I initially came to Japan to learn about Shinto and Buddhism as each was lived and practiced.

I became compelled to know why Buddhists told me that "IMAOKA *sensei*"[5] was a *bodhisattva* (a living Buddha) and Shintoists said he was *kami* (a divine figure). Christian Unitarians claimed him too, some thinking him to be a saint, if only they had such a category. Various academics referred to him as the "Emerson of Japan."

His idea of religion was such that a majority of Westerners and mainstream Christians would not even think him religious at all. His mysticism was suspect and his theology "heretical." Paradoxically, he questioned theism, while he accepted multiple religious identities of liberal Christian, Buddhist and Shintoist. Literally, a renunciation of theism makes one an *atheist* – *a* (not) + [believing in] *theos* (God). Yet he only rejected the concept of

5. Again, *sensei* (teacher) is an honorific that will only be used in quotations and when personal accounts are related. Otherwise, the academic style will be followed, using only the family name except for clarity or emphasis.

theism, making him a non-theist. He lived a spirituality that had begun in theistic beliefs but had grown *beyond* them, he admitted. He rejected the concept of an Absolute God as authoritarian and anathema to freedom. He thought that one cancelled the other.

I wanted to meet this exemplar of a different type of spirituality! I had returned to California to teach for the spring semester. On an impulse, I borrowed three thousand dollars and flew back to Japan that summer to meet this key figure who appeared to have influenced so many. Although I too am small by American standards, my surprise could not have been greater. This tiny, elderly man was not even five feet in height, frail and a year shy of a century. How could one so small have so great an influence? But his eyes shone with enormous wisdom, peace and happiness (or was it contentment?). He seemed overjoyed that an American who was studying Asian religions would come to him, since he had gone to America to study Western religions. His laugh, actually more a chuckle, contradicted any idea that he was taking himself seriously. Initially, he would tell me absolutely nothing about himself. He had accomplished nothing of note, he would often say. That was meant sincerely. He credited others with what he had assisted. He would say that students must stand on the shoulders of their teachers, so it is the student that should be honored. At least it should be true of his students, and he was principal or headmaster to 10,000 at Seisoku Academy during 50 years. And there had been more at Nihon University, where he taught for a decade. However, he outlived most of them. Pointing to their greater accomplishments, he recounted that they had become professors, bankers, politicians, labor leaders, writers and even a prime minister or two.

His tiny religious community was mistranslated as the "Tokyo Unitarian Church" (*Kiitsu Kyōkai,* literally *unity* or *oneness fellowship*). Before the formal meeting on Sunday mornings, there would be a gathering of those who joined him in a kind of Zen-type meditation of "just sitting." It was *seiza.* He would not claim anything about its significance or purpose. The group often included a Zen master, several Buddhist and Shinto priests, professors, bankers, a publisher, an occasional foreigner, whomever. IMAOKA had been practicing *seiza* for almost nine decades, both in groups and individually.

During my initial three-week visit with IMAOKA, I had the good fortune of daily, hour-long visits. We always exceeded his family's suggestion of that hour, and IMAOKA pleaded for me to stay longer and return earlier the next day. I came to know a man who would rather listen than talk, learn than teach, question and ponder the other's answers rather than provide polished truths.

Then he sent me on a trip around Japan to find answers to my questions about him from persons who had known him and his activities. For these interviews I had to read their books and articles, first talk with them about their views and leadership of their own Buddhist or Shinto group, then ask about IMAOKA. They were all famous in their own right, powerful leaders of huge religious institutions. The academics were heads of departments, tenured, well-published, erudite. A Zen master was internationally known. It was an exhausting but extraordinary introduction to progressive religions in Japan in one-on-one encounters that could not have been accomplished without IMAOKA's request that they talk with me.

Yet, none of these great leaders had known Dr. IMAOKA before he was 60 years old. A few had been in close association with him for four decades. He would so often say that he had just been too slow to die. Or, avoiding his customary play on words, he had outlived those who knew him and could tell me about the first six decades of his life. Further, IMAOKA flatly stated on my first visit that he had not done or written anything of merit. And when asked about any degrees or awards he had received, he chuckled, paused, and he spoke of "an honorary doctorate from Meadville" (referring to the American Unitarian seminary in Chicago).

The central problem, methodologically, in writing about his life and thought was how to learn of someone who assisted others "egolessly," ever behind the scenes or in the background. And, almost maddeningly, when people could be interviewed for the last half of his life, they spoke in admiration without specifics. And there was a reason. His questions reversed any flow of information. IMAOKA did that to me repeatedly. The joy of talking to him or just sitting with him in *seiza* was enough. That is, unless one wished to write about him.

How could IMAOKA be "an Emerson" if there was no collection of writings, no archive or repository, not even quotations and sayings spread in some way? When he said that he had published nothing of merit, even professors at Japan's leading universities who had both studied with him and later worked with him could not mention any influential publication from memory. That would be corrected as they gathered together one hundred plus essays for his 100th birthday. (I wanted to believe that it was possibly in response to my question concerning what he had written, and the embarrassment it had caused when no one could immediately put their hands on a single article. I was a brash, young professor who was asking very direct questions that a more knowledgeable person of Japanese culture would have quailed to ask.) The rediscovered essays were found in a range of periodicals that covered the spectrum of Japanese religious and secular traditions. This proved the breadth of his influence. But the essays did not an Emerson make – not in literary form or cultural importance. They had been momentary and contextual, relevant for a single publication, timely, but easily forgotten. A specialist in Japanese history, culture and religion was needed; I had no such pretense. I offered all my research and notes to specialists I knew. None took over my responsibility.

The International Association for Religious Freedom (IARF) Congress in 1984 gave me a fourth visit to Japan. IMAOKA's daughter-in-law, Emi-san, shared a family album. In it were pictures of two Imperial Awards for his contribution to education, photos of the Doctor of Divinity given by Meadville and more of honors from interfaith organizations. There were also pictures of the academic and religious leaders he had assisted. No one that I interviewed, other than his family, knew of the Imperial awards. He was concerned that I might focus on such matters, thinking that no one should.

A pattern of mesmerizing visits with IMAOKA continued after the 1984 IARF Congress, as I was invited back to Japan to assist with interfaith projects for Buddhist and Shinto organizations. He seemed to strengthen from our conversations, extending the time of each to two and three hours. He continued demonstrating his reputation as a listener and questioner. He sensed what was important in the moment and knew how to gently ask a clarifying or transformative question. At one moment, he wanted to know more about "free religion" and Emerson's involvement in the [American] Free Religious Association (FRA). He asked me: "What is free religion?" I did not know that this was a central concern of his life, as he listened to my lengthy, academic description of this idea in the West. I would only discover IMAOKA's leadership in the Japan Free Religious Association by confronting him a year later with a direct question about "free religion" in Japan. I had to become more attentive to what might lie behind any of his questions or comments. And when my month or so visit would end, he would promise to be waiting for me on my next visit.

A breakthrough came the next year at the Harvard Divinity School library. I had arrived early to do some research before attending Collegium, an academic association for the study of liberal religion. I was its history chair that year as well as the next – and then its president. Alan Seaburg, Harvard Divinity School's librarian and an old friend, asked me to examine a large box of materials that seemed to be from Japan. The box had been found by an intern that morning in the library's basement, untouched for decades. These end-of-the-19th century, hand-written letters and reports took some patience to read. Almost everything was in English and involved field reports to the American Unitarian Association's headquarters in Boston, detailing the operations of their Japanese Unitarian Mission.

While I had studied liberal Christianity in America under Prof. Sidney Mead and free religion with Prof. Stow Persons, I had specialized in religion in modern India. Reports from a Unitarian missionary to the American Unitarian Association (AUA) in Boston had not been on my list of interests. Yet, I continued to work through hundreds of pages as a favor to a good friend – to assess their value and recommend whether or not they should be saved and catalogued. Suddenly, an "*N. Imaoka*" appeared in a letter that was asking Unitarians to quit their mission and leave Japan. Was IMAOKA Shin'ichirō the last secretary for the American Unitarian mission? Was he somehow "*N. Imaoka*"? What had Unitarians done to be asked to go home?

I had only enough cash to have about a third of the letters and documents copied – no credit cards accepted. I was also given permission to photograph all the old pictures from the box. Hand-holding my 35mm slide camera that evening, using a desk lamp whose temperature (Kelvin) was a bit too hot, I managed to copy both slides and old photos. I was assured that all of this would be available and catalogued by my next visit. However, that box disappeared completely prior to cataloguing.[6] Its pictures and documents had vanished, so that my almost-too-light-to-read xerox copies and my "hot" slides were invaluable. Fortunately, some of the correspondence and reports in the lost box had duplicates that were preserved in the American Unitarian Association (AUA) archive at Harvard University. The discovery of "N. Imaoka" and the field reports sent to Boston would be a turning point. I could study

[6] Four or more students were involved in the xeroxing with others coming to see the documents, photos and hand-painted glass slides, as word spread of the discovery. Alan Seaburg said that this loss was the only material that disappeared during his entire career.

hundreds of primary documents that I had copied about IMAOKA's presence in the Japanese Unitarian movement in the 1920s. Had I been at a major university, I would have gotten a grant and followed these leads with research at the Harvard archive.[7] No such support was available at my university, so I shared my findings with anyone who might take it further. But each time, they came to the conclusion that there was not enough historical data to finish a biography or an intellectual history.

A professor at the University of Hawai'i, John Charlot, introduced me to Michel Mohr, professor of Japanese religion and specialist of Buddhism in the Meiji era. After years of sharing my research with others and encouraging them to write about liberal religion in Japan and of IMAOKA Shin'ichirō's place in it, I became Prof. Mohr's reader as he completed his groundbreaking tome on Buddhist and Unitarian dialogue in Japan.[8] It was the foundation that I needed to better understand the Meiji period of IMAOKA's life. That era was one of tumultuous change in which Japanese values, education, professions, religions, culture, politics, economics and much more were in flux. I am deeply indebted to Michel Mohr for his patient guidance in the complexities of the Meiji era. Specifics of that indebtedness will be acknowledged throughout this study; his forgiveness will be sought for any conversation wrongly appropriated as my own insight. And, of course, all the mistakes are mine.

•••

IMAOKA Shin'ichirō left no institution that he created or that took his name. He left no spiritual teachings meant for others to

---

7. I would finance my visits by making films and videos for Risshō Kōseikai, four in all; and editing publications for Tsubaki Grand Shrine, creating the largest Shinto website of that era and helping a Shinto priest make the first HyperCard database on Japanese religion and culture. There was no academic funding for religious studies at my teaching university during my 30+ years there. The reader is alerted to any possible conflict of interest in funding my research, which could be a scholarly transgression.

8. Michel Mohr, *Buddhism, Unitarianism, and the Meiji Competition for Universality* (Cambridge, Mass.: Harvard University Press, 2014).

adopt as religious truths. His was a complex spirituality that defied labels.

Yet no one who sat with him in *seiza* remained untouched in his presence. That was why this book has been written: to explore that influence, to probe the paradox of freedom, to follow the faith journey of the "prophet of free religion." For him, each segment of life was like a school, a place of learning "with its time for graduation," as IMAOKA would say. Each graduation was remembered and valued as it had contributed to one's life and growth.

He would find transformation in the search for true freedom, a freedom that has multiple spiritual dimensions. He called it *jiyū shūkyō* (*free religion*). He thought it possible for all religions to be part of the process of spiritual liberation, although none completely. Sadly, organized religion could also enslave. All religions' true purpose was to liberate, he thought: to foster creativity in humans, to end meaningless imitation, to promote an ennobling life of joy and compassion. *Jiyū shūkyō* should permeate all of society and culture, the so-called secular – art, music, literature, science, nature, business.

IMAOKA, like Raja Rammohan Roy, the great reformer of Hinduism (1772-1833), would never attack another's faith – those personal truths that are from one's own direct experience of life and offer the possibility of coming into the presence of the unknowable. These experiences motivate one to be kinder, more compassionate, loving and generous. Such experienced truths are personal; they are existential truths. What IMAOKA would question was the human mistake of leaping from personal truths to ontological truth (somehow claiming it to be "God's Truth," an absolute, "inerrant revelation," etc.). Trying to experience truth claims would compose much of his spiritual journey. Wisdom would come from existential crises along the way. Yet, his crises and what he learned directly from them would remain personal and largely untold, as he lived by the Buddhist discipline of "egolessness." He claimed no realization or enlightenment. He disappeared as he related to others by being a mirror of their best.

IMAOKA's spiritual journey would take him into non-theism. This is the realm of philosophers, both ancient and modern. Their reasoning developed an ability to handle greater uncertainties and complexities. Just as the *notion of uncertainty* functions in scientific models like those of Thomas Kuhn[9] or Michael Polanyi,[10] IMAOKA's spirituality embraced complexity and *pure freedom.* Such a spirituality begins in a temporary truth until a better understanding replaces it. IMAOKA grew from one "truth" to the next, uniting any true elements into a new faith commitment.[11] His faith stance merged rational and mystical experience without losing devotion or transformative ritual. Appendix B will explore studies and theories about such thought.

IMAOKA often said he was not a philosopher nor a scholar. The facts about his life will question that modesty – an assertion he fully meant. Thus, calling him a *sage* must disprove his denial. However, he did love the word *cosmic.* It was a term that expressed the ideal from the *yuniterian* movement about becoming a true human being. One who practiced *free religion* was striving to become a *cosmic person.*

His own professed ideal was to become *a true human being.* He certainly was an exemplar of one, and perhaps much more. Hopefully, the evidence of his life journey will fully support him as being seen as a mystic and a rational, a *Cosmic Sage* – an exemplar of an integral spirituality.

---

9. Thomas Kuhn, *The Structure of Scientific Revolutions* (1962), especially concerning "paradigm shift."

10. See Michael Polanyi, *Science, Faith and Society* (1946); *Personal Knowledge* (1958); *Personal Knowledge* (1958), etc.

11. IMAOKA had an annual practice of writing a Tentative Statement of Faith. It represented the truths he had learned that year and a spiritual vision for the coming year.

"In the university of human life there is no graduation."

Calligraphy by IMAOKA *Shin'ichirō*

Dr. IMAOKA *Shin'ichirō and Prof. George Williams,* 1981

SECTION TWO: AS A JAPANESE CHRISTIAN

Chapter 2

Converting to the "Devil's Religion"

The one-century life-span of IMAOKA[12] Nobuichirō [which can also be read Shin'ichirō] predestined him to witness profound transformations of his homeland, Imperial Japan.

Japan's horizon changed dramatically after the arrival of Commodore Perry and the Convention of Kanagawa (1854) forced its insular society into an era of radical transition. IMAOKA Nobuichirō[13] was born only three decades later on September 16, 1881,[14] a year before Ralph Waldo Emerson died. Americans joked that he was almost the reincarnation of Emerson. He liked the joke and would honor the Sage of Concord with a life focused on *free religion.*

---

12. The family name will be written in small caps to help non-specialists – with the exception of quotations. The proper order is often reversed in communications in English with the West during the first half of IMAOKA's lifetime. Names will be used according to academic custom without titles or honorifics; no disrespect is intended or implied. Then in the sections where I am reflecting on personal interviews, an honorific will be used – i.e., IMAOKA sensei.

13. IMAOKA's birth was registered at the local Buddhist temple by a priest who chose *kanji* phonetically for the name his parents gave him – Nobuichirō. Most Japanese would read that *kanji* as Shin'ichirō, the *kun'yomi* pronunciation. Nobuichirō would be the *on'yomi* pronunciation which he often used late into his life.

14. Dating precisely is a problem as Japanese dating was based on the beginning month of each new Imperial era. Even one's age would vary by a year, as time in the womb was also counted.

These decades had been a time when Japan moved from feudalism under a shogunate to the restoration of imperial rule, from hereditary occupations and status to new possibilities: economic, educational, cultural, linguistic, religious – and many more unseen. It was a time of excitement and fear, embraced or fought. Emperor Meiji had become Japan's ruler (1868–1912) as Japan struggled to avoid being carved up like China, as yet another colonial territory seized by Western powers. An imperial worldview was being created with a question concerning just how many non-Japanese elements could be accepted in a Japan that intended to be independent of and equal with these colonial powers.

Nobuichirō was born the third son of faithful Buddhist farmers in Matsue, approximately one hundred miles from Nagasaki up the western coast, the area of earlier Roman Catholic missions in the 16th century – and then their suppression.[15] IMAOKA recalled: "I was not fed until I prayed before the Buddhist altar. I memorized the "Shoshinge" and the "Gobunsho" (sacred texts) without knowing what they meant."[16]

His parents were Pure Land Buddhists in the denomination known as Jōdo Shinshū. All of Buddhism was being challenged religiously on two fronts. Buddhism had been privileged during the Tokugawa shogunate, but now State Shinto was being recast with a new national identity embedded in Imperial rule. That ideology threatened Buddhism's place and privileges. Christianity had returned with the unequal treaties forced upon Japan, and its missionaries were now in the countryside, converting Japanese to become members of an exclusive religion – the only true one. Japan had been a culture of multiple religious identities, not exclusive loyalty to just one.

---

15. Japan had prided itself as a nation of religious toleration; yet Christianity became an enemy of the state in 16th century Japan. See IMAOKA's future university mentor, ANESAKI Masaharu (1873-1949), *History of Japanese Religion* (1930).

16. IMAOKA, "My Articles of Faith at 103" (1984).

In another era, not one of transition, Nobuichirō could have become a nominal worshiper of Amida Buddha, relying on Amida's grace (*tariki*), affirming acceptance with the *nenbutsu* ("I take refuge in Amida Buddha") as his assurance of rebirth in the Pure Land, a Paradise in the metaphorical West (that is, toward the setting Sun). And he would have most likely have become a farmer.

Being Baptized an Anglican Christian

A bewildering array of Christian religions rushed into Japan after the ban on Christianity was lifted in 1872. All claimed in one way or another to be the very Church of Jesus Christ (Roman Catholic; Russian Orthodox Catholic; German Lutheran, American Lutheran, British Lutheran; British Anglican and American Episcopalians, Calvinists and Presbyterians of many nationalities; Baptists, Methodists, and non-denominationals like Holiness or Latter Day Saints). To what would be called mainstream or orthodox Christian missions could be added three tiny liberal Christian mission efforts: British and American Unitarians, American Universalists, and the German Evangelical Mission (*Allgemeine Evangelisch-Protestantischen Missionsverein*). IMAOKA's life would be touched first by Anglicans, then Congregationalists and finally Unitarians.

Anglican missionaries reached Matsue in 1890 when Nobuichirō was nine. Rev. Barclay Fowell Buxton led a missionary company to Matsue, making it their headquarters. They were affiliated with the Church Missionary Society of the Church of England. Initially the new mission was known as the "*One by One Band of Japan*," being dedicated to personal holiness and committed to evangelism.[17]

Paget Wilkes, a graduate of Oxford, joined Buxton in

17. Otis Cary's *A History of Christianity in Japan: Protestant Missions*, Vol. 2 (London and Edinburgh: Fleming H. Revel, 1909) is a "mission history" that catches the flavor of this period and cites reports from the various missionary societies.

1897.[18] Wilkes employed the most effective missionary approach of that era, which was to offer English lessons for free. Yet, Nobuichirō never intended to become a Christian, even after he accepted the opportunity to learn English from the missionaries. Wilkes had his students, including Nobuichirō, read the New Testament in English and became familiar with the notion of God's loving grace and salvation from sin by accepting Jesus Christ's sacrifice.

Barclay Buxton

PagentWilkes and two fellow Ministers

IMAOKA recalled:

> ... my conscious religious life began in my high school days when I happened to come in contact with Rev. B. F. Buxton, an Anglican Church missionary. ... [T]his was the beginning of my contact with the white man, Western culture and Christianity. Rev. Paget Wilkes, a co-worker of Rev. Buxton, invited us to a class of English conversation and Bible study. I was a very diligent boy to attend the class, being very much interested in English conversation. I had no interest in the Bible at first, but I was attracted to Christianity through the noble characters of the missionaries and was baptized at last at the Matsue Episcopal Church.
>
> In those days (1898) in Japan, Christianity was taken for *a religion of devils*, and Christians were taken for *traitors to the state*. The fact that I was baptized, therefore, was a great shock to my parents. My father seriously considered exiling me from the parental roof. My mother was more lenient than my father, but it saddened her more.[19]

Wilkes felt a great need to save others from eternal damnation – those outside of God's love. He had copied a method used by a

---

18. Paget Wilkes, *Missionary Joys in Japan or The Leaves from My Journal* (New York: George H. Doran, 1903/1913).

19. IMAOKA. "My Spiritual Pilgrimage," (1970) *italics added.* Episcopal and Anglican are the same.

non-missionary teacher, a Captain Leroy Lansing Janes.[20] Brought to Japan in the last years of the Tokugawa shogunate by a regional *daimyō* (a samurai lord), Janes taught Western military arts and sciences in Kumamoto. But the Restoration of the Emperor, in 1868, made these regional (military) schools illegal, so Janes was used to teach English. Although Christianity was banned as treason, Janes mixed memorization of Christian Bible verses about sin and salvation and reading the Christian Bible into his English lessons. This led to the conversion of the famous Kumamoto Band,[21] some forty young (former) samurai who became the first class at Joseph NIISHIMA's Christian school in Kyoto, the future Dōshisha University. It began as a "native" or indigenous Congregational religious school. EBINA Danjō (1856-1937) was one of "Janes' Forty" [converts], soon to be helping Imaoka overcome his first doubts about his new religious identity.[22] (The adult IMAOKA would work with many of Dōshisha's graduates and professors – EBINA, KISHIMOTO, Abe, MURAI, and

20. Otis Cary, *A History of Christianity in Japan* pp. 122-124.

21. KANAMORI, *Kanamori's Life-Story Told by Himself: How higher criticism wrecked a Japanese-Christian – and how he came back* (Philadelphia: The Sunday School Times Company, 1921).

22. EBINA Danjō (1856-1937), one of the "Kumamoto Band of Brothers," was a young samurai who then illegally converted them to Christianity by his English teacher–even before the death penalty for such treason had been lifted in 1874. Leroy Janes (1838-1909) took the Kumamoto Band with him to Kyoto when their domainal school was closed. They studied together at Dōshisha school (which would become Dōshisha University (同志社大学 Dōshisha daigaku) and merged with Congregational Christianity. The Christian Missions' historian, Otis Cary, noted in his *History of Christianity in Japan* (and repeated in *Japan and Its Regeneration,* 1903, p. 88):

> It is still too early for the sadder side of this story to be written in full. Suffice it now to say that in later years Captain Janes was not in sympathy with revealed religion. In 1893 he again came to Japan and became a teacher in a government school in Kyoto. The love that his former pupils had for their teacher combined with other influences to lead a few of them to join him in opposition to the teaching of the missionaries. Though his course was such as soon loosened his hold upon them, all did not recover the faith that was so shaken by the very one who had been the instrument for arousing it. (p.151)

others.[23] These "former samurai" ministers, along with YOKOI Tokio and KOZAKI Hiromichi, would later gather in Tokyo at Unity Hall, headquarters of the American Unitarian Mission.)

Wilkes was able to convert Nobuichirō from the nominal Buddhism of his childhood to a more intense devotional religious life.[24] However, at this point in the missionary careers both Wilkes and Buxton brought sacramental Christianity with all its dogmas. Its emphasis on the two most important sacraments, baptism and the Lord's Supper or Holy Eucharist, was troublesome for a score of Japanese Christian converts in the period prior to IMAOKA. In fact, at this very moment indigenous Japanese Christian leaders whom he would soon come to know were already questioning these rituals as they seemed to be of the very type that any Confucian scholar would reject as superstition. These former samurai ministers, the Kumamoto Band, began calling for a truly Japanese form of Christianity based only of the teaching of Jesus without any of these European or Western accretions.

IMAOKA later recalled, "I was baptized when I was attracted by his character and spirituality and was converted by him."[25] His conversion was not a dramatic, life-changing in-breaking of divine grace, as Wilkes would describe of so many of his converts in his mission reports. Young Nobuichirō followed a pattern of conversion that involved the positive influence of an exemplary missionary whose personality invited a trusting relationship and served as a life model. This human relationship opened a more expansive meaning to life than what he had as a child in his devotional Buddhist practices. At sixteen he was in a period developmentally in which he was

23. They will all become part of the *Rational Christian* movement. See Section Two.

24. For more on the characteristics of *devotional religion*, see Appendix 2: Religious Types.

25. IMAOKA. "My Articles of Faith at 103." (1984)

emotionally ready for such expansion, and IMAOKA always felt fortunate that such an ethical figure as Wilkes touched his life. That pointed him to something higher and greater than he knew before. It gave him a new sense of identity and purpose. There was, for him, no break with his former self. No "sickness unto death" of a Kierkegaard, no overwhelming sense of unworthiness of a John Bunyan. This was the "boring" type of gradual conversion that William James chose not to study in depth.[26] IMAOKA had grown into a fuller identity, a larger humanity, with wider horizons. But where would this take him?

Wilkes is strangely silent in his books about this period of his work in Japan and his missionary achievements in Matsue. As head of the mission, Buxton would be praised by the leading orthodox missionary organ, *Mission News*, for the conversion of a unique Japanese youth. IMAOKA Nobuichirō would graduate from the elite Imperial University and – in spite of that – remained a Christian, even became a Congregationalist minister. But, this very silence invites a closer look at IMAOKA's few reflections on his conversion as a high school student.

Nobuichirō was converted by missionaries who later became so zealous that both Buxton and Wilkes would not remain high-church Anglicans. In fact, they would return briefly to England in 1901, where they joined the Evangelistic Band, a group so zealous that it would eventually have to leave the Church of England. They had been influenced by a rising Pentecostal fervor that focused on signs or gifts from the Holy Spirit. Wilkes especially began what other missionaries called "aggressive evangelism," with street preaching, revivals, and intense altar calls to repentance. His journal, *Missionary Joys*, does not mention IMAOKA who was his most celebrated convert, and IMAOKA barely mentioned the man who led

26. William James, *The Varieties of Religious Experience.* New York, 1902.

him to become a Christian.[27] By the time Wilkes returned from England to make Kobe the center of the Evangelistic Band for his fervent activity, IMAOKA would be there as a minister of an indigenous Japanese Kumi-ai church, affiliated loosely with the American Congregationalist Mission.

Both the missionaries who converted him and IMAOKA had gone through intra-faith conversions. They had moved from one form of Christianity to another. IMAOKA's intra-faith conversion from Anglican to Congregational Christianity had a new feature: his questioning mind wanted better answers to the questions that had caused his doubts.[28] At the same time, Buxton and Wilkes changed religious identities from sacramental orthodoxy to evangelistic pietism. Wilkes sought to bring Japanese ministers of all denominations to the experience of a Pentecostal blessing of the Holy Spirit:

> Our Japanese leaders, men who have had a definite personal Pentecost, have but little use for even interesting Bible 'studies,' if they do not lead souls into a clear and definite experience, and bring the seeking heart to a first-hand dealing with the Lord in the quiet of their room or the silent mountain-side.[29]

Wilkes not only proselytized by street preaching and revivals but also by teaching throughout the Empire at the invitation of other missionary groups, sharing the message of a second blessing, that of

---

27. Paget Wilkes, *Missionary Joys in Japan or Leaves from My Journal* (New York: George H. Doran Co., 1913).

28. This change is a second type of conversion: inside of the Christian faith from one denomination to another – from sacramental, belief-centered Christianity to a more individual, faith-centered practice. Buxton and Wilkes had a similar type of experiential change. However, theirs was from sacramental, belief-centered Anglican Christianity to a holiness, pentecostal, experiential faith with signs of a *second blessing* from the Holy Spirit, such as speaking in tongues, faith healing and/or ecstatic experiences.

29. *Missionary Joy*, op.cit., pp. 32-3.

the fire of baptism by the Holy Ghost.[30]

Nearly six decades after his conversion, IMAOKA would remember that remaining a Christian was not easy during his high school years. He was obviously quizzed by both his parents (as mentioned earlier) and by his fellow students and teachers. This was a common experience for almost all young Christian converts.[31] They would have an initial euphoria, an overwhelming experience of love and joy, a period of heartfelt transformation into a *new life*. But he, as they, had to explain this *new life* to others inquiring about its meaning in a part of Japan that viewed being a Christian as disloyalty to the Emperor and dishonor to one's parents and ancestors. The Christianity, that they had learned primarily in English, had to be defended in Japanese. And that would not be easy.

Nobuichirō reported that doubts came almost immediately. So, he turned to Japanese sources. Earlier Christian converts had written about their struggles to express the Christian message of salvation in the Japanese language. But, what he read from them only increased his doubts. One book especially, by one of the Kumamoto Band, now a famous leader of one indigenous form of Japanese Christianity, was by UCHIMURA Kanzō (1861–1930). He questioned what the missionaries were teaching and how they were administering their missions in Japan.

> ... pouring over UCHIMURA Kanzo's prophetic book, I boiled over with righteous indignation. But as I progressed through the Kumamoto Fifth High School, my doubts about Christianity gradually increased. Did the Virgin Mary give birth to Christ? Was he resurrected after three days on the cross? I began to doubt some of the miracles in the Bible. When I was very troubled about this, I met EBINA Danjo and he

---

30. Paget Wilkes, *op. cit.*

31. For example, see KANAMORI, *op. cit.*; and examples especially of Unitarian converts: Clay MacCauley, *The Unitarian Movement in Japan: Sketches of the Lives and Religious Work of Ten Representative Japanese Unitarians.* (1900)

> said that it is all right if you do not believe the miracles in the Bible, Christ is an ordinary man. But you should believe that there is a God. Professor EBINA's thinking was based on the teachings of Free Christian churches as distinct from so-called orthodox Christianity. This teaching saved me.[32]

These questions were common for many educated Japanese Christians, especially those who were studying for Christian ministry, or studied about religion in government schools and colleges.[33] In the high schools, many of the Japanese teachers would be Confucian in their worldview, especially concerning their rational denial of miracles. Virgin births and resurrections would be strongly questioned by them, as all miracles were in Confucian philosophy. So, young IMAOKA searched the writings of these first generation Christians like UCHIMURA for answers.

UCHIMURA had questioned European doctrines and additions that were not found in the Bible. For example, the doctrine of Trinity, translated into Japanese as *san-ichi* (three-one) or as *san ichi kami* (the 3-1 god), sounded strange to him,[34] although there was a parallel with the three bodies of the Buddha and one essence (the *trikāya* doctrine in Buddhism).[35] UCHIMURA's condemnation of some missionaries' attitudes of racial and intellectual superiority would hardly meet young IMAOKA's need for certainty in defense of his *new life* as a Japanese Christian. He turned to a Japanese pastor in the Kumi-ai movement, another indigenous Christian development.

---

32. IMAOKA, "My Articles of Faith at 103" (1984)

33. Some of the questions of converts who remained Christian despite their doubts about the dogmas: "KISHIMOTO; MURAI and others among the ten representative Japanese Unitarians expressed similar issues. MacCauley, *Sketches, op.cit.* (to be discussed in later chapters).

34. Trinity was translated by Christians as *sanmi ittai* 三位一体, where the Chinese character 位 is read with the unusual pronunciation *mi*, suggesting "body" 身. See https://ja.wikipedia.org/wiki/三位一体, suggested by Prof. Michel Mohr.

35. Later IMAOKA will study this comparatively with his professor, ANESAKI. See ANESAKI, "The Fundamental Character of Buddhism and Its Branches" (1912) presents the *trikāya* doctrine of the three bodies of the one Buddha.

EBINA Danjō would come into Nobuichirō's life at this point and begin a relationship that would continue until EBINA's death in 1937. For young IMAOKA, EBINA became the bridge between orthodox and liberal Christianity. But the Japanese fault line was not just exclusive religion (Christianity as the only true faith) versus inclusive, universal salvation. EBINA, like other elite Japanese of his era – that is, of samurai birth, knew inclusivity from his early schooling according to the Bushido code – the moral principles of the old samurai class, combining Confucian, Buddhist and Shinto values (rectitude, courage, benevolence, politeness, sense of honor, loyalty, self-control, etc.).

IMAOKA would honor EBINA's memory as a teacher who taught him to address his doubts with reason and honesty while forging a humanistic Christianity. EBINA's portrait would grace IMAOKA's bedroom until the end of his life in 1988.

Some Observations about Imaoka's Youthful Religious Experience

Nobuichirō would say that he did not have a classical conversion experience. By that he meant specifically the kind of sudden conversion experience William James had focused upon in his classic 1902 study.[36] IMAOKA had confessed his sins as a teenager by coming into the Christian faith and receiving the love of Christ. Yet, he had not experienced a *new birth* or significantly different being. He had experienced unmerited love, at least partially through the unusual kindness and engagement of his British missionary teachers, Baxton and Wilkes. They were undergoing their own experiential transformation at that very moment, returning to England where they broke with the established Anglican Church's missionary enterprise. They became evangelicals, returning not to the Anglican mission in Matsue but to Kobe.

36. James, *Varieties, op. cit.*

IMAOKA had been exposed to high church sacraments, especially baptism and communion with its belief in miracles of redemption and of the transformation of bread and wine into the body and blood of Christ. With its focus on the physical presence of God in the Eucharist, one received these as proof of one's conversion to Christianity, washed in the blood of Christ for the remission of one's sins and partaking of the body and blood of Christ in the miracle of the holy communion. These were symbolic – yet, also a real presence. Despite what it meant for him initially, he would later doubt the need to administer either sacrament in his Kobe ministry. There was something foreign, European, about these rituals and their literal meaning of washing away sin and eating and drinking God's presence. Even non-sacramental Japanese Christian denominations would share these concerns about baptism and communion. They searched for some other religious experience to anchor their Christian faith.

IMAOKA's Conversion to Episcopal/Anglican Christianity

High Church Anglicanism wished to foster an experience of the *Transcendent* as immanent. In the ritual of *Holy Communion* bread and wine became Christ's flesh and blood. Its rituals portrayed the divine in symbolic vestments, images and icons, ceremonies, music, and word. Yet, even Buxton and Wilkes needed something more than these rituals and symbols to anchor their own faith as they tried to express it in Japanese. They came under the influence of Methodist pietism and a pentecostal movement that would lead both into a more holiness faith and practice. They had first come to Japan with a certainty that their message was directly from Christ, through the Apostolic Church and its authorities (Bible, Creed, ordained leadership, apostolic succession, etc.). This type of religious experience had been transformative of an "old self" of sin and rebellion against God into a "reborn self," forgiven and in the process of sanctification. The love of God and "His grace" were mediated by the Church of Christ in relationship (fellowship) with the human agents of grace (his ministers, missionaries, and fellow church members). God was both transcendent, completely other than his creation, and immanent, flesh and blood, fully incarnated as Jesus Christ – and miraculously available in the Eucharist. But, something had occurred as they shared sacramental religion in Japan. It did not translate well. Even they would undergo intra-faith conversion to another subtype of devotional religion, the *immanental*[37] presence of the Holy Ghost and a second blessing of pentecostal gifts to the *sanctified* [another level of commitment and dedication in their faith].

IMAOKA's conversion was not sufficient for him to remain a "sacramental Christian." And, according to Wilkes' own account when he revisited Matsue a decade later, no convert from this period could be found.[38] IMAOKA had left Anglican Christianity and joined Congregationalism, only three years after his initial conversion and baptism, in 1901 under the influence of EBINA Danjō. This was an intra-faith conversion, within Christianity. It was not a renunciation of the initial conversion as a Christian, but, according to his later reflections on his lifelong pilgrimage, it was a *graduation* that did not reject the past. Each change would come to be seen as *graduating* in a process of growth and maturation, not denial or rejection of some error or falsehood.

IMAOKA's reflection, decades later, does not rule out the possibility that, in 1901, there could have been an existential crisis. What he first believed had become his core identity, his new self-

37. "Immanental" is a *terminus technicus* [technical termonology]: a term of theological import that indicates divine or sacred presence in nature or ordinary reality. It is used as the opposite of "transcendental," a term for something that is beyond nature, a privileged "reality," in Abrahamic religions, God (in English).

38. Wilkes, *Missionary Joys, op.cit.*

understanding as a particular type of Christian in that specific community. The experience was primary; the explanation or understanding of it by himself or others was secondary and would be evaluated differently as he grew and developed.

Not only had certain explanations, Western doctrines, been questioned and left behind, but also the human agents of his conversion, Buxton and Wilkes. There is a great silence in their missionary records: IMAOKA was never mentioned, the star convert of their work in Matsue, according to the *Mission News* of 1908. That silence is indirect evidence of some emotional pain as the relationships and commitments were questioned – and broken.

From the viewpoint of experiential phenomenology (that is, the structure of religious experience within a particular religious type), sacramental Christianity with its immanental aids (images, icons, rituals, and human agents of grace) was of the same type as his childhood's devotional Buddhism. Jōdo Shinshū faith and practice, from which he converted, also had sacred objects to experience the Buddha and his grace (images, icons, rituals, and human agents of grace). However, he had been a child without any of the "heartfelt feeling" possible in devotional religion. He confessed that he had no understanding of his Buddhist heritage at that time. Later, at the university under the instruction of Professor ANESAKI, he would gain a new appreciation of Buddhism.

Conversion to Congregational Christianity

The context of this conversion is complicated in a number of ways. To simplify, the human agent of his second conversion was a charismatic member of the Kumamoto Band, a former samurai and a Christian convert educated at Dōshisha college under its founder NIISHIMA Jō (1843-1890). EBINA Danjō was now part of the growing native (that is, Japanese) Christian independence church movement, the *Kumi-ai*. The leaders of this movement would become part of his life, directly and indirectly, positively and negatively influencing him.

IMAOKA's intrafaith conversion was initially fueled by reading the works of the anti-missionary Christian leader, UCHIMURA Kanzō who was so unbending in his anti-war and anti-idolatry stances that he had touched off a national crisis. It was called the *Uchimura Incident* of 1891 since he would not bow before the portrait of the Emperor, as he thought that made the portrait an idol.[39]

EBINA helped IMAOKA retain his identity as a Christian, shifting from the certainty of sacramental Christianity (Bible, creed and dogmas, True Church of Christ, etc.) to the authority of his own religious experience. He facilitated and affirmed IMAOKA's change from dependence on "other-authority" to "own-authority." That is, IMAOKA should question any element in the narrative that Western missionaries had preached as Christianity in their foreign language and see what made experiential sense in Japanese. Supernaturalism (virgin births, miracles, resurrections) made no sense for someone with a good Japanese education, even a high school student. Learning in Japan was colored by a Confucian worldview of naturalism and humanism. Nature followed laws that were not violated with miracles.[40]

While his second conversion was not sacramental, it still resembled the belief-centered, ritualization of the first. While a creed from the West in English (or other foreign languages) was rejected and the convert was freed from it, there was a link to the "essence of Christianity" or the "religion of Jesus Christ" that still had to be validated by a testimony or a message of one's own personal

39. UCHIMURA taught that Japanese needed to abandon Western creeds, form fellowships without a paid ministry, and develop a uniquely Japanese Christianity based only of the teachings of Christ.

40. Concerning how scientific Chinese influenced thinking, see Joseph Needham, *Science and Civilization in China.* 17 Vols.

salvation. This link of testimony and personal experience meant articulating one's faith in Japanese – formulating a belief system. This placed young IMAOKA in the same quandary that all *Kumi-ai* ministers were facing: each searching for the true religion of Jesus and having to reconstruct their faith and practice according to its original form before Christianity had been westernized and had become sectarian, and then split into many groups and denominations questioning the others and often not having communion with them. (The sectarian spirit was clearly seen in "closed communion." Another denomination's baptism into the Christian faith was not recognized, and, therefore, members of other churches were not allowed to share the Lord's Supper in their church.)

IMAOKA had converted from an orthodox and conservative faith and practice to a more fluid Japanese development – "heterodoxy within orthodoxy," as it was called. This movement was condemned by Congregational missionaries as liberal and rationalistic. But, it was also feared as anti-missionary. This latter fear was not true of EBINA's version of an independent Japanese Christianity, as he remained friendly and cooperative with his denomination's missionaries. By forming an independent organization within Congregationalism, EBINA was free of foreign authority and "dollar-rule" by missionaries. And, by insisting that the individual churches be self-sufficient, they were free of foreign funding and control. They could declare to the government that they were truly Japanese, free and independent.

A word should be said about the morphology or form of this conversion. It seems to be composed of two pillars: experience and free belief. Experience was personal and direct but it would have the coloration of the particular religious community with the individual's appropriation of that experience. IMAOKA did not recall any difference in religious experiences, only in growth and maturity. His recollection may be a secondary reflection. EBINA's method of evangelism was tuned to a sudden or dramatic conversion, marked by a conversion experience from a sinful past self to a new birth in Christ. Baptism brought one into the community of faith, the Church. Yet, even the requirement of baptism would lessen in the years to come among Kumi-ai churches. It would become just one of many questions for IMAOKA in the next period of his life.

From Matsue, so far from the center of the Empire, IMAOKA Nobuichirō was chosen to enter the Imperial University of Tokyo. Good fortune would have it that EBINA would accept a pastorate in Tokyo, and IMAOKA would attend his church every Sunday during his university years. But would that be enough to save him from a secular education? Christian schools had been established to keep converts from being lost to secular education's rationalism, materialism, skepticism, and/or atheism. No Christian convert had gone to the Imperial University and then become a Christian minister. Would young IMAOKA be the first?

TIMELINE

1881	IMAOKA's birth in Matsue, Sept 16.
1890	Arrival of the Anglican Mission in Matsue
1891	*UCHIMURA Incident*
1897	Arrival of Paget Wilkes of Anglican Mission
1898	IMAOKA baptized in the Episcopal [Anglican] Church in Matsue
1902	IMAOKA travels to Tokyo to attend the Imperial University

Major Japanese and International Events

1853-54	Admiral Perry "visits" Japan
1868	Restoration of Imperial Rule
1872	Ban on Christianity lifted
1874	Taiwan Expedition by Imperial forces
1890	Imperial Edict on Education
1893	World's Parliament of Religions, Chicago – 8 Japanese participated
1894-95	First Sino-Japanese War. Treaty of Shimonoseki in 1895.

His father and mother, a photo in his study

"In those days (1898) in Japan, Christianity was taken for *a religion of devils*, and Christians were taken for *traitors to the state.* The fact that I was baptized, therefore, was a great shock to my parents. My father seriously considered exiling me from the parental roof. My mother was more lenient than my father, but it saddened her more"

--from "My Spiritual Pilgrimage"

Chapter 3
At the Imperial University as a Christian

Young IMAOKA was chosen, based on the national exam, for admission into the newly established philosophy program within the Literature Department of the Imperial University of Tokyo in 1903. He would not speak or write about this honor – how a provincial would make it to the center of the Empire, at the heart of a caldron of change to its social structures and its educational system. Christian schools had been established to make sure that young converts did not have to struggle with the dissonance between academic questioning and committed belief in eternal Christian verities. He did not follow the missionaries' advice to attend Dōshisha, the Congregational Mission's college.

His university experience would have two main focuses: academic study of religion at the Imperial University and participation in EBINA Danjō's Kumi-ai[41] Congregational church in Tokyo. EBINA had moved to Tokyo, coinciding with IMAOKA's arrival there. He had helped IMAOKA with his high school doubts, and now he would assist him with the dissonance he would experience in his university studies. There could have been many possible outcomes. His doubts could have increased to the point where he would

Ebina Danjō

41. The Kumi-ai movement was not unified but had three divisions of which EBINA Danjo (1856-1937) had become one of its leaders. The main purpose of the movement was to become independent of foreign authority and finances. Many complex issues were involved in which IMAOKA would become entangled.

renounce his Christian conversion and faith or just become a Sunday Christian and weekday skeptic. The goal that IMAOKA sought was to harmonize his faith with Japan's thrust for "modern" learning – rich with science, psychology and historical criticism. Could EBINA help him remain a Christian?

IMAOKA's Study at Tōdai

Nobuichirō, who now registered as Shin'ichirō, entered the Imperial University of Tokyo (Tōkyō Teikoku Daigaku, often called Tōdai), in 1903, and would study with some of the best scholars of that era. While all the Christian missions, conservative and liberal, were attempting to establish training schools for young Christians, the best young people in the land were heading to secular or government schools – Keiō, Waseda and schools attempting to become universities. The conservative missionaries feared that their converts would not survive being exposed to science, history, textual criticism, philosophy, and the theory of evolution – as well as the attitudes of skepticism, materialism, and even free inquiry.

IMAOKA flourished in his studies, even as his doubts about specific Christian beliefs grew. Out of the entire student body, only forty at Tōdai began as Christian.[42] None faced a greater challenge to their faith than he did in the academic study of religion. IMAOKA exposed himself to all of these new streams of thought as well as studying his own culture at a deeper and more critical level. Speaking in 1981 about "A Universal Cooperative Society," IMAOKA reflected on his college experience about 75 years later. He mentioned his important relationships with two teachers. He did not mention the rigor of the program and the fame he achieved among Japanese Christians. He recalled:

> At the University (Tokyo Imperial University), I chose the

42. KISHIMOTO Nobuta, translated by John F. Howes, *Japanese Religion in the Meiji Era* (Tokyo: Ōbunsha, 1954), Vol II.

> philosophy department. Professor Anesaki Masaharu,[43] who was lecturing for the first time on "The Study of Religion," made a great impression on me. The professor's very first lecture was on "Mysticism." He commented broadly on the mystical aspects of various religions in a profoundly interesting manner. Professor Anesaki was a Buddhist but he had also studied Christianity. I was surprised to hear him express his religious attitude so lucidly, 'Because I am a Buddhist, I am a Christian, and because I am a Christian, I am a Buddhist.' And so, my eyes were once again opened to Buddhism.
>
> It was during my university days that I admired Professor Tsunashima Ryosen. The professor was an exceptional philosopher and a logician. On the occasion of his illness, he achieved a deep religious experience which he announced in the journal, *New Person*, under the title of "An Actual Experience of Seeing God." His was a vivid religious experience of the union of God and himself in the heart of the universe. This can be seen as a broad religious insight transcending Christianity and Buddhism. This article affected me greatly and taught me much.[44]

IMAOKA joined a new area in the Philosophy Section of the College of Literature. It was called the Science of Religion, being formed by a new professor, ANESAKI Masaharu. He had been affiliated[45] with the Unitarian Mission's School of Advanced Learning (*Senshi Gakuin*), lecturing there at the School for Advanced Learning and at both Unity Hall and in the Summer School training program. ANESAKI's involvement with Unitarian Christianity began through his invitations to lecture at the School. Their strategy was to acquaint scholars with the "unitarian

43. ANESAKI Masaharu (1873-1949) became his mentor and a lifelong colleague. He had been connected to the Unitarian Mission's school, the School of Advanced Learning, before it closed in 1900. He was also affiliated with the New Buddhist movement. Anesaki was a rapidly emerging scholar.

44. IMAOKA, Shin'ichirō, "I Believe in a Universal Cooperative Society" first published in *Rinri*, No. 384, Special Edition "Search for Faith" (Ethics).

45. How deeply involved with and sympathetic ANESAKI was with the American Unitarian Mission is a matter of scholarly debate. The Mission's second director, Clay MacCauley, would inform the American Unitarian Association that ANESAKI was a sympathizer.

philosophy" of free inquiry.[46] Within a year of his graduation from the philosophy program at the Imperial University, ANESAKI lectured about the issue of pathology in religion at Unity Hall,[47] arguing against claims that religious experience was pathological. He continued that interest by offering a course on the psychology of religion at Tōdai, a course that IMAOKA took.

IMAOKA's first publication was an essay *"Discussing Hero Worship from a Religious Perspective."*[48] It was published by his former school, Kumamoto Academy, back in his home province. He had begun a lifetime of writing essays about a current concern. His essay focused on a fear of Western psychology (that is, the Freudian school of psychology) and its claim that religious experience was but a pathology. Young Nobuichirō defended religions in general. Prof. Michel Mohr summarized IMAOKA's argument "against three main reductionist interpretations of religion":

> In short, religion can by no means be reduced to miracles, to a pathology, or to hypocrisy, and it should not be suppressed; it is a universal (*fuhenteki*) and necessary phenomenon that is generated by the inborn demand of the human mind.[49]

Not too bad a defense of religion and religious experience by a young student of religious studies. Yet, it was defensive against the *new*

---

46. Tatsushi NARITA, "About Masaharu Anesaki: Chronology" Chronological Notes 1873-1949. tatsushinarita.wordpress.com/masaharu-aesaki-chronology/ Accessed May 2013.

47. NARITA, *ibid.*

48. *"Shūkyō no kenchi ni tachite eiyū sūhai o ronzu"* translated by Michel Mohr, personal communications dated 10/20/2013 and 11/27/2013. Journal *Ryūnankai zasshi* No. 94 (October 1902), pp. 18-34. This periodical was issued between November 1891 and August 1919 by the *Daigo kōtō gakkō,* the school that later became Kumamoto University. Reprinted in IMAOKA Shin'ichirō. 1982. *Jinsei hyakunen.* [hereafter referenced as *Hundred Year Human Being*] Tokyo: *Daizō shuppan*, pp. 17-31. IMAOKA studied at Kumamoto school from 1900 to 1902.

49. Michel Mohr, *Buddhism, Unitarianism, and the Meiji Competition for Universality* (Cambridge, MA: Harvard University Press, 2014), p. 97.

psychological knowledge from the West.

ANESAKI identified strongly with Nichiren Buddhism, which normally was quite conservative and narrow in its openness to other views, even Buddhist ones. It preached an exclusive interpretation of *ekayāna* – which it understood as only one way of truth. Yet, ANESAKI had become a Buddhist universalist. *Ekāyana*, he taught, was the unity of all truth, in all forms of Buddhism, and in all religions. This universality would influence IMAOKA's viewpoint.

Through his Buddhist professor, IMAOKA was becoming a Christian universalist: that truth was not exclusive and the "plan of salvation" he had learned from Buxton and Wilkes was inadequate. God's grace was for all his children. IMAOKA loved to quote ANESAKI's words: "Because I am a Buddhist, I am a Christian, and because I am a Christian, I am a Buddhist." IMAOKA would learn much more about Buddhism in ANESAKI's classes, reading Buddhist scripture and essays in Japanese, Chinese and Sanskrit. This would become a future problem: how to be an evangelistic pastor who converted individuals from their own faith and also be a universalist who found truths in every faith?

There is no coincidence that the program in the scientific study of religion that ANESAKI put together at Tōdai resembled the one at the School for Advanced Learning.[50] Both used practicing scholars of their own tradition to teach about their faith – accurately, critically, historically, comparatively. In the "liberal" (specifically meaning "free inquiry") setting at the Unitarian's Unity Hall, where the School for Advanced Learning met, Christianity was treated in the very same way as other religions. There was an implied equality without one religion and its history or its scripture being privileged. This was

50. The School for Advanced Learning was a central part of the first period of the Japan Unitarian Mission and will be discussed in the next Section on Japanese Unitarianism and IMAOKA's involvement in it.

fully developed later in the Science of Religion program of the Philosophy Section at the Imperial University. The curriculum there was demanding, even for the most brilliant.

As a philosophy/religious studies student, IMAOKA had to pass exams in two Western languages of the three taught (English, German, French). He passed English and German. Plus, he would also have two semesters each of Greek and Sanskrit. These languages were important for scriptural studies: Greek for Christianity and Sanskrit for Indian religions, including Mahayana Buddhism.

The courses that he is known to have taken were among the minimum requirements to graduate with a degree in the Science of Religion. He had to take seven courses a semester: five semesters of the Science of Religion, two of Indian Philosophy, one of Chinese Philosophy, one of [Occidental] Philosophy, one of the History of Oriental Philosophy (*sic.*), one of the History of Occidental Philosophy, one of Ethics, one of Psychology, one of an Introduction to Aesthetics, one of the Fundamental Principles of Sociology, one of Anthropology, one of the Outline of Japanese History, and two semesters each of the aforementioned scriptural languages, Greek and Sanskrit.[51]

There was a richness available in the Philosophy Section, with its nine areas, as well as the College of Literature. He might have taken or just "sat in" – Philosophy, Chinese Philosophy, Indian Philosophy, Psychology, Ethics, Science of Religion, Aesthetics, Pedagogics, Sociology. He had only to sample these areas in his religious studies major, while concentrating on the scientific study of religion. He did mention fondly, decades later, about a visiting German philosopher whom he enjoyed and from whom he had acquired a lifelong habit: "one cannot be a philosopher if he does not smoke." IMAOKA cheerfully quoted his German professor, while

51. *Catalogue of Tokyo Imperial University*, Tokyo, 1903.

denying that he, himself, was a philosopher or a scholar. The Imperial University of Tokyo was bringing scholars from the best universities of Germany, England, and America to enrich its programs. Its professors and graduate students were also involved in exchanges with these universities.

It was in his university classes that IMAOKA engaged in textual criticism of the Christian New Testament. This is what Wilkes and missionaries feared: higher criticism of the Bible, comparing the Gospel stories of Jesus' life and finding contradictions, thus threatening the doctrine of Infallibility of the Bible.

IMAOKA recalled:

> Soon after I entered college, I began to doubt the historicity of the New Testament story concerning Jesus' life, and the validity of orthodox Christian doctrines. I moved, therefore, to a Congregational Church that was quite liberal in contrast to the Episcopal Church.[52]

He had turned to EBINA Danjō and his openness to *new knowledge* about Christianity.

As a Member of the Hongo Church of EBINA Danjō

EBINA acknowledged the difficulties that educated Japanese had with what the missionaries taught them. He published in 1909 what he had been preaching and what IMAOKA was attempting to use in his faith struggles:

> What, then, is Christianity? Educated Japanese answer: It is the religion taught by most of the Protestant missionaries in the last forty years—that the world was created in six days through periodical divine interventions, and that man was formed from the dust of the earth by the divine hand; that God was existent as the Holy Trinity before the creation; that death entered into the world through the sin of Adam, the ancestor of all mankind; that one of the three persons in the Godhead came down from heaven to save mankind from eternal death, was incarnated in the Virgin Mary,

52. "My Spiritual Pilgrimage," delivered before the Tokyo Unitarian Fellowship sometime in 1970.

performed many miracles, died on the cross to propitiate a wrathful God, was buried, and rose again bodily from the grave on the third day; that God lives somewhere in heaven, surrounded by angels and archangels, but sometimes comes down to earth to amend his work by supernatural operations; that Christ will come on the clouds of heaven to judge the world and separate the righteous from the wicked—and so forth. We once tried, they say, to believe this teaching, but could not. The God of Christians is a creation of their own imagination. Christians are good men, doing good works, encouraging temperance and philanthropy, but their doctrines are unreasonable and contradictory to science. Christianity is a relic of the past; it does not deserve the faith of students.[53]

Ebina, an ex-samurai who had also studied Confucian logic and ethics just as Imaoka did, acknowledged how primitive the missionaries' presentations of Christian dogmas sounded in Japanese. Ebina also met the arguments of Japanese intellectuals who rejected Christianity by using current European Enlightenment scholarship from Feuerbach[54] and Schleiermacher,[55] from *new theology*,[56] and from Christian Socialists. He was especially critical of the shortcomings of Liberal Christianity – the Universalists, Unitarians and German Free Church (whom Imaoka would soon meet). Ebina found his answer to all these critics in the message of Paul and the Sermon of the Mount:

But the God of Christ and his apostles has been ever present with the missionaries and the Christians of Japan, to will and to work in them for the furtherance of the eternal living gospel, the fatherhood of God and the brotherhood of mankind. Christianity has succeeded at many points. The people have recognized the truth taught in the Sermon on the Mount—the fatherhood of God, the inner righteousness of spiritual disposition, the worth of the individual soul, chastity, monogamy as the basis of the family, and

53. EBINA Danjo, "The Evangelization of Japan Viewed in Its Intellectual Aspect," *Harvard Theological Review* (April 1, 1909) Vol. 2 pp. 199-200.

54. Ludwig Feuerbach's *Essence of Jesus* was translated into English by Marian Evans (*aka* George Eliot) in 1855. By 1900 it was well know in Japan.

55. Friedrich Schleiermacher, *Der Christliche Glaube,* translated as *The Christian Faith* (1830).

56. IMAOKA would later translate Campbell's book on *The New Theology* as ANESAKI's assistant in the next phase of his spiritual pilgrimage.

the brotherhood of man.[57]

IMAOKA now heard EBINA preach a subtle form of *national consciousness*, not the uniqueness of nationalistic State Shinto that was propelling Japan toward perpetual war. But EBINA's call for a unique form of Japanese Christianity had in its implied nationalism a contradiction of ANESAKI's universalism. EBINA taught that a true Christian would be a true citizen, a true Japanese, independent of foreigners. Japanese Christianity would be uniquely Japanese. "Japan longs after the essence and kernel, not the formal hell of Christianity."[58] EBINA did not reject non-Japanese scholarship but stated that it must be suited to Japan's needs. This concern became more nationalistic as Japan's military voiced doubts that Christians could make good and loyal soldiers. IMAOKA sensed a dilemma.

At this time IMAOKA was being torn between the views of EBINA in the pulpit and ANESAKI in the classroom. (ANESAKI had joined Christian socialists and pacifists – KISHIMOTO, ABE, MURAI, and others – in both study groups and societies concerning socialism and pacifism.) For a time, IMAOKA followed EBINA, even becoming his assistant in Tokyo before accepting a pastorate of his own in Kobe. But the dissonance would grow with time.

An Imperial University Graduate

IMAOKA graduated from the Imperial University in 1906, the second graduating class of the Science of Religion within the Philosophy Section of the College of Literature.[59] Emperor Meiji attended the graduation on July 10, 1906.

His graduation was recorded in the Imperial University of Japan's *1910-11 Catalogue*. He was listed in the section of Gakushi and Other Graduates of 1906. The catalog was published in English and his name was transliterated as Shin'ichirō. In the future, he

57. EBINA, *op. cit.*, p. 200.
58. *Ibid.*, p. 201.
59. *Bungakushi* graduating from the *Imperial University of Tokyo (Tokyo Teikoku Daigaku) Calendar/Catalog*, p. 200.

would be Shin'ichirō in his dealing with his mentor, Prof. ANESAKI, and Nobuichirō in the countryside. That is, until he finally decided that the more common pronunciation of Shin'ichirō would be easier for others to remember.

	1906	
Seiji Itō	Sōbu Kurozumi	Kinzō Satō
Kankyō Moriya	Shyūhō Tsukahara	Gyōshō Yoshida
Shinichirō Imaoka		

From page 200 of the Imperial University of Japan's *1910-11 Catalogue.*

Marriage after Graduation

At EBINA's church, in its youth group, IMAOKA met FUKUDA Utayo. Her family was of the former samurai class. By every account of those who knew her, she was an "alpha female." She ordered, led, commanded. She would prove to be innovative and was an early adopter of the new possibilities for women. In time, she would become a national feminist leader in Japan.

They married in 1907, shortly after IMAOKA graduated and had served some months as EBINA's assistant. That was the only real preparation that IMAOKA had for ministry. He was the first graduate from the Imperial University to become a Christian pastor.

Yet how could his studies in the Science of Religion program prepare him for ministry? One answer is that it didn't just as missionaries and Japanese Christian leaders other than EBINA had said. They had strongly advised him to attend a Christian school. Another answer is that he was experiencing what a minister's life could be by participating in EBINA's church and youth group by observing ministry and its possibilities for leadership and study. EBINA modeled an openness to liberal Christianity – that is, free inquiry – as long as it did not threaten the quest for a true, independent, Japanese faith and practice – and loyalty to Japan and its Emperor. EBINA drew the line just before that liberalism would have taken him out of mainstream Christianity into Unitarianism or Universalism.

IMAOKA was recommended by EBINA for one of the largest and most important congregations of the Kumi-ai movement in Kobe. Since each congregation was independent, EBINA's recommendation of his star disciple had to await their decision. It came almost immediately. In 1907 Utayo and Nobuichirō left Tokyo for Kobe and a life together there.

•••

A Note about Conversions and Religious Experience

Experientially, IMAOKA professed no new religious experience during his university years. He spoke of this period as one of learning and growing. He had learned to cognize carefully and critically. He became comfortable in academia with its open inquiry and its quest for demonstrable truths. Above all, he learned to use reason and logic to express his views and accept appropriate judgments and criticism of them.

Under EBINA's influence, there seems to have been a consolidation of a special kind of devotional religion. He attended worship every Sunday and was part of an active youth group. He became EBINA's assistant. Worship involved public prayer, church music, Bible readings, and a sermon. Combining a rational religious approach to Christianity with his deep devotional faith and practice, EBINA helped IMAOKA to be comfortable with questions that could not be answered immediately, if at all. But there was tension, if not contradiction, in EBINA's approach. In the classroom with ANESAKI, IMAOKA experienced a belief that free inquiry would lead to verifiable truths, possibly even universal ones. At church, EBINA utilized free inquiry in his quest for a Japanese Christianity that had some hidden norms. EBINA's not-so-hidden nationalism would justify loyal Christian citizens to fight for Japan in just wars. But when were wars just? Another tension was EBINA's adapted evolutionary model of religion with a rationalized, devotional Japanese Christianity as the truest and best religion. Therefore, conversion to Christianity was necessary, and it would usher in the Kingdom of God. Evangelism is presupposed, and a Christian's duty was to convert others.

IMAOKA Nobuichirō did not have a spiritual or existential crisis in Tokyo as had been feared by Congregational missionaries. He matured and grew in his faith and practice, but his internalized dissonance would soon manifest in his Kobe ministry.

TIMELINE (Imaoka, Age 22-25)

1903 Entered Tokyo Imperial University, College of Literature, Philosophy, Science of Religion program.

1906 Graduated Tokyo Imperial University

1907 Married FUKUDA Utayo

1907 Accepts call to be the pastor of Hyogo Kyokai

Japanese Events

1872 First Protestant Christian church was founded at Yokohama

1888 Viscount MORI, a Christian statesman, was assassinated. [End of Period of Acceptance and Light, Beginning of Period of Struggle and Criticism]

1889 Promulgation of the Japanese Constitution with freedom of religion [Christianity was no longer banned]

1890 Imperial Rescript on Education

1893 World's Parliament of Religions, Chicago. Eight Japanese delegates, including KISHIMOTO, attended, whom IMAOKA will meet in the next period of his life

1894-95 Sino-Japanese War

Chapter 4
Pastoring a Kumi-ai Church (1907-10)

Arrival in Kobe

IMAOKA Nobuichirō[60] arrived in Kobe in 1907 with his bride, FUKUDA Utayo, seemingly fired by a zeal to evangelize like his mentor EBINA Danjō. EBINA had nominated him, and the Hyogo Kumi-ai (Congregational) church had called him to be their pastor. This church was historic among the Congregational Kumi-ai churches. It was one of the original congregations that had been lead by NIISHIMA Jō to organize into an independent association within the American Congregational Mission.[61] They wanted to be free of foreign rule, both directly from missionaries or indirectly from foreign funding. These churches became self-supporting – almost, although they did receive small foreign mission offerings at Christmas and occasional gifts of foreign support. But Japanese Christians wanted and needed to be able to say to the government that they were independent, loyal to the state, and not a hidden asset of a colonial power.

Some call it *Zeitgeist*, the spirit of the times. There had been a major shift in the country's attitude toward Westernization (*ōkashugi*). Until about 1890, Japan was open to Western science, technology, military arts, culture and even religion. But as Japan was still being treated as an inferior, even after its victory over Russia in 1905, and

---

60. Away from the sophistication of Tokyo and the Imperial University, he was again Nobuichirō. The same Chinese character 信 can be read Shin or Nobu. "Nobu" would be difficult for others to remember. He would finally change for their sake later in life.

61. The Indigenous Japanese Congregation Association adopted the name *Kumi-ai*, meaning union or "brotherhood".

the unequal treaties had not been revised, the national mood had an effect even on Japanese Christianity.

Ready to Serve

IMAOKA never spoke about his extraordinary education at the Imperial University. Yet, not attending the denominational Bible college for ministers, Dōshisha, may have meant that IMAOKA lacked some pastoral skills and would have struggled in his first ministry. But, that seemed not to have been the case as he attended EBINA's church in Tokyo and had seen how EBINA handled the worship services with hour-long sermons (at least), altar calls for conversion, celebrations, weddings, funerals, baptisms, and the Lord's Supper. Any one of these might have been a challenge, but he seemed to have had no problems. Nor was there any complaint known to come from his congregation.

Even the financial difficulties that accompanied ministry did not seem to matter – at least for him. Salaries for ministers in Kumi-ai churches were barely enough for survival, coming from the offerings of the congregation. Yet, both churches and ministers were proud of being independent of any foreign assistance. A minister was called to serve and to sacrifice. IMAOKA gladly adopted this mode of living and continued practicing it the rest of his life.

Within a year, IMAOKA would receive national recognition in the larger Christian community (which included the mainstream Christian denominations). Others saw a bright future for this Imperial University graduate. He had only to learn how to lead a congregation ritually, educationally and experientially. Young and enthusiastic, he seemed ready for great success as a Kumi-ai minister.

Some of the most promising Kumi-ai ministers had not been able to continue in the ministry because of their questioning. TOYOSAKI Zennosuke, another leader from Kobe, had been a zealot in converting others throughout high school and his Bible college days.

TOYOSAKI explained: "But when I entered a preacher's life, I was placed exactly in the same situation as Mr. Emerson in the pastorate of a Boston Congregational Church. As a pastor I should have preached the salvation of souls, but my mind was clouded with doubts."[62]

Almost every Kumi-ai minister had been converted to Christianity, as MURAI Tomoyoshi (1861-1944) had put it, because of "the high and noble aspirations of the Christian life, and ...[being] possessed with the idea of devoting my life to the work of the moral elevation of my country."[63] He had found Channing's sermons[64] in the Dōshisha library and determined that he would go to America and study "Christianity thoroughly and critically so as to solve [his] theological doubts."[65] He did and returned to tell other Kumi-ai ministers about his discoveries. They were about a liberal Christianity of free inquiry that the missionaries feared.

ABE Isō (1865-1949) began as a minister but discovered that he "could not preach the Christian doctrines with a bold spirit unless [he] grasped some foundation firmer than what [he] had before. ... [I]n the Dōshisha college [he] was so overwhelmed with the kindness of the teachers and my fellow students that I felt no need of investigating its doctrinal side. But as a minister [he] could not evade the questions which one might ask me. ... In a word [he] felt the need of studying

---

62. Japan Unitarian Mission [Clay MacCauley], *The Unitarian Movement in Japan, Sketches of the Lives and Religious Work of Ten Representative Japanese Unitarians.* Tokyo, 1898; 1890, p. 49. The reference is to Ralph Waldo Emerson, who resigned his Unitarian pastorate and later was the senior member of the Free Religious Association. Emerson's writings were published by the Japan Unitarian Mission and were influential during this period.

63. *Sketches, ibid.,* p. 36.

64. William Ellery Channing (1780-1842) was an early "unitarian" and humanist in revolt against the Standing Order of Congregationalism in New England. His sermons were a major influence both there and in Japan.

65. *Sketches, ibid, p.* 37.

the nature of the Bible scientifically."[66]

KISHIMOTO Nobuta (1866-1945), who left teaching at Dōshisha school and became editor of the YMCA magazine, *Rikugō Zasshi*, was one of a growing group of Kumi-ai liberals returning from foreign theological studies. While in America, KISHIMOTO had even participated in the 1893 World's Parliament of Religions. His questions arose during his ministry before going to America and Germany for further studies:

> Why should an all-wise and all-merciful God allow sin and evil to enter into this world? Is this the best world God can create? Why was not Christ born in Japan? Is there no salvation but through Christ? Is Confucius saved? If God is omniscient, what is the use of praying to Him? Why must Christians, God's own people, lead a poor and despised life, full of trials and persecutions? Did Christ actually perform the miracles ascribed to him? Were the prophecies really foretold and fulfilled as they are said to have been? Did Christ claim himself to be divine? If so, in what sense? How can the infallibility of the Bible be proved? Are there not many things in which the teachings of science and philosophy cannot be reconciled with those of the Bible? Can one be justified in believing as true what he cannot but think to be contradictory?[67]

These returning ministers with their *new knowledge* from their studies in America and Europe were accepted in Kumi-ai pulpits and invited to speak at ministerial meetings. What they shared was a challenge to the views of Congregational missionaries – and to young ministers like IMAOKA.

Preaching Expository Sermons

Young IMAOKA seemed well aware of all this questioning, but his immediate focus was learning to be a good minister. That meant that he needed to be prepared every Sunday to preach and lead in worship. Of course, there were many other duties and responsibilities, but he saw the sermon as the means by which he

---

66. *Ibid.*, p. 50. *"He" replaces "I" in this quotation, as it expresses what most of this group thought.*

67. *Sketches, ibid,* p. 31.

educated his congregation. He did not burden his congregation with his doubts. Instead, he preached "expository sermons" from passages in New Testament focusing of the life and ethics of Jesus. The Sermon of the Mount (Matthew 5) was his favorite, as it was also EBINA's. IMAOKA translated directly from Greek, trying to use Japanese words that were open to insight. He avoided concepts that had given him doubt (virgin birth, miracles, resurrection) and focused on the joy of the new life of following the example of Jesus.

While Biblical literalism had been taught at Dōshisha (that the Bible is absolute truth because it is the very Word of God), IMAOKA had been taught literary criticism at Tōdai. That was how the Confucian Classics had been studied for centuries. Students were taught to question the authorship of each book in the "Confucian Canon," its approximate date, its literary form (whether history, story, myth, legend, etc.) and much more. Ministers trained at Dōshisha were taught not to see literary differences in the Christian Bible since the Holy Spirit was its author; they were shocked by higher criticism that came from fellow ministers fresh returning from advanced studies in New Testament and Christian theology.

IMAOKA's studies at Tōdai did not seem to lead to the problems of KOZAKI Hiromichi who complained about the way he had been taught at Dōshisha. KOZAKI said that it was "ludicrous in the extreme" that a missionary professor at Dōshisha had treated the Old Testament like a scientific textbook. He tried to force his students to believe literally in the stories in Genesis "as if he were teaching children in Sunday school or inhabitants of the South Seas."[68] KOZAKI was a brilliant student, a former samurai, one of the original Kumamoto Band who had fled to Dōshisha and was now a

68. Yosuke NIREI, "Toward a Modern Belief: Modernist Protestantism and Problems of National Belief in Meiji Japan," *Japanese Journal of Religious Studies,* 34/1 (2007), p. 159.

Kumi-ai minister. IMAOKA's Old Testament studies had been in English and not Hebrew, but the narratives in each book were studied at Tōdai as Jewish wisdom rather than science or history.

Depending on how rigorous his year of Greek study of the New Testament had been, IMAOKA should have had no problem translating a fresh and vital message. His main focus in 1907 was to know the original teachings of Jesus. The literary forms that he studied in the Confucian Classics would have certainly helped as he found different types of literature in the New Testament: parables, one primary saying from Jesus in Aramaic ("My God, My God, why have you forsaken me?"),[69] Hebraisms in some of the books, and so much more. But, he focused on the Sermon on the Mount and its vision of the Kingdom of God as the truest and most authentic message of Jesus.

Leading in Worship

The Kumi-ai (Congregational) "Order of Service" gave a certain amount of freedom wherein the minister could pray spontaneously or use prepared prayers, choose hymns, pick a sermon topic, and even decide how long to preach. He prayed orally in church but would not petition or beg for God's favor. He prayed in thanksgiving and for guidance. The offertory prayer was moved from before the congregation gave their tithes and offerings to afterwards – thus becoming a blessing for the congregation's generosity rather than an emotional appeal for a greater gift.

Picking the hymns was an art to be learned. The Doxology was common to all orthodox missions and churches ("Praise God from whom all blessings flow..."). Japanese hymnology had made significant progress since he became a Christian. The Episcopal [Anglican] worship service in Matsue suffered from hymns that were strange both in their wording and music. Early translations were poor and had to be revised many times. But by 1903, a joint effort by the

---

69. "*Eli, Eli, lama sabachthani*?" Matthew 5:46, quoting Psalm 22:1.

major missions had resulted in a unified hymnal that had 125 shared hymns as well as a number of Japanese originals. Eiko Matsumoto NAGAI [Western name order], a Methodist hymn writer, wrote "Heavenly streams so pure and dear." It was one of the oldest hymns from 1884 and sang of the living water that Jesus talked about with the woman at the well.[70] Yet, IMAOKA struggled with the hymns inherited from a inter-denomination committee whose theology stressed the devotional and emotional aspects of faith and practice with questionable theology.

Despite his care to be personally honest as he led in worship, there were areas of worship that caused concern. For most Kumi-ai ministers (and the majority were conservative), these concerns had been addressed before the new century. Their attention was consumed by the *new theology* reaching them at ministerial meetings and in *liberal* publications. However, IMAOKA conscientiously approached public worship as his immediate responsibility. Even what had been decided a decade before in the Kumi-ai churches had to be examined afresh by him.

A Sunday worship service customarily had the congregation recite either the Apostles' Creed or a Declaration of Faith. IMAOKA knew the Apostles' Creed from his days as an Anglican at Matsue. He would have been free to lead his congregation in reciting it but did not.

> I believe in *God* the Father Almighty,
> *Maker* of heaven and earth, [*creator – ex nihilo* as taught at Dōshisha]
> And in Jesus Christ his *only Son* our Lord, [Son of God, i.e, the Emperor]
> Who was *conceived* by the Holy Ghost,
> Born of the *Virgin* Mary, [virgin birth]

---

70. Pauline Smith McAlpine, "Japanese Hymnody: Its Background and Development," *The Hymn*, vol. 32, 1981, p. 41.

Suffered under Pontius Pilate,
Was *crucified*, dead, and buried:
He descended into *hell*;
The third day he *rose again from the dead*; [resurrection from the dead]
He ascended into heaven,
And sitteth on the right hand of God the Father Almighty;
From thence he shall come to judge the quick and the dead.
I believe in the *Holy Ghost*; [ghost or spirit – problematic]
The holy Catholic Church;
The Communion of Saints;
The Forgiveness of sins;
The *Resurrection* of the body, [again, resurrection]
And the *Life everlasting*. Amen.

Each of the italicized English words provided special problems for Japanese converts: linguistically, philosophically and even scientifically. For instance, the only Chinese characters (kanji) for the word "God" were *tiān* (天, "Heaven") and *shàngdì* (上帝, "Highest Deity" or "Highest Emperor"), *dì* (帝, Lord) and *shén* (神, God, Supernatural Being; J: *Kami*). Most Protestant missions chose the Chinese character, *shén* (神), whose *on'yomi* reading or Sino-Japanese pronunciation is *shin* (the Japanese kanji 神). The *kun'yomi* reading or pronunciation is *kami*, the Shinto word for God or Gods. Modifiers make the word singular or plural. Teaching a plurality of Gods or even one God (*Kami*) as undistinguished from all other Gods (Kami) was hardly acceptable. For any literary person, a specific kanji had to be chosen to identify the Christian God. Translating "God's Son" into literary Japanese was even more problematic. In China and Japan, "son of God" (*tenshi* 天子, *tiān zǐ* in Chinese) was the Emperor, Heaven's adopted son.

Kumi-ai theologians moved away from the Apostles' Creed toward a nominal Confession of Faith with some latitude for personal interpretation. They tried to explain Christianity in "simple and brief" terms. In 1891, the Kumi-ai churches had adopted a "statement of faith" declaring their beliefs with the proviso that it was not a creed. No one had to believe every word or phrase. (They were moving away from a belief-centered Christianity toward a more experiential one.)

> "We believe in one God, infinite, perfect, who is made known in the Bible as Holy Father, Holy Son, and Holy Spirit.
> We believe in Jesus Christ, who, being God, became man; who suffered and died and rose again that He might save sinners. We believe in the Holy Spirit, who bestows the new life.
> We believe in the Bible, which was given by the inspiration of God and makes us wise unto salvation.
> We believe in the Holy Church, baptism by water, the Lord's Supper, the Holy Lord's Day, eternal life, the resurrection of the dead, and in just rewards and punishments."[71]

And yet again in 1895, they gathered in Nara to make a "declaration of faith" to the deputation of the American Board of the Congregational Mission who were investigating the latest "belief" crisis at Dōshisha college. The American Board came because missionaries reported that their Japanese ministers and churches were becoming too liberal and were not accepting Christianity literally. The new "Declaration of Faith" stated:

> We who, believing and revering Jesus Christ as Saviour, are called of God; do greatly mourn over the present condition of the world, and assembled here in prayer unto God and in the rich enjoyment of the Holy Spirit's gracious influence, we determine to proclaim the Gospel and to establish the kingdom of God according to the following principles:
> 1. That all men should repent of all sin, and through Christ should return unto obedience to the Heavenly Father.
> 2. That all men being the children of God, the great principles of love and sympathy should be upheld among them.
> 3. That the home should be purified by maintaining the principles

[71] Otis Cary, *A History of Christianity in Japan: Protestant Missions* (New York: Fleming H. Revell Co., 1909)., p. 259.

of monogamy; and the mutual duties of parents and children, elder and younger brothers, should be fulfilled.
4. That the nation should be elevated and the welfare of mankind promoted.
5. That the hope of eternal life should be perfected through faith and righteousness.[72]

This concern about a declaration or statement of one's faith became a lifelong habit. Even after moving beyond Kumi-ai (Congregational) ministry, IMAOKA would write a tentative "Statement of Faith" each New Year.

He had found a way to lead in worship as a celebration of God's love and the joy of living ethically. Church life had become rich and fulfilling – in stark contrast to the poverty which the IMAOKAS shared that first year.

Ordination and Recognition

There were external signs that he was succeeding. The *Mission News* proudly announced his ordination on April 11th, 1907. He was ordained at the Hyogo Association's semi-annual meeting. The *Mission News* commented further: "His conversion and choice of the ministry may be regarded as one of the results of Rev. T. F. Buxton's work at Matsuyo [Matsue]."[73] Buxton was by then the supervisor of the Evangelical Band that he and Wilkes had established in Kobe; it was Buxton's name that was associated with this rising star in the Kumi-ai movement. A year later in 1908, *The Christian Movement in Japan: Sixth Annual Issue* published by the Methodist Publishing House mentioned IMAOKA twice: "The first Imperial University alumnus to enter the ministry is Rev. N. Imaoka who has recently become pastor of the Kumi-ai (Cong.) Church at Hyogo."[74] IMAOKA seems to have spoken at a Y.M.C.A gathering and is mentioned

72. *Ibid.,* p. 260.
73. *Mission News*, vol. XL, No. 2 (Kobe, Japan. April 15, 1908) p. 112.
74. *The Christian Movement*: *Sixth Annual Issue.* Published for the Standing Committee of Co-operating Missions (Tokyo: Methodist Publishing House, 1908), p.47. [Cong. = Congregational]

prominently in their section:

> The [YMCA] Association secretaries have attempted more systematically than ever before to press upon the attention of young men the opportunity of the Christian ministry. This has been done by addresses, conferences, and by articles in the Association organ, 'The Pioneer.' One of the most helpful influences in the direction of securing graduates of the Imperial Universities for the ministry is the ordination of Rev. S. Imaoka, a graduate of the Tokyo Imperial University, to the ministry at Hyogo."[75]

His contact with the YMCA would be rewarded several years later when he would become one of the editorial assistants for their magazine, the *Cosmos* (*Rikugō Zasshi*).

His ordination in 1907 had come almost immediately, showing the approval of his congregation and the association of Kumi-ai churches. Everything seemed to be going well in that first year of ministry. There was one exception to all this success; Utayo decided to leave Kobe and go back to Tokyo. She left to attend NARUSE Jinzō's Tokyo Women's College and study Japanese literature. She had been in Kobe less than a year. She asserted her right of independence; IMAOKA did not voice any objection. (He had married above his "station" – she from a former samurai family, he a farmer. Poverty could have been the tipping point. Her freedom would become a lifelong theme as she developed her interests.)

Ministerial Meetings

As a pastor, IMAOKA was expected to participate in numerous ministerial meetings, conferences and retreats. He was not yet used as a speaker but was there to learn from others' experiences and insights. An earlier generation of ministers were returning from universities and seminaries or universities in Europe and America, mainly New England – the main region of Congregational Christianity. This made these meetings exciting and exhilarating, but probably only for the ministers who did not fear questioning their beliefs and risking

75. *Ibid.*, p. 246.

change in their religious identities. IMAOKA loved open inquiry. They brought news of the *new learning*, and its theological questions and scholarship. He would get to know the members of the Kumamoto Band who were now leaders in the Kumi-ai churches. Some would become his associates for life.

The shift in Japanese Christianity, in general, and the Kumi-ai movement in particular, had mirrored his own development. During Imaoka's short time as a conservative Christian, a belief-centered, orthodox faith had shifted as dramatically as had his own. It was becoming less creedal, insisting that one did not have to believe all the doctrines arriving from America and Europe. The teachings of Jesus were being pursued critically and *scientifically*[76] by the most educated ministers. And, importantly, they were not being forced out of the Kumi-ai movement. These liberals were in the minority, but they were tolerated.

All this had led to a split along theological lines as conservatives and liberals (using labels from the West), and another split according to the burning issues of the day. The majority of ministers were uncomfortable with the vastness of change that had come in every area of their lives. They turned to leaders who defended the Christianity that the missionaries had taught them. And, they gladly called themselves evangelistic and conservative. Former Anglican Paget Wilkes, now a non-denominational missionary evangelist, used these meeting to press ministers to holiness and a Pentecostal religious experience rather than liberal studies. He pressed them to seek a second conversion by the Holy Ghost with signs of a true Pentecost.[77]

---

76. Again, italicized words are used to signal terms which are normative, technical or weighted ideologically. Simply, they have a privileged usage by a group or individual.

77. Paget Wilkes, *Missionary Joys in Japan or Leaves from My Journal* (New York: George H. Doran Co., 1913), p. 32.

One group of ministers were part of the Kumamoto Band and had graduated from Dōshisha along with EBINA. They would become a part of IMAOKA's life, both in this period and later – ABE Isō, KISHIMOTO Nobuta and MURAI Tomoyoshi – known later as the Dōshisha Trio. ABE and KISHIMOTO began teaching at Dōshisha, but they had to leave when missionaries and the mission board fought back against the college's growing religious liberalism.

Already, there had been two major crises at Dōshisha, the last actually bringing consensus among the ministers. The Japanese board of directors was criticized for trying to make Dōshisha a secular college in order to receive state funds. The American Congregational Church threatened to withhold its funding because Dōshisha had, from their point of view, become too liberal. The board had attempted to become free of mission control. But their solution was to make Dōshisha, the pride of Japanese indigenous Christianity, into a non-Christian institution. The board was forced to resign. But then, the ablest professors and the college president resigned as well. That is when ABE and KISHIMOTO left Dōshisha.

Japanese church historian KISHIMOTO Hideo (1903-64), son of KISHIMOTO Nobuta, described the mood of Japanese Christianity a generation later:

> The churches longed for theological discussion. They had become dissatisfied with American orthodoxy. They turned to the comparatively free interpretations of European theology which were introduced to Japan by the German Universal Evangelical Mission. Unitarianism with its tradition of British deism and American theology followed shortly afterward. Its claim that the Bible was the work of man rather than the word of God satisfied the intellectualism of Meiji Christians.[78]

The contest between liberal studies or *new knowledge* ("New Theology" as it would come to be called) and an evangelical, pietistic

---

[78] Kishimoto Hideo, trans. by John F. Howes, *Japanese Religion in the Meiji Era*, vol. II. (Tokyo: Ōbunsha, 1954), p. 270.

faith (with some becoming Holiness or Pentecostal) was not the most important issue for Kumi-ai ministers. They were disturbed by the struggle of three charismatic leaders – EBINA Danjō (1856-1937), UEMURA Masahira (1858-1925) and UCHIMURA Kanzō (1861-1930) – who challenged ministers with issues they thought would make the Gospel more accessible to Japanese, less creedal and more independent of foreign control. The issues were complicated and often heated. They feared that Christianity could be outlawed again, and they had very different approaches to that fear.

As IMAOKA listened at these meetings and read the discussions in the many publications of that era, both liberal and conservative, he found bits of truth that would become part of his lifelong quest. He had an inner stability that was both loyal to past religious experience (his conversions) and open to new change and growth. He believed one did not need to renounce their earlier religious identity, only add what one learned from direct experience.

KISHIMOTO Hideo, writing as a conservative church historian, was critical of the theological debates of three leaders (EBINA, UEMURA and UCHIMURA) during this period.[79] Imaoka had come into the Kumi-ai movement sponsored by the smallest group's leader, Ebina, who identified his group as "national-spiritual."[80] He had debated creedalism with UEMURA Masahira and the divinity of Jesus with UCHIMURA Kanzō in 1902. The majority had followed the more conservative leaders, defending the full historicity of the Gospels and the truth of doctrinal or creedal Christianity.

The Ethos of Kumi-ai Christianity

One issue that caused division along liberal-conservative lines was the infallibility of the Bible. The majority of ministers believed

79. KISHIMOTO Hideo, *op. cit.*, p. 273.

80. Danjo Ebina [EBINA Danjō], "The Evangelization of Japan viewed in its Intellectual Aspect," *Harvard Theological Review* (Tokyo, Japan, April 1, 1909), Vol. 2., pp. 186-201.

that the Bible was absolutely true, as they had been taught by the missionaries. They privileged the Bible as divinely authored and defended their position with ever diminishing claims. (How could there be two Davids who killed Goliath? How could there have been enough rain to have covered the earth in forty days?) UEMURA defended God's perfect revelation in the Bible and the creeds that made it clear. EBINA openly attacked UEMURA's biblicism and demonstrated the benefits of not fearing a more open study of the Bible. But, inerrancy of the Bible was hardly IMAOKA's issue as he had been trained in the scientific study of religion to see all texts as human. The Word of God was, for most Dōshisha ministers, literally, the very words of God. But, they seemed not to know, that the Protestant Reformation began when the simple question was asked: in which language did God speak his Word? Latin had to yield to the Biblical languages of Greek and Hebrew. That led to a search for an original text which was dictated by the Holy Spirit. All existing Biblical manuscripts had variances, some slight, some major (like the missing last verses in the Gospel of Mark concerning the resurrection). By nineteen century, textual or higher criticism struggled with the differing accounts of the life and sayings of Jesus. Three of the Gospels, the synoptics (Matthew, Mark and Luke), were very different from John's Gospel. And their theological differences were becoming the focus of German theologians. Kishimoto brought back German scholarship to Congregational ministers. (Besides liberal publications that were getting wide circulation, a German liberal mission had arrived in the 1890s with an advanced training in "higher criticism" or modern Biblical studies.)

The fallacy of literalism and its privileging the Bible as absolutely true was obvious to those who had studied Chinese literature and Confucianism. One studied the Chinese Classics and searched for wisdom and ethical principles in a literature that contained history, biography, fable, poetry, etc. One needed to know the genre of the literature in order to understand and interpret it properly.[81] All of the Kumamoto Band were former samurai who had begun their education attempting to find nuanced principles for ethical living. By the beginning of the twentieth century, most of the Kumi-ai ministers were of a different class – laborers and farmers, without this kind of literary and ethical background.

A moderating position was suggested by KOZAKI Hiromichi, one of the Kumamoto Band and Dōshisha trained. KOZAKI defended the Bible acknowledging the inspiration of human authors. "The authors of the Bible wrote under the grace of the holy spirit which inspired their reason, emotions, and intelligence. Therefore, the thoughts expressed in the Bible do not transcend those of humans."[82] KOZAKI said that the Bible was the irrefutable standard for faith and morals, emphasizing an ethical life. Some missionaries and orthodox ministers called him a heretic. KISHIMOTO Hideo characterized KOZAKI's party as "ecclesiastical and spiritual." Their devotional and evangelical spirit was intense, their loyalty firm. IMAOKA saw the truth of KOZAKI's loyalty, not to the Bible, but to his experienced faith, his spiritual life. IMAOKA never denigrated devotional religion but affirmed its truths that gave assurance and support for sustained moral action. Conservative Christians were often exemplary in living sacrificial lives, and they were generous in both time and resources. IMAOKA affirmed their practice of their faith even when he could not accept their beliefs or perspective.

UCHIMURA Kanzō led those who were concerned about how economics influenced religion – specifically the Kumi-ai ministers.

---

81. See, for example, a modern study by John Charlot trained in French Roman Catholic biblical studies: *New Testament Disunity: Its Significance for Christianity Today* (New York: E. P. Dutton, 1970), 260pp.

82. KISHIMOTO Hideo, *op. cit.,* p. 272.

Receiving foreign money from America or even a salary from a church corrupted ministers, UCHIMURA believed. The very ecclesiastical structure of a paid ministry or priesthood corrupted religion. He started the "no church" (*mu kyōkai*) movement based on his Biblical interpretation of the lives of Jesus and Paul. Neither, he said, were paid to lead their flock. Neither constructed or owned church buildings. In fact, "there was no ecclesiastical order as it is today to be found in the New Testament."[83] IMAOKA was deeply impressed by the notion of an unpaid ministry and Christian fellowships or communities who met without buying and maintaining expensive churches – that is, buildings. IMAOKA was deeply moved by this aspect of UCHIMURA's concept of the Christian life. KISHIMOTO Hideo called UCHIMURA's approach to ministry "spiritual and individualistic."[84]

UCHIMURA had attacked the *new theology* of EBINA in 1902, especially EBINA's doubt in the "divinity of Christ."[85] That debate moved from the ministerial meetings to each creating a journal to champion their ideas.[86] UCHIMURA believed firmly in Biblical revelation. He attacked denominationalism (the lack of unity and cooperation among Christian missions and missionaries), the inappropriateness of missionaries bringing their divisions and jealousies to Japan, their mixing American culture with religion (another way of condemning views of cultural and racial superiority),

83. UCHIMURA Kanzō, *The Diary of a Japanese Convert* (1895). See also Carlo Caldarola, *Christianity: The Japanese Way* (1919) and Mark Mullins, "Christianity as a Transnational Social Movement," *Japanese Religions,* Vol. 32 (1 & 2): 69-87.

84. KISHIMOTO Hideo, *op. cit.*, p. 273.

85. EBINA was debating the "divinity of Jesus" as Jesus refers to a human being. UCHIMURA framed the debate the way theologians had for centuries, as in the creeds, that Jesus was fully man, and Christ was fully God. The "divinity of Christ" would be seen logically, as those with Confucian training would argue, an unproven tautology. Gordon Melton in the *Encyclopedia of Protestantism,* 2005.

86. UCHIMURA in *Fukuin Shimpo* and EBINA in *New Man*, cited in KISHIMOTO Hideo, *op. cit.,* p. 275.

and the simple fact that these denominations were not found in the New Testament nor were their church hierarchies. He taught Christian morality: "to love the one and only true God, sovereign of the universe, with all your heart and strength, and to love neighbors as oneself." He insisted that Japanese Christianity conform with the Japanese structure of spirituality.[87]

EBINA Danjō broke with the Evangelical Alliance in 1902, after his debates with UEMURA and UCHIMURA.[88] Both the parties of UCHIMURA and UEMURA remained in the Alliance, which was beginning to see itself as a bulwark for orthodoxy against free inquiry and Biblical criticism. Most missionaries, including the leaders of the Evangelical Band (Buxton and Wilkes) were solidly orthodox-conservative-evangelical. This kind of questioning was condemned by most missionaries of all mainstream Protestant denominations (Congregational, Presbyterian-Reformed, Methodist, Baptist, Anglican-Episcopal, etc.). The non-denominational bridge between them all was the Evangelical Band and its leaders, Buxton and Wilkes. In his *Missionary Joys in Japan: Leaves from my Journal*, Wilkes summed up his criticism with a little vitriol:

> Only saved from heathenism a few years at most, without any careful training in the perusal and study of the Scriptures, they are plunged into surroundings where all the vapourings of German, English, and American critics are at their disposal. It seems the proper thing nowadays to stock the libraries of theological colleges with this kind of literature; and these young men, already predisposed to a sort of think-as-you-please attitude, find plenty of pabulum for their intellectual pride.[89]

Wilkes devoted a final chapter of his diary to a condemnation of "free inquiry" and "Higher Criticism" of the Bible. He had feared the result when his star conversion had gone to the Imperial

87. Melton, *ibid.*. See also, UCHIMURA Kanzō, *The Diary of a Japanese Convert* (New York, F.H. Revell Co., [c1895], p. 171

88. Melton, *ibid.*.

89. Wilkes, *op. cit.*, p. 317.

University in Tokyo. Now he saw what might be his future as Kumi-ai ministers were returning to Japan after more liberal theological studies.

> For sixteen years I have been labouring in this country, and have travelled many thousands of miles in all directions, met Missionaries of all denominations, seen all kinds of work, mixed with Christians of all classes and persuasions, and have never yet seen or heard of any individual or any body of Christians brought nearer to Christ, and made more earnest or intelligent workers in His Kingdom, through the influence of Modern Criticism. I have, on the contrary, seen and heard of many bewildered, deceived and spiritually ruined thereby.[90]

With yet another twist in the use of textual criticism, EBINA Danjō, whose party KISHIMOTO Hideo called "national-spiritual," used *new theology* to refute Western accretions in Christianity, finding them incompatible with the Japanese spirit. EBINA wrote:

> Jesus and the apostles did not preach doctrines like the Trinity, which are used to judge whether people are believers or not. The doctrine of the Trinity and the Incarnation of the Logos are nothing but explanations of the religious consciousness of Christians in the ancient world. Nobody can turn their assertions into eternal and unchangeable truth.[91]

Decades later, KISHIMOTO Hideo wrote that EBINA understood the relationship between God and man in terms of the Confucian ethics of the relationship; "the difference between Christ and us is not one of substance, but in the degree of development."[92] Kishimoto continued:

> Ebina Danjō was not a nationalist in the jingoistic sense of the word. But the nationalistic strains in his patriotism influenced him to favor Japanese Christianity in order to make it comprehensible to as many Japanese as possible. Other Christian leaders, for similar reasons, attempted to fuse Christianity to Buddhism and

---

90. *Ibid.,* p. 318.

91. EBINA, "Evangelization," *op. city,* p. 189.

92. EBINA, *The Essence of Christianity, 1903, cited in Iwai Shuma,* "Toward a critical analysis and constructive engagement of Ebina Danjo's contextualized theology and worldview" by Iwai, Shuma, Ph.D. dissertation, Reformed Theological Seminary, 2009, p. 253.

Confucianism.[93]

EBINA preached a nascent nationalism not to be confused with a glorification of the militaristic state, but a national uniqueness and the "chosenness" of Japan by God – "His Chosen People." He attempted to "harmonize" Christianity with the indigenous religion of Japan, Shinto. He found that Shinto's God of creation was the same as Jehovah. And, his uncritical expressions of support for the war with Russia (1904-1905) could not have been more troubling for IMAOKA, already fully committed to "Sermon-on-the-Mount Christianity" and its explicit non-violence. Reconciling "turning the other cheek" with a just war was not possible for the young minister. It would only be a few more years before he was completely aligned with Christian pacifists (ABE, Kishimoto, MURAI – and KANAMORI Tsūrin (1857-1945), who began using a bicycle to spread the gospel of thrift to lessen poverty and economic inequality).

EBINA said he was almost Unitarian, but Unitarianism was "too liberal." "I can agree," he said, "with Unitarianism and their theology. But in terms of emotions, experience, and ethical motivation, I find it very difficult to agree with them."[94] Hearing his mentor approve of *new theology,* and almost approve of Unitarianism, would point IMAOKA toward those who had firsthand theological studies in America and Europe – and toward Japanese Unitarianism.

The final party or group among Kumi-ai ministers, visible and invisible in those Kobe area ministerial meetings, were the liberals – ministers studying the *new knowledge* and *new theology* who self-identified as "Unitarian Congregationalists" (including the Dōshisha Trio). Some had just left Dōshisha theological school for Tokyo – ABE, KISHIMOTO, and MURAI. Others began gathering there.

The Unitarians had come from America in 1888 as a new

---

93. KISHIMOTO Hideo, *op. cit.,* p. 275

94. KISHIMOTO, *ibid.* p. 274.

Christian theological perspective for Japan. Two other tiny missions followed, bringing what was known derisively as liberal, a substitute label for heretical or apostate. These three liberal Christian groups were the German Liberal Mission led by Wilfred Spinner, the American Unitarian Association led by Arthur Knapp, and the American Universalist Church led by George Perin. Even though EBINA was dismissive of these tiny liberal groups, their philosophy of "free inquiry" was evident in the ministerial meetings in and around Kobe. IMAOKA was to be influenced by their spirit as were the Dōshisha graduates who were speaking at the Kumi-ai pastors' meetings. Their talks and publications, especially in the YMCA journal, the *Cosmos* (*Rikugō Zasshi*) which the Dōshisha liberals had taken over, were ever present. Whether by circumstance or by persuasion, their message and method of free inquiry would link IMAOKA to these liberals and their joint future.

A New Type of Religious Experience: Meditation

Almost two years after his wife left Kobe, IMAOKA found a practice that helped his struggle with an evangelical ministry and with the loneliness he felt as a separated husband.[95] He found NISHIDA Tenkō (later to be known as Tenkō-san) who would teach him a method of quiet sitting. IMAOKA recalled:

> … my doubts grew about how Christianity should be practiced and I gradually lost confidence in carrying out my duties as pastor. About that time I met Nishida Tenko. It was before he established Ittō-en.
>
> I should comment that the religious people I had met up to that time were all living in another world. They were Buddhist or Zen and some were Christian. They seemed to be practicing literally the teaching of the Sermon on the Mount. "Do not think about tomorrow. Don't worry about life and the economy. Above all, first

[95] He had already listened to Prof. RYOSEN's meditational experience at Tōdai and read Dean Inge's book on Christian mysticism. In these later accounts, he avoided any claim of merging with the divine or cosmos. He did not want to encourage imitation.

seek the morality of the Kingdom of God."

Tenko-san taught, "Give up egotism." As a minister I believed that it was my mission as a Christian to teach and lecture, to resent and deplore the corruption of society, to criticize the decline of my superiors and to save sinful society. But in Tenko-san's view, this was no more than egotism. "I indeed am correct. Therefore, I will be saved." Throw away the "I". Then one must become ego-less. He thought that the universe will become one's world if, by first cleaning the detestable toilets of other people, one does away with the self. This teaching of Tenko-san's was shocking. At the same time the vacillation in my way of life was foolish, and I could not make up my mind to leave the ministry. But soon I could not go on.[96]

Tenkō-san's Memorial picture at Ittō-en

Tenkō-san taught IMAOKA a meditational practice for laymen modeled on the Zen practice of *seizahō*, quiet sitting. For a year, IMAOKA learned *seiza* directly from NISHIDA Tenkō. It involved deep, abdominal breathing and quieting the "thinking mind," the chattering monkey. As IMAOKA would practice it, his silencing of the rational mind was not forced. It was the observation of its flow, its chatter and noise. It was goal-less, not seeking anything – not enlightenment, not

---

96. IMAOKA, Shin'ichirō, "My Articles of Faith at 100," 1981. Erik H. Erickson, in *Gandhi's Truth,* found dissonance in different re-tellings by Gandhi that led him to discovery when Gandhi had felt an existential or emotional crisis. There is reason to believe that more was involved than just the issue of evangelization.

mystical experience, not even happiness. It was just going into silence, perhaps nothingness, but IMAOKA avoided any term that might suggest a goal or a claim of his own achievement. He reflected about his teacher:

> Tenko is one of a few seniors who influenced me most in my whole life. He practiced the Sermon on the Mount literally. In Tenko's daily life and way of thinking, I found something which I had not found among Christians. That was selflessness or detachment. It seems to be [a] quite negative way of life, superficially, but it is quite positive in reality. It seems to be more Buddhist than Christian. What do you think, however, about the fact that Jesus taught in the Sermon on the Mount and on another occasion as follows: "When you do some act of charity, do not let your left hand know what your right is doing. Your good deeds must be secret."
>
> "If any one wishes to be a follower of mine, he must leave his self behind, he must take up his cross and come with me. Whoever cares for his own safety he is lost, but if a man will let himself be lost for my sake, he will find his true self."[97]

When IMAOKA resigned his church in 1910 and decided to move back to Tokyo to join his wife, Tenkō-san recommended that he contact OKADA Torajirō (1872-1920) to continue *seiza* practice with him. OKADA would become famous for teaching the Okada Method of meditation. IMAOKA would practice *seiza* under his guidance for ten years until OKADA's death in 1920.

Resigning from his Church

In 1910 IMAOKA learned that his wife was pregnant. He resigned his pastorate in Kobe and joined her in Tokyo, becoming the manager of a boarding house (a job she had arranged for him). His public explanation may have only told part of the story; it recounted a reluctance in being an evangelistic minister and of converting Buddhists and Shintoists to Christianity.

IMAOKA recalled later:

> After graduating from Tokyo University, in 1906, I took a position as Minister of a Congregational Church in the city of Kobe.

97. Imaoka, "My Spiritual Pilgrimage," 1970.

> But after three years service, I resigned. The main reason was that I became unable to try to proselytize Buddhists and Shintoists into Christianity. I began to think that the mission of a minister was not proselytizing, but making people more honest believers in their own religions.[98]

Why was it so hard for the young minister to *proselytize* Buddhists and Shintoists – a word that did not have the negative connotation it does today? With a chuckle, he simply told a story about a missionary and a Buddhist in the Meiji era:

> The Buddhist asked the missionary "My parents were earnest and ardent Buddhists and died without the chance to learn Christianity. Where are they now, in paradise or in hell ?" The missionary answered "Of course, in hell." The Buddhist said "I will never be converted to Christianity. As you say, if there is truly a hell and my parents are there, I am very anxious to go to hell to see my parents and renew our ideal home life there. Then the hell will become paradise."[99]

"There are some very exceptional points about Buddhism," he reflected, "so isn't it wrong to convert Buddhists to Christianity? So then I left the ministry after three years, and once more endeavored to redo my research. Since this was in 1910, I was 29 years old."[100]

Combining Rational and Mystical Religious Experience

IMAOKA's spiritual journey had moved from belief-centered religious experience with a gradual conversion to a more fervent devotional and evangelistic one with EBINA's mentoring. IMAOKA's reflections point only to a maturation or developmental process of growth and learning. Later in life, he described this as a process of graduation without any disruption or rejection of his past. He did not mind others calling him Christian, and he did not refrain from identifying himself as a follower or disciple of Jesus. He meant this in a precise way: a follower or disciple of Jesus without imitation. But that understanding of his process will become clearer later in his life.

---

98. IMAOKA, "Speech to IARF Congress: Morning Devotion," 1969.
99. IMAOKA, "What I have learned about Buddhist and Christianity," 1984.
100. IMAOKA, "My Articles of Faith at 103," 1984.

What had occurred in this period of immense importance was his introduction to a specific kind of meditation. When others wrote of their practice with OKADA Torajirō, there is more than a hint of goal-oriented meditation. IMAOKA made it quite clear that he sat without a goal. Thus, he would say that he had no achievement about which to brag. He had learned the practice in the "set and setting" of ego-less-ness. This practice would both reinforce and shape his personality, emotionally and religiously. The discipline of *seiza* would continue for more than eighty years – alone or with others, just being silent, breathing. He stated that he had no goal, no desire for gain or enlightenment, not even some mystical experience. Because he wanted no imitators, he would not speak of any special moments or experiences. But from the silence, he began each day in gratitude and with a readiness to grow.[101]

Evaluating the Kobe Crisis

IMAOKA confessed at the end of his life that there had been two existential crises that brought him almost to suicide. Why he left Kobe seems not to be one of them. It was definitely a crisis but not one of the two major ones – those would arise in his future. He doubted his "calling" as a Kumi-ai minister. His wife's pregnancy provided the crisis needed to make a major change in his life. He had the courage to accept the birth of his daughter as his own.

IMAOKA could look back on this period in his life and say that it was a time of growth. His was a desire for more learning. There had been a rich opportunity for that as a Kumi-ai minister. His network of thinkers, of ministers who were drawn to free inquiry, had been broadened. Many would be a part of his life into the future, for they too were moving to Tokyo and the new opportunities there. He had learned to see unity in diversity. He had seen and admired the conservatives'

---

101. Personal conversations with IMAOKA about *seiza* from 1981 to 1988, as well as practice with him.

loyalty, sincerity and dedication – especially their generosity and sacrifices. He also knew that he was more comfortable with rational, questioning ministers and their vision of *freedom*.

NISHIDA Tenkō *would continue to be linked to* IMAOKA *over the next decades, staying with him after World War II when he visited Tokyo as a member of the House of Councillors.*
He was the founder of Ittō-en and joined the Japan Free Religious Association in 1949.

SECTION THREE: JAPANESE UNITARIANISM

Chapter 5

Joining Unitarians:
An Introduction to IMAOKA'S Unitarian Period (1910-1922)

When IMAOKA arrived back in Tokyo, he joined his wife after a two year separation and became a boarding house manager. They awaited the arrival of a daughter. He began putting together a new life of study and assisting others.

Although he said and wrote nothing concrete about this period, fingerprints were everywhere. He joined some of the most influential people of that era in religion, education and progressive politics, as well as social reform. While they were center stage, he worked with them with unusual energy and efficiency in their shadows. However, progressive or liberal activity would be on the losing side of Japanese history as militarism, imperialism and fascism would erase their attempts for constitutional democracy, social and economic equality, rule by law, modern education, and an independent Japan.

IMAOKA would not succeed financially as he started a life of assisting others. This would eventually prompt his wife, IMAOKA Utayo, to pioneer women's entrepreneurship at a time when that was illegal. She would attempt to work around those laws, having her husband borrow for her business attempts. Finances were a constant worry until she eventually succeeded later in life. She continued to assert her freedom in every aspect of her life.[102] During this period, IMAOKA was indefatigable as a graduate assistant, working on special translation projects for Prof. ANESAKI, beginning as a junior editor at a prestigious journal, and becoming involved with the Unitarian Mission.

Graduate Studies at Tōdai

IMAOKA started a newly created program of graduate studies at Tōdai as ANESAKI's special assistant, pursuing an advanced degree in Christian history and thought at 29 years of age. ANESAKI, an assistant professor of Buddhist studies, had a reason for taking IMAOKA as his assistance. ANESAKI had begun to have a major influence with the national departments of education and interior in their attempts to use Japanese religions, including Japanese Christianity, to find modern values to be taught in public education. IMAOKA was given the task of translating two "Christian" books, one of *new theology* and the other on *modern ethics* or *morality.*[103] IMAOKA would complete these translations in due course, more as projects for his mentor's quest for ethical universals among Japan's religions than for his own advanced degree. Even so, he would use what he learned from these works during the next two decades while teaching about Christian thought and history at Nihon University. With all his other tasks these translations into Japanese would only be completed and published by 1915.

What started gradually and then became his central focus, along with his slowly progressing graduate work, was his involvement in liberal Christianity. IMAOKA could have sought part time employment at EBINA Danjō's church in Tokyo or at a Congregational Christian preaching station. For some reason he did

---

102. Ms. IMAOKA Utayo's successes and failures will be explored in chapter 8.

103. The specifics of IMAOKA's work with ANESAKI, NARUSE and Association Concordia is the focus of chapter 9.

not. In fact, he broke his relationship with the Congregational Kumi-ai ministry, just as Kumi-ai's most liberal ministers were doing as they gathered in Tokyo. Some were in charge of the former YMCA magazine, *Rikugō Zasshi* (*Cosmos*), that had evolved into a Unitarian journal. The chief editor was KISHIMOTO Nobuta, one of the Dōshisha Trio whom he already knew, as well as the other two of the trio – ABE Isō and MURAI Tomoyoshi, both assistant editors there as well. Besides their work at *Cosmos*, they all became leaders at the American Unitarian Mission, headquartered at Unity Hall in Mita-ku (also referred to in reports as located in Shiba or Mita-Shiba). They encouraged IMAOKA to help them, and they introduced him to the newly returned American missionary, the Rev. Clay MacCauley (b.1843- d.1925). He would serve two terms in Japan, 1888-1900 and 1909-1920.

Some scholars have thought that ANESAKI was never really involved with Unitarians or was negative toward their activity. Two events are cited to prove that conclusion.[104] Just before IMAOKA arrived in Tokyo, a controversy had occurred at Unity Hall when the president of the Japanese Unitarian Association (JUA) and the main minister of the Unitarian congregation, SAJI Jitsunen, was forced out of the movement. SAJI had introduced his fellow Buddhist, ANESAKI, to Unity Hall where ANESAKI received his first teaching position. They were both *new* or progressive *Buddhists,* and SAJI proudly called himself a "Buddhist Unitarian." The firing of SAJI happened in 1909.[105] Three years later in 1912, ANESAKI warned a colleague not to allow American Unitarians to co-opt their work in Association

104. See Mohr, *op. cit.,* p. 198, fn. 67, citing the "perspicacious article" by TSUCHIYA Hiromasa, "*Nihon Yuniterian Kyōkai no funkyū ni kansuru ichikōsatsu* (A study on the split in the Japanese Unitarian Association)," 1998 and summarized by MATSUOKA Hidetaka, *Saji Jitsunen no shōgai* (The life of SAJI Jitsunen), Kobe: Kōyū puranningu sentā, 2006, pp. 176-86.

105. His firing will be explored in Chapter 8.

Concordia.[106] These two instances have been taken as proof that ANESAKI had soured on any Unitarian connection. If so, he might have warned his assistant away from Unitarianism. In fact, his connection with Unitarianism ran deep. There is ample evidence to demonstrate ANESAKI's use of IMAOKA as his link with the *yuniterian*[107] movement and its activities in liberal education, politics and economic reform.

ANESAKI's involvement with the Unitarian Mission as a "sympathizer" (a word used by MacCauley for important individuals affiliated with the Unitarian Mission) reveals the complexity of the *yuniterian* movement. It began with ANESAKI's invitations to lecture in their theological school. A year after his graduation from Tōdai in philosophy (1896), he became a lecturer there and taught a course on "An Introduction to Pathology in Religion" (*Shūkyō-byori Soron*). This School for Advanced Learning (*Senshin Gakuin*) was located in Unity Hall, a building of multiple uses for the Unitarian Mission and the Japanese Unitarian Association. ANESAKI joined a study group of *Senshin Gakuin* lectùrers in 1897.[108] There, he met and would teach alongside MINAMI Hajime (1865-1940) who had designed a course on the comparative study of Japanese religions. ANESAKI would go with lecturers from *Senshin Gakuin* to a study group on comparative religion, which became a major interest – one he would apply later at Tōdai. In this group he met KISHIMOTO Nobuta, and together they launched the Society of Comparative Religion that November. KISHIMOTO and ANESAKI formed a lifelong bond, and KISHIMOTO

---

106. See page 48 and chapter 10.

107. *Yuniterian* had become a term not only designating Japanese Unitarian but also things liberal, progressive, scientific, or innovative. The different usages of this term will unfold in later chapters. It is therefore a *contextual* term.

108. Tatsushi NARITA, "Masaharu Anesaki: A Life Chronology" Word Press (tatsushinarita.wordpress.com/masaharu-aesaki-chronology/). The Teiyu Study group for research about (social) ethics (and morality) also included KISHIMOTO, ONISHI, ANESAKI, and YOKOI.

would help ANESAKI during the next years through his doctorate and into a professorship back at his alma mater, the Imperial University of Tokyo.

KISHIMOTO Nobuta and wife

ANESAKI joined KISHIMOTO and the rest of the Dōshisha trio in several other liberal study groups: social reconstruction (also known as religious socialism), peace, and poverty and social reform.[109] (As Japan became more militaristic, ANESAKI would become a person of interest to the police as one whose "thoughts need[ed] to be under surveillance."[110]) ANESAKI would continue his publishing in *Rikugō Zasshi* and speaking at Unity Hall, although the frequency declined as his vistas moved past Japan academically, and into the international peace movement in Association Concordia. In 1912 two years after IMAOKA returned to Tokyo, ANESAKI would even take a prominent role at American Unitarian's first missionary

---

109. Narita's biographical note on ANESAKI: "In October 1898 the Dōshisha Trio (ABE, KISHIMOTO, MURAI as President) found[ed] the Research Society of Socialism at Unity Hall with ANESAKI, SAJI, KANDA, TOYOSAKI, HIRAI, KATAYAMA, KOTOKU, KAWAKAMI, TAKAGI." And from KISHIMOTO, Hideo, *Japanese Religion in the Meiji Era* (Tokyo: Ōbunsha, 1956), vol. 2, p. 305: In 1898, they joined in "The Society for Studying Poverty."

110. Mohr, *op.cit.,* pp. 131-2.

conference in Boston. He delivered an address with the lengthy title, "Influence of a better knowledge and appreciation of other peoples and religions, in conjunction with the recent rise of Oriental nations in racial, national, and religious self-consciousness." It was soon thereafter that ANESAKI warned NARUSE to be careful not to affiliate Association Concordia,[111] their pet project, with Unitarians. He feared that American Unitarians might co-opt their program. But this was not animus. Their work needed to be free of any foreign control – or even any claim of foreign influence.

Thus, in 1910, when IMAOKA arrived, ANESAKI still worked with Unitarians, especially the idealists he had joined in study groups and organizations that would get him on that surveillance list a decade later for those who were dangerous to the rise of Japanese imperialism. IMAOKA would be assisting these very idealists for the next decade at Unity Hall and at *Cosmos*. IMAOKA had found his home in work for international peace and Japanese religious unity.

Assistant Editor at *Cosmos*

IMAOKA first volunteered at *Rikugō Zasshi* (*Cosmos*), helping the Dōshisha Trio (ABE, KISHIMOTO and MURAI). This led to another part-time but unpaid job as an assistant editor. *Rikugō Zasshi* was becoming more liberal both religiously and socially. It had become the most academic religious journal in Japan and was publishing young scholars who were either Unitarian in philosophy or were part of the *new knowledge* movement.[112] IMAOKA would also publish in *Cosmos*. Yet, IMAOKA would disappear in the background without mention for years in reports to the Boston AUA headquarters that he was among the editorial staff. Only later would Boston be informed that he was an editor and part of their movement. But, none of this

---

111. Chapter 10 will focus on ANESAKI and NARUSE's work together in Association Concordia.

112. "Unitarian" quickly became a term adopted to connote "modern, scientific, progressive, liberal" and became Japanese as *Yuniterian*. See also footnote 107.

provided any financial support for his family. He seemed happy with Tenkō-san's economic simplicity and the near-poverty of Kumi-ai ministry. Utayo-san, the family recalled, was not.

Beginning at Unity Hall

The Dōshisha Trio had maintained their Kumi-ai (Congregational) connection as they still preached in both Kumi-ai pulpits and at the Unitarian's "First Church," Unity Hall. IMAOKA, for unexplained reasons, lost his direct relationship with the Congregational Mission and its Kumi-ai movement, and strangely, with his former mentor and sponsor, EBINA Danjō. He did not return to be EBINA's assistant minister or join his church. One possible explanation was EBINA's nationalistic support of Japan's military ventures.

However, the gulf between EBINA and IMAOKA concerning their commitments about war and peace remained. IMAOKA joined an editorial staff deeply involved in the quest for world peace and international cooperation and understanding. All were opposed to Japan's militarism. ABE was a leading activist, publishing calls for world peace and Christian socialism. This resonated with the "Sermon-on-the-Mount" Christianity that IMAOKA identified with, even having heard his *seiza* master, Tenkō-san, praise the "Sermon-on-the-Mount" back in Kobe.

It would be almost two years before MacCauley first mentioned IMAOKA in his reports to AUA headquarters in Boston. IMAOKA was teaching in the 1912 Summer School extension program on the "Psychology of Religion," copying one of ANESAKI's favorite courses. His work as an assistant editor was only mentioned in 1915 in an introductory letter that was penned to Charles Wendte (1844-1931). IMAOKA would soon meet him, giving Wendte credit for influencing his involvement in the interfaith movement later in his life.

Helping Uchigasaki at an Independent Unitarian Church

UCHIGASAKI Sakusaburō (1877-1947) arrived in Japan fresh from his theological studies at the British Unitarian's Manchester College at Oxford. In 1912 he brought back to Japan a form of British Unitarianism with confirmation, baptism and explicit membership. UCHIGASAKI's leadership was more devotional and worship-oriented than the lecture approach that had become the style at Unity Hall. Baptism was retained as the symbolism of one being buried to the old and raised to a new life. But, the Lord's Supper was rejected as a pagan addition after the time of Jesus – among Japanese liberals, some even hinting at its being cannibalism. The Jewish Passover meal, UCHIGASAKI claimed, was reformulated to fit a later blood atonement theology arising no earlier than the late second or early third century. Higher Criticism, that he had studied in England, maintained that a Jew would have never conceived of the wine and bread of Passover becoming Jesus' own flesh and blood, foretelling his own death on the cross for the remission of the sins of all humankind.[113] UCHIGASAKI's rational use of *new theology* was attractive to IMAOKA. When UCHIGASAKI invited IMAOKA and MINAMI to join him as assistant ministers, both accepted.

Yet, something strange needs to be noted. IMAOKA mentioned with certainty in 1986 that he did not become a Unitarian until 1917, implying that he had not been a member at this point. Is there any significance to this discrepancy? In fact, it is a key to understanding how reports to the American Unitarian Association in Boston could claim so many prominent Japanese, like ANESAKI and even FUKUZAWA

113. Some modern scholarship supports what UCHIGASAKI learned at the end of the 19th century. Robert Funk and the Jesus Seminar found very few teachings that could be attributed to Jesus. For example, see Funk, *et. al., The Parables of Jesus* (1988) and *The Five Gospels* (1996). UCHIGASAKI would not have gone that far.

Yukichi (1835-1901), the founder of Keiō college, as "almost Unitarians," and as "sympathizers".

Joining the *yuniterian* movement and working for the betterment of Japan was not the same as becoming a member of this liberal Christian group. The ambiguity of being a *yuniterian* worked well for MacCauley when he reported Unitarian influence back to America. It would cause problems for Unitarians' future in Japan.

GROUP OF DELEGATES TO THE MEETING OF THE INTERNATIONAL CONGRESS, BOSTON, 1920
rom left to right: Rev. Clay MacCauley, Rev. T. Rhondda Williams, Prof. S. Ushigasaki, Rev. Jabez T. Sunderland, Swami Yogananda Giri, Rev. Charles W. Wendte, Rev. Samuel A. Eliot, Rev. Basil Martin, Rev. Christopher J. Street, Rev. Samuel M. Crothers

Rev. *Uchigasaki,* third from left, at 1920 AUA May meeting in Boston

A Mission or a Movement?

Something deeper was involved. American Unitarians had come to Japan in 1887 with a profoundly different idea of Christian missions. Their first representative, the Rev. Arthur Knapp (1841-1921) said that he came as a fieldworker, not as a missionary. He came to work with Japanese liberals, the progressives who were inclusive in religion, culture and society. He was anti-missionary and worked with an almost indefinable movement of thinkers, visionaries, reformers and activists who were not afraid of innovation and change.

They sought *new knowledge* not only in science, business, industry, education but also in religion, politics and social structure. Knapp served as the Japan Unitarian Mission's fieldworker-director from 1887-1890.

All the later Unitarian ministers who came to Japan, including MacCauley, were conflicted about their role. They spoke of being fieldworkers ("not in Japan to convert, but to confer, to assist"), but they formed churches, converted leaders of other Christian missions to Unitarianism, and generally measured their success by church membership. They made Japanese into Unitarians. The tension between fieldworker and missionary would set in motion a fundamental contradiction that would lead to the mission's eventual demise.

Once in Tokyo, IMAOKA would begin to learn about the Unitarian Mission and the varieties of "Unitarianism" that each missionary had brought to Japan. His primary sources would have been the former teachers from the failed School for Advanced Learning (*Senshin Gakuin, 1894-1900*) and those who preached at Unity Hall, the "First Unitarian Church of Tokyo." And there would be Clay MacCauley (1843-1925), the sixty-seven year old superintendent of the American Unitarian Mission, in his second appointment to the mission.

There was one more source to learn of the history of the American Unitarian Mission. Once IMAOKA began attending Unitarian Sunday services and assisting at Unity Hall, he found their library. It contained all their own publications, tracts and books in both English and Japanese. It also had almost every copy of Unitarian journals and magazines – the *Christian Register*; a few issues of *Unity* and of *The Radical;* a number of copies of Abbot's *Index;* and current copies of the *Pacific Unitarian*. The American Unitarians Channing, Emerson, Parker, Potter, Adler, Hale, and Martineau were there, and

IMAOKA devoured their writings.

American Unitarians

The American Unitarians who arrived in Japan were just one branch of those who were called Unitarian over the centuries. The name came from Christians who rejected the idea of a Trinity, with its absolute God and creator of the universe being of one essence and three persons or personalities in the Godhead. There might be some validity to the Unitarian claim that some type of anti-trinitarianism existed in most of the twenty centuries of Christianity – but almost never without opposition and even persecution. The historical and cultural differences of these "*Unitarianisms*" were so great that, in most cases, only Unitarians could identify their own religious DNA in all this variety. Otherwise, European Unitarianism began in the 16th century with Dávid Ferenc (Francis David, 1510-1579) in the Principality of Transylvania in the fourth and most radical stage of the Protestant Reformation.[114]

American Unitarianism was birthed by ministers of the Congregational Church of the Massachusetts Bay Colony. Congregationalism was theologically Calvinist and creedal. The colonists were soon struggling to protect their established church order in an occupied native land when a non-creedal Christianity with a variety of expressions disrupted their churches. The dissenters would begin opposing the doctrine of the Trinity as irrational, thus getting the negative label of anti-Trinitarian or Unitarian. It was easier for them to dissent than to formulate a positive belief system that could bind together an association or denomination of "nay-sayers." So from 1825 (their agreed date of origin), for nearly 60 years, Unitarians just affirmed that their faith and practice was "the pure Christianity of Jesus." Their divisions would be transmitted to Japan

114. For a thorough treatment, see George Huntston Williams, *The Radical Reformation* (First Edition, 1962, revised and expanded, 1992).

with competing visions of this pure and rational Christianity and what its mission should be in Japan. (The diversity of faith and practice would affect IMAOKA practically and spiritually, culminating in what would happen in 1922.)

There was great pride in Boston, the American Unitarian Association's headquarters, at its early success. There were smaller Christian groups in 19th century America, but few who were trying to become the unifying form of future Christianity. Unitarian self-understanding was as large as its pride. They had won over Harvard College and its Divinity School, at least in their own minds. Harvard Divinity School was teaching a liberal, rational Christianity based on the latest text-critical studies of the Christian Bible (the Old and New Testaments) as literature in the original languages of its oldest extant manuscripts. The quest for the historical Jesus had developed from European scholarship until it was part of ordinary Unitarian sermons heard throughout New England. Then they put a mission program together from their weak associational organization, poor financial resources and without a theological foundation or a biblical commission to convert others to their faith.

Without a creed but in the name of the religion of Jesus – and without his words except in Greek, a language that Jesus most likely did not know or speak – Unitarians adopted the same purpose of missionizing in a foreign culture that they had adopted a few decades earlier when they had joined British Unitarians in a mission to India.[115] As they had gone to India as fieldworkers, not to convert, but to help others realize the rational truths of their own faith and practice, American missionaries set out for Japan. That was the goal and self-understanding that they professed publicly. Yet, there was

---

115. Spencer Lavan, *Unitarians in India: a Study of Encounter and Response* (Boston: Unitarian Universalist Association, 1977; Exploration Press; 3rd edition, 1991)

always the hidden desire to turn Indians, and now Japanese, into (American) Unitarians. However, Japanese culture cautioned against taking proclamations of ideals as reality. They, and IMAOKA, would look at how ideals were actualized. When the ideal was so high concerning truth, equality, freedom and cooperation, the actual practice of this liberal faith in a Japanese setting would become paramount. Acts trumped words. Deeds proved ideals. And to know the deeds IMAOKA would learn as much as he could of the Mission's history.

A Brief Overview of the Japan Unitarian Mission's Three Periods

True about joining any movement or institution, its prior history is learned in full only later, if at all. There had been two periods of the Unitarian Mission that had come before IMAOKA. The first period of the Mission (1887-1900) was directly administered by American Unitarian missionary-fieldworkers, while the second period (1900-1909) had no foreign missionary presence.[116] The American Japan Unitarian Mission was closed in 1900 and turned over to Japanese Unitarians without missionaries as a sign of their success in creating a self-sustaining mission. And Japanese Unitarianism ran smoothly until 1909. The two periods of just over twenty years were the background as IMAOKA took up a role in this liberal Christian movement. The third period began in 1909, a year before he arrived, with a complex crisis that divided its leadership and raised the issue of the contradictory ideals of missionary and fieldworker. The third period (1909-1922) found IMAOKA moving from an assistant to becoming the last Secretary of both the Mission and the Japanese Association. MacCauley would be replaced the Rev. John Boynton

116. See Chapter 6 for Period One and Chapter 7 for Period One and Two from a Japanese perspective.

Wilson Day in 1919.[117] Day would close the Mission in 1922. For reasons that will become clear, this history has never been written.

IMAOKA's Faith Journey

A resignation of the Kumi-ai ministry in Kobe and his wife's pregnancy brought IMAOKA to Tokyo. The depth of his spiritual and psychological struggle was never revealed. At this point one can only see movement on the surface of his life – from a liberal devotionalism in the Kumi-ai movement to an attempt to merge devotion and reason as he assisted at Unity Hall with publishing, teaching and even occasional preaching.

He chose ANESAKI's universalism and abandoned EBINA Danjō's Christian nationalism.

He affirmed Utayo's exercise of her personal freedom and continued their marriage.

He remained a rational Christian. (Yet, his notion of personal and religious identity had expanded, not rejecting past identities.)

(The next chapters will attempt to bring his spiritual pilgrimage during this period out from the shadows, as he will face two life crises either of which could have ended in suicide.)

Jiyū Shin Gakko, School of Liberal Theology, c.1892

Some of the early *Yuniterian* leaders, c. 1900

117. See Chapter 8 for Period Three, limited to extant AUA sources. There is a great Japanese silence about this period.

Timeline of the Japanese Unitarian Mission, 1889-1921

1885 Sept. Arrival of German Evangelical missionary (Wilfred Spinner)

1884 YANO Fumio writes article about Unitarianism in Yiibin Hochi newspaper.

1886 Letter to AUA and British Unitarians asking for help from prominent Japanese leaders. AUA Secretary Batchelor chooses Knapp.

1887 Death of MacCauley's Wife. He leaves ministry. Newspaper man.

German Evangelical mission [GEM] founded the New Religious School in Ikizaka, Hongo

Arrival of Unitarian Arthur Knapp on "research trip."

1889 Arrival of "team" Authur May Knapp (1888-92) returns with W.J. Liscomb (Literature), Garrett Droppers (Econ), J.H. Wigmore (Law. 1889-98), Clay MacCauley (1889-90; 1909-1921). KANDA Saichirō returns with them as translator and first Secretary of Mission.

1890-1895 Rev. Henry.W. Hawkes of British Unitarians arrives, 1890.

1890 Knapp leaves (reported illness)

Feb. Establish Unitarian Association at Iikura-cho, Azabu

March. First issue of *Unitarian* magazine

April. Arrival of Universalists: George Perin, Issac Cody, Margaret Schouler

1891 W. I. Lawrance arrives. Starts Free Theological School

1891 Bought Building In Iguri. Established "Japanese Unitarian Mission'. Hawkes Recruited SAJI.

1891-1909 SAJI. Buddhist Unitarian. President of JUM [or JUA]. Pastor of churches

1893 World's Parliament of Religions. Six Buddhists and two Christians participated in it from Japan; three of the eight later converted to Unitarianism: KISHIMOTO, HIRAI and NOGUCHI.

On 25 March, the construction of the Unitarian *Yuiitsukan* completed at Mita-shikokumachi, Tokyo.

Fire destroys Kanda Building

1894 Unity Hall completed

First Unitarian Controversy with mainstream missions

1894-1899 Senshin Gakuin.(School for Advanced Learning) at Unity Hall.

1897 ANESAKI Masahiro, Imaoka's mentor, teaches at Senshin Gakuin.

1898 Three Dōshisha Unitarians founded "The Research Society of Socialism: MIRAI, KISHIMOTO, and ABE.

1899	Starting to close down Japan Unitarian Mission
1900	Closure of Japanese Unitarian Mission; Departure of MacCauley SAJI & KANDA left as administrative heads MURAI and HIRAI attend AUA General Meeting in Boston.
1903	Visit by Thomas Lamb Eliot; AUA inspection tours begin.
1905	MacCauley visits Tokyo and Torii Memorial to Emperor at Unity Hall.
1908	Trouble between SAJI and KANDA. Ethical Society controversy.
1909	Return of MacCauley. A third of Unity Hall leave with SAJI and HIROI.
1910	SUZUKI Bunji becomes 2nd Secretary of JUM and JUA
c.1911	UCHIGASAKI Sakusaburō returns from Manchester College and founds Kanda Church
1912	Yūaikai (Friendly Society) labor organization begun in Unity Hall, founded by SUZUKI.
1912	June. Kiitsu Kyōkai (Association Concordia) founded by ANESAKI, NARUSE Jinzō and SHIBUSAWA Eiichi.
1917-1921	IMAOKA becomes Secretary of JUM, JUA. Resigns Dec. 31, 1921.
1919	Day arrives and forces MacCauley to retire. Then attempts to make the mission evangelistic. Defunds *Rikugō Zasshi* (Cosmos). Orders SUZUKI and Yūaikai out of Unity Hall.
1920	Kanda Church disbands.
1922	Feb. Day hires OYABE as his personal secretary. Ends up trying to sell Unity Hall. March 26. JUA asks AUA to close mission and leave Japan June. Day Closes Mission, leaves Japan.
1923	Sept 1. Kantō Earthquake. Unity Hall spared.

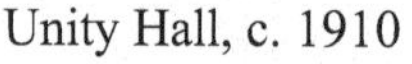

Unity Hall, c. 1910

A postcard from MacCauley with a picture of Unity Hall c. 1916

Chapter 6

American Unitarians in Japan – Period One (1887-1900)

Watching China being carved up slowly by colonial powers, Japanese political and military strategists sought to prevent such a fate for Japan. They immediately sent students to study and learn what was needed and could be done to preserve Japan's independence and its national identity. How easily the colonial powers had forced unequal treaties upon Japan prompted them to look for solutions, even drastic changes for Japanese society. Much of this happened before IMAOKA's birth, but it was the background for his involvement with liberal movements, specifically Unitarianism.

An Unexpected Invitation

By the late 1880's, prominent Japanese leaders were traveling to the West with both a desire to glean what was useful from Western education and technology (its political, legal, economic, military, and possibly, even its religious institutions) and also a primary but contradictory concern: to remain Japanese, "pure" and equal to Westerners, if not "superior."[118]

In 1886 YANO Fumio (1850-1931) returned from studies in the West and became editor of a newspaper which he founded, the *Hochi*

---

118. The primary sources for this period are letters written by the Unitarian fieldworker-missionaries to the AUA, articles they wrote for Unitarian journals, primarily *The Christian Register*, AUA Annual Reports, and AUA Board of Director's meetings reported in the *Register.* There are multiple accounts as well as one in the Clay MacCauley-John B. W. Day, "History of the Japan Unitarian Mission, 1888-1921," a typed, unpublished report to the AUA, dated April 22, 1931. This report was filed by Day, the last Unitarian missionary to Japan, at the insistence of Samuel Eliot, AUA president. It will be cited hereafter as "Day, *History.*" Viewpoints in this account will be noted in chapter 8. Day, *History,* p. 55.

Shimbun. He began championing Unitarianism as the proper form of Western religion for Japan. It should be adopted, he wrote, because it was "enormously adaptable to Japanese needs."

At about the same time TOKUGAWA Yoshiakira (1863-1908) – who would have been the *shogun* of Japan were it not for the Restoration of the Emperor and who was given the title of Marquis under the new nobility system – reportedly converted to Anglican Christianity in England. He heard of British Unitarianism from his friend YANO and gave verbal support for the proposal to have the English Unitarian Association send a minister to Japan to help YANO introduce liberal Christianity.

It was not that Japanese leaders thought that Japan needed more religion. Reformers like the educator, FUKUZAWA Yukichi (1835-1901), wanted a moral foundation for the Japanese masses.[119] Indigenous religions, Buddhism and Shinto, FUKUZAWA thought, had become stagnant and ineffective as the moral fiber for a nation in transition. Japan had been shaken by the invasion of superior technology – first military but also industrial and agricultural with their methods and implements. Science, philosophy and "new thought" had destabilized Japanese society. Even Confucian ethics for the educated ruling class were no longer effective. FUKUZAWA and the former student of his Keiō college, YANO, concluded that Unitarianism would support Christian morality without unscientific beliefs and dogmas.

These leading figures, and some lesser ones, came to the same conclusion: Japan needed a different type of religion that did not deny science, one free from supernaturalism containing fables, miracles

[119] KIYOOKA Eiichi, FUKUZAWA's grandson, published *Keiō gijuku daigakubu no tanjo: Habado daigaku yori no shinshiryo* (*The Birth of Keiō Gijuku University: New Materials from Harvard University*) in 1983. See also Mohr, *Universality, op.cit.*

and stories of hells and heavens (Buddhist or Christian). Such a rational religion would not be belief-centered, fighting over Christian creeds and beliefs or Buddhist dogmas and scriptures. These elites had discovered Unitarianism and made some entreaties during 1886 to bring this rational religion to Japan, first to British and then to American Unitarians.

Fukuzawa Yukichi (1835-1901),
founder of Keiō University

The two most important calls came from the Marquis Tokugawa and Fukuzawa Yukichi. Fukuzawa's call contained the desire to turn his college into a modern university, equal to the Imperial University of Tokyo. British Unitarians thought that they were too small to undertake such a mission and passed the request to their American co-religionists, the American Unitarian Association (AUA). Fukuzawa, as the American Unitarian's president Samuel Eliot remembered later, asked "for conference and cooperation from someone authorized to tell them about the Unitarian habit of mind."[120]

Timing is almost everything, and the death of Rev. Charles Dall (1816-1886) made a new foreign project financially feasible. He had been the last Unitarian missionary to India and had been funded by earnings from a bequest by James Hayward "in aid of Christian

120. Day, *op. cit.*

Mission in foreign lands." Rev. Arthur M. Knapp (1841-1921), a Unitarian minister then without a parish, was chosen for an "errand" to the Orient to check into this new "planting." (Legend has it that George Batchelor, then the AUA's chief officer, chose Knapp after a brief conversation on the steps of the old Beacon Hill headquarters.)[121] Knapp met and befriended two Japanese brothers who were studying in Boston at that precise moment. They were so impressed that their letters home opened the hospitality of their father, FUKUZAWA Yukichi, to Knapp upon his arrival. Without that support, many things would have gone differently.

The Errand to the Empire of the Rising Sun

Knapp and his wife arrived in Yokohama on December 21, 1887, and were immediately taken to FUKUZAWA. Knapp and his "cultured" Unitarianism impressed FUKUZAWA. His introductions allowed Knapp to meet with the highest officials in the Empire. Knapp began publishing essays in FUKUZAWA's newspaper as well as YANO's. Knapp wrote home on December 28, 1888, of his remarkable progress, which was printed in *The Unitarian Review.* He told of writing "daily articles alternately for the *Jiji Shimpo* and *Hochi Shimbun,*" reaching a readership of "thirty thousand every day." Invitations came for him to dine with political and commercial leaders or speak to their associations (almost beyond belief for his fellow American Unitarians like Charles W. Wendte – later to become

---

[121] George Batchelor, in his *Personal Reminisces* (Boston: George H. Ellis, 1916), p. 67, would correct that legend as follows: "When, incited by Americans who had been in Japan (Prof. E. S. Morse and Prof. Ernest Fenollosa), I offered a motion to appropriate money to begin a mission there, Dr. Reynolds gave me a free hand, but said that he could take no active part in raising the money. He had already too many irons in the fire. When I came down from the directors' room after our vote, I met Rev. Arthur M. Knapp and told him what we had done. He asked, "Whom will you send?" I laid my hand on his shoulder and said, with no serious intention, "We will send you." He came to me soon afterward and said he would like to go, whereupon he was appointed; and he, together with Clay MacCauley and others, has, with scanty resources, done a great work."

important in interfaith work – who was his sharpest critic[122]). One of these talks to a society that FUKUZAWA had founded in 1880 for entrepreneurs, largely Keiō graduates, was important enough to be remembered and published seven years later after Knapp had left Japan.[123] To these business leaders, Knapp proclaimed that there was something universal in all religions: "we discover the essential elements within the foundations of [all] religions; whatever sect, whatever teaching, none of them lacks these essential elements."[124] He saw these essential elements to be less obscure in a rational religion like Unitarianism, one without superstition. Yet, he was not in Japan as a missionary to set up Unitarian churches. Knapp's so-called "empire-for-the-taking" letter (Feb.12,1889) to Grindall Reynolds (1822-1894), the secretary and chief officer of the AUA from 1881-94, was an outline for a different type of missions. He explained why he had not started by organizing "a Unitarian church."[125] Knapp allowed meetings, societies, and "churches" to

122. Ltr. Wendte to Knapp, Aug. 7, 1889. "In fact, my only fear for you, and for our cause, lies in your rapid and bewildering success, which is both dangerous for your own spiritual health and our enduring usefulness. Whether it is worthwhile to start an extensive and expensive Mission in Japan at the cost of crippling our domestic enterprises may fairly be asked. The *nearer call is a duty*, Japan a privilege. [*emphasis is Wendte's*] ...It is the profound conviction that you and your Japanese coadjuters are animated by motives more speculative, social, and personal than moral and religious. ...You are dealing only or mainly with the upper educated classes." Documents will be cited from a collection of Clay MacCauley's Japanese materials found in the basement of Harvard Divinity School; its librarian, Dr. Alan Seaburg, had me examine and gave me permission to copy them before they were sent to the current archive. Their current numbering in the Harvard Archive will not be used, as these materials were not yet there.

123. Personal communication from Prof. Michel Mohr: talk to the Kōjun Society on May 16, 1888. Arthur May Knapp and Saichirō KANDA, *Unitarian Doctrine* [ユニテリアンの教義] (Tokyo: Nihon Yuniterian Kōdōkai, Meiji 28 [1895]). The translation of 教義 might better be rendered "teaching principles." Unitarianism claimed to be non-doctrinaire, non-dogmatic.

124. *Ibid.* Translation by Mohr, personal communication.

125. Ltr. Knapp to Reynolds, Feb.12,1889.

arise among Japanese in various places but did not dictate a precise ecclesiastical structure. These were started by Japanese from the influence of his newspaper articles or talks, according to their own design and needs. (Perhaps because they expected financial support from America, these "Unitarian churches" soon vanished.[126] Other missions provided attractive employment for ministers. Thus, the term "rice Christians" came into use.) Knapp's claimed that he was not there to convert Japanese from their native religions but to help in a "sympathy of religions." Some Japanese students were particularly interested in Unitarian principles:

> The young men who have recently returned from America, and while there became interested in Unitarianism, are standing by me nobly. They meet at my house one evening each week, to discuss practical plans for organization; and they are also doing good service in ascertaining for me the character of the material upon which we are to depend, it being impossible, of course, for me to follow up all my correspondents and callers in person, besides being cut off from so many of them by the barrier of language.
>
> I am now engaged in preparing my most important address for this season, that before the Educational Society, a national organization of the leading men of Japan. I have been recently elected a member, and, as is usual on entrance, I am expected to make an elaborate address.
>
> I have taken for my subject "The Practical Uses of Religion," the Japanese being as a nation the most thorough-going utilitarian people on the globe. It will be my greatest opportunity, and I hope to make a worthy use of it.[127]

---

[126] When an orthodox Japanese Christian minister [Yoshimura Hidezo – source: Parker] converted to Unitarianism and founded a church, Knapp would write home why he had not started with organizing "a Unitarian church." His statement signaled that he was not a missionary to organize churches. He had not come to convert, yet a Japanese pastor had converted and founded a Unitarian church. Yoshimura Hidezo, having studied Channing at Dōshisha school in Kyoto built a church in Kudanshita, Tokyo. It was dedicated on Christmas day, 1890. Author's interview with IMAOKA and confirmed by William Parker, "The Unitarian Mission in Japan," n.p., talk given at International Unitarian Fellowship of Tokyo, n.d.

[127] *The Unitarian Review, ibid.*

Arthur May Knapp (1841 -1921)

Knapp worked with translators and published the first two pamphlets on Unitarianism in Japanese and distributed them by mail to inquirers. He cooperated with FUKUZAWA in devising a plan that would mutually benefit both: FUKUZAWA would have a university with three departments taught by three American professors, whom Knapp would bring back with him upon his return. Knapp and the Unitarians would have an open invitation to influence his students with that particular brand of rationality and liberality that FUKUZAWA had seen demonstrated by Knapp and associated with Unitarianism.

Knapp wrote to American Unitarians:

> Now Mr. F[ukuzawa] of course does not wish to have his great institution transformed into a sectarian college, but his impressions of Unitarianism gathered from its work here during the 1st year and from the reports of his sons who have watched its aspects and influence in America have been of so favorable a character that he will be very glad to have it come under Unitarian influences and to enjoy the benefits of the Unitarian atmosphere.[128]

A famous art historian and philosopher, Ernest Fenollosa, would write an evaluation of Knapp's work almost eight years after he left the Japan Mission. Fenollosa captured Knapp's amazing success

---

128. Knapp to Reynolds, Feb.6,1889.

and made a prognosis of the Unitarian's future:

> That Unitarianism has great positive merits of its own I should be the last to deny. But, after all, the key to the situation is the fullness of time. Mr. Knapp, has had the good fortune to be able to offer the Japanese exactly what they think they want. I write in this way because I write to you my belief in the importance of the mission on the present grounds. Whether what the Japanese think they want is what they really want is another question. It would perhaps be premature to argue from their eager curiosity to a great degree of spiritual earnestness.[129]

Knapp prepared for his report at the General Meeting of the AUA with a listing of his accomplishments. He had laid the groundwork for more newspaper work, a magazine that Unitarians could call their own, classes about religious principles, public speaking tours, a post office mission, tracts and publications in English and Japanese, scholarship funds for Japanese students to attend Harvard, and the creation of a "distinctively Unitarian school ...calling it the 'Emmanuel Tokugawa school' after its benefactor."[130] Knapp exhorted American Unitarians: "It may certainly be urged with much force that if for an Empire ready to fall into its hands the [American Unitarian] Association cannot raise the very small sum required, it would be well for it to abandon entirely all thought of entering the field of Foreign Missions."[131]

The opinion shapers of the new Japan, like YANO, editor of the *Hochi Shimbun*, the Marquis TOKUGAWA, and representatives of almost "every leading element in the Empire" heard from Knapp what they wanted to hear: there was a rational form of Christianity that would respect their culture and provide it with a moral basis. These "leading elements" were the old Tokugawa regime, the emerging order of the Imperial Restoration, the intellectuals who favored

---

129. Ernest Francisco Fenollosa to George Batchelor dated June 5, 1889, from Tokyo. AUA Archives bMS 01446 Inactive minister files, Box 106, Arthur Knapp. I am indebted to Mohr, *op.cit.,* for this citation.

130. Knapp to Reynolds, Feb.6,1889.

131. Knapp to Reynolds, Feb.6,1889.

democracy, and even industrial and military leaders. Knapp's letter to Reynolds cited receptions by this diverse leadership that was almost unbelievable.[132]

The Knapps returned to New England in May, 1889, just in time for the AUA annual meeting. They had completed their exploratory visit and now had to convince the American Unitarian Association to undertake a Mission in Japan. It was much to the credit of an Unitarian minister, George Batchelor, before he became the new chief officer of the AUA, that the mission happened at all. Many could find a host of reasons why a group so small should not undertake any mission, especially when some considered themselves a non-missionary faith and practice.

To the 1888 AUA annual meeting Knapp had written:

> The unique character of the Unitarian mission to Japan precludes anything like the usual missionary report. Sent to the men of other religions, not in the spirit of assumption or propagandism, but in that of respect and amity, the Unitarian envoy sends home no lists of converts. It is his good fortune, however, though only three months have elapsed since his arrival, to communicate the most gratifying information in regard to the special objects for which he was accredited. ...There is scarcely a doubt that Christianity is destined to come in and possess the land, along with everything which belongs to Western civilization.[133]

He continued with a hint of what might lie ahead.

> … It remains to be seen whether the liberal interpretation of Christianity, as organized in modern Unitarianism, will meet their wants.
>
> That the existence of such an interpretation of Christianity is a new revelation to them, is evidenced by the eagerness of the response with which every measure taken by its envoy to "acquaint them with the status of liberal opinion in America" has been met. A single notice in one of the Tokyo newspapers, announcing his purpose, drew forth a multitude of letters, one of them seven feet long, from all parts of the empire. This, of course, has suggested the

132. Ltr. Knapp to Reynolds, Feb.12,1889. The AUA would later make its president the paid, chief officer in 1894.

133. *AUA Annual Report, 1888*, p. 31-2.

employment of the instrumentality called the "Post-Office Mission," which will soon be in full operation distributing printed matter throughout the land.[134]

Despite strong objections from important Unitarian leaders from the western states, like Charles Wendte, the AUA voted to fund the Japan Mission. The money came from the Hayward Fund for foreign missions, previously used in India. The AUA had not yet figured out how to change the legal purpose of a bequest, and it was not a Yankee fault to waste a gift. So the Mission to Japan began.

Knapp Returned With His Co-Workers

In October 1889, the Knapps would start back for Japan with three professors, a minister and a returning Japanese who had been studying at Meadville Theological School in Pennsylvania and would become the Mission's first secretary, KANDA Saichirō (1863-1944). Upon Knapp's return in late 1889 with his team of co-workers, Keiō campus would be opened for both his American faculty of Henry Wigmore (1863-1943), Garret Droppers (1860-1927), and William Liscomb (1848-93), as well as to his co-fieldworker/missionary, the Rev. Clay MacCauley (1843-1925), to speak about Unitarianism.[135]

The Mission's first religious controversy occurred almost completely in the Japanese press. They charged FUKUZAWA of becoming, or at least allowing his college to become a sectarian Christian (*i.e.*, Unitarian) institution. The religious press attacked Unitarianism, but Knapp wrote Boston that he "proved that Unitarianism was not sectarian" and its approach to missions was unique. Knapp had argued that Unitarianism could be taught at Keiō as

---

134. *AUA Annual Report, 1888*, p. 33-4.

135. KANDA Saichirō, a Unitarian convert studying at Meadville Theological School, returned as translator and secretary of the Mission.

The professors came, each to found a college at FUKUZAWA's Keiō school, thus creating a university: John Henry Wigmore, law (staying from 1889-92); William Liscomb, literature (1889-93); Garrett Droppers, political economics (1889-1898). Clay MacCauley had been a Unitarian minister, currently publishing a newspaper (serving from 1889-1900; and again from 1909-1920).

it was rational and without dogma. However, Unitarianism remained a heresy to the orthodox for years to come.

The Rev. Henry W. Hawkes arrived from England in January 1889, paying his own way to serve. Hawkes had two interests: developing Unitarian worship in Japan and engaging Buddhists. He prepared a huge worship manual that was translated into Japanese, and he intended to publish an Unitarian hymnal. However, his lasting contribution was his ability to cultivate trust and friendships with Buddhist intellectuals, especially the *New* Buddhists who were open to Western science and moral reform.

Faculty and Graduates of the Japan Unitarian Mission's first School of Liberal Theology, 1889. Rev. W. H, Hawkes*, British Unitarian, insert upper left;* Rev. Arthur Knapp, *insert upper right.*

Knapp and MacCauley made an annual report by mail in 1889 to the American Unitarian Association, essentially describing what Knapp had begun. MacCauley took credit for dividing the work into three departments: education, publication, and worship. They returned to Boston in 1890 to report directly to the AUA board of directors and to the annual meeting in May of the Association. The 1890 AUA Annual Report maintained enthusiasm for their mission, even as they realized that there was "no Empire for the taking." The mood of the Japanese leaders had changed, and anti-Western sentiment was evident. The West was still imposing unequal treaties upon Japan despite all of its efforts to be taken as an equal. Yet, they could report that they had started a journal, the *Unitarian* (*Yuniterian*).[136]

Keiō's transformation into a university was becoming a reality, as was access to its students. Unitarian clubs were being formed for those who were interested. Members of the mission spoke regularly at the "speaking house" in the center of the campus. The two other liberal missions, the Universalists and the German Liberal Mission, seemed prepared to form a strong liberal Christian alliance. MacCauley added that they were thinking of beginning a seminary together.[137]

FUKUZAWA Yukichi, who became known as the father of Japanese modern education, had requested help to turn his school into a modern university. This brought the Unitarian mission to his Keiō College in the Mita district of Tokyo. While many doors had closed even before their arrival in 1889, FUKUZAWA opened his Keiō school and his newspaper to Knapp and his team. The professors worked in their spare time with the Mission and received small stipends from the AUA. As long as Knapp was there and keeping these tasks non-sectarian, no problem arose. Departments of law, literature and political economics transformed the college into a university. FUKUZAWA was pleased.

The Unity Club formed by MacCauley, hoping it would become a church, tested how much evangelism could be attempted on campus. The relationship with FUKUZAWA was based on a bond of respect and mutual labor. FUKUZAWA said that he had no taste for religion but wanted Unitarianism for his students. He saw its moral benefits. This stance of FUKUZAWA would be forgotten by MacCauley when he led the mission alone, vacillating between fieldworker and missionary.

---

136. The *Yuniterian* (ゆにてりあん, 1890–1891) would soon become the *Shūkyō* (宗教, *Religion,* 1891–1898) and then merge with the *Rikugō Zasshi* 六合雑誌 (*Cosmos Journal*), 1880–1921. There was also the *Shinri* (真理, 1889–1900).

137. *AUA Annual Report, 1890.*

Perhaps FUKUZAWA's vision for his university contained a similar contradiction with MacCauley's conflicted Unitarian approach. He wanted his students to learn about Unitarianism, not as a religion but as a system of values to live by its principles. He wanted Unitarianism to replace Confucianism, which he also took as a value system and not a religion. To that end, he and Knapp were in agreement. Japanese intellectuals like FUKUZAWA wanted rational religion for the masses based on knowledge and reason. They despised devotional and ritualistic religions (both devotional Buddhism and Christianity or ritualistic Shinto). FUKUZAWA wanted Unitarianism to create a new Japanese intelligentsia, whose existential core for life choices would be moral and altruistic. Neo-Confucianism had taught him to choose ethical rationality and principled altruism. It took years of study that had been well-suited for the old samurai class which was more leisured. This new generation was not so inclined. When he invited Knapp's Unitarianism to his campus, it would not be apparent for years that it included elements that were not rational – especially its New England customs and nineteenth century ideas of representative democracy but governance by a privileged elite.

Knapp continued moving in the highest echelon of society even with the change in national mood. Knapp's letters reflected this constant intercourse with the most powerful and most educated. Representative was the letter of Feb. 20, 1890, mentioning:

> Mr. Fukuzawa, Count Soyeshima, the Vice President of the Privy Council and the Tutor of the Emperor, Mr. Kato the former President of the Imperial University, Mr. Nakamura the leading Chinese scholar of the Empire and Mr. Sugiura the leader of the moral movement among the Japanese students.[138]

The plan that Knapp had outlined to Reynolds in 1888 materialized with one major exception: the Marquis TOKUGAWA did

[138] Knapp Book, p. 57.

not sponsor a Unitarian school. Actually, by locating at Keiō University in Mita-ku [also referred to as Shiba] in the new industrial district, they did not have a presence in the student district of Kanda-ku, the locale of Imperial University and Waseda [a school also becoming a university]. FUKUZAWA gave them housing and classrooms for their talks and lectures, but Knapp asked Boston for more funding to have a second station in Kanda-ku. Knapp envisioned an educational presence; MacCauley imagined a church.

Knapp and the other members of the Mission interpreted the first losses of powerful Japanese leaders as effected by the political climate in the fall of 1889. Knapp wrote home specifically about the Marquis TOKUGAWA:

> … against all these favorable and encouraging features of the situation must be set the defection of the Marquis Tokugawa who ever since the present anti-foreign reaction began has been under tremendous family pressure to force him to give up all open connection with Christianity. He has at last been obliged to give way though personally at heart he is as much with us as ever and his friendship remains intact. His struggles between loyalty to his faith and loyalty to his family have been in the highest degree pathetic, and I regard his defection as simply and only an indication of the strength of the prevailing political reaction.[139]

Already Knapp was severely criticized from the "Western" Unitarian missionary perspective for his "top down" approach to missions (that is, not winning the masses). These leaders in the Western United States, like Wendte, also disparaged his methods as not truly religious.[140] For Wendte, there was not a true emphasis on worship and devotion. MacCauley's approach, which pressed for more preaching tours to the provinces and for building of Unitarian churches, not classrooms and lecture halls, was more to his liking.

---

139. Ltr. Knapp to George Fox, Nov.11, 1889. Also, Knapp Book, p. 78.

140. Ltr. Wendte to Knapp, *ibid.* Knapp and MacCauley complained that their letters and reports were not being published, while the British Unitarians showed more interest and were publishing Hawke's report of the Japan Mission.

Unitarian Fieldworkers or Evangelistic Missionaries

Both Knapp and MacCauley had been members of the Free Religious Association (FRA).[141] MacCauley had been more prominent.[142] Some of his lectures had been published in FRA organs. The essence of free religion, if one can even be abstracted, was religious freedom for individual faith and practice. Each member had their own perspective about religion, Unitarianism, Christianity and whatever their life purpose might be. Knapp and MacCauley had their own ideas what the mission in Japan should be. They particularly differed on the importance of ecclesiastical organization. MacCauley had become quite conservative compared with other members of the FRA, going back into institutional Unitarianism. He adopted "propagandizing" (his term) the "true or rational religion of Jesus" and established churches in Jesus' name as Liberal Christian (i.e., Unitarian). MacCauley was a Spencerian evolutionist,[143] following those who applied Darwin to social history and seeing Western civilization and rational Christianity at the top of progressive evolution. Yet, MacCauley could recite the old mantra from the India Mission: we have come to confer, not to convert. MacCauley could not sense a contradiction between his profession and his actions. He believed in organizing churches, holding solemn worship services,

---

141. William J. Potter, *The Free Religious Association: Its Twenty Five Years And Their Meaning* (1892). Stow Persons, *Free Religion: An American Faith* (Boston, Beacon Press, 1963). Members of the Free Religious Association followed their fellow FRA colleagues, Knapp and MacCauley, in organs like *The Unitarian Review, The Unitarian*, and *Unity*. See also, Richard A. Kellaway, *William James Potter from Convinced Quaker to Free Religion* (Xlibris, 2014).

142. Clay MacCauley, *Memories and Memorials: Gatherings from an Eventful Life* (Tokyo: Fukuin Printing of Yokohama, 1914). The literary quality of MacCauley's 1914 publication differs from what Day places in his mouth only 5 years later in their MacCauley/Day, "History of the Unitarian Mission in Japan: 1889-1921," manuscript, n.p., c. 1931.

143. "Spencerian evolutionism" was a theory of cultural progress derived from Herbert Spencer (1820-1903).

making speaking tours, creating an association of churches, evangelizing – or the term he used most often, "proselytizing" – especially of orthodox ministers already trained by other Christian denominations. He wanted to get individuals to identify as Unitarian. He liked calling Japanese "Unitarians," or "nearly Unitarian," or "Unitarian sympathizers," in his reports to Boston because of his idea of the importance of membership giving true identity. Counting Japanese as members, or near members, was important to his evangelistic approach.

Knapp had remained a free religionist, but sided with the radicals, unlike MacCauley and Wendte who had both become institutional and loyal to the AUA. Knapp was as close to being anti-institutional, anti-ecclesiastical, and anti-clergy as an Unitarian minister could be. His anti-sectarianism had resonated with FUKUZAWA and those leaders who had wondered about using rational Christianity for the masses. Knapp sought to be a true "fieldworker," learning from Japanese culturally and religiously. In Japan, he had become less missionary and less tolerant of mission duties. He had achieved what Charles Dall never became in India – a non-sectarian fieldworker.[144] And, most importantly, he did not practice any form of racial or religious superiority.

Despite the contradictory approaches of differing "Unitarianisms" dividing Knapp and MacCauley, there had been a unified vision and message foretelling the World's Parliament of Religions' themes of 1893: sympathy of religions, unity of truth, brotherhood of man, and fatherhood of God. This message had resonated with the Japanese ruling and educated classes' desire for national independence, racial equality, scientific and practical

144. Spencer Lavan's study is a must read: *Unitarians and India: a study in Encounter and Response* (Boston: Skinner House, 1977). More broadly, David Kopf, *The Brahmo Samaj and the Making of the Modern Indian Mind* (1979).

knowledge, higher morality, and rejection of superstition. Unitarianism's message seemed a good and rational religion for the masses. These very slogans would adorn the front wall of their future headquarters of Unity Hall, dedicated in 1894. (They would greet IMAOKA when he arrived in 1910 at the beginning of the third period of Unitarians in Japan.)

Trouble on the Horizon

There was something that Knapp might not have been able to see as an American, even with his background as a journalist. The Japanese nation-builders, especially the Marquis, were watching America's territorial expansion into the Pacific. America needed refueling stations to compete with Western colonial powers for China. To prevent warships from refueling with wood charcoal in its ports, the Hawaiian Kingdom in 1854 had declared itself a neutral nation, supposedly the first nation in history to do so.[145] Its indigenous rulers had accepted Christianity and declared the Hawaiian Kingdom to be Christian. They had been accepted into the "Family of Nations," entering into treaties of trade and recognition of sovereignty with more than forty nations, including the United States.

One unsuccessful plan was to make Japan a nominally Christian nation, having proceeded so far as to begin exploration of an engagement between the Prince KOMATSU Akihito (1846-1903)[146] and Princess Ka'iulani (1875-1899) of the Hawaiian Kingdom. The implications of this were staggering. Perhaps Princess Ka'iulani's early death ended this dream; perhaps it never had a chance. Hawai'i was not occupied by the United States until 1893. Until then, its "Christianization" had been an example to Japan of a way to avoid

---

145. Declared by King Kamehameha III, http://www.hawaiiankingdom.org/hawn-territory.shtml.

146. Taken from a letter from Queen Lili'uokalani to the Princess. Others claim the proposed marriage was to Prince KOMATSU's half-brother, Prince HIGASHIFUSHIMI Yorihito (1867-1922).

colonization by foreign powers. This illustrates why the Marquis Tokugawa's interest in or flirtation with Unitarianism was not alone – that others among the highest officials and cultural shapers in the Meiji era were looking for practical ways to save Japan from colonization.

New Englanders, with their shipping interests and desire for trade with China, had been proposing annexation of Hawai'i for decades. America would encourage a coup by plantation owners and "the bayonet constitution" by which the United States acquired Pearl Harbor from the Kingdom of Hawai'i in 1887. Then, warships were stationed at the world's first neutral nation. In 1893 America assisted a puppet overthrow, putting Queen Lili'uokalani under house arrest.[147] America failed to gain possession of the island kingdom until the war with Spain in 1897. Although U.S. President Grover Cleveland had apologized for the illegal action in 1893, America needed Hawai'i for a refueling and staging station. The U.S. took Hawai'i by occupation – and the Philippines and other Spanish possessions by conquest.

Some Congregational missionaries and their children were implicated in America's territorial advance into the Pacific. The Dole family came to Hawai'i typically divided between Congregationalists and Unitarians: Sanford Dole, a Congregational, took part in the Hawaiian coup and became the President of the Republic of Hawai'i; his cousin James, a nominal Unitarian, founded Dole Pineapple. Japanese nation-builders were quite aware of America's move into the Pacific. For the Marquis Tokugawa and Imperial planners, Hawaii's example showed that Christianization had not protected the Hawaiian Kingdom nor would it protect Japan's sovereignty. The perceived use of Christianity in the Pacific by colonial powers was seen as a "fifth

---

147. Two U.S. Presidents, Cleveland and Clinton, would apologize for this illegal act, but... neither would find a remedy. There are major dissertations and a slew of recent publications to suggest that this should be common knowledge.

column" of potential traitors, and remembered later during Japan's occupation of Korea in 1910, as Korean Christians were brutally punished.[148]

Something Happened

With sensed resistance to his vision of the mission both from powerful Japanese leaders and from his co-workers, Knapp "became ill" in the winter of 1891. He said: "I leave with the assurance that my initial errand is fully accomplished, that strong organization is effected in spite of the untoward political influences at least and that the future is left in the best of hands."[149] He left Japan, and the Mission changed directions. Knapp followed the ministerial etiquette of not criticizing his successor – for almost twelve years.[150]

In the "official reports," first Knapp in 1890 and Hawkes in 1891 would become ill and return home. There are starkly differing accounts of their departures. Knapp had written a letter to George Fox, assistant secretary of the AUA, in September 1890, that he had a kidney problem and believed that a three-month leave would return him to normal health.[151] MacCauley wrote one month later to Fox, stating "since Knight Arthur will be gone from the field... As I now look at our affairs it seems advisable that there should be no hurry in

148. In 1910 Prince Itō was quoted concerning Japan's occupation: "I consider that one of the gravest perils to Japan is the Christian Church in Korea." Repeated in Wilkes, *Missionary Joys, op. cit.*, p. 142, when he visited Korea and saw the persecution first hand. Parenthetically, New England Unitarian and Congregational families were closely related. The Doles were one example. Annexation of Hawai'i had been a major concern for New Englanders for decades with little protest from Unitarians. The Japanese power elites tempered their open welcome of American Unitarians as these events unfolded in the Pacific.

149. *Ibid.*

150. In 1903 Knapp told Thomas Eliot, sent by the AUA to Japan to investigate its "assets," how badly he thought MacCauley had done. Concerning speculation why Fukuzawa "expelled" MacCauley from his Keiō residence, see Mohr, *ibid.,* p. 56, exploring Tsuchiya's hypothesis about these tensions. John B. W. Day's account of Knapp's departure in his *History* puts the blame on MacCauley.

151. Ltr. Knapp to George Fox, Sept. 12, 1890, cited in Mohr, *ibid.,* p.24-5.

sending some one to take Mr. Knapp's place."[152] Day's "history," which claimed to be the faithful account dictated by MacCauley in 1919, as he retired and was leaving Japan, claimed: "Upon MacCauley's and others remonstrating with him, he resigned."[153] Knapp is also accused in Day's account of being more interested in purchasing curios than winning converts.[154]

Knapp published a two-volume work on Japan in 1900, the year that we founded the Yokohama *Japan Advertiser,* giving only a brief comment on Unitarianism. It was prophetic:

> The Christianity which gains a foothold or any lasting influence in the Empire will be neither Presbyterian, nor Episcopalian, nor Baptist, nor Methodist, nor Unitarian Christianity. It will not be even American, nor English, nor German, nor Roman Christianity. It will be, if anything at all, an essentially Japanese faith based upon and assimilated with the old loyalties. What has happened in every other department of the nation's life, the dismissal of foreign teachers and employees just as soon as natives have been educated to take their places, is the manifest destiny of the foreign religious propagandist. The Japanese will, as always, give him a patient and hospitable hearing, with a view to ascertain whether what he has to offer will be of use to the nation's life. If it shall be found to be of service in enhancing the power of that life, the office of administering it and of moulding its future developments will be directed by native influences, and the self-appointed foreign directors of the nation's religious and moral well-being will find their occupation gone. And thus the only invasion of the Empire which ever had a hope of success will prove a failure. In her faith, as in her polity, Japan will remain, as always in the past, the unconquered Island Realm.[155]

William Irvin Lawrance (1853-1935) arrived to replace Knapp in 1891 but would only stay until 1894. Lawrance wrote years later that "In the early months of 1891 Knapp withdrew and I was

---

152. Ltr. MacCauley to Fox, October Oct. 6, 1890, cited in Mohr, *ibid.*, p. 25.

153. Day/MacCauley, *op. cit.,* p. 32.

154. Day/MacCauley, *ibid.* This passage in Day's report is clearly in Day's style and vocabulary rather than MacCauley's.

155. Arthur May Knapp, *Feudal and Modern Japan*, 2 vols. (Boston: L. C. Page & Co., 1900), Vol. 2, p. 221.

appointed in his place."[156] Possibly, he meant that he was just appointed in early 1891, as Knapp was reported leaving in December 1890. Lawrance summarized his own service for an article commemorating the closure of the Mission in 1900. It was a modest summary of his excellent contribution but left out his most lasting gift; he had introduced Christian socialism to liberal seminarians coming to him from the more orthodox missions.

> About the time I arrived our monthly magazine, known as the *Unitarian*, was enlarged in scope, and made more distinctly helpful to our cause, its name being changed to *Shukyo*, meaning Religion. More recently it has been combined with one of the largest and most influential magazines in the empire [*Rikugō zashhi*], and, still issued from our own headquarters, has a wide influence. Tracts and translations from our best authors have been sent out in increased numbers, many thousands of them going through the mails to the intelligent people of the country. Letters began to come in with increasing frequency, so many coming, in fact, as to require almost the entire time of our efficient secretary, Mr. Kanda, to answer their inquiries. A branch mission was begun in a part of Tokyo swarming with students of the Imperial University and other schools. Here I preached, lectured, and conversed with young men until the mission was burned in a conflagration that laid waste a whole section or ward of the city. This loss so stimulated interest and sympathy among our friends in America as to secure for the mission the erection of a new headquarters, second to none in the city in beauty and adaptation to mission uses.
>
> Climatic conditions rendering my further stay in Japan hazardous, I returned to America in January, 1894.[157]

MacCauley took over as director or supervisor of the mission in 1891, with the desire to lead the mission according to his distinctive vision of a Unitarian mission. Yet, Knapp's leadership as a fieldworker continued to bear fruit. The *Unitarian* (*Yuniterian*) journal he started was renamed *Religion* (*Shūkyō*). A school begun by Lawrance for young men interested in liberal Christian studies became the famed School for Advanced Learning. Along with it,

156. Lawrance, *Christian Register*, April 12 1900, p.21.

157. *Ibid.*

Lawrance started a second church in the student district. Both would thrive until a fire would destroy a huge portion of the student district, also destroying their month-old building.

The 1893 Annual Report to the AUA told how the loss of their building had led to major fundraising with only a small portion coming from the American Association. There were five 'out-stations' to distribute Unitarian literature. Lawrance's school had become the School of Liberal Theology (*Jiyū Shin Gakko*). A "Mr. TAKATA" (who changed his name to MAYEKAWA) had started the Yagembori church.[158] SAJI Jitsunen, the New Buddhist priest who was recruited by Hawkes before he left the mission, had advanced from an assistant editor at their journal to become the "superintendent" of "The Tokyo First Unitarian Church" and was "delivering excellent addresses from week to week." The publication department distributed 25,000 tracts and 13,000 copies of *Shūkyō*. MacCauley gave that annual meeting a taste of the kinds of questions that Secretary KANDA and pastor SAJI were answering, each handling about a thousand letters a year to Japanese inquirers:

> How is social morality to be best established? Is capital punishment justifiable from a moral and religious standpoint? Are religion and State education reconcilable (a burning question now in Japan)? What is the most pressing present moral need? Why is marriage between near relatives immoral? How shall the abolition of prostitution be effected? What is the fundamental principle of Christianity?[159]

Waning Interest in Foreign Missions (1894-1899)

International tensions between nations and changing attitudes toward foreigners were not the only things that MacCauley and Lawrance had to contend with. Criticism was coming from

[158] The church was so short-lived and so quickly disappears from the reports that one is probably justified in suspecting TAKATA of being an adventurer.

[159] *1893 Annual Report* [of the AUA]. April 21, pp. 47-53, signed by MacCauley as "Superintendent of American Unitarian Association in Japan."

evangelical Unitarians who wanted human and financial resources refocused. Charles Wendte wanted the AUA's funding for home missions, since he was a minister in the western United States. In his earlier criticism of Knapp, Wendte predicted that Japan might only be a momentary fad, "Do you not sometimes fear that fickleness and disaffection at home, as well as in Japan, will make it impossible to keep up such a work over so long a term of years?"[160] But it would require actions from Boston headquarters for that prediction to become true. Stories in the *Christian Register* and visits from Japanese Unitarian leaders to Boston kept up interest and support. And as importantly, the Hayward Fund financed the work which was a designated behest only for foreign missions. Something had to change for the Japan mission to end.

The AUA board had tried to prevent any new expenses in Japan as the United States experienced "the Panic of 1893." It would last for four more years.[161] Prof. Mohr concluded that the fate of the Japan mission was decided at the September 1893 meeting of the AUA board, just after Reynolds died and the AUA's own financial crisis was discovered. George Batchelor, who had previously helped the Japan Mission at every point, was appointed head of the Association in 1894 – the top office was henceforth president instead of secretary. He found the Association so deeply in debt that he began cutting the mission programs in America and Japan. As a financial realist, he needed to close the Japan Mission. He wrote Ernest Fenollosa and FUKUZAWA Yukichi for evaluations of the mission but their responses were too positive to be useful.[162] KISHIMOTO wrote a powerful defense of the work and a plea to American Unitarians not

160. Ltr. Wendte to Knapp, *op. cit.*

161. The Panic began in 1891 and ended in 1897.

162. FUKUZAWA to Batchelor, Oct. 26, 1895 and Fenollosa to Batchelor, June 5, 1889. Fenollosa was a professor of art history at the Imperial University; his response to Batchelor's inquiries was not timely but was supportive of the JUM.

to close the school, renamed *Senshin Gakuin* (the School for Advanced Learning).[163] The Japan Mission and its various departments including the school were not closed immediately, because of its continued popularity in America. From this point on, the Mission would receive a third of what had been the earnings from the Hayward Fund. Lawrance resigned in 1894; the official reason was illness.[164] He returned to the AUA to become head of its Sunday School department. He would remain an ardent defender of the Japan Mission. His position in Japan was not replaced; MacCauley was left alone as the AUA's last missionary.[165]

The three professors began leaving Keiō University. Wigmore departed to become president of the University of North Dakota in 1892. Liscomb became seriously ill in 1893, returned home and died. Droppers would remain at Keiō until 1898. MacCauley would state that the professors' services had been of little value to the Mission. This evaluation of their service is only found in Day's redacted history – placed in MacCauley's mouth.[166]

From 1893 to 1899 Batchelor and the AUA Board cut the funds going to Japan. They ordered its School of Advanced Learning to be transformed into an educational extension program by 1899. This was done over the objections of MacCauley, the faculty and Japan Unitarian Association leaders. Lastly, the AUA Board closed the Japan Mission by bringing its last missionary, MacCauley, home in 1900.

---

163. KISHIMOTO to Batchelor, Nov. 3, 1895. KISHIMOTO soon resigned as chief editor of *Rikugō Zasshi* and began as a lecturer at Waseda school – on its way to become a university.

164. Day's *History* blames Lawrance's resignation from the Mission on MacCauley's criticism of him. This remark follows a pattern: Day does not miss an opportunity to criticize MacCauley.

165. An extended exploration of this first period of JUM and the intricacies of its ending is found in Mohr, *ibid.,* pp. 18-60.

166. John B. W. Day was the AUA's missionary during the third period of the American Unitarian Mission.

Their public justification was that the Mission had been such a success that it warranted a dramatic change – no American missionaries were needed. The *1900 Annual Report* would proudly state: "In the course of the present year the Mission will take another step in advance. The entire local charge and direction of the Mission will hereafter be intrusted [*sic.*] to native workers."[167]

The financial panic in 1893 led to Boston trying to reduce its programs, including the Japan Mission. But, that panic was long over when they were finally able to drastically reduce such a popular program as the Japan Unitarian Mission without it appearing to be a failure. All expenses during the period of financial panic were met by the Hayward Fund, indicating that it had not only recovered any losses, but that extra funds were available for an expanded program in foreign missions. In 1900 there was no financial reason to close the Mission. The reason would lie elsewhere.

Retreat to Advance

By cutting the expense of the Japan Mission and redefining how the Hayward Fund could be used for "foreign mission," Batchelor could solve a larger problem: its struggle with the Western Conference. Batchelor would use the saved funds to bring its leader, Charles Wendte, a critic of the Japan Mission, into the AUA as its Foreign Affairs director. In 1899 Wendte had called for an international interfaith organization.[168] At the 1900 General Assembly of the AUA, the International Council of Unitarian and Other Liberal Religious Thinkers and Workers was born. It would be renamed repeatedly until it finally became the International Association for Religious Freedom in 1969 (IARF). Wendte would be its first

167. *1900 AUA Annual Report*, p. 21. This section of the report was repeated verbatim in the coming years.

168. The June 1, 1899 *Christian Register* contained Wendte's invitation to the first meeting of the international organization to be known as the International Council of Unitarians and Liberal Christians.

executive secretary. He would also be the director of Foreign Affairs for the AUA, overseeing the AUA's mission program. Wendte would finance his international travels and the Congresses held every four or so years with the Hayward Fund. This did require a drastic reduction in funds for Japan, resulting in what the AUA headquarters euphorically called the Japanese success that allowed them to take over their own mission "without any loss of programs."[169]

Lawrance wrote in an April 12, 1900, *Christian Register* article, praising the former mission as the "largest enterprise undertaken by AUA in [its] 75 year history..." He continued: "Finally, Mr. MacCauley has resigned, and will soon be in America. The mission is now to be intrusted [*sic.*] to native workers, whose eminent attainments and acquaintance with local conditions make them especially capable of doing efficient work; while their characters and careers are such as to inspire confidence in their zeal and devotion to our high principles."[170]

MURAI Tomoyoshi wrote an article for the November 29, 1900, *Christian Register* (pp. 1323-4 and republished as a booklet, *The Unitarian Movement in Japan*) which pointed out why Unitarianism as an idea or philosophy was so important.

> It means that the Unitarian kind of religion is to be introduced into our educational system. Such is the trend of thought concerning religion among scholars and educational leaders in Japan.
>
> The Unitarian tendency is very strong among native orthodox Christians. ...The Unitarian tendency of thought is not confined within the Christian circle, but is also prevailing rapidly among the Buddhistic thinkers.[171]

---

169. For those wishing to explore the closing of the Japan Unitarian Mission in 1900, links to the *Christian Register* and the *Unitarian Yearbooks* of these years, especially 1888 through 1907 (the next crisis), are easily available at hathitrust.com. Quotations in the *Christian Register* and the *Unitarian Yearbooks* are from this archival website.

170. *Christian Register*, April 12, 1900.

171. *Christian Register*, Nov. 29, 1900.

Rev. Murai Tomoyoshi, one of the Dōshisha Trio

Murai asked for continued funding of Japanese Unitarianism, saying that they had "not been able to do much because of the deficiency of money, in spite of the fact that there are coming a number of strong and earnest invitations from various districts. ...Another interesting feature of the Japanese Unitarian movement is the social work." He again asked for help to build in the "intellectual quarters as Kanda[-ku] in Tokyo. All other bodies have their own churches or lecture halls in that part of the city, which they are willing to rent for any purpose except for Unitarian preaching. … [A] new hall is only ten thousand dollars."[172]

While the *Christian Register* published these articles looking back upon a decade of success, nothing came of the appeal for funding of a second hall in Tokyo.[173] The annual appropriation had been cut so that the four departments of education, worship, publication and social work had to be drastically reduced.

First Period: Accomplishments and Failures

Considering the tiny expenditure and the brief number of years, the Japan Unitarian Mission was an amazing success. That very success was used as the reason for closing the American Japan Unitarian Mission in 1900. The accomplishments remained and

172. *Ibid.*

173. Another appeal in 1903 by Thomas Eliot would have a positive response, chapter 7.

greeted IMAOKA as he arrived in Tokyo. The failures, as of any institution, were glossed over, then and into the future. Failures were more evident to Japanese Unitarians, and IMAOKA would have soon learned of them.

In 1900 MacCauley left an extraordinary collection of innovators but a fragile institution. As IMAOKA would say, its strength was also its weakness. The magnificent Unity Hall was "a gift to the Japanese people," with an endowment for its upkeep. Because the Association (JUA) had not become a *zaidan*, a foundation, it did not own its own hall or the endowment to maintain it with insurance, repairs, etc.[174] That was owned first by KANDA Saichirō, the secretary of JUA. Before he left in 1900, MacCauley transferred ownership to a Japanese real estate lawyer, a Mr. MUSUIJIMA. He held real estate titles for foreigners – in this case, for the secretary of the AUA, Charles St. John, who was holding this "foreign asset" for the AUA.[175] Suddenly, the gift of Unity Hall was no longer owned by the Japan Unitarian Association. The consequences of this action would not be known for two decades. (Unity Hall would seem to prove UCHIMURA Kanzō's thesis that a building would create dependence, not independence. And with foreign funding came foreign control, interference and governmental suspicion. But that lesson was to be learned in period three and its endpoint in 1922.)

Another weakness was MacCauley's example of micro-management of finances. In theory, the Japan Association received an annual or biannual grant. It went to the Association's treasurer and would not be interfered with by MacCauley or the AUA. The rhetoric claimed a unique approach to missions that freed rather than made Japanese dependent. Unitarians were blind to their own ecclesiastical

174. The majority of the JUA board were deeply influenced by UCHIMURA's "no church" movement, which avoided expensive church buildings – their cost, upkeep, and foreign dependence. Yet, they enjoyed and benefited from this building.

175. This becomes a major issue in the demise of the Mission in 1922.

controls, especially through finances. And, Unity Hall was the albatross that made the Japan Unitarian Association subservient. Yet, this very building was the centerpiece of their program – their school, publication department, worship hall, social work center and meeting place for progressive organizations.

The closure of the School for Advanced Learning had a consequence known immediately. The progressives and innovators who had taught or studied there went out into the Empire as liberals in a variety of fields, mainly education. The students, who had been taught there and became progressive leaders, ceased to flow back into Japanese society.

The teaching of each religion by a reputable scholar of that tradition would be one influence from the 1893 World's Parliament of Religions in Chicago. The University of Iowa claimed it was the first state university in the United States to institute that model. Harvard and Oxford would also have visiting scholars teach their own religious tradition. MacCauley thought that the School for Advanced Learning, with its faculty in 1893, was the first in modern times to accomplish this ideal.[176] The Imperial University in Tokyo would use the approach of the School for Advanced Learning in teaching about Japan's religions.

In education, some went to the great universities, like KISHIMOTO, who had already anticipated the closing of the School and had gone to Waseda to help it become a university. Others, who had

---

176. *Catalogue of Shinshen Gakuin* 1893-1894, p. 58. The faculty consisted with MacCauley as President and professor of Philosophic and Historic Theology, William Lawrance secretary and professor of Biblical Criticism and Exegesis, Garrett Droppers was professor at Keiōgijuku (university) and lecturer of sociology and social ethics, ONISHI Hajime was lecturer of psychology, ethics and history of philosophy; SAJI Jitsunen was lecturer on religions of Japan; KIKUCHI Hisato was lecturer on Japanese Classical Literature; MASHINO Yetsukeo was lecturer on Christian Theology and HAGA Yaichi was lecturer on Japanese grammar and rhetoric. A number of young scholars would become lecturers in the following years.

been or were still lecturers at its closing, like ANESAKI, returned to their alma maters – ANESAKI to Tokyo Imperial University. He founded the program in which IMAOKA studied. YOKOI Tokio returned to Dōshisha to become its second president. Many would stay in the programs at Unity Hall to make the second period of Japanese Unitarianism quite remarkable in its own right. But, the educational extension program said to replace the School for Advanced Learning could not erase the truth that the school's closure was one of the greatest blunders in AUA history. The school had been a magnet the effects of which could not be duplicated.

Although it was not even noted at the time, Keiō University was closed to American Unitarians. MacCauley had been asked in 1897 to quit the free residence provided by FUKUZAWA on the campus. FUKUZAWA so distanced himself from MacCauley and Unitarianism, that when he died in 1901, the connection would be forgotten.[177] His grandson, KIYOOKA Eiichi, accidentally learned of Unitarian help in Keiō's becoming a university when he wrote its history.[178] What Knapp had gained with his "cultured Unitarianism" and his unadulterated fieldworker approach was now lost.

The most subtle failure of the first period involved contradictions between practical assistance and church-building – and that might be blamed on freedom's ambiguity. Unitarians came to Japan bearing the standard of freedom's religion: freedom of conscience, freedom of new ideas and philosophies, freedom to study

177. Mohr, *Universality, op.cit.*, pp.50ff., explores the complexities of these events.

178. KIYOOKA Eiichi, *The Autography of Fukuzawa Yukichi* (Tokyo: The Hokuseido Press, 1981) and *The Birth of Keiō Gijuku University* (Tokyo: Keiō gijuku, 1983). I am grateful to him for his gift of these books and his guided tour of the historic sites on Keiō's main campus, as well as a visit to the plaque that commemorates the location of Unity Hall's Friendly Society.

science and evolution, freedom from dogmas, freedom from ecclesiastical hierarchies, freedom from foreign dependencies, and so much more. These freedoms were wrapped in individualism. Developing individual freedom had been the focus of the first period. Its social dimension would be the focus of the second Japanese period.

Japanese progressives had fallen in love with freedom's call. They self-identified as *yuniterian*.[179] That freedom let them examine religion in general and in specifics. They had already begun linking freedom with responsibility, in their lectures and publications, making liberating religion of service to their new Japanese society and creative of a moral, just and free character in community. Many had been converted into Christianity by orthodox missionaries of sterling character. But their belief-centered religion, filled with ideas that did not make sense culturally or intellectually, had brought them to Unitarianism. This religion of free thought and religious liberty had the highest of ideals and intentions. But ideals have to be applied in one's life and in community. That test was to come.

Suddenly, the missionaries of individual freedom were gone. They left a building, some programs and an organization that seemed

---

179. MacCauley's reports do not inform Boston AUA headquarters or the Unitarian public of the malleable nature of Unitarian church membership, enjoying the benefits of multiple identities. As mentioned earlier, *yuniterian* had become a word for members, sympathizers, progressives as well as non-church members. A high percentage of its leadership were both Unitarians and Congregationalists, like ABE, KISHIMOTO and MURAI. They served actively in both organizations. MacCauley bragged about Japanese tolerance and how these leaders were not ostracized for being Unitarian; and that was true. He did not inform American Unitarians, or perhaps he did not even understand, that dual identities were part of Japanese religious history. Knapp had understood that there was no reason for conversions as liberal influence could transform Japanese faiths. He did not count or report membership in the American Unitarian Mission. This was MacCauley's strength and weakness, his introduction of the missionary-evangelistic contradiction of membership into fieldworker experiment. For MacCauley, a planting in Japan required a harvest, and the fruit of the harvest was members.

democratic and constitutional. Japanese Unitarianism seemed to have been well "planted" – and that success was being celebrated in New England. Yet, the constitutional democracy that MacCauley left them was an American replica – more precisely, a "Boston Brahmin" design with unseen flaws.[180] Planted in Japanese soil, Unitarianism and its religious freedom would grow fruits of a liberal community that sought to be truly Japanese.

[180.] American Unitarianism came to Japan as liberal and democratic. Their form of democratic organization came with the same contradictions they had developed in New England. It was minister-controlled and was modeled after a business cartel. The AUA, although adopting the word "association," was struggling to centralize free churches into a denomination with a liberal ideology. Independence of ministers and congregations were being expressed in movements that contested centralization under the AUA (the Free Religious Association, the conferences, the independent newspapers and periodicals, etc.).

There was a second contradiction born from the Mission's rhetoric. That is more obvious. The Mission claimed to be uniquely run by Japanese through their own association, free of foreign control. The foreign funds came from the AUA to MacCauley who turned them over to the Japan Unitarian Association's treasurer. In theory, they were free to do with it as they saw fit for "liberal religious" purposes consistent with Japanese culture. MacCauley had overseen the use of the funds simply because they were so meager.

Chapter 7

Japanese Unitarians: Their Perspectives in the First Two Periods (1888-1900, 1900-1909)

This chapter will attempt to construct a "native," non-missionary history of Japanese Unitarianism in full recognition that none of the major Japanese leaders published such a history. The son of one of the most prominent leaders, KISHIMOTO Nobuta, whose participation spanned all three periods of Japanese Unitarian history, wrote a scathing critique of Unitarianism's failure as a religious movement. The son, KISHIMOTO Hideo, hid his father's leadership in all liberal organizations by never mentioning him by name.[181] He wrote his own father out of Japanese Unitarian history. IMAOKA never spoke more than a sentence or two about his participation in Japanese Unitarianism, barely admitting that he was the Japan Unitarian Association and Japan Unitarian Mission's last secretary.[182] Such a lack of "native" remembrances, perhaps only in memoirs and diaries yet to be researched, signals that something traumatic happened.[183] There was a richness in the successes of the first missionary period (1888-1900) so that the failures in closing the flourishing School for Advanced Learning and its Mission in 1900 could be accepted as a financial necessity. This chapter revisits the missionary period from another point of view and combines that with the decade when there were no American Unitarian missionaries in

---

181. KISHIMOTO Hideo, *op.cit.*

182. Technically, he was the last secretary of the Japanese Unitarian Association (JUA) and the next-to-last secretary of the Mission (JUM). A "rogue figure" would be hired as the last JUM secretary. See chapter 8.

183. The traumatic closing of the Mission will be the subject of chapter 8.

Japan (1900-1909). Both periods formed the background of the movement that IMAOKA joined.[184]

Because of the scarcity or absence of contemporaneous Japanese accounts, the extant data from the American Mission reports will be reexamined to learn non-missionary perspectives on Japanese Unitarianism. *Missionary histories* are a special genre dedicated to the successes of their institutions and actors. So it is telling that there was no official AUA account of the Japan Unitarian Mission or any analysis by Unitarian historians.[185] One will search in vain from Earl Morse Wilbur[186] to current historians of Unitarian Universalism like David Robinson.[187] Two small reports were compiled a decade after the mission's second attempt and closure in 1922. The third director of the Japan Mission, John B. W. Day (serving from 1919-1922), completed his report in 1931, writing only an introduction and attributing fifty more pages to an interview of MacCauley. Day's "MacCauley History" only raises questions. The reasons for this will become clear in the next chapter as Day "closes"

184. If Japanese Unitarianism becomes a field of study, future scholars will probe Japanese journals and diaries, attempting to find accounts of participants in *yuniterian* activities. Perhaps something has survived the ravages of time, war, and neglect. As mentioned, IMAOKA did not become an Unitarian until the third period, but contemporaneous studies of the *yuniterian* movement as such have not been found.

185. Brief accounts of the history were repeated in articles in the *Christian Register* by MacCauley, Lawrance, Eliot, Wendte, MURAI and others during these years. The MacCauley history allegedly dictated to John B. W. Day in 1919 was never published but filed as a report. Even Cornish, Day's mentor at the AUA, found it unworthy of publication.

186. For example, Wilbur, *A History of Unitarianism: Socinianism and Its Antecedents*, 1945, and *A History of Unitarianism In Transylvania, England, and America to 1900*, 1952, or Robinson, *The Unitarians and the Universalists* (1985).

187. One might argue that there are two current accounts: William Parker gave a brief summary in a talk for the English-speaking Tokyo Unitarian Fellowship, and Mark Harris' notes on IMAOKA's "Unitarian congregation" with its "syncretistic theological outlook" – both should not to be considered carefully researched histories.

the American Unitarian Mission to Japan – and defends the reasons for doing so.[188] AUA President Samuel Eliot (1862-1950) found no answers in what Day had written and why the Japanese had told the AUA to leave Japan. Eliot's sad reflection, in his own hand-written manuscript, "An Unexpected Call and a Broken Connection," was not published. It mentioned MacCauley's death in 1926, making that the earliest possible date that his reflection was written. It is likely that Eliot reflected on Day's 1931 report and then attempted to solve what remained for him a mystery: the 1922 failure of the Unitarian mission to Japan.

Early Japanese Representatives and Sympathizers

William Lawrance (fieldworker from 1891 to 1900) had a special talent for attracting young Japanese ministers from orthodox Christian missions who had unanswered questions, cherry-picking their best. Henry Hawkes (British fieldworker from 1891 to 1894) developed relationships with young Buddhists who wished to reform their denominations, discovering SAJI Jitsunen and gaining him as a Buddhist Unitarian. MacCauley chose ten "influential individuals" as representatives of the quality of those who had become Unitarian "members," yet most of them retained a dual religious identity. He published their biographies and pictures in the closing publication of the first period of the mission as *The Unitarian Movement in Japan: Sketches of the Lives and Religious Work of Ten Representative Japanese Unitarians* (1900).[189] This development of dual religious memberships and identities was not reported.

The way liberal Christian, New Buddhists and academics networked together in "activities at Unity Hall" reveals another

188. See chapter 8.

189. [Japan Unitarian Mission, Clay MacCauley], *The Unitarian Movement in Japan, Sketches of the Lives and Religious Work of Ten Representative Japanese Unitarians* (n.p., 1900). In the 1990s Starr King School for the Ministry still had an original copy, as well as SAJI Jitstunen's personal image of Kannon.

dimension and suggests convictions that would influence IMAOKA when he arrived in its third period. The dimension of conversion to a Unitarian identity stressed by MacCauley came from his missionary perspective. What membership did not reveal was indigenous perspectives of progressives having found a home in the *yuniterian* movement. Few seemed to give up their previous identity. *Yuniterian* had entered the Japanese language less as a word for religion than as a philosophy of innovation. Charting the *yuniterian* activities or movements at Unity Hall reveals its significance during the second period of Unitarianism in Japan. As a religion, Unitarianism had failed to conquer an Empire, becoming localized in Tokyo. As a *yuniterian* movement, its activities evidence an advance into many important arenas of a changing society.

MacCauley's *Sketches* gave a brief history of the Mission and asked *members*: how did they become Unitarian?

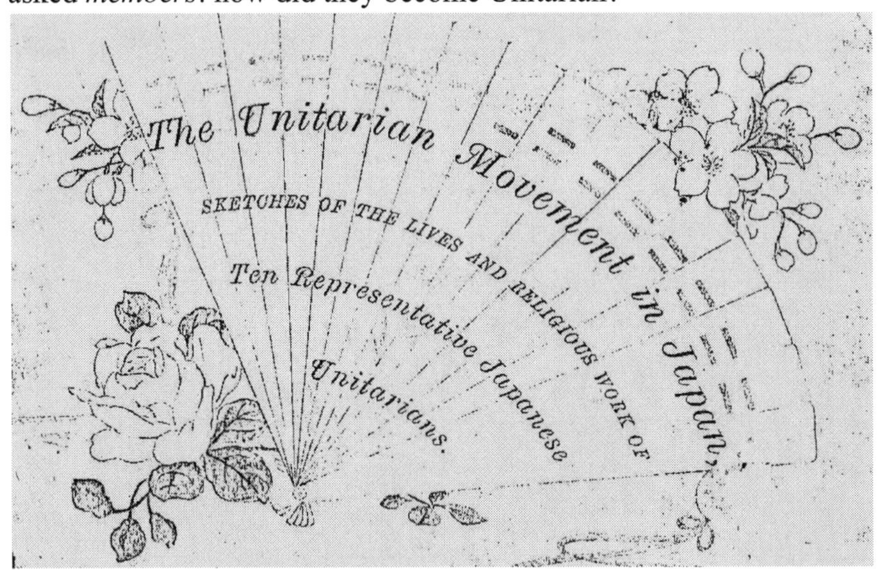

Sketches described the "conversions" ten of the 1900 leaders led to run the Mission.

The question only revealed their various backgrounds – Buddhist, Confucian, conservative Christian. Their essays were lightly edited by MacCauley "keeping their quaint English"[190] and hastily published to show how successful the mission had been as it closed in 1900. Although the booklet was published in Japan, it was written in English for American supporters. It attempted to justify the American effort and assure supporters of its success despite leaving. These ten would certainly guarantee success without an American presence, as the *Christian Register* and Annual Reports reassured American Unitarians.

The ten leaders of the Japan Unitarian Association wrote briefly about themselves and why they converted to Unitarianism. Three had attended the World's Parliament of Religions: KISHIMOTO Nobuta, a Congregationalist Christian; HIRAI Kinza, a Zen priest, and NOGUCHI Zenshirō, who had interpreted for the four attendees who were Buddhist priests. SAJI Jitsunen, president of JUA and chief minister at Unity Hall, was a New Buddhist, recruited by Hawkes. The three Buddhists (SAJI, HIRAI, and NOGUCHI) were joined by SHIMADA Saburo, an orthodox Confucian. Five prominent leaders came from various Christian missions: KISHIMOTO Nobuta, MURAI Tomoyoshi, ABE Isō, TOYOSAKI Zennosuke, and OGASAWARA Yoshio. Only KANDA Saichirō came to the Mission directly from Unitarianism, having become a Unitarian in San Francisco. They were all "first generation Christians." Their families were Buddhist, Shinto, Confucian or a blending of Japan's three religions. The Buddhists were from orthodox, priestly families.[191]

MacCauley's organizing question was why they had become Unitarians. All mentioned some aspect of rational freedom. Each explained how their religious experience or outlook was too narrow, even irrational. They had found a community at Unity Hall. "I

190. MacCauley Ltr. to Eliot, March 8, 1900.

191. Those with whom IMAOKA worked and could have influenced his spiritual journey and thought will be mentioned in the "Glossary of Key Terms and Figures."

revolted against orthodox Confucianism," wrote SHIMADA. Almost everyone explicitly mentioned some aspect of a theological, intellectual or psychological quest for liberation and the freedom that they had found.

In his 1900 annual report MacCauley proudly stated that five orthodox Christian converts were helping with the preaching at Unity Hall:

> ...Prof. Hajime Onishi, late dean of Senshin Gakuin and now president of the "College of Literature" of the New Imperial University at Kyoto; Prof. Nobuta Kishimoto, graduate of Harvard, and now professor of ethics in the "Imperial Normal School;" Rev. Tomoyoshi Murai, of Andover, now professor of English in the "Foreign Languages School" of Japan ; Prof. Isoo Abe, of Hartford Seminary, and lately professor in the "Doshisha University;" and Rev. Zennosuke Toyosaki, now professor in the Kokumin Eigakukai, Tokyo – all coming to us through Orthodox Christianity.[192]

There were dozens, perhaps hundreds, of others who joined in the Unitarian movement during the first period as *yuniterian* activists and sympathizers. Students would study in Tokyo for three years, complete their program and return to their homes. Some graduates of the schools, colleges and universities taught at Unity Hall's School of Advanced Learning or preached on Sundays or Thursdays. Most came from the educated of the upper classes. They were the new intelligentsia, or soon to be. An important figure not mentioned in the group of ten was ANESAKI Masaharu, probably asked but declined to be in the booklet, in age a junior to the ten but from a samurai background as were several of the others. He had recently taught at the School for Advanced Learning. He, like many of the other sympathizers associated with Unity Hall, would speak, teach, and publish in the *yuniterian* movement, and then rise as a major academician in his chosen field. In fact, he had already become important with allies like KISHIMOTO and ABE, whom he joined in founding several societies for study and action. This is an aspect of

192. Also included in MacCauley, *Memorials*, *op. cit., p. 516.*

the *yuniterian* movement that received scant notice in MacCauley's reports to Boston and will be explored as "native" activities.[193] Ideals that IMAOKA would be influenced by, positively or negatively, may be deduced from these activities.

MacCauley left two leaders in charge of the mission and its church work: SAJI Jitsunen and KANDA Saichirō. SAJI, a former Pure Land Buddhist priest, brought his personal fame to Japan Unitarian Mission and served as its President. KANDA continued to serve as secretary of Japan Unitarian Association, having been secretary for both the Mission and the Japanese association (JUA). They led Unity Hall and its churchly functions, that is, worship and preaching, as well as the use of the AUA annual subsidy. SAJI and KANDA were the first two representatives described in *Sketches*. For lack of a better term, they can be identified as "ecclesiastical liberals." Only the administrators, SAJI and KANDA, received a salary. They were joined at Unity Hall by a network of members or sympathizers who preached and lectured but had some other source of income. Unity Hall was fortunate to have members who followed the Kumi-ai practice of non-paid ministry. Some, like the Dōshisha Trio, preached regularly at both Unitarian and Congregational churches. It was a time when liberal sermons about the *new theology,* free of Calvinist doctrine, were desired in both groups' pulpits.

Two more seminary trained preachers arrived in the second period to have prominent roles in Japan Unitarian Association. MINAMI Hajime and HIROI Tatsutarō became Unitarians during the non-missionary period and would preach regularly in the Unity Hall pulpit. MINAMI came from the liberal Evangelical German mission and was considered by IMAOKA to be the best New Testament scholar of that era. HIROI, arriving from the Methodist mission, had been

193. "Native" is used here to denote activities that MacCauley did not brag about or report to the AUA with their "Boston Brahman" perspective. MacCauley was clever and knew that Christian socialism and its social agenda were not to be reported.

expelled for heresy. He was almost as charismatic as SAJI and became SAJI's assistant pastor at Unity Hall. HIROI remained his firm ally until around 1906, the beginning of internal troubles over finances in the Japanese Unitarian movement. SAJI and HIROI's leadership at Unity Hall, as its main ministers, will be discussed later in this chapter.

While the Japanese Unitarian Association and its Unity Hall congregation had attracted a group of scholar-preachers who served without pay and preached to hundreds of students and people with an intellectual bent, it was numerically insignificant. It had shrunk to one "church" and one preaching station. The few studies that have glanced at this liberal faith have concluded that its decline began in 1894 when the AUA started trying to close the Mission. That closure occurred in 1900. That would be correct from a missionary or ecclesiastical point of view. An indigenous perspective would come to a different conclusion.

Constructing Japanese Unitarian Perspectives

Knapp once wrote that Japanese "were the most utilitarian people in the world." This was certainly true at Unity Hall. Most wanted to do something with their *new knowledge* and liberal religion for society, for the new Japan. A few, and one of those was probably KANDA who came from a conservative banking family, joined in the study groups and even in the formal societies, but would not become an activist, especially as social activism aroused opposition from the government. The Dōshisha Trio (KISHIMOTO, ABE and MURAI) led first in founding study groups, then societies, and finally practical activities, soon angering government authorities. In 1900 the Peace Preservation Act gave officials who supported fascism new powers to suppress protesters and organizations, especially those involving the labor and peace movements.

Arguably, Unity Hall was becoming the most active locus of such organizations in Tokyo, if not the nation.

Most of these activities were begun as an extension of the classroom during the first period of Japanese Unitarianism. There was little or no participation by the missionaries except in classes or workshops, as Lawrance had begun with Christian socialism. An exception had been the peace movement joined later by MacCauley. There were so many activities going on at Unity Hall that most members of the Japan Unitarian Association could only join a few. Charting the individual interests and their reasons for further activism will involve future studies. These overlapping memberships in activist organizations made Unity Hall both dynamic and dangerous, "the most dangerous place in the Empire," according to a retired police official.[194]

Viewing Japanese Unitarianism through the lens of its *yuniterian* activities, Unity Hall was far more than a place of liberal preaching. It involved social and academic education and publishing; Christian socialism and social issues (legal, penal, women's rights and freedoms); the peace and international movements; labor and political action, and a general ferment for liberal causes. These *yuniterian* actions will be summarized in relation to Unity Hall. Since all are quite dynamic and the individuals involved were active in one society or another, only a sketch can be made to suggest some of their *yuniterian* perspectives.

Unity Hall as a Liberal Religious Center

SAJI Jitsunen, a Buddhist Unitarian, and his assistant HIROI Tatsutarō, a radical unitarianized-Methodist, led the religious services at Unity Hall. This combination drew full attendance for years. There was a gradual evolution, moving toward more practical religion. The second Sunday morning sermon focused on Christian

---

194. Mohr, *op.cit.,* p. 131, and personal conversation.

Socialism by applying Christian principles to social problems of economic inequality; labor/capitalism issues as religious concerns; women's suffrage, contraception, prostitution; a more just legal and penal system; democratic or representative political parties. This became the *social gospel* in Japan before the Social Gospel in America. But, it would not be looked upon favorably by Boston's AUA leadership. As labor and social unrest increased in America during the next two decades, an anti-labor and anti-working class attitude was projected onto the situation in Japan. And American Unitarianism did not come from the working classes.

SAJI Jitsunen

HIROI Tatsutarō

As already mentioned, SAJI and HIROI led a corps of unpaid educator-preachers employed in the various schools, colleges and universities of Tokyo. SAJI balanced the two Sunday morning sermons, with one by a Buddhist and the second by a Christian followed by discussion. There was also a sermon or lecture Sunday evening, as well as a study or Bible class on Thursday night.[195] The success of this dimension of Unitarianism was verified by the Rev. Thomas Eliot (1841-1936) when he visited Japan in 1903. It is

[195] MURAI, "The Unitarian Movement in Japan," *Christian Register*, Nov. 19, 1900.

important to note at this point that he found no disagreements among leaders at Unity Hall or in the Unitarian movement. He only noted one point of alarm: there was a tendency toward Christian socialism, especially among the editors of *Rikugō Zasshi*, the Unitarian journal.[196] Perhaps that motivated his question to KANDA about the preaching at Unity Hall: "But can you preach Jesus?"[197] (His presence on an AUA commission to investigate what was happening and his report will be returned to later in this chapter.) Even when the AUA had closed their Mission and given complete control to the Japan Unitarian Association, commissioners began to appear to check on the mission. Eliot admonished the Japanese to "keep religious" and be "true representatives of Christianity and Jesus himself." He strongly discouraged the social and practical focus.[198]

There was a religious education program for children with Sunday School classes, celebrations of the various holidays, and plays which the children presented to the congregation. Of note, Eliot's report mentioned that there was almost an equal number of women present and active in the discussions at church and in the classes.

Biblical and theological classes were a remnant of the once successful School for Advanced Learning. However, *Senshin Gakuin* had become a extension school for seminarians from orthodox missions wanting to study the Bible critically. Some very qualified scholar-preachers would contribute their knowledge in these programs. Of special note was MINAMI Hajime, German trained New Testament scholar who would eventually become the professor of Christian studies at the Imperial University of Tokyo.

---

196. John Frederick Scheck, *Transplanting a Tradition: Thomas Lamb Eliot and the Unitarian Conscience in the Pacific Northwest, 1864-1905* (Ph.D. dissertation, Univ. of Oregon, 1969), p. 358.

197. Scheck, *ibid.*

198. Scheck, *ibid.*

In an article in the *Christian Register* in 1900, just before he would attend the annual meeting in Boston, MURAI Tomoyoshi, one of the Dōshisha Trio, wrote that there were nine educator-preachers at Unity Hall and at a Tokyo preaching station that had survived the closing of the American Mission. MURAI described what was happening at Unity Hall as "the First Unitarian Church of Tokyo." Two sentences would be taken from this article and repeated in the *AUA Annual Reports* of the next several years. Even Thomas Eliot's visit in 1903 did not change this description of the now independent movement in Japan. MURAI wrote:

> Every Sunday we meet twice, both morning and evening; and each service lasts more than two hours, two preachers occupying the same pulpit in turn, and thus two long sermons are preached at each service. The writer understands that American Unitarians are not very enthusiastic church-goers, but the case is quite different in Japan. Our hall is crowded with devout and anxious hearers every Sunday. They do not come from any other motives but to hear sermons. Our church music is no attraction to them. The fact is we have no music in our services excepting a few minutes of marching organ played by a lady previous to preaching, and all the rest of the time is devoted to sermons. While our Unitarian church is so well attended, orthodox churches are always very thinly attended. There are more than fifty churches of orthodox denominations in the city of Tokyo; and there is no single church among them which has attendants of one hundred in number, the average attendance being about forty. Our people are not fools. They know just where to go for the real spiritual and intellectual nourishment.[199]

MacCauley clearly stated his perspective on the importance of the Sunday services and preaching in the 1900 *Sketches*:

> Our lectures are unique, because they are not prescribed within the limit of any doctrinal teaching, but touch upon any subject, ethical, social and political. At the same time they differ from ordinary lectures, because they are thoroughly religious. We believe

199. MURAI Tomoyoshi, "The Unitarian Movement in Japan," *Christian Register,* November 19, 1900.

our Sunday lecture is the most important and effective means of spreading our principles at present.[200]

With Unity Hall's unpaid, part-time minsters there was an acknowledged lack of pastoral care, often having to use Buddhist priests for some church-member funerals. However, Japanese Unitarianism's "religious" character and activities were not faulted by any AUA commissioner; each reported that their investment and property were being used properly. The Congregational mission had caused a rebellion by the way it administered its grants and property. Capable Japanese leaders chaffed at being treated as incompetent; similiar tension with Boston would be slow to manifest. Somehow, even with his authoritarian ways, MacCauley was able to salve over this difficulty with Boston as long as he served in the Mission.

Unity Hall as a Center for Interfaith Cooperation

In America an interfaith movement had not succeeded in overcoming denominational differences. The World's Parliament of Religions in Chicago in 1893 had a simultaneous program of denominational congresses. Although there was almost a fifty-fifty split between conservatives and liberals, the liberals only united in a several organizations that lasted but a few years. One did survive and would evolve into the future International Association for Religious Freedom [IARF]. But it would only become truly international in the 1960s when IMAOKA brought Japanese organizations into IARF.

Protestantism supposedly recognized the individual's freedom of belief – that one was free to join a church that one believed. Protestantism had naturally led to divergent doctrinal interpretations. Many small denominations had arisen as a result of these differences. Each had sent missionaries to Japan. Few gained more than a thousand members during the Meiji era. The large denominations tended to lose their prophetic voice and to compromise with the

200. *Sketches, op.cit.* p. 9-10.

government, according to KISHIMOTO Hideo, an orthodox voice for the history of Christianity in Japan.[201] The smaller groups, KISHIMOTO continued, accustomed to suspicion and extremely strong in their faith, continued to speak out against official policy. The Society of the Friends and the Holiness Church were particularly outstanding. The larger denominations tended to lose evangelistic fervor and to preoccupy themselves with problems of church organization. The smaller denominations, on the other hand, each bent on establishing a separate branch in Japan developed new methods like tent meetings and street evangelism. KISHIMOTO Hideo failed to see the liberal missions' attempt to merge or cooperate. Since Unitarians were not trying cooperative efforts with Universalists in America, this *native* activity was under-reported in the *Christian Register.*

Already noted was one type of interfaith cooperation at Unity Hall with Buddhist and Christian services. Classes in the graduate school and then in the extension courses were interfaith in intention and content, almost always taught by someone practicing that faith. What was surprising and must be addressed was the fact that the three liberal Christian missions (Unitarian, Universalist, and German Liberal Evangelical) could not even join in establishing a joint seminary, or even a college. This seems a result of the American Unitarian posture that did not credit the other two missions as being liberal or rational enough. Both these missions had missionaries with academic credentials equal or higher than MacCauley's. But they tended to be more rigid in their pedagogy. Unitarians continued to cherry-pick the brightest and best converts from these missions who wanted freer inquiry. (In the third period, Rudolf Otto would visit the German Liberal Evangelical and suggest that they merge with the other two liberal missions. Again, that suggestion met an American Unitarian refusal from Boston.)

201. KISHIMOTO Hideo, *op. cit.*

Despite the American attitudes or administrative difficulties that prevented cooperation and interfaith work, Japanese *yuniterian* interfaith activity was extensive. It happened both at Unity Hall as a meeting place and elsewhere with *yuniterian* leaders who organized interfaith meetings and societies. The 1904 Congress of Japanese Religionists was but one example of the New Buddhists (like SAJI, HIRAI and ANESAKI), the Dōshisha Trio and other Congregational-Unitarians leading in a quest for religious unity. And that quest would have many forms, one lasting long beyond official Japanese Unitarianism and extending into Association Concordia (which we will meet in the next chapters), the Japan Free Religion Association, and in IARF (chapter 10). ANESAKI and HIRAI both explored an experiential dimension of interfaith participation with Theosophy (chapter 9), HIRAI even bringing Col. Olcott of the Theosophical Society to Japan.

From Japanese perspectives, there was a notion of the purification of Christianity. Western and American accretions contained many distortions of the "pure religion of Jesus." The missionaries fought over doctrines and beliefs that were not even in the New Testament – no Trinity, no Popes, but also no denominations and specifically cultural additions like Western music and order of services or church holidays. A pure religion of Jesus should unify rather than divide humanity.

Unity Hall as an Educational Institution – And More

The School for Advanced Learning (*Senshin Gakuin*) – the more Confucian title, suggested by FUKUZAWA himself – was an experiment in religious education that pioneered learning about another's faith as well as advanced study of one's own. It took place in the *hall of unity*, a *unity* that was yet to be discovered. That *unity* did not divide worship and education (even though for clarity in presentation they are divided here). Lecturers had learned Buddhism and Confucianism in the languages of their traditions. Christianity required study of Greek and Hebrew. All struggled with the problems of translating religious traditions into the Japanese language. (ANESAKI experienced this model when he taught at the School of Advanced Learning and was able to see it implemented at the Imperial University. IMAOKA benefited from studying in one of richest religious studies programs in the world at that time.)

Outside Unity Hall, c. 1916

KISHIMOTO returned from Harvard just short of finishing his dissertation. He had participated in the 1893 World's Parliament of Religions where there was an attempt to listen to others' presentations concerning their faiths without privileging one's own. At least, that had been the ideal. It was not done perfectly, but it had been a goal—to listen and learn. KISHIMOTO's publication of "About Research in Comparative Religious Studies" in *Rikugō Zasshi* in 1894 brought the comparative and scientific study of religion to Japan. Then, he taught comparative religions at the newly opened Unity Hall's *Senshin*

Gakuin and served as its dean.[202] When Boston threatened to close the School in 1896, KISHIMOTO led in the creation of study groups of scholars with different perspectives and faith commitments. He organized a Roundtable Conference on Religion that became the Study Group of Religious Leaders. Noteworthy was the way lecturers from Unity Hall brought young scholars like ANESAKI into their circle. Within two months of the first Roundtable meeting, KISHIMOTO and ANESAKI, who was still a graduate student at the Imperial University, joined in founding the Society for the Study of Comparative Religion (*Hikaku Shūkyō Gakkai*). In 1897 KISHIMOTO established *Teiyū rinrikai* (the Teiyû Association for Ethics). In 1898 he and ABE helped found the Society for Studying Poverty, which later the same year changed its name to the Society for Studying Socialism. The closure of the School for Advanced Learning in 1900 moved the focus of academic activity to the new schools where they taught, and to publishing, with its center being *Rikugō Zasshi* (*Cosmos*). Study of poverty led to social action, while the academic study of religion led to interfaith dialogue with such encounters as the 1904 Congress of Japanese Religions credited to *yuniterian* leaders like ABE.

Unity Hall and Publishing

YANO Fumio and FUKUZAWA Yukichi had provided thousands of their readers across the Empire with information from Knapp about Unitarianism. The magazine, *Yuniterian* was started in 1890 and renamed *Shūkyō* (*Religion*), as *yuniterian* had become a term for almost anything that was liberal and progressive. The main emphasis during the missionary period was publishing and distributing

202. *Catalogue of Senshin Gakuin*, Tokyo, 1894, KISHOMOTO's lectures on comparative religion were first gathered in 1895 in a volume entitled *Shukyo no hikaku kenkya: Tokyo Senmon Gakko hogo bungaku dai ikkai daininenkyii kogiroku* (Studies in Comparative Religion: Transcript of Courses Given at the Vocational College in the Class of Japanese Literature First Session for Second Year Students). See Mohr, *op.cit.*, chapter 5.

pamphlets through their "Post-Office department." By 1900 KANDA reported that 100,000 pamphlets had been distributed during the previous year.[203] Most had been in English, but some were published in Japanese.

It was not pamphlets from the New England divines nor even the few in Japanese that spread the full range of *new knowledge*—from the scientific and comparative study of religion to the acceptance of science and scientific method in evolution or psychology or critical analysis of social issues. It was Japanese independent questioning in their published studies that drew other thinkers to Unity Hall. KISHIMOTO was just one example of someone who returned from study abroad with *yuniterian* questions, ideas, and methods.

KISHIMOTO moved from a contributor and assistant editor at *Rikugō Zasshi* to its editorial board, finally becoming its chief editor. He facilitated its merger in 1898 with *Shūkyō*, making it the center for propagation of *yuniterian* ideas. When he left to teach full time at the future Waseda University, he left *yuniterian* editors and writers, a *yuniterian* board of directors, and his even more activist *yuniterian* colleague, ABE Isō, as the new chief editor. Located at Unity Hall, nothing had changed in its commitment to *yuniterian* issues during the non-missionary period, except possibly that it had become more activist. (Thomas Eliot's inspection of Japanese Unitarianism in 1903 confirmed that. It was the heart of Christian socialism.)

Unity Hall as a Center of Christian Socialism

There was always a strong desire for a rational religion that was more than reasoned ideas, more than just talk about liberal principles. Lawrance had introduced the study of Christian socialism

203. *Sketches*, p. 12. KANDA, the JUM and JUA secretary, is given the credit by librarians as editor of *Sketches,* although MacCauley claimed in his writings that he was editor, "lightly editing" its ten biographical essays of Japanese leaders.

in his classes at the School for Advanced Learning, reading books like Yale professor Woolsey's *Communism and Socialism* (published in 1888). Droppers, one of the professors that the Mission brought to Keiō, had discussed inequities and injustices in the West in his sociology and economics classes. These, he said, should not be repeated as Japan entered a new era. Lawrance did not become a social activist. He returned to Boston in 1894 and became the director of the Sunday School department of the AUA. His Japanese students had a particular loyalty to their conversion to Christianity and in their desire to live the "religion of Jesus." Study and talk was not enough. Their practical natures required action. They began to use the ideas of Sermon-on-the-Mount Christianity, Matthew 5, and the Book of James to address what needed to be done to correct what was rapidly becoming a capitalist-militarist-authoritarian society. They were simultaneously preaching at Unity Hall, giving lectures on liberal topics with critical discussions in their classes at breaks during the school year and in summer courses, and publishing in *Rikugō Zasshi* (*Cosmos* journal). However, that was mere talk and just writing. They began to form societies about Christian socialism, world peace, economics, politics and women's issues that led to action – many of these societies were meeting government resistance to the point of repression.

The religious socialists of Unity Hall were Christian and Buddhist, as was the organization that they formed in 1898, the Research Society for Socialism. The Dōshisha Trio (KISHIMOTO, ABE, MURAI), some New Buddhists (ANESAKI, SAJI, HIRAI,), and a host of *yuniterian* leaders (KANDA Saichirō, TOYOSAKI Zennosuke, KAWAKAMI Kiyoshi, TAKAGI Masayoshi, KATAYAMA Sen, and KŌTOKU Shūsui) began studying socialism.[204] Conservative-liberal theological

[204] Both Mohr, *op. cit.* and Narita, *op. cit.* list this study group. Mohr goes into greater detail.

lines did not seem to apply as UCHIMURA also joined in these studies, only to leave as soon as he felt that they had interpreted the Kingdom of God to be in this world instead of the next. Yet, he remained a friend of Christian socialism, even though he thought it to be too idealistic in thinking God's justice could be brought into this world.

The studies divided between gradualists and radicals. Those who were more "ecclesiastical Unitarians" and gradualists focused on preaching and building a larger Unitarian membership. They would be praised by the first commissioner sent by the AUA in 1903, Thomas Eliot. The more activist members placed little importance on church membership and more on activities that had a chance to change or mold Japanese society. It was this majority at Unity Hall that Boston discouraged and sincerely believed was too secular and not religious enough.

Some went only as far as joining the Society for the Study of Socialism, like KANDA. He was definitely a gradualist and would use his power to prevent the Socialist party from using Unity Hall. ANESAKI had joined in the society for study of socialism but seemed not to proceed further as he had gone to Berlin to finish his dissertation. KATAYAMA Sen and more radical elements moved quickly to secular socialism and then to Marxism. KŌTOKU Shūsui became an anarchist. They would publish the Communist Manifesto for the first time in Japan. One of the radicals, KŌTOKU, would be executed in 1911, soon after IMAOKA arrived in Tokyo.

ABE, MURAI, KISHIMOTO, and TAKAHASHI were committed to parliamentary democracy and world peace. They would attempt to form political parties. Their motivation came from a specific understanding of the religion of Jesus, which was non-violent, choosing peace and persuasion in pursuit of social justice.

Under the Peace Preservation Act of 1900, a law giving repressive police powers, some of their publications were seized with the threat of more punitive action against individuals. ABE, in particular, was a target for his activities. At first, the government did not fear socialism as much as democracy, which might empower the masses, especially workers. Study at Unity Hall moved freely from social issues to economics to labor to opposition against Japan's endless wars. Each study spawned societies that led to direct action. Needless to say, *yuniterians* were attracting police interest.

Socialism had a specific and narrow meaning for them: *what was beneficial to all of Japanese society.* It did not mean the end of private property, nor was it against the private use of capital, but it addressed poverty, economic inequity, misuse of state and natural resources. Labor and social welfare were collateral issues, sometimes implied by socialism. ABE, joined by his colleagues from *Senshin Gakuin* and Unity Hall, helped found The Research Society of Socialism in 1898, with ANESAKI joining them. In 1900 they formed the Association of Socialism. It was at this point, under threat of the new Peace Protection act, that KANDA acted on his authority as secretary of JUA to prevent their meeting at Unity Hall. They moved from Unity Hall's library to KATAYAMA's house in 1903.[205] By 1903 ABE joined more activist socialists, like KATAYAMA, but when KATAYAMA became a Marxist socialist, ABE remained a radical Christian socialist.[206] ABE later published *The Present Situation of the Socialist Party in Europe* on May 25, 1917, which was seized by the police the same day.[207]

After a rather lengthy period of cooperation with the secular socialists—until they became Marxist and anarchists, ABE and the Christian socialists moved away from them into peaceful movements to quiet labor unrest and address militarism. They had decided on

---

205. Mohr, *op.cit.,* pp. 111-5; also see Narita, *op.cit.*, citing Iguchi, 124.

206. ABE wrote *Solving of Social Problems* and *The Ideal Man,* seminal documents for both labor and socialist movements.

207. Mohr covers the tumultuous period well; *op.cit.,* chapter 6.

forming political parties using parliamentary democracy to reshape Japanese society. Despite KANDA's prevention of socialism working out of Unity Hall, *Rikugō Zasshi*'s offices were never moved. *Rikugō zasshi*'s hundreds of articles on Christian socialism await comprehensive study. Beginning with KISHIMOTO's editorship, there was a column on socialism in every issue all the way to No. 481, February 1921.[208] Tentatively, one can say that a rational theology was emerging that applied ideas in the New Testament—the Sermon on the Mount, Matthew 5, and the Book of James—to problems confronting any form of economic or social exploitation.

Unity Hall as the Center for Peace: for a world without war

IMAOKA recalled how leaders at Unity Hall encouraged prominent figures to head the movements while they did all the difficult tasks. Count ŌKUMA Shigenobu, founder of what became Waseda University, is credited with beginning the Peace Society of Japan and becoming its first president. Pacifist *yuniterian* leaders like ABE not only joined him but also provided space for the society at Unity Hall. MacCauley later bragged to Boston about a connection that had begun before he returned for his second missionary tour in 1909:

> You will be interested at learning that the Peace Society of Japan may soon have its main office in one of the unused rooms of our Unity Hall. Count Okuma is its President and it numbers some of the best of Japan's citizens in its membership.[209]

The peace movement had a variety of approaches. Some *yuniterians* were total pacifists; others were internationalists who prioritized negotiation and just (fair, moral) compromise – with a range of anti-war advocates. Japan had been at war with only one significant interlude since 1875. The idealists believed that they could transform Japan and lead the entire world to peace without

208. Mohr, *op.cit.*, p. 158.

209. MacCauley Ltr. to Eliot, June 19, 1911. See also, Mohr, *op.cit.* pp. 101-2.

war; almost all their activities at Unity Hall overlapped on this issue with other movements like Association Concordia, the original Kiitsu Kyōkai (chapter 9). Not surprisingly, there were generals and admirals in the peace movements because they believed that military power was for defense of the nation, not aggression or violence against others.

The militarists, joined by the *zaibatsu* (the financial-industrial clique), propelled Japan from one conflict to the next, creating almost a state of continual warfare. ABE protested how it taxed the worker and wasted national resources. National conscription began in 1873. Christians were portrayed as disloyal to the Emperor and the nation, as they questioned the growing militarism and refused to swear allegiance to the Emperor as God's Son.

These are the dates of Japan's military successes during this era. Success bred pride and a desire to continue on the path of empire and military conquest.

1875 – Expeditionary force to Formosa.
1875 – Japan took the Kuril Islands.
1876 – Japan seized the Bonin Islands.
1879 – The Ryukyu Islands were formally annexed and became the prefecture of Okinawa.
1882 – Japanese troops sent to Korea to restore order.
1885 – War between Japan and China was averted by the Treaty of Tientsin.
1894-1895 – First Sino-Japanese War. It secured Taiwan for Japan.
[1898 – Americans defeated Spain and occupied the Philippines, Guam, and the Hawaiian Kingdom. [America had become the primary military threat to Japan in the Pacific]
1899-1901 – Japan sent troops to help end the Boxer Rebellion in China
1904-1905 – The Russo-Japanese War with Japan victorious

1910 – Japan annexes the Kingdom of Korea
1914-1918 – First World War. Japan acquires possessions of Germany.

The defeat of Imperial Russia in 1905 affected perceptions of Japan's strength both at home and abroad. Japan was now an imperial power to compete with others on an equal basis. Yet, equality did not come. Controlling the military became more difficult as its most aggressive elements attempted unsuccessful coups but successful assassinations of civilian leaders in the 1920s. For example, HARA Takashi, a commoner and liberal leader of the Rikken Seiyūkai party (Friends of Constitutional Government), had become prime minister in 1918, with the rallying cry of "Militarism is dead." Three years later, however, HARA was assassinated.

Parallel activity to the search for peace among nations was internationalism, at a time when only nationalism was viewed as loyalty to the Emperor and thus to the nation. Just as the ultra-nationalists attempted to get the public to view the peace movement as traitorous, internationalism was projected as disloyalty to Japan's national spirit.

In the coming chapters, IMAOKA and other *yuniterian* members continued these activities long after Unity Hall was closed.

Unity Hall as the Center for the Labor Movement

As their district became industrialized and workers' slums grew around Unity Hall, the social issues of workers and their families were addressed from the pulpit, in the classroom and in their publications. Again, the various study groups and societies (ethics, Christian socialism, poverty, etc.) converged in labor issues. ABE, MURAI, KATAYAMA, YOKOI and others spelled out the frightful conditions of the working class. For example, *Rikugō Zasshi* published KATAYAMA's "The Japanese Labor Problem" and TOYOSAKI's "Gospel of Socialism" in the late 1890's. KŌTOKU

Shūsui's "The Degeneration of Society: Its Causes and Cures" was studied, and he was invited to join them at Unity Hall.[210]

Labor conditions and organizing workers would become the central task of Unity Hall in the third Unitarian period under its new JUA and JUM secretary, SUZUKI Bunji. (This will be a major part of the next chapter and, along with Christian socialism, a primary cause for the Mission's crises beginning in 1919.[211])

Unity Hall as a Foundry for Japan's First Political Parties

By 1900 the study groups began seeing themselves as idealists. They actually formed a Society of Idealists in 1901, pouring those ideals into the first Social-Democratic Party. ABE became its president. He was joined, of course, by the rest of the Dōshisha Trio and by KAWAKAMI Kiyoshi, KATAYAMA Sen, KŌTOKU Shūsui, KINOSHITA Shoko and NISHIKAWA Kojiro. Most of these became famous, but KŌTOKU became infamous as an anarchist.[212] They published a declaration in the Japanese and English press that, among other things, called for the repeal of the Peace Preservation Act of 1900, the law with repressive police powers. Within a day that very law would be used to outlaw their political party. KISHIMOTO's son, Hideo, would not mention his father's involvement with these idealists whom he described as having "their heads ... in the clouds."[213] (His father would always be subordinated among "the others" of the liberal movements that Hideo described.) KISHIMOTO Hideo, the son, summarized their declaration as being too far in advance of the times. (IMAOKA would live long enough to bring out KISHIMOTO Hideo's own idealism as they would work together in 1948 founding another idealist movement, the Japan Free Religion

210. Mohr, *op. cit.*, p. 111-112.

211. Chapter 8. See also Mohr, *op. cit.,* chapter 6.

212. High Treason Incident, May 1910.

213. KISHIMOTO, Hideo, *op.cit.*, p. 305.

Association – to be addressed in chapter 9.)

ABE and the Social-Democrats listed eight objectives and twenty-eight proposals for specific action. "The objectives were (1) the elimination of racial discrimination; (2) the elimination of military preparations; (3) the elimination of class distinctions; (4) national ownership of the means of production; (5) national ownership of public transportation; (6) equitable distribution of property; (7) equal opportunity for everyone to obtain political office; and (8) equal opportunity for education. The 28 proposals for action included the limitation of armaments, elimination of the House of Peers, tax reduction, prohibition of child labor, a national labor law, universal suffrage, and repeal of the Peace Preservation Act of 1900.[214] As already mentioned, the government dissolved the party instantly. It would have to be re-founded several years later, credit being given to KATAYAMA Sen as the new founder with ABE and others joining.

A decade later in 1910 the High Treason Incident would snare KŌTOKU among the conspirators planning to assassinate the Emperor.[215] While it may have frightened the *yuniterian* activists as was intended, they continued to publish and further organize political parties – peace, socialist and labor. They hired the very law school trained journalist who had interviewed KŌTOKU in his death cell, SUZUKI Bunji, as their new executive secretary of JUA and JUM, replacing KANDA who had resigned.

Unity Hall as a foundry of political activity sent many into politics with the goal to realize *yuniterian* ideals of peace, social justice and international cooperation. SAJI Jitsunen became a district representative and then the mayor of Tokyo. ABE helped found the Social-Democratic Party. ABE and UCHIGASAKI (whom we will meet again in the next chapter) were elected to the House of

---

214. KISHIMOTO, Hideo, *ibid.,* p 305.
215. Mohr, *op. cit.,* p. 119-120.

Representatives, and ANESAKI was appointed to the House of Peers. NISHIDA Tenkō (Tenkō-san of Ittō-en) also served in the House of Representatives. IMAOKA recalled many more of this era as *yuniterian* leaders, such as SOYADA (member of Cabinet, head of Hochi Shimbun), KANEKO (member of the Privy Council) and NITOBE (Secretary of the Japan chapter of the League of Nations). Their efforts would be crushed by the forces of militarism as parliamentary democracy was swept away.[216]

The Crisis that Brought MacCauley's Return

The crisis that brought MacCauley's return has been researched with quite different conclusions. A brief summary of the crisis of 1909 in the firing of SAJI will show why it had little effect on IMAOKA's involvement at Unity Hall.

One interpretation of the crisis sees it beginning with KANDA's ejection of the socialist group from Unity Hall in 1902. KANDA would be protecting the Unitarian movement from its more radical figures like ABE, MURAI and KISHIMOTO. Yet, they remained on the boards of JUA and the Unity Hall church board and, more to the point, continued speaking at Unity Hall, which SAJI and KANDA administered. ABE remained as chief editor of *Rikugō Zasshi*, and the others continued as writers and editors.

A second interpretation depends on how a date of a handwritten letter is read. HIRAI, the former Zen Buddhist priest, wrote to Knapp indicating that the board of directors was withdrawing from Unity Hall. The letter has been interpreted as having been written on November 19, 1904. HIRAI's numeral "4" in

216. Unity Hall would also become a home for the beginning of the early feminist movement in Japan. Eliot in 1903 had noted that nearly half of the participants at Unity Hall were women. But there is nothing yet found of their *yuniterian* activities in this period. Some evidence of a powerful feminist movement is hinted at by Prof. Caroline Furness in 1921. Ms. IMAOKA Utayo was very much a part of that history yet to be uncovered.

the 1904 is not fully legible and could be a "European 7" with a line through it. Dating the time of the board's threatened resignation in 1907 leads to a more reasonable narrative. This was the time that the JUA/Unity Hall church board contacted the AUA President Samuel Eliot and characterized Unity Hall as no longer being "liberal Christian" but having become "ethical culture."[217] Eliot sent MacCauley to Japan, and he arrived in 1909. Ethical culture was anathema for Boston.

The precise reason for the crisis may not be solved. The explanations range from personality conflicts, religious differences, money and power. They pit KANDA against the Dōshisha Trio, Christian Unitarians versus Buddhist Unitarians, a personality clash between KANDA and SAJI, a fight over the funding from America, or the more serious charge of SAJI's misuse of funds. HIROI, the radical, unitarianized-Methodist and SAJI's loyal assistant minister, wrote

217. Day's "MacCauley history" contains a mixture of viewpoints and rationalizations: "S. Kanda, however, was troubled over the increasing non-Christian character of the services of the church. Jitsunen Saji, the minister, and Hiroi, his assistant, were, to all appearances, turning the movement into an Ethical Culture Society and S. Kanda who was a devout Christian, together with a large majority of the church, was much concerned over the change." p. 35. "Frequent letters came to America concerning the de-Christianizing of the church. … MacCauley, being commissioned to resuscitate it, returned in 1909 to find Saji and the church at odds. The Bible had been laid aside, prayer had been given up, and lectures that had no religious character were being given. The meetings were largely attended but the movement was purely an Ethical Culture work. MacCauley at once announced that he could not direct a work of this character nor support one that is not carried on as professedly Christian. This greatly heartened S. Kanda and Saji and Hiroi were soon obliged to leave the pulpit. " p. 36

Day's Preface to his "MacCauley's history" contained the following: "For a matter of ten years the Japanese continued the work, financially assisted by the American Unitarian Association. Matters did not prosper, however, for the church at Mita fell into the hands of a bright but unscrupulous leader who used the funds and the prestige of the movement to further an ethical culture society. Complaints having reached America of the non-Christian character of the work then going on, Dr. MacCauley was returned to his former post in 1910, where he remained for nine years." (unnumbered, approximately p. 2.)

These passages concerning "ethical culture" are not contained in the edited version (typed but without page numbers) that Cornish placed in the AUA archive.

extensively against MacCauley's handling of the crisis, defending SAJI, perhaps too one-sidedly.[218] HIROI does clearly critique the contradictions of MacCauley's return to fire SAJI, when the Mission had been proclaimed all these years as independently liberal (free) and Japanese (independent of foreign control and its money). Ideals were now judged by actions. What is clear is this: ANESAKI did not find the situation at Unity Hall disturbing enough to suggest that IMAOKA not become involved there, and IMAOKA began to serve there and said nothing about this event.

Following the Money

During the independent period of the Japan Unitarian Association in 1903, the only serious criticism from Thomas Eliot's inspection concerned their having become too socialist (or too concerned about social issues). He had recommended to his cousin Samuel Eliot and the AUA board that money be released for a second church hall in Kanda-ku, the educational district. Funds for a property and hall in Kanda-ku resulted in two grants from the Hayward Fund. The one in 1905 was for $2,330[219] and in 1906 "an appropriation of $3000 [was to] be made, for the year beginning May 1, 1906, to include the amount held for a new hall in Tokyo."[220] The grants failed to reach the ten thousand needed, with SAJI and KANDA each squirreling away a grant. MacCauley came in 1909 and ordered them to surrender what they held. KANDA did immediately, while SAJI only did so after the threat of a lawsuit. SAJI would leave Unity Hall taking more than a third of the members with him. (This was the basis for erroneously coming to the conclusion of a Buddhist-

218. Mohr explored this controversy in detail in the context of Buddhist-Unitarian dialogue, *op.cit.,* pp. 198-208.

219. *Christian Register*, May 18, 1905, p. 554, the Director's Report, "for a new hall in Tokyo" not taken from the general budget but seemingly from the Hayward Fund.

220. *Christian Register*, June 21, 1906, p. 696.

Unitarian split.) He and his assistant, the radical Methodist-Unitarian HIROI, started a rival Unitarian church and association and conducted a publicity campaign against MacCauley. They claimed to be the true *Yuniterian* movement.

MacCauley would rename the American Mission *To-itsu Kurisuto-Kyo Kodokwai* and the Unity Hall congregation *To-istu Kurisuto-Kyo Kyokwai.* MacCauley explained these terms in the *Christian Register* as:

> The words To-itsu are a translation, as near as may be, of the word 'Unitarian,' meaning 'Uniting under One (God).' The word should be hyphenated, To-itsu. Our church is a very active organization just now. Last evening the last of a series of three mission meetings was held. Several persons united with the church Saturday and Sunday. Last evening twenty young men requested to be enrolled, and they signed the Constitution and Bond of Union. One of the Japanese papers has had several columns in reference to these meetings. The name of the church was turned into Japanese so that the Japanese might feel more at home in their confession.[221]

He wrote a new constitution for the Association which they adopted.[222] This 1909 "Constitution of the Tō-itsū Kuristo-Kyō Kōdōkwan of Japan (Unitarian Christian Association & Mission)" was written in his unmistakable hand.[223] Only someone who loved organizations could have imposed four classes of members (active, associate, life, and honorary) based on a pledge of signed membership and annual dues with a Board of Management consisting of its elected officers. MacCauley was tacitly admitting that he had failed to clarify the president and secretary's roles when Japanese Unitarians were given their independence, if there had in

221. *Christian Register*, Feb 29, 1912: page 211 See also Mohr, *op.cit.*, p. 122, fn. 51, for a proper translation.

222. MacCauley, "Constitution of the Tō-itsū Kuristo-Kyō Kōdōkwai of Japan (Unitarian Christian Association) & Mission," handwritten by MacCauley in 1909. Copy in Harvard Divinity box found in the basement!

223. Note the new name of the Association, the Mission and the movement was changed to Unified or Unity Christian.

fact been any – because of the constant arrival of AUA commissioners inspecting the program during its second period and the fiscal controls imposed by Boston on the annual grants.[224]

MacCauley's choice of a new name and structure was largely ignored by Japanese Unitarians. Neither had utility. So they would continue to use *yuniterian* for their progressive religion and its activities. In Boston, the *Unitarian Year Book* and the *AUA Annual Report* would continue to use Unitarian as the official English translation for the Tokyo church and the Japanese Association.

The beginning, duration and causes of the crisis of 1909 and the splintering of the *yuniterian* movement did not have sufficient enough consequences for IMAOKA's graduate advisor, Prof. ANESAKI, to suggest that IMAOKA stay away from Unity Hall or from its journal, *Rikugō Zasshi.* An end to Buddhist and Unitarian cooperation is contradicted by the fact that Buddhists and Unitarians would still be working together at Unity Hall, for the journal and in their shared societies and groups. A new progressive movement, Association Concordia (*Kiitsu Kyōkai*), would begin in 1912 with participation of *yuniterian* leaders – and with IMAOKA, ANESAKI's graduate assistant, one of the working secretaries (elucidated in chapter 10).

The money, which MacCauley recovered from SAJI and KANDA, was not used to buy property and build a hall in the educational district of Kanda-ku. The AUA directed that it be used for operational expenses of the Mission (MacCauley's salary and upkeep of Unity Hall) for the next two years. Funds were freed so

224. The ideal of being a unique and independent mission involved a contradiction with the mission's message of equality of religions and races – or put another way, *native leadership* in their own land of their own churches. After MacCauley became the only foreign missionary during his first term (1888-1900), he assumed the title of director (alternatively, supervisor or superintendent) of the Mission and president of the School of Higher Learning. But there was never independence from AUA annual grants.

that the Hayward Fund could be used for an upcoming interfaith congress in Berlin led by Charles W. Wendte in 1910.

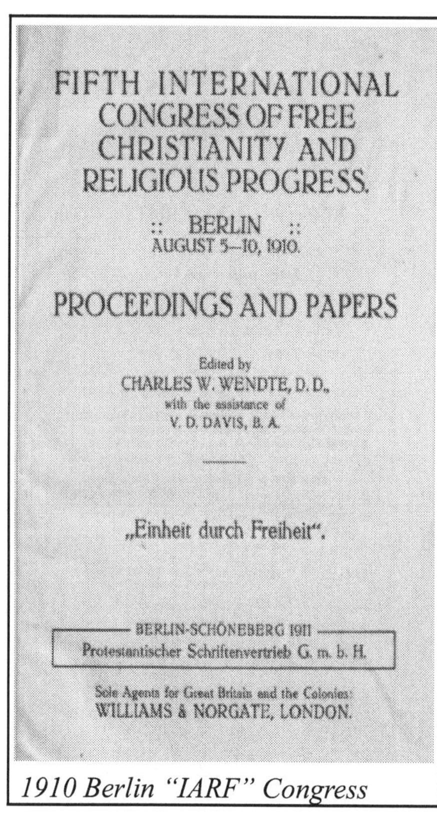

FIFTH INTERNATIONAL CONGRESS OF FREE CHRISTIANITY AND RELIGIOUS PROGRESS.

:: BERLIN ::
AUGUST 5—10, 1910.

PROCEEDINGS AND PAPERS

Edited by
CHARLES W. WENDTE, D. D.,
with the assistance of
V. D. DAVIS, B. A.

„Einheit durch Freiheit".

BERLIN-SCHÖNEBERG 1911
Protestantischer Schriftenvertrieb G. m. b. H.

Sole Agents for Great Britain and the Colonies:
WILLIAMS & NORGATE, LONDON.

1910 Berlin "IARF" Congress

Charles Wendte, 1st Executive Secretary of ICFCRP [which became "IARF"]

Chapter 8

Japanese Unitarianism, Period Three (1909-19)

Upon his arrival in Tokyo in 1910, IMAOKA joined Unity Hall and its editorial staff at *Rikugō Zasshi*. Yet, he was barely mentioned in the wide variety of documents of this third period of Unitarians in Japan.[225] The Japanese leaders mentioned in the reports to the AUA and in the articles of the AUA's *Christian Register* were minister-professors of the new educational institutions or distinguished members in politics or commerce. MacCauley liked to mention the

[225.] This chapter must sort through an enormous amount of material: letters and reports from the last two superintendents of the JUM, Clay MacCauley and John B. W. Day; a document that "many hands" touched in two versions. A paged version is entitled: "Clay MacCauley 's History of the Japan Unitarian Mission: *Apologia Sua Vitae"* with "a memorandum for Mrs. Patterson from Dr. Cornish." Cornish wrote:

> "At our request Rev. John B. W. Day has written out the story of Clay MacCauley in Japan, as Clay MacCauley dictated it to him when they were together in Tokyo. [MacCauley left Japan in 1919. This was given to Cornish in 1931] The manuscript is exactly as Dr. MacCauley himself wished it to be. Please put it in some permanent file and keep it in the library."

Cornish attached a note stating that these were the exact words dictated to Day in 1919 just before MacCauley retired from the Mission and left Japan. Yet, Day contradicted Cornish's claim within his five page Preface: "The main part of this is here reproduced, much as he spoke it, in somewhat permanent form." Day's report had been asked for by Louis Cornish, Day's mentor and guide throughout his tenure with the Mission – and upon his return to Boston in 1922. Cornish had Ms. Patterson, a secretary at the AUA, file the typed manuscript in which someone had made obvious spelling and grammatical corrections, probably Ms. Patterson as she typed Day's handwritten report. There are two filed copies, one having a note by Cornish to her, both unnumbered. One has a brief Preface that seems to be a draft of an obituary for MacCauley in the style of Cornish, the other has a signed introduction by Day, dated April 22, 1931. AUA Pres. Samuel Eliot's lament, "An Unexpected Call and a Broken Connection," containing an internal date of 1926 also inferred the use of Day's 1931 handwritten report. Eliot's manuscript is undated, probably 1931. Thus, the reports were not contemporaneous.

quality of the Mission's leadership; IMAOKA was only a graduate student at Tōdai. IMAOKA spoke little in personal interviews about his activities during this period, only admitting he had served as the last secretary of the Mission and the Association.

IMAOKA would remain invisible until he went to Harvard in 1915 with his professor, ANESAKI, serving him as a special assistant. When he returned, only his consistent *modus operandi* of assisting others from behind the scenes kept him from leadership roles until late 1917. He had been reliable, hard working, and without ego. But necessity would make him secretary of both the American Japan Unitarian Mission and the Japanese Unitarian Association when SUZUKI Bunji, the second secretary of JUM and JUA, needed to resign to devote all his efforts to the labor movement. That change would place IMAOKA at the center of the movement to face the largest crisis of the mission's brief history.

As mentioned in a previous chapter, IMAOKA's wife, Utayo, had obtained for him the position of manager of a boarding house which he began upon his arrival in Tokyo in 1910. She actually ran the boarding house, directing two maids, but seemed to chafe at the family's relative poverty. She may have already been part of the Japanese women's movement pressing for more freedom, especially in the area of business ownership and management. Her personal quest for freedom had brought IMAOKA back to Tokyo.

IMAOKA had completely adopted Tenkō-san's Buddhist message of *egolessness* and EBINA's of Christ as the invisible servant ("do not let your right hand know what your left is doing"), accepting material scarcity. He continued his spiritual practices much as he had done in Kobe as a Kumi-ai minister begun with Tenkō-san – a type of meditation called *seiza-ho*. His quest for intellectual freedom would flourish as rational or cognitional religion. Questioning, studying and addressing social problems of a new Japan evolved into moral principles and disciplined living. Tenkō-san's introduction to the *seiza* group of OKADA Torahirō deepened his meditational practice, turning what might have been a cold religious rationalism into a blend of Zen-like meditation and rational Christianity. He would regularly attend daily *seiza-ho* practice until OKADA's death in 1920.

> Returning to Tokyo, I did meditation with Professor Okada Torajirō. This was recommended by Tenko-san. There was a meditation group every morning from 6 to 7 at the Buddhist temple, Hongyoji, in Nippori. I went there every morning. Professor Okada taught us, "Breathe correctly with correct posture and meditation will make you one with the universe." He also said, "My method of meditation is basically the same as Master Dogen's Zen meditation method." The fact that I was able to take private lessons from Professor Okada during the remaining seven years of his life was a vital force in my career. I continued to practice meditation thereafter, and even now do not neglect it, so that it is my only discipline.[226]

IMAOKA had arrived a year after the end of the period of Japanese Unitarian independence. KANDA Saichirō (1885-1946) would resign his dual position as Mission (JUM) and Association (JUA) secretary within a few months. He had held both of these offices since the official beginning of the Mission in 1888, when he returned with the first missionary party. Both illness and the demand of his family to run their bank were given as reasons for his resignation.[227]

---

226. IMAOKA, "My Articles of Faith, at 103." September 16, 1984. Note a possible discrepancy of seven years until the end of OKADA's life in 1920.

227. There had been a division between secretary KANDA of the JUA/JUM and the Dōshisha Unitarians concerning socialism. KISHIMOTO and ABE were willing to work with the more radical Marxist socialists and went to the new meeting place at KATAYAMA's house. Yet there was continuity in the publishing network from *Yunitarian* [the magazine] to *Shūkyō* to *Rikugō Zasshi*. KISHIMOTO was its chief

MacCauley needed a secretary whose primary role was translation. Despite winning an honorary doctorate from Princeton for his Japanese grammar, he needed constant help from his secretary as a translator to accompany him when only Japanese was spoken. But, he was not able to hire a secretary for over a year. He had slipped back into the role of chief representative of Western Civilization in Japan, becoming president, vice president or secretary of a dozen expatriate organizations, almost all only using English. An Imperial award gave him court rank and prestige that helped the Mission, especially from police interference or surveillance.[228] His reports and articles to American Unitarians would allow the *yuniterian* movement at Unity Hall to flourish without too much interference from the AUA.

1910 Farewell party for K*ANDA*, *from MacCauley's 1914 book, Memories and Memorials.*
The description in the List of Illustrations simply states:

"Farewell testimonial to Secretary Saichiro Kanda after his twenty years of service." 1890-1910.

American Unitarians were told of renewed vitality in liberal worship, publishing, teaching and social work – MacCauley's four original departments. To tell them about a much larger network of dynamic, even dangerous programs would have been

---

editor and then in 1899 passed that role to ABE. Other continuities will be shown in this chapter.

228. His first Imperial award came in recognition of his support of Japan in the Russo-Japanese War of 1904-05. His articles in the New York Times were widely praised in Japan. A second Imperial Award came on his 75th birthday, making him one of the most honored foreigners of this era.

counterproductive. Articles and reports in Samuel Eliot's presidential column and Charles Wendte's "Foreign Notes" repeated the same themes about a unique mission of the most talented and best-educated *native* leaders in Japan. In the December 15, 1910, *Christian Register* Wendte wrote: "The withdrawal of Mr. Kanda will necessitate a new alignment and distribution of our missionary work in that country; but it will always retain the impress of the gentle, affectionate, and devoted spirit of him who has so exemplified the precept of the Master, 'Whosoever will be great among you, let him be as one that doth serve.'" Wendte continued to mention that ABE would preach in the morning and MINAMI on Sunday evenings with MacCauley, "the general adviser and helper, bringing to this work his ripe culture, large experience, profound sympathy with Japanese national and ethical aspirations, and wise, conciliatory spirit."

A year later, the September 1st *Christian Register* appraised readers that "the Rev. S. Uchigasaki, arrived from a three-year study at Manchester College, Oxford, and has been called to the ministry of the Tokio church." Eliot and Wendte characteristically used that spelling of the capitol as Tokio. Eliot mentioned two interfaith meetings at Unity Hall: a "Liberal Christian or Interdenominational Congress" with presentations from "Christian, orthodox, liberal, Buddhist, Shinto, and speeches without creedal association on behalf of education and social reform." These presentations were published in "Progressive Religion." A rally was led by the "Japan's Women's Association" concerning "interests of social purity" that were addressed by JUA officers, MINAMI, ABE, and SHIMADA.[229] An all-day meeting of "Count Okuma's Japan Peace Society" would soon take place, Eliot reported. Three of the five primary activities of the

229. SHIMADA Saburo (1858-1923) was mentioned in the 1900 *Sketches,* active in the labor movement, later a member of the Diet and was head of the Printer's Union until it was outlawed.

yuniterian movement are evidenced in this 1911 *Register* article: interfaith dialogue, women's issues, and peace. Only economic (or labor) and political issues were not noted. Spelling out the significance or importance of these activities escaped both writers and readers.

When a third of the Unity Hall congregation left with SAJI and HIRAI, attendance had to be rebuilt. ABE and MINAMI were not as dynamic as their Buddhist-Unitarian (SAJI) and Methodist-Unitarian (HIRAI) predecessors. And, the times had changed. Other denominations, especially the Congregationalists, had become more liberal, less dogmatic and open to science and new knowledge (Note that IMAOKA's translation of Campbell's *New Theology* had been awaited in Kumi-ai circles only to be found "old" by the time it was published.). It was not Sunday worship that filled Unity Hall, but the progressive activities joined by others: conferences, congresses and rallies that brought together all the faith communities in a growing sense of social progress and hope. Because all liberal movements suffered a traumatic ending with the victory of Japanese fascism in the 1930s, the type of recovery at Unity Hall from the SAJI crisis has been missed by the few scholars who have studied this religious movement. In fact, how IMAOKA spoke of a *yuniterian* spirit during the final decade of the Japan Unitarian Association was full of hope. It would continue past the Mission's crisis of 1922. The *yuniterian* spirit would evolve into a social and political movement that only national events could extinguish in the 1930s.

SUZUKI – the Second Dual Secretary

It took some time for MacCauley to find and convince a brilliant young lawyer to take KANDA's position. SUZUKI Bunji had started his professional career as a journalist. He had graduated from the law school at the Imperial University of Tokyo and gained national prominence in his first job, being the law reporter for the

Asahi Shinbun. He was assigned to cover the High Treason trials following the May 1910 arrests of dozens of conspirators against the Emperor. SUZUKI's interviews of some of the "traitors," especially KŌTOKU, who had been a part of *yuniterian* activities at Unity Hall until he became an anarchist, showed the fairness of the legal system to be in question. SUZUKI was fired for an "unspecified error" – a euphemism for his being too honest and dangerous for the newspaper. Both IMAOKA, who had attended the Imperial University during the same years as SUZUKI, and UCHIGASAKI, a close friend, were helpful in persuading SUZUKI to become the dual secretary of MacCauley and of the Association.

What had been a major duty during the period of independence became a constant source of shared responsibility as more and more American Unitarian dignitaries came on commissions, or just introductions from the AUA, for a month or more stay. The more important visitors included Thomas Eliot, Charles Eliot, Samuel Eliot, George Peabody, Charles Wendte, Jabez Sunderland, Caroline Furness – and many minor Unitarian divines. Some came with promises though none materialized. Not one visitor seemed to be aware of the extraordinary era that Japan was experiencing. It was a time of democratic hope in the Taishō Era.[230] Their reports

230. The Taishō period or era (*Taishō jidai*) is a time in the history of Japan that dates from July 30, 1912, to December 25, 1926. It coincides with the reign of the Emperor Taishō. The new emperor was sickly, which prompted the shift in political power from the old oligarchic group of elder statesmen (*genrō*) to the Imperial Diet of Japan and the democratic parties. Thus, the era is considered the time of the liberal movement known as the "Taishō democracy". It is usually distinguished from the preceding chaotic Meiji period and the following militarism of the first part of the Shōwa period.

During the Taishō democracy there were several diplomatic attempts made to encourage peace, such as the Washington Naval Treaty and participation in the League of Nations. However, with the beginning of the Shōwa era, the apparent collapse of the world economic order with the Great Depression starting in 1929, coupled with the imposition of trade barriers by western nations and an increasing radicalism in Japanese politics including issues of domestic terrorist violence

simultaneously chided Japanese Unitarians for not knowing the latest American principles of social work yet faulted them for their interest in and promotion of Christian socialism.

Charles William Eliot visited Japan for the AUA Mission in 1909. He again raised the prospect of AUA help in building another hall in the student district of Kanda-ku. The grants for that hall, given in 1905 and 1906, and recovered by MacCauley in 1909 had been absorbed for operational expenses of the Mission.[231] Challenged by Eliot's proposal, the Japanese immediately raised their share by 1910, but the promised funding from the AUA never came. The AUA was focused on a new interest – international liberal religion under the leadership of Charles Wendte and the 1910 [IARF] Congress in Berlin.

Labor, Poverty, Social Work

Until SUZUKI became the secretary of both the JUM and JUA in 1911, labor issues had not developed into concrete and sustained actions. Slums, poverty, even gardening, health and thrift habits touching upon alcoholism and prostitution were studied and solutions were approached on an individualistic basis. The poor needed to be educated and reform themselves, they thought. The poor's habits needed to change. Change was not undertaken systematically or nationally, with ABE Isō the rare exception. He attempted to test the limits of legality in starting a political party and supporting a labor movement (more about JUA's amazing president later in this chapter). KANAMORI Tsūrin was an example of those who focused on

(including an assassination attempt on the emperor in 1932 and a number of attempted coups d'état by ultra-nationalist secret societies) led to a resurgence of so-called "jingoistic" patriotism, a weakening of democratic forces and a belief that the military could solve all threats both domestic and foreign. Patriotic education also strengthened the sense of a *hakko ichiu*, or a divine mission to unify Asia under Japanese rule.

231. Funding for the Berlin 1910 "Fifth International Congress of Free Christianity and Religious Progress" [IARF] absorbed the annual grants to the Japan Mission. MacCauley was instructed to use what he had recovered from SAJI and KANDA to run the Mission without additional resources from the Hayward Fund.

individual change, bicycling to lecture to poor working families on how savings and thrift would lift them from poverty.

MacCauley took some credit for teaching SUZUKI about social concern, especially interest in the laborers around Unity Hall and their slums. MacCauley had written a book called *Thought and Fact for Today* in 1911,[232] which discussed the relation between capital and labor. MacCauley proposed a working relationship within industry and how both labor and capital could work in harmony. This could have influenced SUZUKI's notion of mutual benefit and harmonious relations between workers and owners. ABE and the Association had been studying these conditions from economic, labor and political perspectives for more than a decade.[233] In the first Unitarian period, Garrett Droppers and William Lawrance had found eager listeners as they taught about socialism, Christian socialism, social theory, economics and political theory at Keiō University and their own School of Advanced Learning. ABE and most of the *yuniterians* of Unity Hall had pulled back from radical and militant socialists like KATAYAMA and KŌTOKU. However, MacCauley's claim ignored a decade of activity without his presence or influence.

SUZUKI's solution was to follow the British model of benevolent societies. He founded a Friendly Society, Yūaikai, in August 12, 1912, with every intention to transform it into a labor union as soon as it became legal to do so. Not surprisingly, almost every member of the Japan Unitarian Association would join Yūaikai, not because they were workers – they weren't – but in solidarity out of a concern for economic justice.

---

232. MacCauley, *Thought and Fact for Today* (Yokohama: Kelly and Walsh, 1911), 95pp. MacCauley believed that he introduced Suzuki to Krause's theories about labor and capitalists working together harmoniously. He, or Day, claimed that he organized Yūaikai, which was incorrect (another example of the unreliability of Day's putting his ideas into *MacCauley's History*), p. 21.

233. Day, *MacCauley's History*, *op.cit.*, p. 21.

Leaders of Yūaikai outside Unity Hall, 1916

However, the AUA's positive attitude concerning free study for systemic change of the economic order had changed with the rise of labor unrest in America. Social concerns were a constant in Japanese sermons, publications and activities, and that had brought early criticism from Thomas Eliot in his 1903 report about too much socialism and a need to refocus, not on workers and their conditions, but on the educated classes and students. Now, the *yuniterian* movement had a lawyer to lead their actions – and almost any action concerning labor conditions and worker rights was illegal as defined by the Peace Protection Act of 1900.

SUZUKI moved quickly after he was hired, finding fourteen workers to study their labor conditions and those of the slums on Unity Hall's doorsteps. They formed the basis for a cadre of labor organizers who would work with him in the factories and slums. The first organizations in Japan had been declared illegal under Article 17 of the Peace Protection Act of 1900, which was invoked to prevent agitation against employers or landlords – or anything that might disturb social order.

Believing this was liberalism's calling, MacCauley made an unusual arrangement with SUZUKI: "The new movement [Yūaikai] grew in importance and the work began to extend throughout the country. We continued to back this up by retaining Suzuki as the Mission's Secretary but *setting him free to devote himself largely to the new work*."[234] Others, including IMAOKA, were called upon to help perform his other duties.

MacCauley's Needs

The secretary's dual work as Association coordinator and as MacCauley's assistant was initially shared by JUA members. SUZUKU would spent more time away from Tokyo as Yūaikai's membership and their role in labor issues increased. The job of the joint secretary provided a number of important services to help MacCauley as well as manage the complex use of Unity Hall by all the societies and action groups that met there. Because of this and his age, secretarial help was the first duty to be shared when SUZUKU was not available – and then he was freed from all responsibilities of the dual secretary. As more American visitors came, that was another responsibility that fell on the JUA officers and workers. The dual secretary needed to be ready to fill in when speakers cancelled, arrange lectures and receptions at Unity Hall, and handle financial matters for the Association. IMAOKA, though junior to the professors and ministers at Unity Hall, would be called upon the most.

MacCauley seems to have lost his fluency in Japanese. He had preached in the first period with KANDA as his translator. MacCauley may have lost some of his language ability during his nine-year absence (1900-09). In his second term of service MacCauley needed constant translation help. Even earlier in 1905 on a visit to make arrangements for the republication of his grammar book, he totally misunderstood a ceremony when he did not have an interpreter. MacCauley was invited to attend the dedication of a *tōrō* to the Emperor on the grounds of Unity Hall. A decade later he still

234. Day's *MacCauley's History*, *op. cit.*, p. 22, Emphasis added.

thought the *tōrō* honored him:[235]

CLAY MACCAULEY MEMORIAL TŌRŌ, TOKYO, 1905

"Japanese friends signalized my return to Japan in 1905, by erecting, in the grounds of Unity Hall, a monumental stone lantern – ancient Nora style, – inscribing on it my name, the date, – 'Nov. 3, 1905,' – and the sentiment KI-NEN-TO, 'Remembrance Cherishing Bearer of Light.'

"Soon after my Second return, in 1909, I received from His Majesty, the Emperor, a decoration of 'The Order of the Rising Sun.'"

-- Quoted from [List of] Illustrations, p. XIII, in MacCauley, *Memories and Memorials: Gatherings from an Eventful Life* (Yokohama: 1914), p. 548.

In Day's transcription of MacCauley's oral history in 1919, Day summarized or paraphrased MacCauley's dictation (with MacCauley speaking in the third person – or Day just putting words into his mouth):

> To his surprise, he was asked to come to the Unitarian Headquarters [Unity Hall] to witness the dedication of a memorial Toro, which is a memorial lantern, to himself. The lantern bore the inscription:
>
> His name and Ki-Nen-To, which being interpreted means:
>
> Here is a Bearer of Light to Cherish
> the Memory of One Who, Like this Lantern,
> Has Shed Light Abroad.
>
> (Ki-Nen-To literally means, "A rememberance [*sic.*] cherishing a Bearer of Light.")[236]

Day continued in his transcript of MacCauley: "such things

[235] MacCauley, *Memories and Memorials: Gatherings from an Eventful Life* (Yokohama: Fukuin,1914).

[236] Day, *History*, *op.cit.*, p. 13.

are usually done in Japan to persons for public service, whether living or dead." MacCauley had been honored, as great as any diplomat or foreigner of that period, but there were times that he did not understand what was happening without help. SUZUKI had been freed from this responsibility to build the Friendly Society, with offices in Unity Hall as its headquarters and free use of the great hall for their meetings. More and more, helping MacCauley would fall upon IMAOKA.

Yūaikai's Attempt to Mediate Economic Justice

The Yūaikai grew rapidly as the only legal organization in Japan to represent workers of all trades and crafts. MacCauley reported: "In 1914, then being only two years, the [Friendly] Society had 194 branches and about fifty thousand members, extending from the northernmost to the southernmost islands, a district of 1200 miles. SUZUKI still remained Secretary of the Mission which he served for five years."[237]

In 1914 the *Friendly Society* struggled to form a labor union, but it was refused by the government. SUZUKI carefully trained a cadre of labor organizers to work in non-violent ways to gain concessions from employers and prevent violence by workers. Economic inequity had reached intolerable levels.

Decades of war profiteering exploited cheap labor, crowding workers into disease-ridden slums and creating conditions for rebellion. Revolt came not against the government but against capitalists. As national feeling still supported military conquests of Korea and China, anger erupted against employers. The radical socialists brought in an era of strikes, increasingly violent. Perhaps

237. Day, *MacCauley's History*, *op.cit.*, p. 22, numbered manuscript. The MacCauley/Day account creates a dating problem. If we ignore dating SUZUKI as having been hired in 1910/11 and take the real date as 1912, five years would mean that he ceased being paid secretary in 1917. IMAOKA would have returned from Harvard in 1916.

this contemporary description of a slum in Kobe, even with its Western agenda and tone, will help in understanding what SUZUKI, Yūaikai, and the *yuniterian* movement faced when they attempted to address the myriad of problems industrialization had brought to the New Japan.

> Industrialism in Japan is like a stream with two forks, the one sparkling and gay, bearing gold and all the delights of modern convenience and luxury, the other putrid and dark with the wreckage of human beings. And they flow close together. Go with me to Kobe to look at the mansion of a ship-building magnate, the head of a plant employing 17,000 men. He is a gentleman of the best blood and breeding, graduated from a famous American University, a patron of arts and philanthropy. He is not a showy spendthrift. His huge profits from wartime contracts have been spent largely in assembling a choice collection of European art... Now let us walk a mile away to that ante-room of hell, the slums of Shinkawa, where twelve thousand human beings swam. Open sewers and germ-haunted kennels multiply disease. Criminals, beggars, gamblers, and abandoned women are the quarter's leading citizens. Dirty children in droves play and fight and ape their elders up and down the goat-path alleys as though theirs was the normal kind of life. These slums represent, it is true, the cess-pool of Japanese industrialism, but it is a pool which is incessantly replenished by the men and women flung off like broken fragments from the fast flying wheels of the economic mill. The Shinkawa slums are duplicated in every large city of the country.[238]

SUZUKI's cadre worked to prevent violence while he and his lieutenants sought potential solutions that would resolve the growing number of strikes. The National Factory Law had been passed, addressing some of the issues raised by *yuniterians* networking together, but it was not enforced until 1916. Even then, children under twelve were still employed. Women and children were used in the mines; and they could be required to work up to 12 hours a day,

---

238. Galen M. Fisher, *Creative Forces in Japan* (New York: National Council, Department of Missions, 1923), p. 76.

ten days in a row. They should not have been required to work between 10 p.m. and 4 a.m. – a provision in the law that was never enforced.[239] Workers were still averaging less than one yen a day in most jobs.

Suzuki represented labor (or workers) nationally, even though it was still illegal to form labor unions. The worst consequences of industrialization – low wages, health-destroying work, lack of adequate medical care or accident insurance, living in squalor and disease infested slums – needed redress. Violent strikes began to erupt. SUZUKI and Yūaikai raced to quell the violence, addressed grievances and negotiated settlements. "In 1914 there were only 50 strikes involving 7,904 workers; in 1917 the number had increased to 398 strikes involving 57,309 workers, and the peak was reached in 1918 with 417 strikes involving 66,457 workers."[240] Yūaikai was given credit for settling nearly fifty major strikes, mostly in shipping and steel manufacturing. As the need for workers in the war-related industries decreased after the Great War (WWI), strikes lessened. But unemployment and low wages continued and brought hunger. The rice riots of 1918 again involved SUZUKI and Yūaikai as mediators. This resulted in the Imperial Household donating the equivalent of $1.5 million for a relief fund, followed by $12 million contributed by wealthy capitalists. SUZUKI and Yūaikai had become national heroes of the moment as evidenced by a song sung by marching workers during a labor struggle in Kobe in 1919:

> Workers of Nippon, awake, awake!
> Old things are done with and passed away.
> Worlds that are new are for you to make.
> Strive, then, and fail not in this your day.
> Farmers and weavers and shipwrights all,
> Miners who labor beneath the soil,

239. *Ibid.*

240. Fisher, *op. cit.,* p. 81, quoting a contemporary study by R. UNNO on "Industrial Education."

You who drop sweat to get bread, we call.
Honors are now for the sons of toil.
Early to work though cold winds bite,
Tired ere homeward their way they take,
Daylight gone and the stars alight,---
So they toil for the whole world's sake.
Workers of Nippon, awake, awake!
Old things are done with and passed away.
Worlds that are new are for you to make.
Strive, then, and fail not in this your day.
Hooray for the Yuai-kai Hooray![241]

SUZUKI and Yūaikai organized cooperative markets[242] and eating houses where workers and their families could be sure of one meal a day. [Ms. IMAOKA, as we will soon learn, became nationally known for her role in this.] With no accident insurance for workers, Yūaikai sought to get employers to provide doctors and nurses, playgrounds and entertainment halls, good ventilation and lighting in the factories, allowances upon retirement, and sick benefits. Unfortunately, these benefits were achieved in only a few factories and plants. For those who heard of these successes but saw no change in their own misery, violent calls for action by militant activists won their support and weakened Yūaikai. Labor unrest became a major fear even before the end of World War I, as Russian workers toppled their government. Fear of Unitarian involvement in labor issues would make Boston rethink its support and supervision of its Mission. The presence of the only legal labor movement – although it was not yet a labor union – at Unity Hall brought both prestige and danger.[243]

For almost seven years, SUZUKI led an unusually peaceful labor movement. He had even gone to the Paris Peace treaty negotiations at the end of WW I as labor's representative in 1918.

---

241. *Japan Chronicle*, August 14, 1919. Emphasis added.

242. Ms. IMAOKA Utayo received national attention for her efforts in organizing these. *MacCauley's History,* p.37 of the numbered manuscript.

243. Mohr, *op. cit.,* chapter 6.

Then everything changed. Yūaikai had become too powerful; government and major manufacturers worked to weaken or destroy it. From 1920 onwards, membership declined, and militants began to gain more concessions than Yūaikai could with its peaceful approach. They also called for the militant overthrow of capitalism – as radical socialists, communists and Bolsheviks won workers' support.

ABE's Leadership

As important to IMAOKA's development as was his assisting SUZUKI was his assisting ABE ISŌ in his indefatigable activities for world peace, a socially just society, interfaith dialogue and cooperation, women's issues, and even liberal politics. ABE had been one of the Kumamoto Band of NIIJIMA JŌ [older transliterations: NEESHIMA, NEESIMA]. ABE was among his original students at Dōshisha, studied abroad at Hartford Theological Seminary in Connecticut, returned to teach at Dōshisha, followed KISHIMOTO as chief editor of the *Cosmos*, and finally became president of the Japan Unitarian Association. (*Nihon Yuniterian Kōdōkai* was renamed by MacCauley as the *Tōitsu Kirisuokyō Kōdōkai* [*Kōdōkwai*].)[244]

ABE Isō (1865-1949)

Before IMAOKA joined the *yuniterian* movement in its third period, as we have already learned, ABE became an officer in the

[244] See entry about ABE in *Sketches, op.cit.*

JUA in 1898 and helped found The Research Society of Socialism in 1898 and Association of Socialism in 1900. He was joined by ANESAKI and instructors from the School for Advanced Learning. More moderate Unitarians like KANDA and SAJI stopped with study as others became more activistic and political. By 1900 the study groups began seeing themselves as idealists. They actually formed a Society of Idealists in 1901, pouring those ideals into the first Social-Democratic Party (Shakai Minshutō), which was outlawed two days later.[245] This would not be ABE's last brush with the authorities.

ABE's idealism in the first two periods of the Unitarian mission continued into the third period, often networked with other groups in activities not directly associated with religion. ABE linked Japan's over-population problems with its wars for territorial expansion, poverty and suppression of women. He became known as the "father of sexology" and the "father of sociology" for his work in the 1920s and 30s – most of which kept him on the police surveillance radar.[246] His actions and writings had the potential of disturbing peace and order. As a professor at Waseda, which was now more progressive than Keiō and had become its rival, ABE taught economics and social issues. His department at Waseda would spawn radical students and faculty, some less judicious than he and getting into more trouble with the law. Incidentally, he started the university's baseball team and thus became known as the father of Japanese baseball, although SUZUKI may have introduced it in Yūaikai's program in 1912 – according to MacCauley. In 1919 MacCauley reported to Boston that ABE was offered the presidency of Dōshisha but turned them down for "personal reasons." ABE had become a protagonist for social change, active in the popular press on

245. Kishimoto H., *loc. cit.*

246. Frühstück, Sabine, *Colonalizing Sex: Sexology and Social Control in Modern Japan* (Berkeley: University of California Press, 2003).

almost every social issue of the day. He had become what we call today "a public intellectual."

Perhaps one of the most interesting issues for IMAOKA was that of women's liberation and rights because of his wife's freedom. IMAOKA Utayo was mentioned a few times in Unitarian literature of the period. MacCauley, later quoted by Eliot and Wendte, wrote that Utayo was "a national figure," "a leader of issues for her sex."[247] A few more details about her were reported to American Unitarians in 1921 by Prof. Caroline Furness of Vassar College.[248]

The idea that women's status, conditions, issues and "rights" were considered important in shaping the new Japan was due in no small part because some men like ABE with progressive values and access to sources of power championed gender equality. These were not the old Meiji influence-shapers but a younger generation who attempted to influence a broader public with their publications and lectures. ABE became one of the most public of the intellectuals of this era. He joined early feminists, publishing their concerns and their works, across a wide variety of issues. In 1901 in the manifesto of Idealists, attempting to found the Idealist Party, ABE had included universal suffrage, seeing women as equals in the political sphere. Educational and economic equality were also affirmed as equal opportunity. Suffrage, property ownership, legal equality, education, prohibition, prostitution, contraceptives and women's health issues were addressed in his popular writings. There was practically no mention of the importance of these *yuniterian* women's activities in reports to America. A scant notice mentioned that

> The hall [Unity Hall] [wa]s regularly used once a month for the meetings of the Society for Temperance, the Society for the Relief of Released Prisoners and Prison Reform, for the Society for Public Sanitation.[249]

247. *MacCauley's History, op.cit.,* p.37 of numbered manuscript.
248. Discussed later in the chapter.
249. *MacCauley's History*, p. 16 in the numbered copy.

These were all led by women with Abe's and the JUA's full support.

Just as ABE had found in allying with activists in the social justice and labor movement, in the women's movement he found himself working with women who were more radical than himself. (Uncharacteristically, MacCauley would not even claim some of these women as "Unitarian sympathizers" as they were too non-conformist.) In 1910 ABE wrote in an article entitled "Free Love" what freedom meant to these early fighters for women's liberation.[250] They called themselves "blue stockings" and so named their journal in 1911. HIRATSUKA Raichō (1886-1971) was their leader. She began her education in the Universalist Mission school and continued at Japan Women's University founded by NARUSE Jinzō. IMAOKA Utayo also attended there as a graduate student. HIRATSUKA may have met UCHIGASAKI, then minister of Unity Hall, at *seiza-ho* since many *yuniterians* practiced with OKADA Torajirō – as did IMAOKA and KISHIMOTO. Wherever she first met UCHIGASAKI, she attended his Bible classes at Waseda University. ABE worked with her and even published in her *Blue Stockings* magazine (*Seitō*) on women's issues like birth control and contraception, when these were considered anti-patriotic, since Japan's oligarchs wanted a larger population to support their war efforts.[251] HIRATSUKA led in a direction that seemed alien – even French libertine – to most of Japanese society. She advocated free love and a woman's choice of her lovers; and she practiced what she preached, openly. Her *nom de plume* was "Raichō" (thunderbird).

250. Cited only by Frühstück in her bibliography.

251. HIRATSUKA was famous enough to be included in an English article in Wikipedia: https://en.wikipedia.org/wiki/Raicho_Hiratsuka. *Blue Stocking* folded in 1915, but Raichō's leadership in the women's movement was firmly established. She had two children by a younger lover, only marrying him in 1941. She died in 1971.

Sabine Frühstück's study, *Colonizing Sex,*[252] found ABE joining almost every aspect of the early women's liberation movement – publicly – when even advocacy was illegal. While Frühstück's work focused on the field of sexology, she found ABE's contributions for the advancement of women in a wider range of issues. ABE and YAMAMOTO Senji were both public men and "well known from their articles in daily papers. Hence, their activities were observed more carefully."[253]

ABE was a cofounder of the Purity Society (Kakuseikai), which guided the anti-prostitution movement with the slogan "liberation of prostitutes" and published the monthly journal *Purity*. At the beginning of the 1920s, ABE became a leading representative of the birth control movement. He promoted his ideas on prostitution, birth control, and eugenics[254] in both medical journals and popular magazines including *Purity, Women's Review, Perverse Psyche,* and *Popular Medicine.*[255]

ABE allied with SUZUKI and KATO Toyohiko, founder of the Japan Salvation Army and cofounder of the Japanese Farmers' Union, to address birth control because of its impact on working women.[256] He also addressed prostitution from multiple perspectives, noting how poverty led parents to sell their daughters; prostitution spread social diseases and destroyed the family. As an economics professor, ABE was convinced that Japan's colonial policy was disastrous. Japan already had "colonies" in Taiwan, Manshu, and Korea, and would soon begin colonization of China by military force. He condemned the military's use of "comfort women" as another exploitation of women.

---

252. Sabine Frühstück, *Colonizing Sex: Sexology and Social Control in Modern Japan.* (Berkeley: University of California Press, 2003).

253. *Ibid.*, p. 166.

254. ABE's love of science led him to think that eugenic research could solve birth defects and lead to a healthier humanity. He did not foresee the ethical problems. Frühstück credits this one mistake for his negative place in history.

255. Frühstück, *op. cit.,* p. 121.

256. *Ibid.,* p. 133-4.

Frühstück concluded that ABE was "Once a savior of the underprivileged as the founder of Japan's first socialist party and a crusader for the abolition of prostitution..."[257] However, ABE advocated two policies that he thought rational with which IMAOKA disagreed: "early marriage as his solution to keep girls from being sold into prostitution" (while IMAOKA sought universal public education as a better solution) and sterilization for the "genetically diseased" because of the burden their descendants placed on society (which IMAOKA rejected completely).[258]

The Constant Flow of AUA Dignitaries

As if Japanese Unitarians did not have enough to do for the betterment of Japanese society, and while *The Christian Register* praised their independence and competence in running their own programs, the AUA would send one commissioner after another to check on "its investment" (the term they actually used) or to promote AUA ideas and purposes.

The issues of the 1913 *Christian Register* described lengthy visits and the reports of Prof. Francis Peabody and the Rev. Jabez T. Sunderland, both sponsored by the AUA as Billings lecturers. Sunderland had a second purpose: to promote "Theistic Congresses or the Congresses of Universal Religion" to be held around the world with the one in Japan to be jointly sponsored by the JUA and the Association Concordia (an organization led by IMAOKA's mentor, ANESAKI). MacCauley's 70th birthday was reported in the June 12th *Register* and featured such prestigious guests as "Prof. and Mrs. Peabody…, Pro. Inouye and Prof. Anesaki of the Imperial University, … Rev. Emil Schroeder of the German Church, … Prof. Abe … and others." The month before, readers were told of a purchase as a fact that never became a reality: "Most recently the American Unitarian

---

257. *Ibid.,* p. 154.

258. *Ibid.* To be historically fair to ABE, American sociologists had pioneered work in eugenics and ABE had followed their lead. See comment above, footnote 249.

Association has bought a desirable site in the heart of the university quarter of Tokio, where a second church is to be erected, designed more especially to accommodate seekers for liberal religious truth among the 16,000 students, 4,000 of them women, who reside in that section of the city."[259] Sunderland's article in the November *Register* revealed an agenda of Wendte's: uniting liberal religionists by "taking a company of eminent representatives from America and England around the world and holding a world-girdling series of congresses with the aim of creating more fraternal relations between the great religions of the world."[260] Sunderland wrote in the November 27, 1913 issue:

> The Association Concordia, an organization of some eighty men, of as great prominence and influence in education, business and public life as could be found in Tokyo or Japan, after full consideration of the matter has authorized me to write Dr. Wendte conveying to him an invitation for one of the congresses to be held in this capital city of the empire, the Association to be its host, to entertain the foreign speakers and visitors, and to make all local arrangements.
>
> How fitting it is that the Congress should be held under the auspices of the Association Concordia, as well as how much this promises for its success, will be seen when I explain that the Association has its existence (as its name suggests) on purpose to promote essentially the same ends which Dr. Wendte and his associates have in view in setting out to create their congresses; namely, better acquaintance and more fraternal relations between the different great religions, only Association Concordia does not confine itself to religions, but goes further.
>
> Some of the leaders of the Association Concordia, among whom were Baron Sakatavia [sic.], the mayor at Tokyo, Baron Shibusawa, formerly a cabinet minister and a man of great wealth and public spirit. Dr Naruse, president of the Women's University, and others... [Co-founder Anesaki was not

259. Charles Wendte, "The Extension of Unitarian Christianity in Foreign Lands: In Motive, Message, and Methods," *The Christian Register,* May 15, 1913, p. 466.

260. Sunderland, "A Billings Lecturer in Japan," *Christian Register*, Nov. 16, 1913, p. 1146.

mentioned.][261]

The plan for Congresses around the globe was thwarted by the beginning of a World War in 1914.

IMAOKA Became Secretary

Early in 1917 IMAOKA was appointed dual secretary of the JUM and JUA. The earliest extant mention of his appointment was in Charles Wendte's "Oriental Notes" column as AUA's director of Foreign Affairs.[262] The account began by reporting on Yūaikai and its celebration at Unity Hall of its fifth anniversary. Then Wendte announced that IMAOKA had become the new secretary.

> The Yuai Kai, Japan's labor society, which was the outcome of the social endeavors of Bunji Suzuki, until recently the secretary of the Unitarian Mission in Tokyo, has now grown to such dimensions that the quarters occupied by it in the Unitarian Building no longer suffice, and it has been decided to erect a labor temple or hall for its activities. ... It is pleasant to think that in Japan, at least, the Unitarian fellowship is among the foremost friends of the labor cause. ... Mr. Suzuki's place as secretary of the Unitarian Mission has been filled by Mr. Imaoka, who not long since was for a time a student at the Harvard Divinity School at Cambridge, Mass. A young man of ability, gentle manners, and religious spirit, he bids fair to be a valuable acquisition to our liberal forces in Japan.[263]

This change does not seem to be particularly noteworthy for MacCauley, as his earliest surviving mention of IMAOKA as secretary was a comment in a letter to AUA President Eliot in 1919.[264] This would logically be the case if IMAOKA had already been performing many, if not all, of SUZUKI's secretarial duties. Thus, IMAOKA remained nearly invisible, consistent with his *modus operandi* of

---

261. ANESAKI's warning to NARUSE not to allow the AUA to co-opt Concordia Association has a broad context.

262. *Christian Register*, May 24, 1917, p. 498.

263. *Ibid.*

264. Ltr. MacCauley to S. Eliot, March 13, 1918. "Our secretary, Mr. Imaoka, is a man of education of a high order, and is both earnestly religious in character and genuinely sympathetic spiritually, with a widely comprehensive liberalism in theology and philosophy."

assisting others from behind the scenes. Necessity had made IMAOKA secretary of both the American Japan Unitarian Mission and of the Japanese Unitarian Association when SUZUKI Bunji, the second secretary of JUM and JUA, needed to resign. IMAOKA began to receive a half-time salary for his service, which he certainly needed with the birth of a second daughter. The fact that Wendte knew of IMAOKA's appointment in early 1917 probably means that MacCauley had informed him, as Wendte was the AUA Director of Foreign Affairs. However, that letter has not survived.

In a span of only seven years, IMAOKA had become the bridge linking different networks of activists, idealists, and dreamers simply by serving in the most progressive movement of that era. These *yuniterians* were overlapping networks of socialists (Christian and radical); internationalists; pacifists; ethical reconstructionists; new Buddhists; educators (of Waseda, Keiō, Imperial University of Tokyo, the remainder of the School of Advanced Learning continuing at Unity Hall, Dōshisha and schools like Nihon University); editors and writers; orthodox Christians (NARUSE, UCHIMURA, EBINA, etc.); politicians (and founders of the Socialist, Peace and Liberal parties); MacCauley's circle (diplomats, old ruling class, new nobility and aristocracy, industrialists, military, foreign journalists); World Parliament of Religions' returning Japanese representatives; and the *seiza* group of OKADA Torahirō. The center of these connections was Unity Hall for those in Tokyo and their *Cosmos* magazine (*Rikugō Zasshi*) for those beyond. And IMAOKA would arrange for many of these activists to speak at Unity Hall during his tenure.[265]

As the third period drew to an end in 1919, IMAOKA would have adopted a cluster of *yuniterian* ideals, having worked with and been influenced by ABE, KISHIMOTO, MURAI, SUZUKI, MINAMI, UCHIGASAKI, as well as MacCauley and the wide range of Unitarians –

265. Personal communication when asked specifically: his answer: "Yes, I did much of the organizing."

yuniterians now called Liberal activists.

Characteristics of IMAOKA's Japanese Unitarianism

By analyzing the ideals of those with whom IMAOKA worked, it is possible to construct the lasting influences he had acquired during these seven years of service in the *yuniterian* movement.

OFFICERS OF JAPAN UNITARIAN ASSOCIATION WITH REV. F. G. PEABODY, D.D., A.U.A. DELEGATE TO JAPAN, 1913

Published in MacCauley's 1914 Memories and Memorials *illustrating the continued strength of the Yuniterian movement. Any picture of the movement after 1910 could have included IMAOKA sensei.*

First and foremost, as Knapp had said in the beginning, a *yuniterian* movement would be Japanese, not alien. Its message and ideals were expressed in Japanese, nested in its traditions and culture, in dialogue with Japan's most progressive elements. This was a commitment to Japanese culture.

Second, *yuniterian* had become a Japanese word for what was progressive, liberal, and open to science. It championed research and new learning, harmonizing it with Japanese culture and its spiritual past.

Third, it is international, open to foreign systems and solutions, and rejecting ultranationalism. Although "birthed" by

American Unitarians, which entailed American influence and funding, it was created as an independent liberal religious philosophy and movement, helped by fieldworkers to evolve as needed in Japan. That independence was loudly and repeatedly proclaimed by Knapp and MacCauley and every visiting AUA dignitaries from Thomas Eliot to George Peabody. All saw "their mission" as unique and different from those administered by orthodox foreign missionaries who governed their missions by the purse strings. IMAOKA would advocate international cooperation even as it was considered disloyal.

Fourth, Japanese Unitarianism was ecumenical in the sense of *ecumené,* a worldwide religious inclusivity, neither sectarian nor denominational, and universal in its most inclusive sense. The goal was always unity, and the term *unity* was constantly used in its self-expression. That had been compromised in 1909 with the expulsion of SAJI, the Buddhist Unitarian chief pastor of Unity Hall. But, cooperation with the New Buddhist or Buddhist Unitarians had not ended, especially with IMAOKA's work with ANESAKI and the quest for a unified ethical code cooperatively constructed by Japan's three religions (Buddhist, Shinto and Christianity – with ethical/religious Confucianism having a significant input as well). The search for unity developed as multi-dimensional religious identities, much as Japanese in the past had demonstrated as Shinto-Buddhist or Buddhist-Confucian or even Shinto-Buddhist-Christian.

Fifth, Japanese Unitarianism had embraced democracy and freedom as a life practice. Their commitment to religious freedom and independence emerged as a stable characteristic. Freedom had two invisible correlates: responsibility and equality. One cannot be part of a free community, they thought, unless responsible to others who are also free and equal. MacCauley's age helped them tolerate his micromanagement, especially of finances. Yet, he wisely facilitated Japanese *yuniterian* independence. However, the issue of independence and equality was a potential problem in every visit to Boston by members of the *yuniterian* movement. They would report condescension and attitudes of racial superiority (to be detailed in the next chapters). This would be experienced for the first time in Japan in 1919 with the arrival of a new director of the mission, the Rev. John B. W. Day.

Sixth, at Unity Hall the movement's religious expression was "lay-led." They were not anti-clerical, as almost all of the "ministers" who preached or spoke regularly on Sundays and Thursdays had come with theological or religious training from Christian or Buddhist traditions. Their salaries were paid by teaching; they were volunteers. They were not receiving salaries to be ministers; they were not "rice Christians," paid with foreign money.

One could argue that this was more a result of lack of AUA funds to facilitate the creation of a professional ministry. It meant that invitations to support churches or even preaching stations in other parts of the Empire had to go unmet. Hundreds of graduates from colleges and universities had been Unitarian members or attendees in Tokyo, had returned to their parts of the country with no institutional support, and had no effective way to stay connected. The AUA saw this problem, but the reality was lack of resources, human and monetary.

IMAOKA continued "lay-led" ministry the rest of his life.

Seventh, Japanese Unitarianism was socially engaged. Unity Hall was a caldron of religious, social, economic, cultural and political concerns. Its program and philosophy was committed to creating a Japan that would solve problems of economic inequity, of the universal right to vote in a democracy, of achieving gender freedom and equality, and of solving social ills from prostitution to overpopulation to health care and care for the elderly.

Eighth, Japanese Unitarianism was committed to peace. It

was anti-war and anti-imperialism. It envisioned Japan leading toward a world without war. This entailed an economic order that did not exploit the worker nor waste human and natural resources in militarism. Its middle path was between capitalism and bolshevism (Russian communism). It sought a type of Christian socialism that was socially responsible.

Ninth, Japanese Unitarianism was wholistic and unitive. Religion, culture and politics were not separate. Liberal religion, *yuniterian-ism*, was not just what happened in church on Sundays. Everything progressive, ethical and liberal were welcome at Unity Hall. So many of Japan's socially progressive organizations had begun there and would continue to have free access to the building until American opposition brought pressure to make them leave. Such was the case with Yūaikai, the Worker's Friendly Society, Japan's oldest surviving labor union.

Tenth, Japanese Unitarianism was practical. It had to be more than talk, prayers, or idealistic dreams. Religion had to be lived, be useful, and solve life problems. That would lead *yuniterians* to have an unusually high representation in national politics. They thought they could guide Japan to become a liberal democracy only to be crushed in the 1930s, as Japan's territorial expansion led to autocratic government, totalitarianism and militarism. Practicing *yuniterianism* openly would become impossible.

IMAOKA's Spiritual Pilgrimage

IMAOKA's mature spiritual identity had been largely shaped by the end of this period. He had completely adopted Tenkō-san's Buddhist message of *egolessness* and his method of meditation called *seiza-ho*. He practiced an economics of needing less and giving to those in need. It was not the life of following Christ, the suffering servant; it was living Jesus' example of ministering and teaching – but not as a minister or teacher, but just as an assistant.

His quest for intellectual freedom would flourish as rational or cognitional religion. Questioning, studying and addressing social problems of a new Japan evolved into moral principles and disciplined living. Tenkō-san's introduction to the *seiza* group of OKADA Torahirō turned what might have been a cold religious rationalism into a blend of Zen-like meditation and rational Christianity. He would regularly attend daily *seiza-ho* practice until OKADA's death in 1920.

The next decades of his life would sorely test his personal (that is, his existential) truths, which he had merged together in a rational mysticism that was dedicated to service.

A group picture with IMAOKA in the second row center, c. 1919. The reports to Boston mentioned that almost as many women as men were involved in the programs and services.

Chapter 9
Closing of the Unitarian Mission
Period Four: 1919-1922

From MacCauley's return in 1909 until the arrival of the Rev. John B. W. Day in 1919, there was little change in the activities and characteristics of the Japan Unitarian Association (JUA) in which IMAOKA had found his religious and philosophical home. Its name was changed by MacCauley when he tried to solve the problems of the 1909 crisis that occasioned his return. But, the new name was largely ignored in Japan. *Yuniterian* had become a proud Japanese word for liberal, progressive, modern; open to science and "universal" education; and Unity Hall as the center of the *yuniterian* movement.

IMAOKA became the last dual secretary of the JUA and of the Mission in 1917. SUZUKI had relied on volunteers for his tasks with MacCauley and the JUA almost immediately after he was hired. His role as president of Yūaikai had grown nationally and internationally as the Japanese representative of labor. However, after the 5th annual meeting of the Yūaikai, SUZUKI needed to put some distance between himself and the American Mission. Charles Wendte mentioned IMAOKA's official appointment in a report in his Foreign Affairs column in the *Christian Register* of May, 1917.

While Japanese Unitarianism and *yunitarian* activities were maintained without any significant changes from 1909 to 1919, several issues from their affiliation with American Unitarians would create a new situation, and from an historian's viewpoint, a new period. One problem was the 1893 gift to Japanese Unitarians of

Unity Hall. The second was the ideal of Japanese independence and management of their own programs. These concerns remained latent with only dissidents like HIROI voicing them.

The Gift: Unity Hall

There had always been a problem about *property ownership* by foreigners in Japan. The Japanese government was trying to prevent foreigners from buying up land or resources, having learned from what colonial powers had done elsewhere in Asia and the Pacific. The first secretary of the mission, KANDA Saichirō, held all the mission property in his name until 1900. Then, when the mission was closed in 1900, Boston declared it a success and its last missionary, MacCauley, was ordered home. He had KANDA institute a complicated transaction that placed Unity Hall and any other asset with AUA secretary Charles St. John as "foreign owner." Since St. John could not have an absolute title as a foreigner, it was held for him by a Japanese real estate lawyer, a Mr. MUSUIJIMA. St. John died leaving Unity Hall to his widow, and she released it to the AUA. MacCauley began trying to get the AUA to release the property back to the Japan Unitarian Association. The problem lingered through the second period and became a focus for MacCauley in the third. MacCauley proposed a *zaidan*, a corporation, as the "legal person" in Japan to own the property. But Boston just stalled, requiring procedures about the structure of the *zaidan* and asking vague questions that they felt were not answered. They feared Japanese involvements in social concerns of the working class. These fears were not revealed to MacCauley. For almost four years, with letters going back and forth, the Japanese Unitarian leaders could not but wonder why Boston did not trust them. Japanese leaders remained polite and patient, yet it was a cancer that would eventually become acute. The property issue would be one of the items that a commissioner would be sent in 1919 to solve once and for all.

Unitarian Ideals or Duplicity?

MacCauley had been sent by the AUA to reestablish the Japan Unitarian Mission in 1909 as a Liberal Christian organization, renaming it as such. Boston asserted its might against the interfaith, ethical culture it feared had evolved after turning over everything to Japanese Unitarians in 1900. As we already know, MacCauley fired SAJI and tried to make order at Unity Hall in 1909.

HIROI Tatsutarō, who had been SAJI's assistant minister, resigned from Unity Hall and joined SAJI in January, 1910. Together, they formed a new *Yuniterian* church, movement and publication – but it survived little over a year. HIROI was the first to make a public criticism of MacCauley and the AUA's duplicity in gifting Unity Hall, having claimed Japanese Unitarianism was unique and independent of foreign control, and then resorting to dollar control of the mission. Others had just left silently. HIROI pointed out the American Unitarian Mission's duplicity at a time when America was being accused of racism against Japanese and Chinese in California. MacCauley reported this controversy to Boston, but it was not told to American Unitarians in their publications.

MacCauley sent to Boston a detailed summary of Hiroi's accusations:

> Our [Japanese Unitarianism's] declaration of principles has been known for 20 years. Mr. MacCauley knows it, and long ago he recognized it; and he encouraged it in the tract I have read before you. And look at this pulpit! Mr. MacCauley designed it. In its outer shape it has a torii, and within its frame are two crosses and three lotus petals. It shows already that [the] J[apan] U[nitarian] A[ssociation] is the full expression of Shinto, Buddhism and Christianity. ...
>
> It is [a] fact that J[apanese] U[nitarianism] is near to Christianity. Its affairs are mostly more or less connected with Christianity. But, in accordance with its principles, we can not now

say it is part of Christianity.

It is above Christianity, above Buddhism. J.U. is the name given to the foregoing, all inclusive principles. It includes all [the] different religious sects. Therefore in its substantial, or formal principles and in its faiths, its members are free. There is no pope, no presbyter, no bishop to interfere in the faiths of its members. Unitarianism is not a part of Christianity, but Christianity is part of Unitarianism. If anyone asks me then "What are you?" I answer "I am a Unitarian." There may be Christian Unitarians, Buddhist U., and Confucian U. The proposal to make Unitarianism a Christian denomination, I utterly reject. Today this is an obsolete thought.

... Gentlemen: I am indeed very, very sorry to see Mr. MacCauley who is the pioneer of our Unitarian movement, trying by his lecture, in this 42nd year of Meiji (1909) to go back to the thinking of the past century, and declare that "Unitarianism is historically Christian." Japanese Unitarianism is Unitarianism only, and not a Christian denomination. ...

Though low in virtue and shallow in learning, yet in my heart I believe there is a speck of conscience. I shall not please myself by discounting my faith and forfeiting my principles in order to receive foreign money. I offer you these words as my farewell.[266]

MacCauley had conveyed HIROI's criticism to Boston, but his *ad hominem* response was brief and condescending:

Unfortunately, there is much in Mr. Hiroi' s history that weakens the force of this address. It can not be accepted as a wholly sincere affect. But it is *interesting as a symptom* of how things can go in this country. Of course it largely misrepresents my positions, as the reader of my address, here criticized, will see.[267]

Something had happened at Unity Hall that Boston and MacCauley did not comprehend. They renamed the Japan Unitarian Association (which only an authoritarian episcopal system could legally do) as Liberal Christian. However, as HIROI articulated, Japanese Unitarianism had evolved into something more than Christianity. Its inclusiveness reached toward the goal of universality

---

266. Ltr. from Clay MacCauley to Charles Wendte and Samuel Atkins Eliot, dated January 22,1910.

267. *Ibid. Emphasis mine.* I am indebted to Prof. Mohr for locating this letter.

– unity of all spiritual paths in their diversity.

ABE and the JUA Board meekly allowed MacCauley to rename the Association and just ignored it. IMAOKA would keep HIROI's insights alive to the end of his life. He became a committed universalist, seeking truths in every religious path.

More Than a Dissident's Problem

Perhaps Japanese Unitarian leaders were polite to a fault about the gift of Unity Hall and the duplicity about leaving Japan and then returning to assert control over JUA's beliefs, practice and structure. Yet, there was a more serious problem that had only been voiced by those who broke entirely with Unitarianism. It involved a potential contradiction of the mission's ideal of equality of religions and races – or put another way, *native inferiority.* The issue of superiority had been there after Knapp, the *free religionist* and cultural egalitarian, left in 1891. New Englanders had come to Japan with mild to strong attitudes of educational, religious and even racial superiority. Japanese leaders with a samurai heritage and superior educations seemed to feel arrogance the quickest. Both Japanese Unitarian members and sympathizers, who participated in educational and religious programs in Boston, almost universally sensed it. Since the Japan Unitarian Association's leadership was mostly professors, they received dual invitations to Boston from Harvard and the AUA, often to participate in the annual May General Assembly. Troubled Japanese returned having felt condescension, a feeling that they were somehow unequal at the AUA, but surprisingly not so at Harvard. ANESAKI, the accredited father of the scientific study of religion in Japan, had distanced himself from religionists who treated Japanese as inferiors. But he was just a sympathizer. Major Japanese Unitarian leaders suffered Bostonian superiority but remained loyal – ABE, KISHIMOTO, MURAI, and IMAOKA. HIRAI, the former Zen priest and Buddhist Unitarian, was the first to leave Japanese Unitarianism after visiting Boston. HIROI, the Methodist Unitarian, found this malignancy also in Japan with the beloved MacCauley.

These issues of working with American Unitarians were not new, but they simmered under the radar to be personified in a new director of the Mission who arrived in 1919.

IMAOKA's Work with MacCauley

IMAOKA's role as the dual secretary would span the third and fourth periods of the Mission. MacCauley needed help keeping his schedule, arranging transportation, and having a translator or arranging for someone to translate. IMAOKA confirmed that MacCauley was not fluent in spoken Japanese and could not read Japanese. Only a single letter remains to demonstrate this aspect of IMAOKA's duties. On Sep. 24, 1919, he wrote to MacCauley asking for permission not to personally take care of him while he attended a memorial service, having made all the necessary arrangements:

> Dear Dr. MacCauley:
>
> I am very sorry to ask you to allow me to go to Sendai tonight for attending the memorial service held there in the honor all the late Hon. Oyama, M.P. and a member of our Association. I am asked to go so unexpectedly that I have no time to see you and ask your allowance. I'm going to take the place of some speakers who became suddenly impossible to participate in the meeting on account of circumstances beyond control. I will be back by next Saturday.
>
> I wrote to Baron Kanda in your name that you are taking Dr. Van Ness to the meeting of the English Speaking Society and ask him to make effort to attend.
>
> I arranged a moto-car to meet you at the Shimbashi Station Saturday morning at 9 o'clock. I gave your name to the car-man. I ask Takahashi, our clerk, to meet you at Shimbashi Station at the same time to help you.
>
> We decided to hold a reception for Dr. Lars Van Ness in our Hall the next Sunday at 4:00 p.m.
>
> I sent out already invitation letters for the dinner in the Monday evening in your name to Profs. Abe, Uchigasaki,

Kishimoto and Mr. Suzuki, most of whom I am sure will come.

Will you please give the cheque for the September account to Takahashi our clerk when he will tomorrow take this letter to you. The cheque should be, as usual, payable to Imaoka on order.

As to the interview with Marquis Okuma, he is sure to have a professor of the University interpret. So I am told by the Steward of the Marquis.

Yours very truly,

N. Imaoka

P.S. I ask Dr. Van Ness to speak on the subject "The Religious Situation in America after the War" or something like that.

The Arrival of Yet Another AUA Commissioner

MacCauley had only himself to blame for Boston sending another commissioner to inspect the Mission. He had begun complaining in 1917 about his age as he became 74, his recurring illnesses and depressions, and his fear of not having any savings for retirement. His monthly, handwritten letters to Eliot (AUA President) seldom were less than 10 barely legible pages. Eliot worked hard to find useful items to extract and place in *The Christian Register*. MacCauley continued to pester him in each letter about putting the Unity Hall property back into the hands of the Japanese Unitarian Association. It had also become a concern for Japanese Unitarians as other missions turned over property and administration of funding to their *native* boards, while the American Unitarians with all their preachment of a unique mission run totally by Japanese had not.

MacCauley had left for the summer of 1917 to recover from a recurring malaise on the Big Island of the Territory of Hawaii, now the center of the American military presence in the Pacific. Upon his return, MacCauley praised how extensive and even prestigious the Unitarian program continued to be. His complaints to Boston were the same year after year, but one paragraph in one of the many long, rambling, almost illegible, handwritten, private scribbles to Samuel

Eliot seemed to press a hot button – Oct. 4, 1919, to be exact.[268] He mentioned that there were new labor problems in Japan with SUZUKI Bunji, former secretary of the Mission (1911-1917), and his Yūaikai (the not yet legal labor union), with Unity Hall in the middle of everything. MacCauley was bragging about JUM's importance and American Unitarianism's great contribution to Japan's working classes. Elliot's assessment of the situation was the opposite of MacCauley's. The very mention of the labor situation being related to Unity Hall set off alarms at the AUA headquarters.

SUZUKI had visited Boston twice. Eliot and the AUA Board had the impression that he was an unsympathetic labor leader in the mold of the AFL president Samuel Gompers – possibly even a Bolshevik. MacCauley's mention of SUZUKI's leadership and renewed problems of labor touched a sensitive nerve. In Eliot's and Cornish's views, the Japanese worker movement was at best socialist and anti-capitalist. For them, SUZUKI was becoming a Bolshevik sympathizer like Albert Rhys Williams, the infamous Congregational minister and writer who had returned from Russia having even worked with Lenin.[269]

Eliot brought the matter to the Board immediately, and a representative was sought to send to Japan. Why the Rev. John Boynton Wilson Day was chosen remains puzzling as he had no qualifications except graduating from Harvard Divinity School, plus being a protégée of the secretary of the AUA, Louis Cornish. This relationship is evidenced by almost all correspondence going directly from Day to Cornish rather than to Eliot or Wendte (the AUA director of Foreign Affairs). Most of Day's letters asked that they be kept

268. MacCauley to Elliot, Oct. 4, 1919.

269. The Rev. Albert Rhys Williams (1883-1962) was a New England minister and activist in the Socialist Party. In 1914 he travelled to Europe and then to Russia, meeting Lenin, returning to the United States in 1918. By the end of 1919 he would have seven books praising socialism and communism. The AUA Board would have had anti-capitalist movements on their mind. The movie, Reds, featured John Reed with whom Williams was involved.

confidential and not seen by the full Board.

Day Arrived with Two Commissions

John B. W. Day arrived in Japan in the autumn of 1919, commissioned to investigate and solve any problem that the Mission might have. At least that was the way it was told to MacCauley and expressed in the AUA Board minutes published in *The Christian Register*. Later in justification of his effort, Day would describe dual marching orders – one public from the Board, another private from Louis C. Cornish, AUA Secretary. There was even a promise from Cornish that if Day was successful in "telling the Board what they wanted to know" that he (Day) could have a career appointment to Japan as the new director of the Mission.

IMAOKA and ABE, as secretary and president of JUA, met regularly with Day and attempted to help him understand the multifaceted programs at Unity Hall. They especially wanted him to know how the Friendly Society, Yūaikai, was the only "legal labor organization" in Japan, and how all Japanese Unitarians supported its efforts for economic justice and for peaceful solutions of workers' issues and concerns. Yūaikai was considered by Japanese Unitarianism their crowning achievement to date.

Rev. John Boynton Wilson Day

Day had been privately told to effect a complete and final divorce of Japanese Unitarians from SUZUKI and his Friendly Society. However, to do that Day needed to get MacCauley to resign as director of the Mission. Day played his commission like a poker hand, revealing one card at a time.

In reports to Boston, his veiled criticism of MacCauley grew from faint praise to contempt. At first he just criticized the "sweet old man" for his social schedule that had nothing to do with evangelism and conversions – which Day saw as the task of a real missionary. All MacCauley's honors – his leadership positions in almost every international organization in Tokyo to his two Imperial awards – were interpreted by Day as time wasted; time away from administering the mission and not increasing membership or building churches. His private reports to Cornish became increasingly sarcastic, so much so that Cornish warned him that something positive was needed in them for him to share with the AUA board for its published reports.[270]

One such letter illustrates Day's relationship to MacCauley and JUA members:

> This Hegelian philosophy, of being rather than doing, which this gang have imbibed with such avidity from Dr. MacCauley is the curse of the whole business. If instead of being "the foremost exponent of western civilization to this great empire," in other words, if instead of being a lamp post, as his memorial lantern erected in front of this building describes him to be, our reverend friend had taken to consuming a little oxygen, matters would not be in such shape. Such shape?
>
> I am wrong. Before you can have shape there must be something to be shaped. You think I am showing feeling? Well, had you had "the foremost exponent etc etc" said to you every day of your stay in this country, you would feel, not only like flinging your typewriter at his head but of inviting him to commit harri kari [*sic*.]. But do not be alarmed. I am sitting "like patience on a monument." I do not show him my feelings.[271]

After almost a year Day returned to report personally to the AUA Board. Upon his return to Boston in December, 1920, and with help from Cornish, he presented a program he had created. In his extant twelve page report to the AUA Board, Day concluded that the

---

270. The letters are well preserved in the AUA archive at Harvard.

271. Ltr. Day to Cornish, January 25, 1920. AUA Archives bMS 520/50. Mohr brought this letter to my attention.

"work is tremendously worth doing."[272] He presented a plan to fix whatever was wrong, especially separating Japanese Unitarianism from laborers and their movement that was centered in Unity Hall. He would refocus the mission on students and educators, moving everything away from the industrial quarter to Kanda-ku, the university district.

Day was rewarded with what already seemed to have been promised in the private communications with Cornish if his findings pleased the Board. And they did. That prize was a five-year appointment as the director of the Japan Liberal Christian Mission with the possibility of a lifetime appointment. News of this reached Japan via a mailed copy of *The Register* before Day returned, including a promise of a tripling of the annual appropriation for Day's missionary plan, together with doubling the salary of its new director.

By the time Day returned, MacCauley had finally left Japan for good. Despite all his neuroses, MacCauley was deeply respected, even admired, by his Japanese colleagues. Though he had returned as director of the "independent mission," he did not direct. He protected them from Boston's constant inquiries, but not from the constant burden of American visits. His Imperial awards were a defense against the pendular swings of the politics toward militarism and fascism. MacCauley had become a fieldworker simply by not being a missionary. Despite his need for recognition and his infirmities, MacCauley was deeply respected and loved. It did not go unobserved that he had been forced to resign by someone who neither understood or respected Japanese Unitarianism. Upon their return, Mr. and Mrs. Day were not met at the dock, and Cornish would angrily scold ABE, the Japan Association's president, for this discourtesy.

---

272. Report: Day, John B. W. sent to the Members of the Board of Directors, dated December 14, 1920. AUA Archives bMS 520/50. Mohr called my attention to this report.

Day's first visit had forced MacCauley into resigning from the Mission, moving him out of his apartment in Unity Hall to Yokohama and then to America. Now Day could reshape the Mission according to his own plan. Day stopped publication of *Rikugō Zasshi* (*Cosmos*) after its 481st issue on the grounds that it was socialist and not Christian – but also that it was not economical. *Cosmos* had been considered "the best and most influential religious journal" in Japan, the most "universal" and academic in the opinions of IMAOKA and ABE.

Next, Day moved against the social work programs connected to Yūaikai and SUZUKI.

Contradictory Projects: More Misunderstandings

Day had arrived back in Japan during the 1921 visit of Prof. Caroline Furness of Vassar, who was researching Japanese social work. The Mission had been instructed by Eliot to help her, which fell on the shoulders of IMAOKA. In return she sought to teach Japanese Unitarians how to do social work. Her accounts of her work in Japan were published regularly in *The Register*. One article mentioned Mrs. IMAOKA as a national leader of the women's movement in Japan. It is invaluable as the only contemporary account of Mrs. IMAOKA in English.[273]

Prof. Furness indirectly revealed that, in a farewell meeting with ABE, UCHIGASAKI and IMAOKA, she learned there were twenty plus Japanese publications concerning social work.[274] The dinner was arranged by IMAOKA to try again to help her understand how developed Japanese social work programs were. Her reports missed everything that was being done by Unitarians at Unity Hall, and her

---

273. Caroline Furness, "Some Japanese Unitarian Friends: Personal Impressions of their homes and children, their good works and spiritual outlook, their candor about the Government – The opportunity to co-operate," *Christian Register,* April 4, 1921, pp. 344ff. IMAOKA Utayo merits major research and recognition.

274. *Ibid.*, p. 346.

recommendations were shallow, in view of what had been accomplished there. Her lack of understanding is mentioned only to show how difficult it was for foreigners like Day and Furness to comprehend what was happening even when both had the full help of IMAOKA as translator, guide and teacher, and authorities like ABE and KISHIMOTO as instructors.

IN THE HOUSEHOLD OF A WELL-KNOWN UNITARIAN FAMILY

STANDING, from left to right—two maids; clerk of the lodging-house; Women's University girl; two ladies from Hawaii, friends of Miss Smith's; Mrs. Imaoka; Miss C. L. Smith; two maids.

SEATED, from left to right—Great-grandmother of children; Ken-ichiro, son of Mr. and Mrs. Imaoka; younger brother of the great-grandmother; Yoshiko, daughter of Mr. and Mrs. Imaoka; and Mr. Imaoka.

After Day forced MacCauley into resigning and attempted to force SUZUKI and Yūaikai from Unity Hall, Day was shunned by JUA members, including IMAOKA. Both Day and Furness tended to see what they had already concluded – that Japanese were still students and Westerners were in Japan to teach or lead. When Day moved against the very social work programs recommended by Furness, a red line was crossed. Japan Unitarian Association's symbiotic relationships with Yūaikai and the workers' movement were seen as an essential *yuniterian* activity and involvement.

There was supreme irony in Boston's aiding contradictory goals: Furness seeking to promote social concern for the working class and Day commissioned to end Japanese Unitarian sponsorship of social programs for their labor movement. Day had also been directed to sell Unity Hall which was in the workers' district of Mita, to distance Unitarianism from the labor movement that Boston knew was Bolshevik or at least socialist, and to move to the Kanda district where the great universities were. The new Mission program would focus exclusively on students, education, and missionary work – evangelism, conversions and building churches.

The Sale of Unity Hall

Day negotiated, failed, ordered, and failed again to have the Japan Liberal Christian Association's board, JUA, make the break with Yūaikai. IMAOKA informed Day that they would not order SUZUKI and the Yūaikai from its offices in Unity Hall or stop its meetings in its large assembly hall. When Day attempted locking them out of the building and started a lawsuit, reports hit the Japanese press and anti-American and anti-foreign feelings boiled over.

On the last day of 1921, IMAOKA resigned as Secretary of the Mission. He remained the secretary of JUA with ABE its president. None of the members of the Japan Liberal Christian Association (that is, the Japan Unitarian Association) would help Day, either as his secretary to replace IMAOKA or his interpreter to hire a new secretary. Cornish wrote ABE, President of the Japan Liberal Christian Association, a stern warning that the AUA would not countenance such behavior to their representative. Threats from Boston were simply ignored.

As 1922 began, Day advertised in the public press and hired a secretary who would last for nearly two months. A "Dr. OYABE" appeared and was hired without being vetted by anyone except Day. OYABE Zen'ichirō was a political arch-conservative, defrocked Congregational minister turned instant Unitarian, who remained employed by Japanese military intelligence. The best one can say was that he was an opportunist.[275] Together, OYABE and Day began the task of denying Yūaikai any use of Unity Hall. Tragically that included Japanese Unitarians, whom Day in his correspondence with Cornish now referred to as "the Japs" who opposed him. Coined in California as a racist slur, Day did not use the term accidentally.

On March 26, 1922, Unity Hall was filled with members of the "Liberal Christian Association of Japan" (title used in the letter to Boston). Both Day and OYABE were denied access as they were not members of the JUA. After long and careful discussion, it was *unanimously* adopted that the American Unitarian Association be asked to close its Mission in Japan as soon as possible and have no foreign representative in Japan. IMAOKA, as secretary of the Japan Liberal Christian Association, composed the letter in English to Eliot and the Board. The extremely polite letter was signed by the Japanese Board comprised of some of Japan's leading educators (ABE, KISHIMOTO, MURAI, UCHIGASAKI, IMAOKA, etc.).[276] ABE, as president of the Association, signed first, IMAOKA last.

What Japanese Unitarians did not see coming was Boston's retaliation. Day was instructed by Eliot and the Board to sell Unity Hall and not give Japanese Unitarians any of the proceeds to buy or rent a replacement. Suddenly being locked out of Unity Hall would have unforeseen consequences for both sides.

Boston's procrastination about meeting the requirements of Japanese real estate law concerning foreign ownership would cost the

---

275. OYABE Zeri'ichiro, *A Japanese Robinson Crusoe (*Honolulu: University of Hawai'i Press, 2009

276. Isoo Abe to the AUA President, dated March 31, 1922. A copy is also filed in AUA Archives bMS 520/50.

American Unitarian Association in both time and money. The legal fees to prevent Unity Hall's use by Yūaikai and Japanese Unitarians were never revealed. They had to be substantial as the process to have the right to sell the property took two years. Day could not complete the sale and returned to Boston becoming a paid member of the AUA staff with a commendation from the Board, written by Cornish, for his successful work in Japan.

The AUA worked through their foreign realtor who struggled to complete the sale of Unity Hall. A Mr. Struthers of Frazar Trust Company, Ltd., was hired. However, Boston's lack of cooperation with MacCauley in arranging a current Japanese surrogate to hold the property for Boston or creating a *zaidan* to allow Japanese Unitarians to own Unity Hall themselves prevented any sale. The property was in danger of reverting to the State.

In March 1923, a year later, Cornish sent a letter to ABE in which he reiterated his strong wish, "We hope that the transaction can be completed without further delay, and that if our agents, the Frazar Trust Company, Ltd., need any assistance from members of your Association, that they will render it to the company."

Day had completed only part of his commission, preventing the Unitarian good name from being besmirched by sponsoring or being affiliated with a labor organization in Japan. Unity Hall had been closed. But, this left Japanese Unitarianism without a building, and more importantly, without the will to exist as Unitarians. They lost both Unity Hall in Mita and the rented Music School hall in Kanda. The two Japanese churches closed as the tiny American appropriation had paid taxes and insurance in Mita and possibly some expenses for UCHIGASAKI's independent Unitarian fellowship at the Music Hall in Kanda.

Exactly when Unity Hall was sold is unknown.[277] It would not be until 1931 that it finally found stable ownership. ABE Isō

277. Mohr speculated that the property was first sold in 1923.

described the fate of their building in the February 1931 issue of the journal *Rodo* (Labor). He reflected on his feelings about the decade-long process:

> I was really disappointed. ... it ... pass[ed] into the hands of a real estate broker, there was nothing we could do. Having no choice, we gave up all hope. Later on, the owner kept changing, ... eventually the General Federation of Labor was able to acquire it.[278] [Ironically, Yuaikai had evolved into the Federation, by then Japan's strongest labor union, reunited with its old home.]

The money, if any survived the process, went to Boston. The Hayward Fund for Missions, having been designated for Unitarian missions in India and then in Japan and then again for Wendte's international mission work, disappeared as a separate listing in the AUA's public accounting records.

The Great Earthquake

The Great Kantō Earthquake of September 1, 1923, would be a factor in the final dissolution of the Japanese Unitarian movement. Few could make it to the liberal religious fellowship that attempted to continue at UCHIGASAKI's home. And that ceased after the earthquake. The building, Unity Hall, was spared devastation in 1923 but later was completely destroyed during the firebombing of Tokyo in World War II.

IMAOKA reminisced that Japanese Unitarians (or were they now just "Liberal Christians"?) moved into society to become the invisible leaven liberalizing all the fields – education, banking, politics, literature, religion, etc. But, his gentle words and forgiving soul hid a wrong that even Samuel Eliot could not quite put out of his mind. Eliot's handwritten reflection of either 1926 or possibly 1931 – "An Unexpected Call and a Broken Connection" – mentioned no lessons learned, just regret. Eliot still struggled with an unacknowledged fear that great harm had been done by American

278. *Rodo (Labor) no. 236, February 1931, p. 6.* Cited by Mohr, *op. cit.*

Unitarians in Japan.[279]

A Sad Reflection

Until March 26, 1922, between 400 (the lowest figure) and 1,000 Japanese Unitarians regularly attended Unity Hall in Mita and the fellowship in the Kanda district. The habit of gathering in a Unitarian or Liberal Christian church led by Unitarian professor-preachers was likely to have survived had there been the will. Or, it could have evolved in other models like home fellowships. Although that was tried by UCHIGASAKI in his home, it only lasted for a few months beyond the Great Tokyo Earthquake of September 1923. There was no longer any desire to survive as Unitarians.

Yuniterian, as a word in Japanese, reverted to the foreignness of the English word "Unitarian" and would no longer be seen by Japanese as the philosophy of liberation and equality, with its openness to science and advanced learning, and its example of equality and unity. Its supposed higher ethical system was no longer experienced as an advance beyond Confucian ethics. This Unitarianism became associated with patronizing superiority. While its American representatives were attempting to be fieldworkers, its commissioners had often shown that they came to direct and not to confer. Unconsciously, American elitists had practiced a form of racial condescension that ranged from mild (Wendte) to medium (Cornish) to severe (Day).

As a religious movement Japanese Unitarianism was broken, and even IMAOKA did not attempt to fix it. Yet, in gratitude, he would praise everything that he could ascribe as positive when he spoke of the American contribution decades later. He kept alive an inspiration that came from his college days at the Imperial University found in

279. Eliot wrote his reflection after finally acquiring Day's report that was only filed in the AUA archives in 1931. It now consists of several versions, one purporting to include the dictated report of MacCauley and another edited by Cornish. Issues about this document are addressed in Chapter 8 (see the first footnote).

Emerson and free religion.[280]

Leaven for the Nation

IMAOKA would say that they did not cease to exist but had become the invisible church, leaven for the entire society. SUZUKI was the father of the labor movement. ABE, and most other Japanese Unitarians, would champion Christian Socialism, internationalism, and Christian pacifism during decades of perpetual war. ANESAKI (a sympathizer) and IMAOKA would promote moral [religious] education and interfaith dialogue for national unity. SAJI and HARAI would lead Unitarian Buddhists in their attempts at uniting religion and culture. In politics, Japanese Unitarians would help found the Liberal, Socialist and Labor parties and enter national politics in the 1920s. Their Japanese magazine, *Rikugō Zasshi* (*Cosmos*), had vanished, but many continued as influential writers, journalists and publishers.

From 1922 until 1948, this liberal leaven would have to be found in the ideas taken into secular institutions.[281] IMAOKA followed his mentor, ANESAKI, into education.

IMAOKA's Spiritual Pilgrimage

One could argue that there was a firm grace in IMAOKA'S drafting of the polite letter to Boston. Japanese Unitarians had been wronged deeply and tragically. IMAOKA only discussed the episode when the author found the documents and asked him directly. He showed no anger and little interest in the topic. He seemed surprised that it had been discovered.

All evidence from this brief period points to a dynamic religious identity and practice as a rational mystic – practical, serving, working, teaching, writing. No religious change was noted; he was continuing *seiza* and living the principles or truths he had found.

---

280. This is a complicated topic is tackled in Chapter 12.

281. For a study from the viewpoint of intellectual history, see Michel Mohr, *Buddhism, Unitarianism, and the Meiji Competition for Universality* (Harvard University Press, 2014).

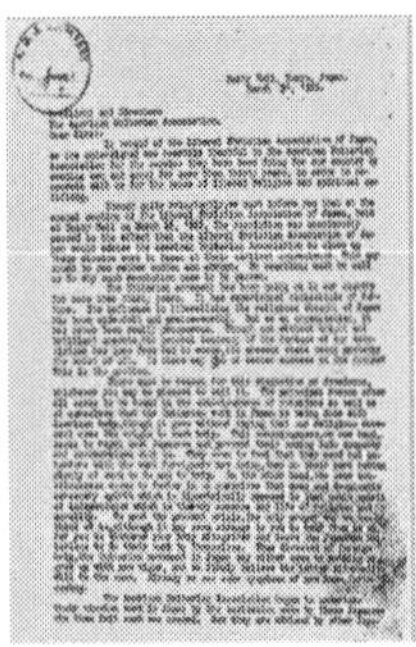

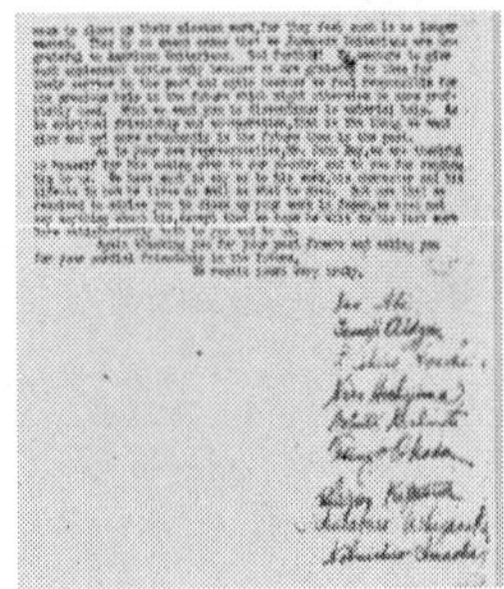

The March 26, 1922 letter used the AUA's own designation of the Japan Unitarian Association. They were unanimous in politely telling American Unitarians to go home. ***Nibuichiro Imaoka's signature is the last one.***

An Unexpected Call and a Broken Connection
By Samuel A. Eliot

How many of the readers of the Christian Register can remember, in these distressful days, the happy relations we once enjoyed with many broad-minded and gentle-mannered fellow-workers in Japan? The Unitarian Mission in Japan, whatever its untoward fate, deserves to have its story recorded. It influenced the thought of thousands of intelligent Japanese. It modified the methods of the older Christian missions and animated them with a new spirit. It broadened the horizons of many more or less provincial Unitarians and gave them, or some of them, a consciousness of their larger fellowships and responsibilities. It was exceptional in origin because it was undertaken at the invitation of the Japanese and not by the initiative of foreigners. It was unique in design because the Unitarian representatives were commissioned "not to convert but to confer". It proposed a procedure which did not concern itself with the defects in other systems of religion but with the discovery of their merits. It assumed

"Samuel Atkins Eliot II (August 24, 1862-October 15, 1950) was the first president of the American Unitarian Association (AUA) to be given executive power; he held this office from 1900 to 1927." *Dictionary of Unitarian & Universalist Biography.*

Dr. Eliot's "Broken Connection," written in longhand but never published.

SECTION FOUR: A LIFE OF ASSISTING OTHERS

Chapter 10
Assisting Prof. ANESAKI Masaharu

When IMAOKA returned to Tokyo in 1910, he joined his Kumi-ai colleagues and YMCA contacts as an editorial assistant at *Cosmos* (*Rikugō Zasshi*). He began *seiza* meditational practice at Tenkō-san's suggestion with OKADA Torajirō in a meditation room at Hongyji Buddhist temple.[282] As already mentioned, he was soon deeply involved at Unity Hall, volunteering and assisting in numerous ways there.

Within two years IMAOKA returned to his alma mater, the Imperial University of Tokyo, to begin graduate studies. Prof. ANESAKI not only welcomed him back but made him one of his unpaid assistants (*fukushu*), not in Buddhist studies, ANESAKI's specialization, but in the history and thought of Christianity.[283]

Prof. ANESAKI Masaharu (1873-1949)

This might seem a bit strange as ANESAKI was the rising star at

282. As mentioned previously, *seiza* was potentially transformational.

283. Mohr, "Missing Link" *op.cit.*: IMAOKA's former mentor ANESAKI Masaharu (1873–1949) took him on as an unpaid assistant (*fukushu*).

the Imperial University in Buddhist studies. He had been given the mantle of leadership in the academic study of religion by KISHIMOTO Nobuta (at that time called the "father of the comparative study of religion"). KISHIMOTO had moved into publishing at *Cosmos* and working toward the social and political transformation of Japan. ANESAKI would become known as the "father of the scientific study of religion" in Japan.[284] He had ventured briefly into comparative religion with an American researcher in the midst of his Buddhist studies, finding parallels in Buddhist and Christian narratives in their respective scriptures.[285] Eighty-eight parallel ideas in the "gospel" stories of the two faiths were found, although each was thought to be independent and not borrowed from the another. Such comparative study was abandoned, and ANESAKI returned to his quest to understand the historical Buddha. However, he had a peripheral interest in constructing a universal ethical system for Japan. And that is where his new graduate student fitted in.

ANESAKI's prodigious publications in Buddhist studies were coming to completion. Previously in the 1890s, his work led to a series of studies, all published in 1898: a translation of Eduard von Hartmann's *Religionsphilosophie* as *Shukyo Tetsugaku* ("*The Philosophy of Religion*") in 394 pages, *Hikaku Shukyo-gaku* ("*The Science of Comparative Religion*") in 344 pages, and *Indo Shukyoshi Ko* ("*A Study of the History of Indic Religion*") in 813 pages. In 1898, remember, he had lectured that autumn at the Japan Unitarian Mission's School of Advanced Learning on the psychology of religion.

Winning a government scholarship to study abroad at the turn of the century, ANESAKI worked with Paul Deussen on his translation

---

[284] See Mohr, *op. cit.* about their relationship.

[285] Albert J. Edmunds and Masahar [*sic.*] Anesaki, *Buddhist and Christian Gospels: Being Gospel Parallels from Pali Texts Now First Compared from the Originals* (Tōkyō: The Yūhōkwan Publishing House, [1905] 1909. 230+ pages.

of the *Bhagavad Gita,* read Sanskrit and Pali texts with Hermann Oldenberg, and completed his dissertation comparing Buddhist texts of the *Agamas* in Chinese with those in the Southern Canon in Pali. ANESAKI had read a "paper on the *Sagātha-vaggo* ... before the XIII International Congress of Orientalists at Hamburg but the research in detail could find no publisher."[286] That led to the comparative study with Edmunds in 1905. That same year, upon returning to Tokyo, he became a professor in the new program at Tokyo Imperial University in religious studies. IMAOKA attended his first classes as an undergraduate.

Parenthetically, while all his research in comparative religious methodology and the text critical studies of Buddhism was still going forward, ANESAKI had joined with his colleagues in the Unitarian movement in their application of religious values to a new Japanese society. As mentioned before, ANESAKI joined the Society for the Study of Socialism and almost every progressive endeavor undertaken by KISHIMOTO, ABE, MURAI, SAJI, HIRAI (a Zen priest and his former school teacher in Kyoto, also a New Buddhist) and others of the *yuniterian* network, or Unitarian movement.

Scholarly studies to date had found ANESAKI's involvement with Unitarians scant –ignoring these memberships or not cognizant of them. The claim is that ANESAKI distanced himself from Japanese *yuniterian*-ism. His use of a graduate student, so closely linked to the *yuniterian* movement, begs a fresh look at ANESAKI's involvement in general education, interfaith dialogue and another interpretation of his activities beyond exegetical studies of Buddhism. All this is pertinent to his relationship with and use of his graduate assistant, IMAOKA Shin'ichirō.

ANESAKI and Japanese Unitarians

When the Unitarian Mission's School for Higher Learning

286. Edmunds and ANESAKI, *ibid.,* p. xi.

(*Senshin Gakuin*) started teaching comparative religions, ANESAKI lectured in 1897 about Buddhism and another of his interests, the new discipline of psychology of religion. He was trying to answer the charge that religion was simply a human pathology, something to be outgrown. MacCauley bragged to Boston that ANESAKI was a sympathizer, almost a Unitarian.

ANESAKI joined ABE, KISHIMOTO and MURAI (the Dōshisha trio) in the socialist movement, the peace movement, and later in pursuit of national political office – and in almost every liberal movement that would modernize and liberate Japan.[287] The movements he joined were started at the Unitarian headquarters, Unity Hall. That is partly why the popular press had begun to use the word *yuniterian* for progressive or liberal ideas and activities.

In 1912 SUZUKI Bunji, the second dual Unitarian executive secretary and a graduate of the Imperial University's law school, would lead the *yuniterian* network into action in a new direction, justice for workers – the beginning of the labor movement. In fact, ANESAKI's name would appear again with the core group of professors at Unity Hall in their concern for labor justice. They were all slightly older than he but the fact that he joined them in all these progressive societies raises the question about his motives, agenda and level of exclusive commitment as an academic to Buddhist studies. He could be paraphrased as saying that because he was Japanese, he was engaged in Japanese society and its progress. Also, because he was Japanese, he wanted that society modernized and unified. He saw religion as its unifier. He could not remain isolated in an academic life of specializing in religion without searching for its applicability to Japan's needs.

---

287. Study Group of Religious Leaders, 1896; Society of Comparative Religion, 1896; plus peace and international movements, etc. These activities would later get ANESAKI on the police surveillance list (Mohr, *op. cit.*, pp. 131-2.).

Before returning to Japan from his studies in Europe, ANESAKI revealed his interest in transformative religious experience only to be sharply criticized by German philosopher of the Unconscious, Eduard von Hartmann.[288] Despite von Hartmann's warning, ANESAKI would not objectify religions and distance himself from religious experience and personal participation. He searched for a unifying essence in religion that would provide Japan with a moral foundation, one not exclusive to one religion but shared by all. His search would take him to Madras and interviews of Annie Besant, a leader in Theosophy who had been a speaker at the World's Parliament of Religions. Conversations and correspondence with William James, just before James' death, led ANESAKI to illustrate the healthy religious experience of Nichiren, immediately crediting William James for the inspiration of drawing scholars "toward men of original religious experience, with emphasis on the psychological point of view, disregarding doctrinal considerations."[289]

His interest in religious experience was emerging as early as 1905, when IMAOKA was attending his classes at Tōdai. ANESAKI published an article that year in the prestigious *Hibbert Journal: A Quarterly Review of Religion, Theology and Philosophy* on "How Christianity Appeals to a Japanese Buddhist." Yet, it did more than address how appealing Christianity might be to Japanese. He signaled a deep interest in finding something in religion that was *universal*, something that transformed life for the betterment of society and unified it. The article sounded themes he was becoming more interested in, a move from mere textual studies to something that would eventuate in the sociological study of Japanese religions – and in its usefulness for society as a whole. He compared the Buddha and

288. Tatsushi Narita, *Chronological Notes 1873-1949*. ONLINE: tatsushinarita.wordpress.com/masaharu-aesaki-chronology/

289. Masaharu Anesaki, *Nichiren, the Buddhist Prophet* (Cambridge: Harvard University Press, 1916), page v.

the Christ, finding a difference in personalities yet a unity in their embodiment of "religious consciousness." Each was a reformer of their own tradition, Hindu and Jewish, with "difference of tastes or modes of expression." "[A]t the fountain-heads of these two streams there appeared the Truth in flesh, the Faith in person, the realisation of this harmony of love and faith...," he would write for a Christian journal.[290]

In 1909 ANESAKI completed his *History of Japanese Religion.* During 1909-10 he contributed articles to the *Encyclopedia of Religion and Ethics* on Buddhist thought and ethics. Except for some later publications on Nichiren and Nichiren Buddhism, his works on primitive Buddhism (*konpon bukkyo*) and the historicity of the Buddha were complete. (He may even have sensed future criticism of his attempt to find the historical Buddha in a privileged set of Buddhist texts as flawed in method and scope. Be that as it may, he would take IMAOKA under his mentorship, not for methodological or textual agendas, but for Japanese religions' practical use for moral education.)

In 1911 ANESAKI completed a study of Imperial lineage tracing it to the "southern court" which was adopted as the official court history. (That gave him a privileged status, giving him some protection for his liberal social and political activities.) He published an article and a study of NICHIREN in 1916, as well as essays from his Japanese civilization course at Harvard.[291] IMAOKA could have helped edit these, but ANESAKI specifically assigned him work concerning his new interest in Christian thought and ethics.

---

290. M. Anesaki, "Impressions of Christianity from the Points of View of the Non-Christian Religions. II. How Christianity Appeals to a Japanese Buddhist," *The Hibbert Journal*, Vol. IV, no. 1, 1905, p. 10.

291. "*Nichiren: The Man Who Lived the Life of the "Lotus of Truth"* and *Nichiren, the Buddhist Prophet* (Harvard University Press, 1916), 167 pages (http://opensiuc.lib.siu.edu/cgi/viewcontent.cgi?article=3094&context=ocj)

Assisting ANESAKI's Quest for a Cultural Unifier

ANESAKI assigned IMAOKA to special research in Christianity, especially new developments in Europe. In 1912 ANESAKI asked him to translate two publications about Christian ethics and thought. This evidenced a shift in ANESAKI's interests in Buddhist textual studies to the practical use of religion for the advancement of Japanese culture and society. He had become focused on the unification of Japanese values and ethics through the scientific study of Japanese religions (Buddhism, Confucianism, Shinto and Christianity).

It may have been coincidental, but IMAOKA's wife, Utayo, had left Kobe to study Japanese literature at the Japan Women's University (*Nihon Joshidai*) with NARUSE Zinzo, a pioneer in higher education for women and a famous Christian leader. The two mentors, ANESAKI and NARUSE, and their two graduate students, Utayo and Shin'ichirō, would begin meeting in ANESAKI's home soon after IMAOKA's arrival in Tokyo. This would be the beginning of Association Concordia (*Kiitsu Kyōkai*).[292]

Rev. Dr. NARUSE Jinzō

ANESAKI would later proudly state that Association Concordia was the only organization at which he was there from the beginning. NARUSE Zinzō (1858-1919) was converted to Christianity by SAWAYAMA Paul (1852-1887). He studied at Andover Theological Seminary and the Univ. of Chicago, struggling with his religious beliefs. NARUSE returned to Japan in 1894. He and ASO Shozo co-authored *Women's Education:* to educate women (1) as human beings, (2) as

---

[292] Interview by author, June 20, 1985. In a talk to the National Conference of Free Religionists in Japan held in Tokyo in 1979 entitled "There is no Graduation from the University of Life," IMAOKA stated that SHIBUSAWA was the true founder of Association Concordia. "It is said generally that the Association Concordia was established by Masaharu ANESAKI, professor of Tokyo University, and Jinzo NARUSE, President of Nippon Women's College. But, this is not correct. ANESAKI and NARUSE took part in setting up the association as a result of earnest persuasion by SHIBUSAWA." That view recognized the crucial importance of SHIBUSAWA's financial support, no matter who began the early discussion of the project.

individuals, and (3) as Japanese. He founded Japan Women's College in 1901 with 510 students and 53 faculty and staff, with its first graduates in 1904. In 1912 he travelled abroad to gain support of his women's university and for Association Concordia. He became a member of government advisory Board on Education.

Association Concordia's founders – with Anesaki, Naruse and Shibusawa.

NARUSE and ANESAKI met with SHIBUSAWA Eiichi (often called "father of Japanese capitalism"), one of the most successful industrialists and bankers in Japan. They issued an invitation in April 1912 for a preliminary set of meetings. The initial group of eight at the first planning meeting were SHIBUSAWA Eiichi (banker, ship builder, and more than 500 business ventures), NARUSE Zinzō (educator), ANESAKI Masaharu (educator), INOUE Tetsujirō (educator), NAKAJIMA Rikizō (educator), UKITA Kazutami (political scientist), UEDA Bin (writer), and Sidney L. Gulick (missionary, educator).

By June 1912, Association Concordia was formally inaugurated. The first article in its prospectus stated:

> The aim of The Association, set in the light of the general tendency in the world towards a concord (kiitsu) in the inner spiritual world, is to undertake research on it, support it, and by forming a sound ideology, thus contribute to the

civilization of the country.[293]

The Concordia movement was not just for Japan but it was also for a changed world. The prospectus continued:

> The Association proposes to bring together leaders of different disciplines, build upon research and cultivation of the minds, and plan a spiritual unification within the country first. And by gradually rallying like-minded people from foreign countries, The Association wishes to lay the foundation for a collective spirit for future civilizations. [*quotation from p.5*]

The organization's initial purpose stated "there is a necessity for contemporary civilizations to illuminate a fundamental oneness, especially among the ideals of different religious faiths." [KENJO, *op. cit.,* p. 4.] They proposed to research, support and form a sound ideology "in the light of the general tendency in the world towards a concord (*kiitsu*) in the inner spiritual world." [*Ibid.*, p. 4] They would meet each month on four issues: 1) Matters of Religious Faith; 2) Customs and Mores; 3) Social, Economic and Political Matters (seen from a spiritual angle); 4) International and Humanitarian Issues.[294] By 1915 they had more than 130 members representing the religions of Japan (Buddhist, Shinto, Confucian, and Christian).

The contention that morality was based upon religion put it in conflict with the ideologists of the State Shinto movement that taught that State Shinto (*Kokka Shinto*) was not a religion but the national morality and ideology of Japan, its national consciousness or essence.[295] When a Manifesto was published in 1916, the Minister of Education attacked the Manifesto and the Association as being in violation of "the state's policy to segregate religion and education" – yet Association Concordia survived. The Manifesto stated:

293. KENJO Teiji, "On Religion and Morality: Shibusawa Ei'ichi's Writings in connection with Kiitsu Association ("The Association Concordia"), p. 4 and from p. 5.

294. KENJO, *ibid.*, p. 5.

295. George Williams, *Shinto* (Philadelphia: Chelsea House Publishers, 2005). See also Mohr, *Universality,* op. cit.

1. We ought to respect the personal characters of both others and ourselves, and thus reinforce the foundation of national morality;

2. We ought to nurture the spirit of the Public domain and thus accomplish the true aim of the Constitution;

3. We ought to encourage voluntary action, while at the same time, pave the way for a development of organizational collaborations;

4. We ought to reform academics, raise the efficacy of education and bring forth genius in all fields;

5. Alongside encouraging fundamental research in science, we ought to place an unshakeable belief at its base and plan for the upliftment of spiritual culture;

6. We ought to respect morality among nations, protect world peace and thus boost the noble cause of nation-building.[296]

What had begun with eight founders in 1912 had grown to seventy-seven named members in 1913 and one hundred thirteen in 1914. Besides its founders of SHIBUSAWA, ANESAKI and NARUSE, there were gathered an extraordinary range of leaders from education, business, government, military, media, and the religious missions. The Unitarian and Universalist missions as well as the *yuniterian* network were participants. Educators from Tōdai, Keiō, Waseda, as well as lesser colleges and universities, were joined by two generals and six admirals, newspaper publishers, diplomats, bankers and religionists from all of Japan's faiths. They came monthly to find and form a "concord (*kiitsu*) in the inner spiritual world." (It is no surprise later that IMAOKA could call upon these influencers of society when he served Unity Hall as its secretary and later at Seisoku Academy as its principal.)

ANESAKI would set the example for the calibre of inquiries that the Association expected. He published *Le Sentiment religieux chez les japonais* (The Religious Sentiment of the Japanese) in the annual report of 1913. This would be followed in 1914 in the Second Report by careful studies of Buddhist doctrine

296. *Ibid.*, p. 6-7.

("The Fundamental Character of Buddhism and its Branches" by Prof. ANESAKI) and Confucian ethics ("Ju-ism and Confucianism" by Prof. HATTORI). These scholarly studies were remarkable in their own right, applying a level of text and form criticism seldom witnessed by non-specialists. Their work presupposed that no particular religion was absolute, each having its own historic construction. Yet, there was the meta-philosophical commitment to the goal of finding a unity or concord in all of Japan's religions (Shinto, Buddhist, Confucian, Christian) that would provide a unified morality or universal ethics for modern Japan.

A short article in the *1914 Second Report* by G. T. Ladd concerning "American Critics on Japan" mentioned aspects of Japanese society needing moral improvement. However, an American was actually speaking about a cultural hypocrisy of his own country. He organized his paper in three sections: (1) disillusionment after finding American "deficiencies, faults, and social, political and more private vices … more accentuated and pervasive"; (2) race-prejudice with its accompaniment of race-conceit (which would soon become full-blown in California: "drive the Mongolian race from America!" was its slogan); and (3) unfair commercial practices. Ladd concluded: "Of the three, the last is the most potent and the most, ethically considered, disgraceful." Ladd had made the unequal treaties and commercial agreements forced upon Japan a moral issue to be discussed by the international Concordia movement.[297] (Almost a decade before the Rev. John Day brought an end to Japanese Unitarianism, Day's behavior of "race-prejudice...with its accompaniment of race-conceit" had been contextualized by Ladd. See chapter 9.)

The notion that a "unifying morality" could be taught in public schools was in direct conflict with the claim of State Shinto that only its ideology and moral code would and could be taught. The political importance of Association Concordia was realized as

---

297. *Second Report of Association Concordia, 1914.*

their members began to be elected to national office over the next two decades. (Note the overlap of members of Association Concordia and the *yuniterian* movement.) The dream of Japan leading the world to international peace would be countered by militarist and nationalist intimidation, special police surveillance, and assassination. The 1920s was the high-water mark of Japanese liberalism (*yuniterian-ism*); and then memory of it faded.

Translating Campbell and Eucken

It was the need for solid research and major papers on Western Christianity that ANESAKI had assigned IMAOKA the task of translating two books: first R. J. Campbell's *New Theology* and then Rudolf Eucken's *Current Thoughts and Modern Ethics.* He had IMAOKA begin with Campbell in 1912 during the beginning phase of the Concordia movement. But the book was too long, some 783 pages, and IMAOKA was still working on it when ANESAKI came back from meeting Eucken at Harvard, where he lectured in 1913. Eucken and Adolph von Harnack were among the first Europeans to join the Association Concordia movement in Europe. ANESAKI wanted Eucken's ethics to be available on the problems in ethics and education.

IMAOKA was already participating in a study group at Unity Hall on Eucken and Bergson led by MINAMI, OKATA and himself.[298] MINAMI would be credited with introducing Eucken to Japan. IMAOKA would finish translating Eucken's *Current Thoughts and Modern Ethics*; it was published in 1914.[299]

---

298. MacCauley to AUA. 1912. MacCauley was probably incorrect in crediting OKADA as one of the team of teachers along with MINAMI and IMAOKA. IMAOKA had arranged for OKADA to teach *seiza* but it was unlikely that OKADA had studied Eucken or Bergson. It would not be long before KISHIMOTO and others would become enthusiastic practicers of *seiza*. See also, Mohr, *op. cit.*, p. 103ff.

299. Rudolf Eucken (1846–1926): Oikken *オイッケン, Gendai shisō to rinri mondai 現代思想と倫理問題* [Contemporary thought and ethical issues], translated by IMAOKA Shin'ichirō 今岡信一良. Kindai shichō sōsho 近代思潮叢書, 第2編, Tokyo: Keiseisha shoten, 1914.

Eucken had won the Nobel Prize in Literature in 1908, and his life work had a singular focus, the spiritual life. It was not based on one particular religion but on something higher than any historic manifestation of religion in a given age or era. Such a view did not have the usual Western conceits. European theologians and philosophers, following Kant and Hegel, had seen Western civilization and liberal Christianity as the highest form of human evolution – a view not acceptable for those who joined Concordia's quest. The "national essence" mentioned in the Imperial Prescript on Education demanded an independent essence of something higher than any religion, even Christianity.[300] (State Shinto challenged this Western claim with Japan's "national essence" as superior.)

An Aristotle specialist, Eucken reasoned without use of special revelation, without privileging any literature or scripture, without miracles or the supernatural. He had not reduced life to naturalism's sensate world nor to determinism's fatalism or to a causality lacking agency or free will. He had found in the universal human desire for something better and higher – the very essence of the life of the spirit. Eucken used what he called the *noological method* (*noologische Methode*), an analysis of the mind or spirit that takes the whole of reality into one's true self, not the small self of the senses, but that something more or greater that anyone may hear and respond to.

> We human beings must realise a higher life within given natural conditions; and to do this, we have first to create and establish a new order of things within our own sphere of existence. This transforms our life into a never ending task, but also imparts to it an incomparable greatness. While thus striving forward, the individual must first of all submerge himself in the new world as a whole, until he finds there his true life, his real and higher self. A complete negation of the little *Ego* and emancipation from it are requisite. This does not mean that the

300. "National essence" of the Japanese nation (*kokutai, kokkyō*).

> individual is to disappear and be absorbed by the infinite. The infinite becomes a living present at this special point, and the individual must take possession of it and assert it. He must also promote the forward movement of life, and must enrich reality by the culture of a spiritual individuality, very different from the one nature has given him. This spiritual individuality can only develop on the basis of the spiritual life, from which it takes its aims and standards; and it must always be in harmony with the movement of the whole.[301]

Eucken grounded the individual's apprehension of "the life of the spirit" in the particular history and culture they had been born into. No other person's apprehension or age's wisdom were enough. One was given (and that was "grace") the innate nature to apprehend the inner spirit of something higher than the senses and the *freedom* to decide to strive for one's own spiritual self.

> We may call the morality arising thence the Ethics of the Spiritual Life, for the centre of life and its ruling motive lie in man's relation to a superior spiritual life, which is at the root of his own being and yet has to be acquired by his own action and effort. Morality represents the principles underlying this great change. Morality grasps the question as a whole. Morality elucidates the fact that all the variety of work is dominated by strife for a spiritual self, a strife which can only be successful if the original situation is reversed.[302]

Eucken argued that each individual has the potential and the freedom *to make their life human* by transcending ordinary sense pleasure and self-interest. By doing so, by exercising one's freedom and independence from nature, from the reality of sensed experience, one could strive towards the good, the beautiful, and the true.

> These are problems which do not originate in ourselves, but which are forced upon us by the movement of history. Their very necessity bids us hope for progression, in spite of all

---

301. Rudolf Eucken, *Current Thoughts and Modern Ethics,* p. 40 (English translation by Margaret von Seydewitz).

302. *Ibid.*, p. 41.

> impediments. The power which has imposed these problems on us will enable us to solve them. But we shall also need to put forth our uttermost strength, and to quicken all our latent spiritual forces; we must grasp our life as a whole, must acknowledge its high aims with all our heart and soul, and must find our real self in these ideals. Only thus can we gain the sense of inner necessity which alone can lead us onward.[303]

Eucken then makes the connection of our possibility to strive for a spiritual life with the moral imperative to do so.

> In this manner, our aspiration becomes closely linked to morality. Let us see wherein we have already recognised the quintessence of morality. Life and aspiration are detached from the little Ego, and take root in a spiritual world in which we find our own essential being, so that while working for this spiritual world, we are at the same time working for our own depth and spiritual self-preservation. Such a change and reaction, such identification with the movement of the spiritual life, means only that our aspiration has gained a moral character. This moral character brings us, at all points, into touch with our time. By means of our own aspiration, we can now grasp, unite, and deepen all the goodwill, genuine feeling, and untiring activity of our day, which was hitherto inadequate only because it lacked inner unity and quickening spiritual power.[304]

Eucken's natural revelation emerging from the natural order, without miracles or any form of supernaturalism, pointed the "soul" to a universal "God" that is *the something higher* in all religions and the ground of all morality – good, beauty, and truth. His ethical system required human freedom, both for moral agency (freedom of choice) and moral responsibility. Eucken provided a way to avoid a mechanistic life causally determined by sensate reality and its resulting environment. He argued against the notion of an autocratic god. His was an argument against anthropomorphism and theism. Yet, it seemed universal enough to include Eastern thought and

---

303. *Ibid.* p. 125.
304. *Ibid.*, pp. 125-6.

religion.

While translating Eucken into Japanese would seem a major achievement, IMAOKA's silence about this task was characteristic. Yet, Eucken's ideas would have a lasting influence on his thought and writing. Eucken had compromised the concept of freedom by hiding (or presupposing) a notion of divine design – that of progress, possibly eternal or infinite. This very idea would be rejected by IMAOKA in his mature thought. For IMAOKA, freedom would necessitate open possibilities – both of progress and regress – that is, uncertainty. He, as ANESAKI and those familiar with the Eastern critiques of theism, rejected theism as a projection of human personality traits upon the universe in general (an observation made by Friedrich Schleiermacher a century before) and incarnation (in-flesh-ment) of a deity in particular. Eucken deepened IMAOKA's notion of freedom as a necessity to becoming *human* (a privileged term and concept in Eucken).

Campbell's *New Theology*

IMAOKA's translation of Campbell's famous *New Theology* had been eagerly awaited by the rapidly liberalizing Japanese Christian community, especially the Kumi-ai ministers.[305] However, when it was finally published in 1915, the *New Theology* was "old news." What had caused so much controversy in England, arrived to Japan's culture of *new knowledge* as already familiar – and paradoxically, affirming what Japanese Christians already knew and had long-ago processed. It had shocked English Christians to their core – but not educated Japanese.

Not only were the controversies of non-dogmatic Christianity and biblical criticism well-known in Japan, Campbell's popularization of the issues for England seemed so watered-down, it fostered little interest. Little or nothing was found in Campbell for the Concordia

---

305. Only the Evangelical movement, typified by Wilkes, remained staunchly orthodox and conservative.

movement, which was demanding the highest level of scholarship from each religious tradition. Campbell had polished his sermons and talks into quite lucid prose. It was a fine, non-dogmatic discussion of Christian issues, but it lacked the scholarly precision to inspire a young scholar like IMAOKA, or even Japanese Christian ministers who had been processing these issues for two decades.

Unity's Problems

ANESAKI and NARUSE would find Eucken compatible with their agendas – but each in their own way. Campbell was not used as his thought lacked the moral guidance sought to assist a modern Japan. IMAOKA's translation of Campbell did join a substantial body of scholarship published by Association Concordia as they worked to find a consensus morality. And, there is no indication that it was used or useful to Japanese Christians who had eagerly awaited it.

NARUSE had begun his participation in Association Concordia as a Christian, then became a syncretist hoping to found a new religion that would bring together the best of all religions. The new religion would be Japanese in its essence and unity. Syncretism would combine the best of particular religions, he thought, and achieve the sought-after unification of Japanese society. NARUSE would be accused by the Christian community of becoming a pantheist, because he advocated non-theistic ethics.

ANESAKI sought to preserve the particularity of each of Japan's religions, even each denomination or sect. He did not need to find something uniquely Japanese. The essence or unity of Japanese morality should be *universal*, true of all religions, but it had to be experientially true. ANESAKI thought that, by understanding each other's religion through study, sharing and dialogue, the individual characteristics of religions could be learned and unity found. (Perhaps that quest never left him and would be why ANESAKI spent the last chapter of his life studying the problem of the martyrdom of Catholic Christians in 16th Century Japan. Their experience in the face of torture and death pointed to something higher than themselves that remained illusive and particular, hiding the *universal* which he sought. Somehow, he thought, universal truth must be found in their commitment in the face of death.)

SHIBUSAWA's vision was based on his commitment to the divinity of the Emperor and the teachings of Confucius, specifically the social code of the *Analects* (*Rongo*).[306] SHIBUSAWA thought that the common basis for all religion and morality was in Confucian rationality without any of the superstition of the religions. He and the fellow industrialist MORIMURA Ichizaemon had provided nearly two-thirds of the financial support of Association Concordia for its initial decade. As it became evident that no concord would come with the adoption of Confucian ethics as the unifying principle of Japanese morality and education, SHIBUSAWA continued his support but withdrew from active leadership.

Other members added Bushido as the core for Japanese morality and its use in education, both public and private. That too failed, as did the suggestions that any particular religion be the center, the organizing principle, for a national ethics. Many quit the quest altogether, shocked by what they learned of the atrocities of the Great War in Europe – and Japan's growing militarism in China and Korea. Those who remained in the association backed the internationalism that led to the League of Nations, believing that Japan could lead the way to world peace.

Association Concordia, like the American Free Religious Association, had become an organization of talk without effective action. UKITA Kazutami, Association Concordia's official (honorary) secretary, watched its inability to do more than present ideas and debate them; "they concurred not to concur," some said. Its Motto had been: "Concord and Cooperation between Classes, Nations,

---

306. KENJO Teiji, "On Religion and Morality: Shibusawa Ei'ichi's Writings in connection with Kiitsu Association ("The Association Concordia")," p. 9 and AZEGAMI Naoki, "'Modernization' (*gendaika*) and the Formation of Religious Nationalism in Pre-War Japanese Society," translated by Ioannis Gaitanidis.

Races and Religions."[307] The First World War brought the rapid decline of the international Concordia movement, but it was not disbanded in Japan until 1942.

KENJO in his study concluded: "The Association provided an opportunity for the participants to get acquainted with their respective ideals, objectives and speculations, as also to provide them with a platform to help come to terms with the reality of their fellow beings."[308] He continued: "they only happen to demonstrate, paradoxically, that a 'concordia' on various issues was not an easy task."[309]

Their publications made their work known nationally and internationally. Ultra-nationalists and militarists began to fear their influence as an addition to the *yuniterian* movement, especially as they moved into national politics. The Concordia's members were all democratic constitutionalists, despising fascism and militarism. Most were for universal suffrage, women's rights, labor rights, anti-war/ pro-peace, and internationalism. These views were intolerable to a rising Japanese fascism, which was formulating its ideology as State Shinto.

IMAOKA attended Association Concordia with ANESAKI, serving as one of the working secretaries and translators. He was assisting, observing, and learning. Many participants in the Association would be invited to speak at Unity Hall, publish in *Cosmos*, and speak at Seisoku Academy during the following decades. IMAOKA, although a junior in the *yuniterian* network, was already exhibiting his remarkable skills as a connector, a "maven," and a network builder.[310]

---

307. KENJO, p. 18.

308. KENJO, p.15.

309. KENJO, p. 17.

310. A "maven" is a Yiddish word meaning one who accumulates knowledge and is a student, teacher and persuader, according to Malcolm Gladwell in his 2002 *Tipping Point*. Gladwell said the ultimate network builder was a connector, maven and salesman. IMAOKA lacked the last element.

Association Concordia, *Kiitsu Kyōkai* in Japanese, would be disbanded in 1942, but IMAOKA continued its memory and its vision in his church, *Kiitsu Kyōkai*. (See more about this in chapter 13.) He would use a different character (*kanji*) in a play on word-symbols as both a reminder of the old *Kiitsu Kyōkai* and a signal of something new. It entailed a slight change of focus from discussion to learning – his emphasis on lifelong learning and growth.

Attending Harvard

IMAOKA was accepted and enrolled in Harvard's "undenominational" (its own term) Divinity School to attend in 1914. ANESAKI was already there, teaching his newly designed course, "Japanese Civilization."[311] IMAOKA was delayed, perhaps to finish the translations of Campbell and Eucken. When he finally arrived in 1915 for the spring semester,[312] ANESAKI was already on a lecture tour of some of America's major universities.

IMAOKA was listed as "Nobuichiro" at Harvard and assigned to Ware Hall as an "Unclassified" graduate student.[313] He would remember Frederick Eliot as a fellow student.[314] He would mention that he met Charles Wendte while in Boston. It is surprising that he did not mention any impression of Harvard's faculty. William Fenn

---

311. KISHIMOTO had finished all but his dissertation at Harvard for a Ph.D. Mohr, *op.cit.,* chap. 5. He was a member of the Harvard Club and gave active support of graduate studies and visiting professorships there.

312. MacCauley to Eliot. Tokyo. Feb 16, 1915. "Dear Doctor Eliot, This note will be handed to you by Rev. Nobuichiro IMAOKA, a member of our Tokyo Church, who is leaving us this week for a course of special study at the Harvard Divinity School. Mr. IMAOKA has been an assistant in the Seminar of Religious Science at the Imperial University. He has also been a collaborator in our magazine the Rikugo Zasshi. I am sure that you will welcome Mr. IMAOKA to his American residence and will give him your kindly counsel…"

313. *Official Register of the Harvard University: The Divinity School*, Vol. XII, March 30, 1915, p. 55; and Vol. XII., p. 55.

314. Frederick May Eliot (1889-1958) attended Harvard Divinity School from 1912-1915. He served as president of the AUA from 1937 to 1958 when he died in office.

was the dean and Kirsopp Lake professor of Early Christian Literature; Crawford Toy and Francis Peabody were Emeriti. In 1916 George Foot Moore was professor of the History of Religion [*sic., not "religions"*]. There was a fascinating array of courses available to launch any young scholar on a lifetime of academic pursuits. IMAOKA would remain fascinated with Christian history, thought and ethics long after he returned from these studies at Harvard, teaching for a decade at Nihon University in the department of literature about Christianity.

But disaster struck, at least for his dream of obtaining a Harvard doctorate in the history of Christianity and being propelled along the fast track in Japanese education. A chair in the scientific study of Christianity was being planned and soon to be created at the Imperial University of Tokyo; there is little doubt that IMAOKA was being groomed to fill it by ANESAKI and his father-in-law, INOUE Tetsujirō, senior professor in philosophy.

IMAOKA briefly mentioned Harvard over the years in his writing and talks. In "My Free Religious Viewpoint" there is a mention of Harvard: "Later, I studied at Harvard Divinity School for two years." In "Thoughts on Emerson," he said: " Also I followed in his [Emerson's] footsteps at Harvard, and since he was a Unitarian and my great teacher of free religion, I feel a great responsibility in accepting his spiritual legacy." In the "Morning Devotion" given at the IARF Congress in 1969, he said: "It was 1915 and 1916 that I studied at Harvard, when Professor Fenn was Dean, and Professor [Henry Wilder] Foote was secretary of the Divinity School. A former President of the Unitarian Association, Frederic [*sic.*] May Eliot, was in the same class. If you will permit me to say I later became a full-fledged Unitarian, it was due to these circumstances." In "IARF Facts and Prospects" IMAOKA stated: "The writer [IMAOKA referring to himself], during his student days at Harvard, first became aware of the international liberal religious movement through Dr. Wendte." In his remarks (read by his son) when receiving the IARF Distinguished Leadership Award in 1981, he wrote: "When I was a Harvard University student in 1915, I happened to meet Mr. Charles Wendte who was then the first general secretary of IRAF [*sic.,* probably just a typo] and kindly explained to me the history, principals and purposes of IRAF [*sic.*]. I was utterly fascinated and realized that my spiritual pilgrimage until then had been nothing but an introduction to IRAF [*sic.*]." In the 1981 "Sources of Learning and Faith" IMAOKA said: "Later, from 1914 through 1915, my esteemed master, Professor ANEZAKI Masaharu, lectured at Harvard University on the history of Japanese culture, and thanks to the professor's good offices, I accompanied him as an assistant and I was fortunate to be able to study religion and philosophy there."

While these brief mentions of Harvard acknowledge the fact that he could be called "a Harvard man," the significance of the portions of the two years spent there – 1915 and 1916 – is lost.

Yet Another Crisis

Word came during the fall semester of 1916 that his wife, Utayo, was pregnant, again. He returned home immediately. Although IMAOKA forever remained "a Harvard man," an almost revered expression in Japanese academia, his dream of obtaining a Harvard Ph.D. was shattered. He had risen from a remote corner of the Empire to join the elite educators of Japan – almost. His return was inglorious. He would never speak of this crisis in his talks or his writings. In an interview, he did say that he had twice visited Mihara-yama crater, the suicide gulch of his day.[315] He did use one of those crises as an illustration of true friendship. He stated:

> Many of my acquaintances would think that I have little to do with monetary affairs. However, as a matter of fact, once I

315. Interview with George Williams July, 1986.

> thought of throwing myself into the crater of Mihara-yama. The reason why I selected Mihara-yama was that it might conceal my ugly remains from people. However, when I confided my plight to one of my friends, he at once lent me some tens of millions of Yen in cash unconditionally, that is without a bond of debt or interest. Through his friendship and assistance, I was renewed and I owe him my long life – over 90 years by now.[316]

This concerned his wife's second business failure – unmentioned in that talk. He had again signed for a loan so that she could begin a business of her own, one she could not own as a woman at that time in Japan. After the first business failed, she tried again running up "tens of millions of Yen" in debt (when the Yen was approximately 2 to 1 to the dollar). On a teacher's salary, there was no way for IMAOKA to ever hope to repay that enormous debt which was in his name. A friend saw his despondency and saved him. IMAOKA Utayo persevered – and eventually succeeded.[317]

Their first crisis had occurred when IMAOKA was in Kobe as a Kumi-ai minister in 1910. The financial crisis cannot be dated, but it was stated as one that took him to suicide leap. The second pregnancy in 1916 seemed a double humiliation, failing an educational goal and the cultural norms for a husband. He had handled the first pregnancy crisis. Of the three crises, only the second (the impossible debt) and third (another pregnancy, combined with the failure at Harvard) seem to be what moved him to the verge of suicide – twice. The very core of his existence and his principles for living seemed to have ended in failure.

---

316. "There is no Graduation from the University of Life," delivered before the National Conference of Free Religionists in Japan held in Tokyo in 1979. Translation by Bill and Dorothy Parker.

317. That rich friend must have been SHIBUSAWA. It was said by a church member that one of IMAOKA Utayo's companies placed the first telecommunications satellite into orbit. She would receive two Imperial awards in her lifetime. IMAOKA once commented in a private conversation with the author: " She gave me much trouble but she also gave me this [the financial resources to travel internationally and work in IARF]." His comment was with his characteristic smile and chuckle – not a hint of ill will or blame of his innovative and sometimes revolutionary wife.

Both crises challenged his belief in freedom (*jiyū*). He sought freedom of thought and religious belief, while his wife sought freedom of action and choice in relationships. He survived, but the paradoxes of freedom – personal, social, existential – would become the major challenge for his thought and life. (Chapter 13) As a scholar and a religionist, freedom had defined his spiritual quest. How could he retain freedom (*jiyū*) as his own ethical principle? Had it not failed for Utayo? These questions would need to be answered in the coming decades.

Continuing Their Work Together

There is no evidence that ANESAKI directly helped IMAOKA when he returned in crisis to Tokyo in 1916. ANESAKI was lecturing abroad. War clouds were on the horizon.

IMAOKA dates his full membership as a Unitarian in 1917 well after his return to Japan, when he became UCHIGASAKI's assistant. This seems odd as he had lectured at Unity Hall's summer school and in its education program, had been an assistant editor at *Cosmos*, and had helped UCHIGASAKI as his assistant minister, both at Unity Hall and then at his Kanda-ku church. MacCauley had assumed IMAOKA to be a member in his reports to Boston. But, MacCauley had assumed others, even ANESAKI, to be Unitarians or Unitarian sympathizers. It seems strange that IMAOKA had not signed the membership roll. He had come to Unity Hall and served. It was the Japanese Unitarian Association that opened to him, accepted him and nurtured him in his personal crises. After Harvard, he stepped back into assisting at Unity Hall, especially with his fellow graduate of the Imperial University, SUZUKI Bunji. In fact, within a year of returning from Harvard, he would officially relieve SUZUKI of his tasks as the secretary of both the Japan Unitarian Association and of the Mission. (That was discussed earlier in Chapter 9.)

After the demise of the Unitarian movement in Japan in 1922,

IMAOKA assisted ANESAKI in a number of conferences, the most important in 1928, the All-Japan Religions Congress, and another in 1931, the Japan Religious Peace Conference. IMAOKA followed his old pattern of doing the work as "the principal organizer" but avoiding having his name on the program.

Not to be lost sight of was IMAOKA's beginnings in public and private education. (They will be discussed in the next chapter and ANESAKI's hand will be seen in this part of IMAOKA's life as well.) In 1919 IMAOKA began teaching Christian history, thought and ethics at Nihon University. In 1925 ANESAKI recommended IMAOKA for an unusual position, principal or headmaster of an elite academy, Seisoku.

Some Takeaways From This Period

ANESAKI'S influence on IMAOKA began at the Imperial University and would continue even after his death. IMAOKA kept ANESAKI'S picture in his study with that of his deceased wife, and those of Tenno-san and his *seiza* teacher, OKADA – until his own death. He saw his life and work built upon the firm foundations they had given him.

Even IMAOKA's involvement with Unity Hall (and the *yuniterian* movement and network) could be interpreted as part of ANESAKI's liberal agenda of openness to *new knowledge* and making that compatible with Japanese culture. Then, after 1922, "the John Day effect" killed any desire for Japanese liberals to be known as Unitarian and made them slow to identify with the term "*yuniterian.*" This effect would last for two and a half decades, until 1948, and a new era in IMAOKA's life – and in that of Japan. It would mark a time when the giants of liberalism in Japan had died, leaving IMAOKA to lead without leading – and without ego. The story of this period would almost die with him.

IMAOKA's openness to *new knowledge* entailed the notion of internationalism. He had broken with his Kumi-ai mentor, EBINA Danjō, because of EBINA's nationalist conceits, a disguised racial essence or uniqueness. That would be a factor in the disappointment with American Unitarianism and John Day. However, that had manifested itself as a more blatant racism. Association Concordia brought together the widest range of Japanese society, including military and government officials, in a quest for international understanding and cooperation – as equal peoples and sovereign nations. This idealism entailed an equality of gender, race, wealth, culture and religion. IMAOKA shared that vision and commitment with ANESAKI. There had been optimism in a universal ideal that would unify humankind and lead toward an era of peace. Such idealism was shattered, first with the results of the First World War and its aftermath and then by the rise of Japanese militarism and nationalism.

Association Concordia had brought together remarkable personalities in Japanese society. Those in education were introducing new disciplines into Japanese universities. IMAOKA would be instrumental in bringing many of them to Unity Hall to speak there. Some joined the Japan Unitarian Association only to be part of the last meeting at Unity Hall in March 1922, when American Unitarians were asked to leave Japan. These leaders would remain part of a network of progressives as IMAOKA moved into the next phase of his life at Seisoku Academy (Chapter 11).

Perhaps the most dangerous thing that IMAOKA was involved in was the peace movement, hardly disguised as internationalism. Unlike SUZUKI Bunji, who was protected by his status as a graduate of the Imperial University law school,[318] IMAOKA's protection came from his very egolessness, that habit of assisting and never stepping to the front of the stage for acclaim from others. In the years ahead, during

---

[318] See Mohr's explanation of SUZUKI's police protection, Mohr, p. 123 fn. 57.

the Second World War, his pacifism and commitment to world peace and internationalism would guide him to search for Shinto, Buddhist and Christian leaders who shared that commitment (soon to manifest in his work with J. W. T. Mason).

The quest to find something transcendent at the heart of religion, thus unifying all religions, would be continued despite Association Concordia's failure. However, his quest was not to find an essence, principle, or concept at the heart of religion. Bergson's use of images rather than concepts pointed to the nature of every principle. Principles are epistemological metaphors. They are symbols created by humans who are striving to grow beyond what they are today. Bergson's intuition would be combined with Eucken's radical concept of freedom. Thus, he needed to reconcile images and conceptualization. IMAOKA had taken Emerson's "free religion" to heart, but it was still too individualistic, too self-centered. It was for him *freedom's paradox*. As a concept, it was an absolute, a value that asserts freedom from bondage of any kind. Yet, absolute freedom was impossible, even for kings and emperors. If it could be understood as an image of a *cosmic* ideal that calls humans to become better and strive for something higher, then *freedom* could be seen as the ideal of all religion.

This vision would lead IMAOKA in 1952 to join the International Association for Religious Freedom and start taking Japanese religious leaders to its international meetings. (And ironically, that only became possible because of his wife's entrepreneurial success.)

Timeline (IMAOKA, 1910-1931)

1910 Began training in *seiza* under the instruction of OKADA Torajiro with Shoko Kinoshita and others.
Began as a graduate student under Prof. ANESAKI at Tōdai

	Worked as an assistant, Tokyo Imperial University's Science of Religion Department
1912-1915	Translated "New Theology" by W. J. Campbell into Japanese.
1914	Translated "Current Thoughts and Modern Ethics" by Rudolf Eucken into Japanese.
1915-1916	Studied at The Divinity School, Harvard University.
1916	Became a Unitarian (formal membership declared by signing membership roll)
1919-1936	Lectured on history of religions and Christian history at Nihon University, Literature Department
1923	Great Tokyo Earthquake
1928	All-Japan Religions Congress
1931	Japan Religious Peace Conference

IMAOKA was enrolled along with two other young scholars in a graduate program at Harvard Divinity School. This would have lead to a doctorate, most likely in preparation for the chair for the scientific study of Christianity at the Imperial University of Tokyo being created by his mentor, Prof. ANESAKI.

UNCLASSIFIED

Imaoka, Nobuichiro, A.M. (*Imperial Univ., Tokyo*) 1906,	*Tokyo, Japan,*	Ware 34
Jalkanen, Aaro Johannes, Gr., *University of Helsingfors, Finland,* 1908,	*Duluth, Minn.*	5 Sumner R'd
Morihira, Shoichi Douglas, S.T.B. (*Boston Univ. School of Theology*) 1914,	*Tokushimaken, Japan,*	[Newton Centre 9 Sturtevant Hall,

From the "General Information and Announcement of Courses," Harvard Divinity School, 1916

Chapter 11
Assisting in Education

Upon his return to Tokyo from Harvard, IMAOKA would give much of his time and energy during the next three years to Unity Hall, assisting UCHIGASAKI and SUZUKI, and serving MacCauley until he resigned. As Unity Hall closed in 1922, a letter and package arrived from his dear friend in liberal religion, John Haynes Holmes. He was a famous ex-Unitarian minister and now, pastor of the Community Church of New York. It mentioned previous correspondence and exchanges of materials.[319] IMAOKA credited Holmes with teaching him about the true nature of the church as a fellowship (a *koinonia* or *gemeinshaft*).[320] Holmes had sent him *New Churches for Old.*[321] His book arrived with an invitation to bring the Japanese Unitarian Association and Unity Hall into his "undenominational" Community Church movement. Timing may not be everything, but the timing of this invitation could not have been worse. Both JUA and Unity Hall were no more. Yet, Holmes' ideas on education would soon find a new context as IMAOKA began a new chapter in his spiritual pilgrimage – education as religion, school as church.

IMAOKA had taught in the educational program at Unity Hall, notably with MINAMI in a seminar on Bergson and Eucken. He had lectured regularly in the holiday and summer programs, the

319. Copy of original letter given author by IMAOKA.

320. "Morning Devotion, July 16, 1969." Terms in Greek and German that Imaoka knew well, indicating the nature of relationship within the spiritual community, but not as a building or structure.

321. John Haynes Holmes, *New Churches for Old: A Plea for Community Religion* (New York: Dodd, Mead and Company, 1922), 341pp.

alternative "adult education program" that attempted to take the place of their School for Advanced Learning. While he assisted SUZUKI who was spending more and more time leading the labor movement than serving as executive secretary for the Unitarian Mission, IMAOKA coordinated the educational program at Unity Hall which extended to the Sunday morning and evening services as they became more educational. (This had been noticed by AUA commissioners who saw this as tending toward Ethical Culture and away from religious Unitarianism.) When SUZUKI finally resigned of necessity to distance his labor movement from any foreign connection, both he and Boston's AUA were in agreement – for different reasons. SUZUKI's duties were now being taken care of by others, but he needed distance from any foreign entanglement and funding. IMAOKA, its new, official secretary, continued the focus on social issues, education, and publication of liberal religious materials.

Everything changed with the arrival of the Rev. John B. W. Day. Once he had forced MacCauley to resign, Day then tried to compel his secretary, IMAOKA, and the Japanese Unitarian Association to begin a standard missionary program including evangelistic trips and preaching stations. Perhaps it was only circumstantial as to timing, but within months of Day's arrival, IMAOKA accepted a lectureship at Nihon University in its Literature Department. He would teach comparative religion and Christian history and thought there from 1919 to 1935.

Day's orders from the AUA to remove SUZUKI and the Yūaikai in fear of Bolshevism and make the "Liberal Christian Mission of Japan" more religious contributed to the demise of Japanese Unitarianism, as previously discussed. Yet, its death might not have happened without three almost simultaneous occurrences: the AUA closed Unity Hall leaving the *yuniterian* movement without a meeting place (and began a protracted process of selling it), the

AUA cut off all funds to the movement, and the 1923 Great Tokyo Earthquake changed their local crisis into a greater national trauma.

The *yuniterian* movement entered the decade of the 1920s with seemingly unrealistic optimism of creating a liberal, progressive, democratic Japan.[322] SUZUKI was fighting a valiant battle against exploitive capitalism in league with rising militarism. Education was a key in attempting to solve labor and economic inequities. ANESAKI had become a national advisor concerning educational policies and curriculum, which could have shaped the quest for Japan's national essence (*kokutai; kokkyō*) toward being more inclusive of all religious values (note his work in Association Concordia and all his allies there) instead of the outcome in militarist state ideology (*Kokka* Shintoism). The way *yuniterian* sympathizers had begun to transform the top universities of Japan (Tōdai, Keiō, Waseda, etc.), the mainstream Christian denominations (especially Congregationalist/Kumi-ai), and even Japanese religions (especially Shinshū Buddhism) reinforced their optimism – until they no longer could come together at Unity Hall or publish their own journal, *Rikugō Zasshi.*

The depth of the spiritual trauma can be guessed by *an unusual silence* from the religious *yuniterian*s – KANDA, SUZUKI and IMAOKA (the three dual secretaries of the Japan Unitarian Mission and the Japan Unitarian Association); KISHIMOTO, ABE, MURAI (the Dōshisha Trio, all Unitarian-Congregationals), and all the educators, publishers, writers and artists who were active members of Unity Hall and the Japan Unitarian Association. Firsthand accounts dealing with the demise of the *yuniterian* movement and of Japanese Unitarianism would be expected from these prolific writers. Yet,

322. Do not read "democratic" as a copy of American democracy, which careful studies published in *Cosmos* had faulted as representative without voting rights for all, socially and economically unequal, racially biased, etc.

there was inexplicable silence. The erasure was of such a nature that none of the major participants in the *yuniterian* movement resurrected it even in their memoirs. Only the son of KISHIMOTO Nobuta, Hideo, wrote of Japanese Unitarianism's place in the history of the modern period – and that not positively. As a mainstream Christian church historian, KISHIMOTO Hideo (1903-1964) would blame Unitarianism for weakening Japanese Christianity and being a primary cause for its lack of further growth.[323] But, this was a secondhand account in which he left out his father's name, including him only in "the others" even when his father was the primary person or leader in an event.[324]

School as Church

IMAOKA had assisted in the educational program at Unity Hall from his arrival in 1910, until the building was closed to Japanese Unitarians in 1922. As the end approached with every step taken by the AUA's John Day, IMAOKA began as a lecturer at Nihon University in its Literature Department. This might have led to a full time professorship if he had not accepted the double challenge of rebuilding a private academy and of implementing the ideas that he and his mentor, ANESAKI, had envisioned. Seisoku Academy[325] was a

---

323. Hideo KISHIMOTO, *op.cit.* Surprisingly, he would join IMAOKA as one of the founders of the Japanese Free Religious Association and work with him until his death in 1964. See mention in Chapter 13.

324. See Chapter 8, "Japanese Unitarians."

325. Seisoku Gakuin will be referred to as Seisoku Academy. It was a private Middle School taking five years to complete until after WWII. During the American Occupation it was divided into a Middle School and a High School, each of three years.

Seisoku Gakuin was an elite preparatory school that had been successful in placing its graduates into the best universities. Its role was a sensitive one: educate young leaders who would direct the nation. That was not unnoticed, and it brought surveillance. An officer was assigned to the school to observe any violation of state educational policy or hint of disloyalty to the Emperor.

Seisoku High School had already produced prominent international leaders: YOSHIDA Shigeru, prime minister and ambassador; SATO Nastake, president of the

college preparatory school with a distinguished history. ANESAKI encouraged him to take the position at Seisoku and later spoke enthusiastically at IMAOKA's installation.

If ANESAKI's goal had been for IMAOKA to join him at Tōdai as the professor of Christian studies, that possibility was foreclosed with IMAOKA's failure at Harvard. It appears that ANESAKI sought to use IMAOKA to accomplish another important task. ANESAKI had long wanted to find a way to teach national morality in public education. IMAOKA had helped him in Association Concordia, gleaning moral principles from all of Japan's religions and trying to make what was common to all the unifier of moral principles taught at an early age. By 1925 it had become clear that Association Concordia would not come to an accord that could be proposed for public – that is, governmental – education. It is reasonable that his encouragement of IMAOKA to "step down" from university to secondary education in a private academy was as much his idea as it could have been IMAOKA's.

On the other hand, if IMAOKA had been one hundred percent behind this new direction, one would logically assume that he would have given up the part-time lectureship at Nihon University when he began at Seisoku. However, IMAOKA held onto the university lectureship for another ten years, well into the time that another chapter in his life had started: assisting J. W. T. Mason's quest to learn about Shinto.

IMAOKA and Higher Education

Why did IMAOKA quit his lectureship at Nihon University in 1935? There might have been a deeply psychological reason. Teaching "religion" and "history" are two of the most conservative

---

Upper House and a Foreign Minister; and IWANAGA Yukichi, the founder of Japan News Agency who succeeded in settling disputes between the Associated Press and the Reuter News Agency.

pursuits in academia. Each discipline struggles with "what was" and must be accurate concerning what happened. It is the psychological opposite of the creative freedom that IMAOKA sought spiritually as we shall see in his future assistance of Mason.

Even liberal religion had disappointed him in its inability to live up to its ideals. From this point on, he would be focused on the process of "going beyond" – beyond liberalism, beyond Unitarianism, beyond religion itself. But that "going beyond" contained a paradox. The spiritual journey would have identities, arrivals, and graduations. He was doing something, practicing something, experiencing something, learning and growing. These are "measureables" – even when he denied he had achieved anything of significance. The process of learning and its paradox of having learned something could be resolved if one could live in a continuous "both/and." Both achieved experiences and their denial as having any final consequence. Some versions of Christianity conceptualized that one could be saved, once and for all. And some versions of Buddhism posited that one could attain enlightenment. However, IMAOKA would profess a dual identity in both, claiming neither to be saved nor to be enlightened. Both identities were for IMAOKA a process of continual learning from different perspectives.

ANESAKI's vision needed a prestigious school where moral education could be legally attempted, and IMAOKA accepted the challenge. But it involved a dual challenge. First, was the rebuilding of a destroyed school, the result of the Great Tokyo Earthquake of 1923. IMAOKA – the networker who had assisted ANESAKI in bringing together such a wide variety of leaders in Association Concordia – now contacted the industrialists, bankers, new aristocracy, and people of wealth, some of whom were graduates of Seisoku Academy. He successfully rebuilt the "Eton of Japan" and began the second part of the challenge: teaching moral values at the very time when nationalists and militarists were attempting to make *kokugaku* (patriotic or national learning) equal to State Shinto (*kokka shinto*) – not a religion at all but the national ideology that was to be inculcated into every aspect of society.

Installing a New Principal

It was only natural that, after recommending IMAOKA for the principalship at Seisoku Academy, ANESAKI would speak at his installation. ANESAKI recounted his student's educational qualifications, also calling attention to his religious affiliation:

> Shin'ichirō IMAOKA is one of the graduates from the department of Religious Studies of the Imperial University. Soon after graduation, he served a Congregational Church in the city of Kobe as its minister. … after three years he came back to Tokyo to renew his studies. As it was just the time that the Imperial University opened the Institute for Religious Studies, I wanted him to work there as my assistant and allowed him to pursue his own research. Four years thereafter when I was in Cambridge, Massachusetts, U.S.A., as an exchange professor at Harvard University I invited him to come to Cambridge as my assistant again and recommended him to Harvard Divinity School as a special student. After almost two years study there, he came back to Japan and has since become a lecturer on Christianity at Nihon University. The fact that Mr. lmaoka, owner of the said career, has been appointed to the principalship of Seisoku High School is indeed putting the right man in the right place.[326]

ANESAKI reminded the school of its famous founders who had influenced both himself and IMAOKA:

> The history of Seisoku High School dates back to 1889 when Dr. Shoichi Toyama, Baron Naibu Kanda and Dr. Jojiro Motora founded the school. They are all my respected professors. I was motivated to specialize in the study of religions by Mr. Toyama. ...Baron Kanda is a fine gentleman who taught me Latin language in my university days. … Dr. Motora, it is needless to say

326. ANESAKI Masaharu, "Introducing Shin-ichiro Inaoka [*sic., misspelling in original*] to Seisoku High School," February 1925. Typed manuscript of talk given to author.

that he was a model scholar who put his whole energy into the research after Truth. It was due to his influence that my conscience as a scholar awoke. It is a matter of course, therefore, that Seisoku Academy has always occupied an outstanding position in the field of education in Japan.[327]

IMAOKA Shin'ichirō, 1930, five years after becoming Principal of Seisoku Academy, teaching at Nihon University, assisting ANESAKI and about to begin working with J. W. T. Mason's project to learn about Shinto.

ANESAKI then mentioned something surprising – that IMAOKA had been educated by the founders. Perhaps he meant that he had been influenced by them as ANESAKI claimed of himself, since there is no evidence that this should be taken literally. He ended with a prediction. Perhaps, one might call it a "head's up" or a fair warning. A new kind of education would be attempted.

> Hence I am exceedingly pleased to learn that Mr. IMAOKA, a former student of mine, who was educated by the founders of Seisoku Academy, becomes now the principal of this school. Although rather a taciturn person, he is an eloquent speaker whenever he expresses his convictions, showing a flash of his personality. If you ask me what his speciality is, I give you a ready answer that he is a human being and has, in addition, all the virtues of the founders in a certain degree. He is not a professional educator and knows very well that character is not built by regulations, examinations and punishments. I am fully convinced that Mr. IMAOKA will not only inherit the spirit of [the] founders but will surely make a new departure in the field of education in Japan, which as a whole has been conventional and formalistic.[328]

Thus, IMAOKA's career change into private, secondary education was launched. He was already 44 years old and should

327. *Ibid.* IMAOKA's list of graduates from Seisoku Academy.
328. *Ibid.*

have only served as principal for two decades before retiring. But, he served as principal from 1925-1960, becoming chair of the board, and then served again as principal from 1969-1973, before again becoming chair of the board. He actually retired just before he was 92.

IMAOKA began at Seisoku Academy as progressives tried to realize their vision of Japan leading the world toward peace at the League of Nations and applying liberal values in all of Japanese society (mentioning just a few examples of the former *yuniterian* visionaries: politics – UCHIGASAKI Sakusaburō, HOSHIJIMA Nirō, ect.; banking – KANDA Saichirō; labor – SUZUKI Bunji; women's rights – IMAOKA Utayo, HIRATSUKA Raichō, and many unnamed women captured in the pictures of Unity Hall.)

His long career in private education produced few written accounts or reflections that survived the second destruction of Seisoku during WWII.[329] IMAOKA did compose a remarkable document in 1928, that survived concerning the three principles of Seisoku as Japan began to see more and more intimidation of progressive and liberal ideas and innovations, especially in education. Seisoku would have a special military officer assigned to see that the national education policy was adhered to, as interpreted by an increasingly militarist and imperialist state. IMAOKA would find a way to evade some of the controls: working with J.W.T. Mason.

Seisoku Educational Policy of 1928

IMAOKA saw his first task after rebuilding the destroyed buildings of the school as providing moral education for a new generation. In the policy statement of 1928, IMAOKA said: "I want to propose three principles of the educational policy of Seisoku Gakuin:

[329] When IMAOKA died in 1988, the author tried to obtain access to anything he had left in the office provided to him in Seisoku. Everything disappeared or was destroyed at his death. His family stated that nothing remained there to bring home. This contradicted my memory of the books and materials that were there during several interviews at his office instead of his home.

Domestication, Socialization and Internationalization."[330] Modeled on parents' love, "school should be like a home or the extension of your home." The familial metaphor suggested the relationships: "the principal is the head of the family, teachers and senior students are brothers of freshmen." The relationships even included teachers and graduates who had died. They would be remembered and honored at an annual ceremony led by students and teachers, but with no priests or ministers.

His next comments were quite unusual in education for elites. "Rules, tests and punishment are not important at our school." Students were encouraged to be themselves, not to just act "well-mannered," "mechanically and passively just like robots" at school but to be themselves as soon they were at home.

> Especially it is wrong to make ranks of students by the results of terminal or annual tests given by stereotyped or standardized curricula. The duty of a real educator should be to draw out individual potential of each student, respecting his personality. It is the most important point to achieve individual personality of each student in true education, not to make him stereotyped.[331]

One innovation was to found the Association of Seisoku Mothers, foreshadowing the Parent Teachers Association in Japan. March 6th of each year, the Empress' birthday, became Mothers' Day for students to think on and honor their mothers.

Socialization was typically demanded as loyalty to the Emperor and the state. IMAOKA expressed it creatively:

> School has a duty to educate young generation in the community. A private school has the same duty as a public school. Any kind of private school should be a public institution morally and ethically. The private school should not be dominated for the Head's or Officials' sake. The community should support and cooperate with the school, too.

IMAOKA observed that "Students are apt to become more and

---

330. All quotations in this section are from "Education Policy of Seisoku Middle School," 1928.

331. *Ibid.* The following quotations are from the same document.

more individualistic or selfish, being forced to study to be elite, to pass the entrance examinations of upper schools." To have his students become community-minded, IMAOKA gave them the experience of democracy, electing and running their own clubs and even their classes.

> Seisoku Students' Association is managed mostly by students. In order to experience social work by themselves, they are very active, belonging to the clubs, such as literary club, speech club, kendo club, judo club, sumo club, tennis club, travel club and pingpong club, after school is over. Each club has a committee elected by students. And I tell the visitors to look at classrooms as well as club activities to understand our real school education.

He was seeking to instill "cooperative prosperity," he said.

> At first they experience self-government and cooperation in a group, and from groups to class, from classes to school. The spirit of democracy is realized through their spontaneous activities in school life.

However, the most controversial principle was internationalism. IMAOKA recalled the history of the founding of Seisoku in 1889. "The founders of our school – Dr. TOYAMA, Baron KANDA and Dr. MOTORA – were excellent pioneers in educational field in Meiji era, having deep and wide insight of international situation." Since the founding of the Seisoku International Association three years earlier in 1925, three types of activities had occurred:

> • Lecture meetings, inviting famous lecturers to address subjects on international situations, etc.
>
> • Writing letters and exchanging paintings with middle school students in foreign countries.
>
> • Learning practical English language.

Members of the Imperial household, both foreign and Japanese ambassadors, officials and dignitaries were invited to speak at Seisoku assemblies. They brought the world to Seisoku's student body. (The fact that they came to Seisoku at all speaks to its importance and IMAOKA's unusual standing and growing influence.)

> Some people say internationalization and patriotism will not be compatible. But I declare to them, "For the Love of our nation, I want to educate young people with internationalism. Japanese people should not stay only in Japan just like a miniature plant in a plant pot. Japanese people should grow in the world just like a tall tree rooted in the great earth." ... The Pacific Ocean era is coming soon. [*spoken to his students in 1928*]

The policy statement of 1928 ended with a roadmap of his own spiritual direction for the next period of his life. It concerned the place of education and religion, or more specifically his growing conviction that education and religion had to be united. Or from another perspective, that there was no distinction since they were one and the same.

> In my view, religion and education should be unified. But Seisoku Middle School should not take a standpoint of a certain conventional sect of religion. To the middle school students who are awakening in religious mind, we should not convert them or disturb awakening. Teachers should lead them very carefully. A teacher should have [his/her] own faith and religious experience. However, he should never preach, nor propagate. We do not need a special school subject for religious education. Religion can be taught in ordinary classes, such as mathematics, science, history, English, music, and so on, when they have their own faith. Teachers are not expected to be religious experts at all.

Already in the handling of national and special school events, one can see IMAOKA maintaining independence from the move toward a fascist and militaristic state.

> On May 5th, Boys' Festival, mothers come to school together in the morning. They prepare for special lunch, such as Red Rice and pounding rice cake with Oak-leaves, etc., for all the students to celebrate their healthy and happy growing. In New Year holiday, the last day of Winter training of Kendo and Judo, mothers come to school to serve them warmest O-shiruko, pounding rice cake with sweet beans soup. On the Graduation Day, each graduate is given something in memory of his awaiting graduation by Association of Mothers of Seisoku. On March 6th, Empress' birthday has been celebrated at girls' schools in Japan in the past, but since 1926 we

have celebrated it as Mothers' Day. I want to give each student a chance to think of admiring his mother. [*This innocuous change may have had a hidden symbolism.*]

Once a year Memorial Service is held at the school auditorium for the teachers and students who passed away, just the same as ordinary families worship ancestors and serve for the dead. But we do not ask any priest to conduct the service. Listening to hearty speeches for them of their classmates and teachers who shared works and pleasure with them, reciting poems and singing songs written and composed by our teachers and students. We are the more deeply impressed than professional religionist's sutra recitation or sermons.[332]

Subversive or Not

What was significant about this policy statement for Japan's Eaton, one of its finest preparatory schools for the elite, was its dedication to an emerging constitutional democracy. Of course, this was seen as subversive by its opponents – not by progressive Japanese leaders of this period, but by the militarists, nationalists and capitalists who profited from authoritarianism.[333] The late 1920s were a prelude of the fascism that was soon to beset Japan with assassinations and coups that would finally end the liberal (*yuniterian*) dream of Japan being the international leader in world peace, disarmament, science serving humanity, and human brother/sisterhood. IMAOKA was a pacifist and an internationalist from the time he graduated from the Imperial University. His differences with his Kumi-ai mentor, EBINA, showed that these convictions came early. He joined the *yuniterian* subversives like ABE, KISHIMOTO, MURAI, UCHIGASAKI, SUZUKI Bunji and similar advocates of non-aggression like Tenkō-san and OKADA. Many of these became successful politicians in the 1920s, even his mentor ANESAKI. Leading Seisoku Academy in this direction was natural but dangerous.

332. "Education Policy," 1928, *ibid.* As mentioned before, all these quotations are from Imaoka's 1928 policy statement.

333. This combination of interests would become known as Japanese fascism.

When I asked for specifics about this period, IMAOKA sent me to students who had been at Seisoku during the Pacific War, WWII. But, they were not aware as students of a covert agenda in having Buddhist and Shinto priests and Christian ministers speak about their ideals or celebrate their religious festivals at the school. They had unusually strong emotional attachments to IMAOKA sensei as an example of how to be a "true human being." The most revelatory interview was with a Zen master who had become internationally famous because of his use of archery to point one toward enlightenment.[334] At one point in the conversation about his master, as he referred by IMAOKA sensei, he decided to shoot an arrow in IMAOKA's honor. His students were shocked that their master had never allowed them to see him shoot – yet he did publicly this once. At the end of the interview, the Zen master wept after speaking about IMAOKA as his principal during the War. For his students, who had escorted me back to the train station, this was the most shocking of all – seeing their Zen master with tears in his eyes.

The interviews led me to conclude that IMAOKA attempted to achieve his ideals of liberal education under the most restrictive of circumstances – police surveillance, enforced educational guidelines, forced compliance concerning unquestioning loyalty to the state, and reverence to the Emperor.

As his values approached becoming subversive of the new order, IMAOKA used a quest with J. W. T. Mason to find the true Shinto as religion and not as an ideology. (That quest to be presented in the next chapter.)

The University of Life

At Seisoku, IMAOKA continued his idealistic vision of education based on religious principles.

The duty of real educator should be to draw out individual

[334] Eugen Herrigel, *Zen in the Art of Archery.* See also, Kenneth Kushner, *Zen Art of the Bow.*

potency of each student, respecting his personality. It is the most important point to achieve individual personality of each student in true education, not to make him stereotyped.[335]

Simultaneous with this liberal and democratic educational experiment in an elite academy, Japan marched toward war and a totalitarian state. Even so, Imaoka attempted to form an ideal community at his school.

His accounts about Seisoku Academy and the Second World War are, as usual, brief acknowledgment of his work and a focus upon the nature of the school, as it became overtly an institution founded on "free religion" (see Chapter 13 as that becomes the final develop of his own spiritual journey). In 1970 he reflected on those decades at Seisoku:

> I cannot omit referring to Seisoku High School to which I have been related for the past 45 years as a principal and chairman of board of directors. I have always thought: If the school does not have a characteristic, it is not necessary to exist. Just in the year we started Japan Free Religious Association, [1948] the board of directors of Seisoku High School decided to declare to the public that all educational activities in the Seisoku High School should be based on Free Religion, pure and creative. *The declaration meant the unity of the secular (education) and the sacred (religion).* In other words, the secular should be as heightened or as deepened as it can be—*and* called sacred at the same time. Seisoku High School does not teach religion to students as a regular course but teachers are urgently required *to study and experience religion personally.* This sort of religious education does not conflict with the Constitution and can be practiced not only in private schools but in public schools too. If you ask me, however, whether Seisoku High School has succeeded to make all its every day secular activities themselves so excellent and so splendid that you can not fail to recognize there something divine and holy, I am sorry to confess "Not yet".[336]

335. "Educational Policy of Seisoku Middle School," 1928.

336. "My Spiritual Pilgrimage," 1970. *Italics added for emphasis.*

Education as Religion

After serving as both as a mainstream Congregational minister and as a liberal Christian (Unitarian) assistant minister with UCHIGASAKI for two decades, IMAOKA would begin in 1919 to frame his leaving ministry for education as a religious direction. "Education is religion,"[337] he would often say and write. The school should be the place to make "true human beings" providing something essential and ultimate in addition to a curriculum.[338] Education should seek to realize "the true, the good and the beautiful which are the ultimate ideals of mankind and nothing but Divinity or Buddhahood."[339] And reversing the metaphor, unlike school, there is *no graduation from life*; ours is a lifetime of learning.[340]

Some of his most memorable word paintings replace the church with the school and with learning rather than worshipping. There was the notion of graduation as an evolution from one stage of one's life to the next. Even life's failings are preparatory and can be diplomas as we learn and grow. In fact, they too are graduations in our life journey not to be forgotten or become ashamed of.

> Education should be continued throughout life, even though one has gone out into the world after graduating from school, since lifelong education follows school education. I should like to say that this lifelong education is given by the University of Life.[341]

Education, as the metaphor for religion, clarified the perspectives on continuous learning and the past achievements simply as graduations. *Both* the experience of oneness with the

---

337. "There Is No Graduation From The University Of Life." *1979.*

338. *Ibid.*

339. *Ibid.*

340. *Ibid. Emphasis added.* Education throughout life may have influenced one of Founder NIWANO Nikkyo's favorite concepts about being a "lifetime beginner." [Founder of Rissho Kosei-kai]

341. *Ibid.*

Universe (with the One) *and* the denial that such an experience as had any real spiritual meaning needed to be held at the same time, he thought. Mystical experiences were just learning experiences, graduations, nothing more.

Seisoku was completely destroyed by the end of World War II. IMAOKA, continuing as its principal, would lead in another reconstruction. During the time that he was principal or chair of the Board of Directors at Seisoku until he was 92, there would be two other distinct aspects of his spiritual pilgrimage – assisting J. W. T. Mason in the quest for the true Shinto and attempting to find *free religion (jiyū shūkyō)* in particular religions and organizations. To those we now turn.

IMAOKA would receive two Imperial awards in education, about which only his family seemed to know in 1980 during interviews by the author.

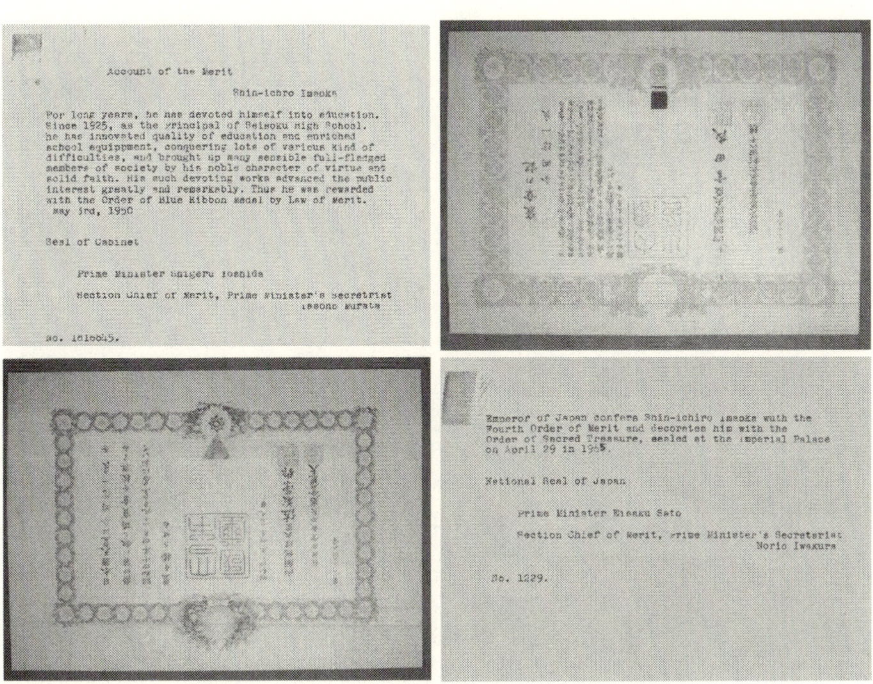

Account of the Merit

Shin-ichro Imaoka

For long years, he has devoted himself into education. Since 1925, as the principal of Seisoku High School, he has innovated quality of education and enriched school equippment, conquering lots of various kind of difficulties, and brought up many sensible full-fledged members of society by his noble character of virtue and solid faith. His such devoting works advanced the public interest greatly and remarkably. Thus he was rewarded with the Order of Blue Ribbon medal by Law of Merit.
May 3rd, 1950

Seal of Cabinet

Prime Minister Shigeru Yoshida

Section Chief of Merit, Prime Minister's Secretriat
Isono Murata

No. 1810645.

Emperor of Japan confers Shin-ichiro Imaoka with the Fourth Order of Merit and decorates him with the Order of Sacred Treasure, sealed at the Imperial Palace on April 29 in 1965.

National Seal of Japan

Prime Minister Eisaku Sato

Section Chief of Merit, Prime Minister's Secretariat
Norio Iwakura

No. 1229.

1950 and 1965 Imperial Award certificates

Standing in front of his wife's company after 1965 Imperial Award

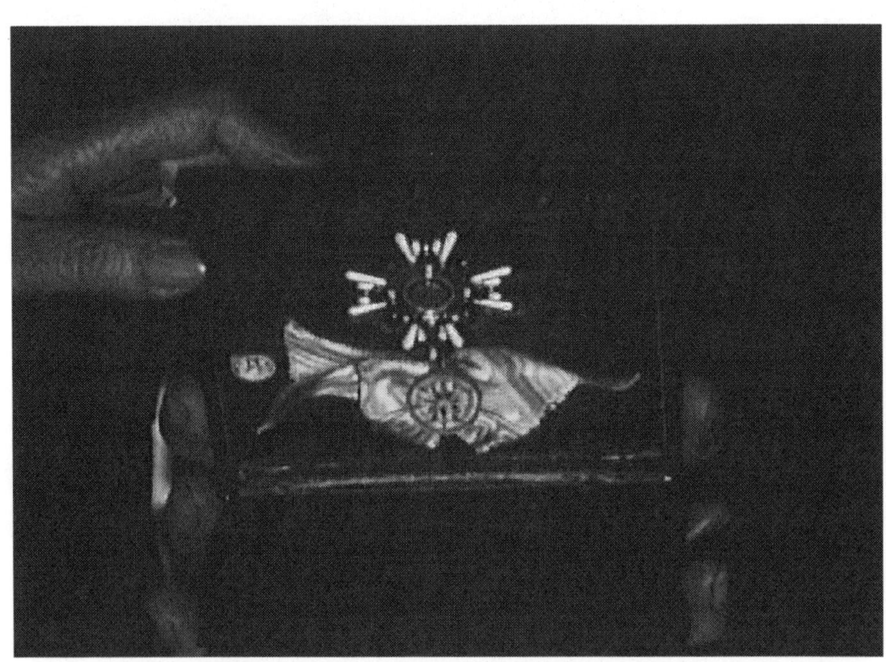

The Fourth Order of Merit with the Sacred Treasure

TIMELINE (IMAOKA, 1910-1976)

1910 Began assisting as editorial assistant at *Cosmos*, teaching at Unity Hall, helping Uchigasaki as his ministerial assistant.

1912 Began assisting ANESAKI as unpaid graduate assistant, translating Campbell and Eucken; became a working secretary of Association Concordia. [*Could have begun as early as 1910.*]

1915 Attended Harvard with Anesaki's blessing. Left in 1916.

1916 Returned to work at Cosmos, Association Concordia, and directly with Suzuki Bunji at Unity Hall as he rose to national and international fame and importance to the labor movement.

1918 Became Secretary of JUM, JUA.

1919 Started at Nihon University in literature department teaching Christian literature and history.

1923 Devoted himself to rebuilding after the school Great Earthquake and fire

1925-1960 Principal, Director; but remained as Head of Directors of Board, Seisoku High School.

Worked as Superintendent for All-Japan Religions Congress held in memory of Enthronement of The Emporer)

1925 Organized Seisoku International Association

1928 Made a three-fold educational policy for Seisoku Gakuin and carried out: Domestication, Socialization and Internationalization of Seisoku Gakuin.

1931 Worked as a Committee Member for Japan Religious Peace Conference held co-operatively by Japan U.N. Society, Tokyo Kiitsu Association and Japan Religious Association.

1932-1940 Studied Shinto and culture of Japan with J. W. T. Mason.

1936 Resigned Lectureship at Nihon University in Department of Literature – working with Mason.

1945 Devoted himself to rebuilding the school after the War for years.

1949 Presented his view on education: all educational activities should be based on Free Religion. Directors of Board of Seisoku High School decided that "Every activity of school education should be based on Free Religion."

1950 Decorated with Blue Ribbon Medal

1965 Honored with the Fourth Order of Merit with the Sacred Treasure.

1969-1973 Reassumed role as Principal in 1969 – in 1973 he is 92 years old.

1973-1976 Resigned as Principal and Chair, served as member of the Board of Directors of Seisoku Gakuin until 1976.

Celebration of 15th year as Principal of Seisoku Academy, 1940

Chapter 12

Assisting Mason: the Quest to Know Shinto

The three visits of an American journalist between 1932 and 1940 would hardly be worth a couple of paragraphs if it were not for IMAOKA's praise of the man and the experiences for own understanding of Shinto. There was an undeniable connection between two of the most different human beings imaginable. That connection provides an understanding of the years leading up to the Second World War and beyond. These years overlap with his work with ANESAKI and his teaching at Seisoku Academy and Nihon University.

Joseph Warren Teets Mason (1879-1941) arrived in Japan in 1932, a 53-year-old retired prize-winning war correspondent.[342] Mason came as an author with a project to explore the sources of Japan's modernization. His second book, the *Creative East,* had already been translated into Japanese in 1928, almost simultaneously with the English publication by Dutton. In the *Creative East,* Mason found only Japan able to modernize and progress while India and China had lost their creative abilities. That book would have a poor reception in both England and America, but Mason came to strengthen his conclusions with an actual visit to Japan, his first.[343] IMAOKA was 51 years old in 1932, his 7th year at Seisoku Academy

342. Mason was present during an assassination attempt on King Alfonso XIII of Spain.

343. While his 1926 *Creative Freedom* had received a few book notices and at least one highly unsympathetic review, his *Creative East* was simply ignored. It meant he had to search for another publisher for his new study of Japan, if he were to be published at all.

and his 13th year at Nihon University. He was a pacifist and an internationalist – humble, assisting others, particularly his mentor, ANESAKI Masaharu. Mason and IMAOKA could hardly have been less alike, as Mason concluded seven years later as he left Japan.

Mason wanted the help of a guide to visit Shinto shrines – and possibly a new translator for his Shinto book. IMAOKA had been recommended. The call to IMAOKA came from the Harvard Club[344] announcing the arrival of yet another visitor who wished to see him. The days of visitors from the American Unitarian Association were long past but the Harvard connection remained strong. This was a visit from an American newspaper correspondent whom IMAOKA mistook as a "Harvard man."[345] What might have been a minor assistance turned into a memorable connection involving almost a decade, IMAOKA acting as translator and guide "all across Japan," as Mason would later describe it. And, from this came the publication of two books in English about Shinto, each translated into Japanese by IMAOKA.

Mason's arrival was on the heels of the Three Religions Conference of 1931, that tried once again to persuade Japanese leaders to renounce militarism and return to the ideals of the "peace constitution." It was one of the last gasps of the *yuniterian* movement before WWII, if it could even be remembered as that, sponsored jointly by democratic and internationalist organizations including Association Concordia and the League of Nations Society. IMAOKA could not have been unaware of the suspicions that would arise from any association with a person of Mason's martial interests. But

344. The Harvard Club was founded by Authur May Knapp, first Unitarian fieldworker, who returned to Japan, bought and published an English language newspaper in Yokohama. Knapp died in 1921.

345. IMAOKA told the author on several times on different occasions that Mason was a "Harvard man," sincerely believing him. Mason actually graduated from New York University.

despite any misgivings and during Japan's constant military conquests in the 1930s, as it was challenged in the Pacific by both Britain and the United States, IMAOKA choose to help Mason.

Mason was especially fascinated with how different the progress of Japan had been than other nations in Asia. Even though he and others characterized it as one of the last nations in Asia to enter the modern era, Japan had resisted colonization and had "modernized" (a term of great weight for Mason).

Joseph Warren Teets Mason (1879-1941) with his wife in Tokyo, 1939

Mason's military interests were peaked by its quick mastery of western military science and tactics. The Russo-Japanese War of 1904 was a particular fascination. Russia had played the racist card of a sacred war against the "yellow hoard" of Japan but had become the first "white Christian nation" to be defeated by "heathen Asians." Mason could have come as a retired journalist and writer interested in this new emerging power in Asia, as an American spy, or both.[346] IMAOKA seemed not to worry, even though he was under constant surveillance at Seisoku Academy to teach within the new guidelines concerning the Imperial Rescript on Education of 1890. These rules were written by the newly formed department on Shinto ideology and required the presentation of Shinto as "national spirit." Shinto was now a state ideology rather than a sectarian religion. The "Taishō democracy" (1912-1926) had ended six years earlier, and an assassination attempt on the Emperor occurred that very year. Japanese armed forces had attacked Shanghai in the First Shanghai Incident that January. A war correspondent arriving at this time would have been noticed.[347]

Yet, Mason came as a "Bergsonian writer," having learned about Shinto from two Japanese officials. In Europe, according to the biographical data in the Columbia University's Mason Archive, Mason had "met Japanese diplomats Suematsu Kenshō and Hayashi Gonsuke, who introduced him to Japanese Shinto, the native religion of Japan, as well as Confucianism. His interest in Eastern civilization grew, and he published two books, *Creative East* (1926) in New York and *Creative Freedom* (1928) in London."[348] Dutton had arranged the

---

346. Due to the lack of resources in Japan, raw materials such as iron, oil, and coal largely had to be imported. The success of Japan in securing Taiwan (1895) and Korea (1910) had brought Japan agricultural colonies. The Japanese military looked toward Manchuria for iron and coal, Indochina for rubber, and China for its vast resources.

347. In November 1936, the Anti-Comintern Pact was signed by Japan and Germany (Italy joined a year later). It was an agreement to exchange information and collaborate in preventing communist activities. The Marco Polo Bridge Incident of July 7, 1937, expanded from a clash near Beijing between Chinese and Japanese troops and quickly escalated into the Second Sino-Japanese War, followed by Soviet-Japanese border wars. The Sino-Japanese War started with the Battle of Lugou Bridge (July 7). Japan captured Peking on July 31 and occupied Nanking on December 13 with the Nanking massacre.

348. From the Columbia University biography in the Mason archive: http://www.columbia.edu/cu/lweb/eresources/archives/eastasian/mason/ldpd.6601952.001b.html, quoted as narrated in this source.]

joint publication with the Chinese Publishing House in Kyoto with MATANI Ryuzō as translator. But, only two things interested IMAOKA enough to mention them during the coming years: the Shinto shrine visits and Mason's having known Bergson, the famous French philosopher. With Mason, IMAOKA could travel to Shinto shrines around Japan as his guide and translator. IMAOKA had his own agenda, finding Shintoists who opposed war and had a non-ideological understanding of Shinto.

A Brief Note about Bergson's Fame

Mason had been led to the thought of Henri Bergson by none other than William James. James and Bergson had begun correspondence around 1903.[349] James introduced Henri Bergson (1859-1941) to America in two publications, in his 1909 *Pluralistic Universe* and his facilitation of the translation of Bergson's *L'évolution créatrice* (1907) which was finished after his death. It was translated by Arthur Mitchell and was published as *Creative Evolution* in 1911. In his Hibbert lectures in London at Oxford, published as *Pluralistic Universe* in 1909, James praised Bergson's thought, thus introducing him, not to England, but to America.

Mason would read *Creative Evolution* and compare its "findings" with a 1895 book written by a New York editor, Henry Mills Alden.[350] This 1913 article for the *North American Review*

---

349. For some recent studies of Bergson and James, see: Paul Ardoin *et al.* (editors) *Understanding Bergson, Understanding Modernism* (Bloomsbury Academic 2013); Keith Ansell-Pearson, Thinking Beyond the Human Condition (Bloomsbury Academic 2018); "Chapter 4. The Comprehensive Meaning of Life in *Bergson,"* Translated from the French by Edward F. McGushin in Scott Campbell and Paul W. Bruno (eds.), *Science, Politics, and Ontology of Life-Philosophy* (Bloomsbury Academic 2013); Rosa Slegers, "James and *Bergson*: Fighting the Beast Intellectualism with Metaphors" (Chapter 7) in David Evans (ed.), *Understanding James, Understanding Modernism* (Bloomsbury Academic, 2015)

350. Henry Mills Alden, *A Study of Death* (New York: Harper and Brothers, 1895), 338pp. Harper would publish Mason's study of Bergson, *Creative Freedom* in 1926.

concluded that Bergson's method of philosophical intuition came to the same insights about the nature of reality and life, as did Henry Mills Alden's *A Study of Death*.[351] Alden's study is an important key to understanding how Mason abridged Bergson. However, Mason's understanding or misunderstanding of Bergson lies outside of IMAOKA's concerns. IMAOKA accepted Mason's self-identification as a Bergsonian even though he hints that he was well aware that Mason was neither a philosopher nor had understood Bergson's key ideas.[352] What he did not say in this regard is revelatory. He did not say (1) that he studied Bergson with Mason or (2) that Mason helped him understand something in Bergson's thought. He and MINAMI had taught Bergson's complex philosophical understanding of evolution's processes at Unity Hall – metaphoric images instead of concepts or principles for duration, creative evolution, a pluralistic universe, freedom without mechanism or determinism, fluid reality apprehended not by intellect but intuition, multiple perspectives as forms of interpenetrating practical and intuitive consciousness, open-ended freedom evolving and devolving, change and becoming with no determined *telos* or end, etc.[353] He would find none of this in Mason's use of Bergson. What he found was much different.

Mason's Use of Bergson

Mason had met Henri Bergson while he was a correspondent

---

351. J.W.T. Mason, "The Bergson Method Confirmed," *The North American Review*, Vol. 197, 1913, pp.90-104, reviewing Henry Mills Alden, *A Study of Death* (New York: Harper and Brothers, 1895), 338pp. Mason states that he begins as an agnostic but finds in Alden confirmation of Bergson's insights.

352. IMAOKA stated: "although I do not completely agree with him…." in 1966 talk, "Re-Examination of Mason's Shinto" (Essay 56 in Imaoka, *Jinsei hyakunen* [Hundred years of a Human Life], Tokyo: Daizō shuppan, 1982.). In an interview July 3, 1985, IMAOKA said: "Mason was a friend of Henri Bergson in France. His ideas were Bergsonian. Mason interpreted Shintoism as creative evolution. Mason thought creative intuition of primitive Japanese people was Shintoism; that it was nothing but creative evolution."

353. There has been renewed study of and interest in Bergson. See also footnote 349.

in Europe. In 1927 when Bergson won the Nobel Prize for Literature, he could be called the most famous philosopher of his day (although other philosophers said his very popularity proved he wasn't a philosopher at all). Mason became one of the many popularizers of Bergson, using elements of his thought in *Creative Freedom* (1926)[354] and in *Creative East* (1928).[355] Mason's books used Bergsonian terms as concepts and principles, especially *creative evolution* and *vital impulse*, arriving in Japan with an almost completed study of the source of Japan's creativity – which according to Mason was Shinto.

In *Creative Freedom,* Mason proudly acknowledged his use of Bergson, quoting him eight times on as many pages.[356] Within Bergson's aura, his theme was the need for freedom to create and to evolve, especially the need for spiritual freedom. On page 397 of the book's 538 pages, *freedom* is used constantly. But even his American reviewers found his usage almost foreign – spiritualized in an evolutionary setting. The review of this first book did not go well. In *The Outlook* of July, 1926, the reviewer wrote:

> "Creative Freedom," says the author in his preface, "is the name given in this book to the quest which stimulates the evolution of existence in its progress away from the disintegration of Absolute Freedom." Quite so. He adds: "The author feels how inadequately he has performed the work of writing and rewriting his book." A perfectly adequate criticism, which happily relieves this reviewer of an ungrateful task. But just one sentence to prove how perfect a self-critic the author is: "The aesthetic reminiscence of the spontaneous creativeness of omnipotence may even cause man to consider himself omnipotently self-efficient when he is deep in aesthetic absorption." Let us pass on.[357]

---

354. J.W.T. Mason, *Creative Freedom* (New York: Harper and Brothers, 1926), 538pp.
355. J.W.T. Mason, *Creative East* (New York: Dutton; London: John Murray, 1928), 144pp.
356. *Creative Freedom* pages xi, 15, 17, 46, 74, 84, 201, 359 twice, and in the index, 520.
357. Review in *The Outlook* (July 21, 1926), p. 421.

Other reviews were not as cruel, but they too pointed out Mason's attempt to be a philosopher about life and its purpose or direction.[358]

Bergsonian Terminology

Bergson's popularizers had attached themselves to weighted terms [*terminus technicus* used by the philosopher] that made them recognized as being his students and needing his aura for their own thought. Bergson had become a refuge from the threat of atheistic evolution, determinism, and materialism.[359] Mason had even attracted a French theologian who wondered if Bergson could be read in support of Christian dogmas.[360] Mason's books seemed to be religious, although he resisted using the term religious and called himself spiritual and agnostic to Western religion. His style of nineteenth century philosophizing with a spiritual bent had not bothered the French reviewer, as it had the American in *The Outlook.* The heaviness of his style would modify slightly in each succeeding book but his use of key or weighted words of Bergson would not.

Creative East introduced Mason's idea that Japan alone had balanced the three creative *fulfilments* [Mason's spelling, and one of

---

358. Cf. reviews in *Ethics (*1926), p. 421; *Bookman* (May 1926), p. 368; and a substantial but disapproving one in a French Catholic journal: J. Dermine's review in *Comples rendus* (1927), pp. 358-60.

359. The revival of the academic study of Bergson has been led by Gilles Deleuze. For more, see Bloomburg publications.

360. Mason's quotations of Bergson declined in *Creative Freedom, Creative East,* and *Meaning of Shinto*. He quoted Bergson directly nine times in the first but only twice in *Meaning*. However, his use of Bergsonian terminology remained substantial. J. Dermine, *op.cit.,* in his review of *Creative Freedom*, concluded: "La synthèse très large et assez logique construite par M. Mason n'a pu être obtenue que par un effort puissant, mais où la « Liberté créatrice » de l'auteur paraît avoir joué un rôle beaucoup plus important que l'objectivité et l'étude vraiment scientifique de la réalité." [The very broad and logical synthesis constructed by Mr. Mason could only be obtained by a powerful effort, but in which the author's "creative freedom" appears to have played a much more important role than the objective and truly scientific study of reality.]

his privileged terms[361]]: *spiritual*, *aesthetic*, and *utilitarian*. India and China had each erred – India becoming too passively *spiritual* and China too impractically *aesthetic*. Japan's ability to achieve this balance of all three came from its openness to "*primaeval* spirit," giving it the creative freedom to modernize, most remarkably in military science. His chapter on "Japan's Creative Religious Discernment" found Shinto to be its source. "All life is spiritual," said Mason. "Kami-Nagata" (the essence of Shinto, he said) meant "being in the state of spirituality." He concluded: "For the essential basis of Shinto is that man descends from the Kami or Original Spirit, individualized in 'The Plain of High Heaven.'"[362] Thus, Mason had already rehearsed most of his ideas about Shinto and Japan, before he arrived in 1932. He would become bolder in transforming Bergsonian images and metaphors into concepts and principles, especially in explaining social development (which he termed racial and national development, in the common usage of the 19th and early 20th centuries).

Without getting too pedantic and only hinting at linguistic usage of technical or weighted terms, a brief excursion will be beneficial. How an author relies on certain words or concepts reveals both the strength and weakness of their thought, as IMAOKA would say. Mason chose terms from Bergson to reinforce his own ideas about Japan and Shinto — and that is one reason that IMAOKA called him "Bergsonian." The frequency of their usage and the use of equivalents also reveals the foci of their arguments. Sometimes, frequency of usage hides a lack of a coherent definition of a term and attempts to convince through repetition. As Mason became more certain of his own thought, his use of direct quotations of Bergson declined.

---

361. Weighted or privileged terms, *terminus technicus*, will be italicized.

362. *Creative East, op.cit.*, pp. 117-18. Mason found no problem in mixing ontology with geography.

Two terms, found on the 538 pages of Mason's *Creative Freedom* (1926), were *impetus* and, or course, *freedom*. Impetus was used on 296 pages with it appearing four times or more on 81 pages. Freedom was used on 397 pages with 74 pages having four or more usages. The following table suggests that Mason used Bergsonian terminology and could easily be identified as a Bergsonian. The *Meaning of Shinto* (1935) continued to use characteristic Bergsonian terminology even after he began working with IMAOKA.

Creative Freedom (1926)	*Creative East* (1928)	*Meaning of Shinto* (1935)
freedom, impetus	progress, "fulfilment"	vitality, creativeness
vitality, creativity	creativeness, spirituality	spirituality, consciousness
life, God	life, God	life, God

Probably more important than frequency or redundancy of words used is the use of technical terms, sometimes called "jargon of the trade." Mason adapted weighted Bergsonian words as *terminus technicus*. Mason found *life* (often a term he substituted for God), *impetus*, *creativeness*, *consciousness*, *intuition*, *understanding*, *spirituality* and *freedom* to be words that he weighted with his own special meanings. Again, he used these power words frequently.[363] In other words, Mason used and adapted Bergsonian language, easily recognizable at the time. What is more important is that Mason's project in Japan was to further prove that the source of Japan's creativity came from Shinto. Shinto had preserved *spiritual intuition*, and that had brought about a unique national and *racial consciousness*. Mason's support of Japan's unique national essence or spirit brought instant attention in Japan, especially among Shintoists.

[363] *Life* was used 306 times on 137 pages and combined with God 23 times on 21 pages; *impetus* 99 times; *creativeness* 17 times; *consciousness* 113 times; *intuition* 98 times and combined with *spiritual* 3 times, *primaeval* 11 times, Shinto 17 times; *instinct* 5 times and instinctive 6 times; *understanding* 67 times, *spirituality* 52 times, and *freedom* 19 times.

Why is all this mentioned? It demonstrates that Mason came to Japan having rehearsed most of his findings about *life* and its *creative direction*, as the *impetus* for *creativeness* in *Creative Freedom* and then as the *impetus* for *fulfilment* (Mason's spelling) in his second book, *Creative East*. This second book had all but given away how Japan had retained its creativity because of Shinto, his thesis for *The Meaning of Shinto*. And within a year of meeting with IMAOKA at the Harvard Club, he would not only give IMAOKA the manuscript, but IMAOKA would have translated and shepherded it into a Japanese publication, *Kami Nagara no Michi*.[364] However, Mason's English manuscript took another two years to get Dutton to print it as *The Meaning of Shinto*.[365] Quite importantly, IMAOKA is mentioned on the title page of the Dutton's 1935 edition as the translator of the Japanese version. Recent reprints by Kennikat (1967 photocopying Dutton's 1st edition) and Trafford (2002 digitizing the text but leaving out any acknowledgement of IMAOKA's translation) have kept *The Meaning of Shinto* available.

Mason continued working while IMAOKA translated the manuscript into Japanese. Mason produced two other books that were printed in Japan but never in English. In 1934 he worked with KANO Hisao and Daito Press to publish *Creative Japan*.[366] By 1935 he and OTANI Tokunō (his translator) brought out *Shintō me de mita Ōbei*

---

364. J.W.T. Mason, author, and IMAOKA Shin'ichiro, translator. J.W.T.メーソン著；今岡信一良訳　神ながらの道 ： 日本人のアイデンティティ(個性)と創造性の再発見 [The Meaning of Shinto: Rediscovering Japanese identity and creativity] たま出版 1989.5 東京　285p [Tama publication, Tokyo, 1989.5]

365. J.W.T. Mason, *The Meaning of Shinto: The Primaeval Foundation of Creative Spirit in Modern Japan* (New York: E. P. Dutton, 1935), 252pp.

366. J・W・Tメーソン述；鹿野久恒編　[J.W.T. Mason; Kano, Hisao], 創造の日本 ： 附諸家のメーソン觀 [Creative Japan], 大東出版社 1934 [Daito Publishing Company, 1934].

(*Shrines May Serve America*).[367] This book had no traction in Japan and was not translated into English.

IMAOKA's translation of *The Meaning of Shinto* became a classic among Shintoists and opened doors for Mason that he immediately took advantage of during his second visit to Japan. Mason took as his purpose in *The Meaning of Shinto* to tell Japanese what they had not brought to self-consciousness and were therefore inarticulate in sharing with the world. He had stated that intention in 1926 before visiting Japan. In 1935 he told Japanese directly how to accomplish this themselves. Saying this in English would have had little consequence and would have seemed arrogant and offensive. But IMAOKA's Japanese, in Mason's name, seemed to meet a need of defending Shinto against Western criticism. Even Mason's English words catch how he presumed to tell Japanese what to find in Shinto and how to defend it. In the Preface, Mason wrote: "Shinto is simple in its outward forms but has profound inward significance. The Japanese have never tried to make Shinto self-expressive in objective analytical ways but have been content to let the inner spirit of Shinto guide them as an integral part of themselves."[368]

His second trip to Japan would include more extensive travel with IMAOKA, visiting shrines and giving presentations to large audiences and small groups of dignitaries – the result of the success of the Japanese translation.[369]

---

367. J・W・T・メーソン著；小谷徳水譯 [J.W.T. Mason; translated by Otani Tokunō], 神道眼で觀た歐米 [Shintō me de mita Ōbei], 立命館出版部 1935.9 [Ritsumeikan Publishing Division, September 1935].

368. J.W.T. Mason, *The Meaning of Shinto: The Primaeval Foundation of Creative Spirit in Modern Japan* (New York: E. P. Dutton, 1935), Preface.

369. There has been a mild revival of Mason's study among American Shintoists, principally affiliated with Tsubaki America. And for that reason, the Harvard Interfaith Project cites Mason as a source on Shinto. J.W.T. Mason, *The Meaning of Shinto: The Primæval Foundation of Creative Spirit in Modern Japan* (Port Washington, N.Y.: Kennikat Press, 1967) and J.W.T. Mason, *The Meaning of Shinto*

The Meaning of Shinto

> "The genius of Henri Bergson has given to the world an understanding of the creative impetus which provides the key to interpreting the character of Japan's creative evolution and the power of Shinto.The creative impetus is the spontaneous impulse of life seeking freedom of action."
>
> – J. W. T. Mason, Meaning of Shinto[370]

Mason would only quote Bergson directly twice in *The Meaning of Shinto,* yet Bergson's key words fill the text. Its main thesis was that in its unconscious myths Shinto has retained *primaeval intuition* of the *vital impetus* for *life* as *creative* and ever *evolving.* This was Japan's genius, its uniqueness, he wrote. It had preserved the knowledge that all *life* is *Kami* [divine, sacred]. As IMAOKA summarized Mason's view years later: "Shinto is primeval and intuitive truth discovered by the Japanese race and has always been the motive power of self-creative activities of Japan as is shown in her history. Bergson's *élan vital* is nothing but the French translation of Shinto Spirit."[371]

IMAOKA would later draw attention to Mason's emphasis that all are Kami, heaven and earth, human and divine:

> His View of Shinto was a Unity Between Heaven and Earth and Man and God as One. ...
>
> One of the many criticisms of Mason is that the Shinto he advocated was Mason's own brand of Shinto and not Japanese Shinto. It is true that Mason did not study the Japanese language, so that he studied Japan and Shinto through English translations of Japanese articles. But Mason excused this by saying, "Were not Nichiren and Shinran great Buddhists despite the fact that they never studied Sanskrit?" In this, we see evidence of his strength as well as of his weakness. Another criticism of Mason is that the

---

(eBook, 2002). Scholars of Japanese religions have not been generous in their assessment of Mason's Shinto. Yet, elderly Shinto priests in Japan still praise it as a fine work of a foreigner.

370. *Ibid.* p. 11.

371. IMAOKA, S., "My Spiritual Pilgrimage," 1970.

Shinto he advocated is nothing more than a rehash of the philosophy of Bergson.[372]

IMAOKA's Invisible Influence in *The Meaning of Shinto*

After the citation on the title page of the 1st edition in 1935, IMAOKA totally disappears.[373] In the Preface of *The Meaning of Shinto* (1935) published in America, Mason gave a sweeping acknowledgment to everyone except IMAOKA:

> The author wishes to thank friends in all parts of Japan who have shown him unfailing kindness and have always been so patient in helping him to understand something of the inner character of the Japanese spirit. Not so much by verbal explanations but attitudes, conduct and the normal activities of life and responses to environment have the Japanese people shown the author their understanding of the meaning of Shinto. The author has tried to translate into words what this meaning is, in some of its fundamental aspects. Where he has failed, the fault is his. If he has been able to reflect the spirit of Shinto in some small way it is because the Japanese people themselves have shown him where the rays fall by their own reactions.[374]

What Mason did not acknowledge was the fact that he did not know Japanese and required a translator to interview his "friends in all parts of Japan" and a guide – IMAOKA. Unless one interprets his

---

372. "Re-examination of Mason's Shinto," 1965. Essay # 65.

373. A comparative study of Imaoka's translation and published Japanese text with Mason's English publications is outside the scope of this study. It would be a worthy dissertation topic and could reveal why the Japanese translations have found deep admiration among Shintoists, while scholars have consistently ignored Mason's English books on Shinto and Japan. There has been use of a reprint of *The Meaning of Shinto* recently among American Shintoists at Tsubaki America.

374. Joseph Warren Teets Mason. *The Meaning of Shinto: The Primaeval Foundation of Creative Spirit in Modern Japan.* New York: E. P. Dutton, 1935. The following quotations in this section are from *The Meaning of Shinto,* chapters instead of pages are referenced as page numbers disappear in electronic reprints.

While Mason was less than generous in acknowledging IMAOKA's role as translator, his meticulous contracts archived at Columbia University library seem exploitive from current sensitivities about indigenous knowledge. IMAOKA served as Mason's guide, translator, and cultural interpreter without the slightest hint of complaint.

carefully crafted sentences about trying "to translate into words what this meaning is," it seems that Mason suggested that he was fluent and quite humble in accepting any fault for his own translations.

Chapters Three and Nine in *The Meaning of Shinto* are interesting in that they required linguistic assistance, undoubtedly IMAOKA's. Since IMAOKA's Japanese version was published in 1933, two years before the English version, there was time to benefit from IMAOKA's help in understanding its very title, *Kami Nagata no Michi.* IMAOKA remained unmentioned in the English version of Chapter Three which is about the "Meaning of Shinto." Mason began by explaining that the Chinese term of "Shinto did not come into use immediately to differentiate Japanese from Chinese conceptions. The original term was Kami Nagata." Mason then worked as a linguist with the elements of the Japanese phrase, *kami nagata*, which WAS chosen for the Japanese title of his book. He told his readers that he dismissed the translation, "Kami-like," since it might "imply that man must strive to be like Kami or man is naturally pure as Kami may be conceived as being." He derived the true meaning from Shinto mythology: "for the inherent Shinto idea is that everything, whatever its nature, good or bad, is Kami-like." Then he told his reader that *kami no michi* was the "Japanese pronunciation of the Chinese ideographs for Shinto…" Importantly, Mason stated that "Further elucidation, however, is necessary to understand what the primeval Japanese mentality sought to express." He turned to Lao-Tze and Taoism [Mason used Wade-Giles spellings from the standard translations of the day] to explain China's choice of extreme spiritual passivity, while *primaeval Japanese spirituality* intuited *creative action* in a unified universe where everything is *Kami*. "That was the Kami way." There was a footnote crediting KATO Genchi with the translation of "michi" as "divine." But, Mason had corrected or expanded his understanding by going deeper than KATO into the spiritual understanding of the terms, so he presented this insight as his own.

Mason acknowledged his written sources in the footnotes, all of which could have been read in the New York Public Library and had been used in his previous books – Aston, Chamberlain, Jeans or Waley. IMAOKA probably suggested the Japanese source that Mason quoted on page 25 – ANESAKI's *History of Japanese Religion*, who coincidentally was IMAOKA's mentor.

In Chapter Nine of *The Meaning of Shinto,* Mason described visits to six Shinto Shrines. Three are natural shrines: a waterfall, a mountain, and a rock. His descriptions are deeply spiritual, the characteristic that IMAOKA admired. Of Hiryu Shrine at the Nachi waterfall, Mason wrote: "Nature has given sanctity to the place; the universal spirit of Nature consecrated the Flying Waterfall for the primitive man's spiritual refreshment. ...for the Falls are Kami or divine spirit." Near Nara the Omiwa Shrine is Mt. Omiwa itself which "represents divine spirit on earth reaching upward toward the Heavenly source of life – the inseparable union of Heaven and earth in universal divinity. … Primaeval Shinto conceived infinity in terms of unconfined freedom; and represented the idea by paying spiritual respect to the living Mountain of Omiwa." Shinto's Rock of Ages, Iishi Shrine in Izumo, is "a reminder of the all-inclusiveness of spirit, perpetuated from the remote ages of the human race."

These natural shrines supported Mason's conception of *primordial intuition* of the unified divinity of *life.* He would write what could easily represent the conclusion of his study often repeated throughout the book with more examples:

> Not at Nachi Falls nor at Omiwa Mountain nor at the Rock of Iishi does Shinto countenance theological worship of the Falls or Mountain or Rock. No spirit, no deity resides in them in any Shinto sense whatever. The Falls, the Mountain and the Rock are themselves Kami, self-creative divine spirit emerging from

> spacelessness and self-developing as the material universe; and man is the same in origin. This primaeval knowledge of reality marks the true greatness of Shinto in understanding the universality of divine spirit. *It is pure monism.* [emphasis added]

Mason then deduced the philosophical and theological corollaries of his findings:

> Shinto denies the dualistic doctrine that imagines a spirit in the Falls or in the Mountain or in the Rock. Kami, divine self-creative spirit, *is* Nature and also is all life, including mankind. There is no separation between the spaceless spiritual source of the universe and any of its objective aspects, any more than there is any separation between immaterial electrons and their emergence into material forms. Immaterial electrons and material elements are the same; and so spaceless divine spirit and Nachi Falls, Omiwa Mountain, the Rock of Iishi and man, himself, are the same. They are spaceless self-creative spirit externalized, and separated from one another in individual formation, but inseparable in spiritual origin. Man, bowing before Nature does not perform a religious rite, in Shinto, but pays respect to Heavenly spirit that is himself and more than himself for it is the entire universe. If the Falls, the Mountain and the Rock were sentient, they, in turn, would bow before man, seeing in his difference from themselves enlargement of creative divine spirit beyond themselves.

This was Mason's profession of faith in Shinto – a Shinto that is monistic, without worship, images, or a Creator God. He had concluded that (1) *Life* is monistic. It is Kami; humans and Nature are Kami. (2) *Primaeval consciousness* knew this intuitively, instinctively. Shinto's inarticulate understanding of reality came directly from *Primaeval Consciousness*. (3) Shinto's creativity is *élan vital*, the *vital impulse* that must be made self-conscious by Japanese themselves so its sacred treasure can be shared with a materialistic, mechanistic world. The corollaries abound: no god of creation, no creation ex nihilo, no worship, no idols, no ecclesiasticism, no ancestor worship (since all are family, the Mikado

[Emperor] is head of the family, and all Japanese are descendants of Amaterasu). Life is one; it can only be understood as everything being divine; he did not attempt to refute the charge that his philosophical conception was simple pantheism.

Mason's concepts would be tested at the three other shrines that they visited on his first trip to Japan, all linked to *Kokka Shintō* (State *Shintō*): Ise, Taisha and Meiji. And Mason's spiritualizing powers in interpreting these shrines again was amply needed. Mason did not experience them as a war correspondent but as a spiritualist and a believer. He dismissed any connections to the "Russo-Japanese War" and ascribed religious meanings to each State Shrine:

> Ise Shrine represents the spiritual unification of the Japanese race in the Shinto meaning of Heavenly divine ancestry. The Taisha Shrine represents the political and geographical unification of the Japanese race through the consolidation of Okuninushi' s territory in the West with Central and Southern Japan – individual parts made permanently cooperative, through human effort. Amaterasu, the first of the Heavenly Kami, is enshrined at Ise. Okuninushi, the first great leader of earthly birth, is enshrined at Taisha. Each is Shinto Kami.

Mason immediately protected his hypothesis, as his eyes saw rituals and images that needed to be explained as symbols.

> Neither Amaterasu nor Okuninushi, however, is an ecclesiastical god in Shinto. ... They are not worshipped in Shinto, but respect is paid to them by living divine spirit whereby the subconscious Shinto intuition of spirituality in its different aspects rises nearer to the surface of the mind.

Meiji Shrine in Tokyo was praised for honoring the human-Kami effort of the past Emperor. Both Meiji and Taisha shrines "represent the continuity of the Shinto impetus of creative action, spreading forth from primitive beginnings into the modern world, carrying progress, through human effort, step by looks to the future [*sic.*, as written by Mason], where increasing creative power depends on the primaeval spiritual intuition of Shinto continuing to endure in

Japan and becoming self-consciously understood by the people."[375]

The most telling invisibility of IMAOKA would be in Mason's conversation with Rev. UDA Ikashemaro. Mason stated: "This saying was written for the author by Rev. Ikashemaro Uda, Chief Executive and Assistant Chief Priest of the Great Shrine at Ise."[376] Neither spoke or wrote the others' language. IMAOKA would reminisce about that visit in 1970 with a different perspective and details:

> When Mason and I visited the Kashiwara Shrine, the chief priest Mr. Uda explained that the door of the sanctuary has been and will be never opened. As soon as the chief priest ended his explanation, Mason cried : "Shinto gods are spiritual! Shinto should keep no image or idol of gods. If any, it should be kept in a museum, not in the sanctuary."[377]

IMAOKA would translate Mason's conceptions of Shinto faithfully because it spiritualized Shinto at a time when religious Shinto contradicted the state ideology. IMAOKA would undoubtedly have been in danger had he attacked State Shinto's ideology of ultranationalism. Helping Mason promote his spiritual interpretations was IMAOKA's way of assisting an American journalist in his quest.

In trying to establish himself in English as a Shinto scholar, Mason's footnotes in the 1st edition and Endnotes in the digital editions reveal ten interviews with Japanese scholars. In each of those cases he would have needed a translator. Prof. INOUYE of the Imperial University, father-in-law of ANESAKI and participant with IMAOKA in many progressive actions, was unapproachable without a proper introduction.

Perhaps all this is too critical of Mason. It was another era in which Western scholars took indigenous knowledge and made it their own. IMAOKA never hinted that he felt misused. Actually, he only

375. Mason's closing paragraph to Chapter Nine, *Meaning, op.cit.*

376. Mason, *Meaning, op.cit.,* Chapter Nine, footnote 3.

377. IMAOKA, "My Spiritual Pilgrimage" (1970).

mentioned having the opportunity to travel with Mason and learn the true meaning of Shinto. What IMAOKA meant by that will be the concluding note of this chapter.

Learning the True Meaning of Shinto

In 1937 IMAOKA and Mason traveled to Mie Prefecture on the route leading down the peninsular to Ise Grand Shrine. In ancient times Tsubaki Shrine had been a huge dual Shinto shrine and Buddhist temple complex with an army to defend this approach to the Imperial Shrine at Ise.[378] Trying to stop the Shogun, IEYASU, from declaring himself Emperor at Ise, brought near destruction to Tsubaki. At Tsubaki Mason and IMAOKA were met by a Shinto scholar and priest, YAMAMOTO Yukiteru. The connection between Tsubaki Shrine and IMAOKA would last. Mason never mentioned the small shrines IMAOKA thought were the most important like Tsubaki and Tepposu. Undoubtedly, the chance to visit these shrines were among the real reasons that IMAOKA assisted Mason. What was important for IMAOKA in his faith journey was meeting an exemplar of Shrine Shinto, the elder YAMAMOTO at Tsubaki Jinja. He was also a pacifist whose three sons would serve in the Pacific War, with only YAMAMOTO Yukitaka surviving to become the future *Guji* of a renewed and transformed Tsubaki Daijinja.[379]

IMAOKA saw the elder YAMAMOTO as a free religionist and at Tsubaki experienced the depth and spirituality of Shinto. This was a different form of religious experience as it approached spiritual transformation through ritualized activity and physical action. Its centering in activity subordinated reason, emotion and intuition to sensed experience (sight, sound, touch, taste, smell – plus motion). Religion was embodied, incarnated – literally. Its activities were

378. Yukitaka YAMAMOTO, *Kami no Michi* (New Horizons Press, 1984).

379. *Ibid.* See also, George Williams, *Shinto* (Philadelphia: Chelsea House Publishers, 2005) in which Tsubaki Shinto is presented to illustrate a progressive movement within Shrine Shinto.

called religious rituals and were easily recognized in the activity of religious worship – bowing, chanting, dancing, to name but a few. These were not exclusive to actional religion. It was their being given priority over rationality, devotion and mystical experience that differentiated this form of religion and its potential for spiritual transformation from other spiritual paths or types. Its experience transformed ugliness into sensed beauty, chaos into harmony and separateness into community.

Mason's Last Trip and Publication

The Spirit of Shinto Mythology was ready in English and published in Japan in 1939, and IMAOKA's translation would be published a year later.[380] Mason with his wife enjoyed speaking to large audiences and attending banquets in his honor. IMAOKA travelled with them and translated. Before leaving Japan in 1940, Mason spoke at IMAOKA's 15th anniversary as principal of Seisoku Academy. Mason praised IMAOKA, saying: "he is the most spiritual and egoless person I ever met..."[381] Mason died upon his return to New York but his ashes were returned in an urn to Tokyo.[382]

IMAOKA recalled: "When he died in New York in 1942, his ashes were brought to Japan to be buried in the Tama Cemetery in Tokyo, although it was the time when the U.S.A. and Japan were at war with one another."[383]

Learning With Mason

IMAOKA used two of his favorite words for the learning experience with Mason: study and research. Both were linked to his

380. J.W.T. Mason, *The spirit of Shinto mythology* (Fuzambo 1939); 神道神話の精神 [*The Spirit of Shinto Mythology*] J・W・T・メーソン著 ; 今岡信一良譯 [J · W · T · Mason's work; Imaoka Shinkiichi [*sic.*], translator] 冨山房 1940.4 [Toyama Publishing House, 1940].

381. Mason, *Papers*, archived at Columbia University.

382. IMAOKA, 1969 IARF morning devotion.

383. Imaoka, "My Spiritual Pilgrimage" (1970).

Mason's grave in Tama Cemetery, Tokyo

having discovered that he was also a Shintoist. And, having found the spiritual vitality of Shinto for growth and creative change, IMAOKA reaffirmed the concept of *multiple spiritual identities*.

> Even now, when I happen to be among Buddhists and Shinto priests, I feel [that I am] coming back home. But I never take off my Christianity. I do not feel a contradiction within myself, being a Christian, a Buddhist, and a Shintoist at the same time. The three are not one, however, having quite different characteristics and individualities, all of them exist in me supplementary of each other.[384]

There is a hint of the moment when IMAOKA knew he was also a Shintoist. That insight was placed in Mason's mouth when he described the "intuition of reality that caused primaeval Shinto to bow in acknowledgment of the divine co-ordination between humanity and the material manifestations of Nature."[385] Bowing to others was also reverence to life and would become a simple example of spiritual growth. For IMAOKA it was a gentle reminder of living in gratitude.

Yet, learning the "true meaning of Shinto" was not credited to Mason, but, oddly, to John Haynes Holmes, the radical ex-Unitarian minister and leader of the Community Church movement. Holmes had never visited Japan or studied Shinto. It was his book that arrived in 1922, as Unity Hall was being closed. Just as IMAOKA gave Mason

384. IMAOKA, talk at 1973 Japan Free Religious Association.
385. Mason, *Meaning,* Chapter Nine.

credit for the opportunity to study Shinto, he gave credit to Holmes, not specifically as his teacher, but for an important insight or moment of growth. In this way of crediting others, he avoided inflating a self-serving ego. He repeated this acknowledgement in many different talks.

"I learned the true nature of Shinto from John Haynes Holmes. That Shinto is a Community Church."[386] From a different perspective in a 1984 talk, IMAOKA would give Holmes credit for teaching him how to interpret Shinto: "It was John H. Holmes who suggested to me how to interpret Shinto in terms of the Community Church."[387] "[From h]is idea of a 'Community Church,' I was awakened to recognize it has been the fundamental idea of Shinto, too. I am fully convinced that Holmes' book suggests the only way in which Shinto becomes relevant to the present needs of Japan."[388] "John Haynes Holmes in America had made me aware of the present day meaning of ancient Shintoism through his Community Church Movement."[389]

In 1973 at the 25th Anniversary celebration of Japan Free Religion Association of which he was a co-founder in 1948, IMAOKA said:

> Since Showa 7 through Showa 15 [1932-1940], about ten years, I eagerly studied Shintoism, Shrine Shinto and Japanese culture with J.W.T. Mason, an American journalist and Shintoist. Even now, when I happen to be among Buddhists and Shinto priests, I feel [that I am] coming back home. But I never take off my Christianity. I do not feel a contradiction within myself, being a Christian, a Buddhist, and a Shintoist at the same time. The three are not one, however, having quite different characteristics and individualities, all of them exist in me supplementary of each

386. IMAOKA, "An Address Of Thanks" for Receiving the IARF Distinguished Leadership Award (1981).

387. IMAOKA, "Impressions of the 25th Congress," 1984.

388. *Ibid.*

389. The IARF Distinguished Leadership Award 1981.

other.[390]

Perhaps that unusual idea can be illustrated in an personal example. A year before his death IMAOKA's son, Professor IMAOKA Kenichirō, invited me to go with him for his annual visit to several Shinto shrines on a New Year's morning. At Meiji Grand Shrine as we were leaving, an announcement informed us that already one million people were on the grounds at 6 a.m. So, one might paraphrase IMAOKA sensei that "on New Years, every Japanese is a Shintoist, and Shinto is the community church of Japan." With simple rituals an inclusive community is created, and without prescribed dogmas a kind of unity is achieved for group consciousness and the potential of working together. But he also said: "Not yet."

IMAOKA's study of the Japanese classics at Tokyo Imperial University, his years of work with ANESAKI and NARUSE in Association Concordia, the conferences in which he was the working secretary (although never the official one who received the honor but not the work), his efforts to bring Shinto leaders into multi-religious programs against war and inequity – all this vast knowledge of Shinto and its practices was sublimated to praise Mason and Holmes. The shrine visits with Mason provided contacts for the final phase of his spiritual journey in interfaith work, but one cannot honestly agree with his crediting others for his insights about Shinto. He would bring together Shintoists who aspired to understand liberating spirituality – *free religion.* (See Chapter 13)

A Reflection on His Spiritual Journey

Since this time with Mason overlaps other periods of his spiritual growth, namely assisting ANESAKI and teaching at Seisoku Academy and Nihon University, the main observations have already been made. His rational mysticism continued. His mystical

390. IMAOKA, "A Viewpoint of Free Religion," given at the 25th Anniversary of the JFRA, November 3, 1973.

experience of *cosmic unity* would soon find a personal resolution to the conundrum of individualistic *free religion* dividing instead of unifying. While Mason was seeing Shinto's *creative vitality* as its source of power and modernization, IMAOKA saw its ritual-oriented practices providing the experience of *community*, or what Holmes had championed as the *community church.* Ritualistic religion, even without reason, could provide communal experience and inspire a group to work together for the common good.

The continuing learning and maturing ethically in difficult circumstances deepened. No existential crises were even hinted at, even though Mason was almost his opposite in numerous ways: one who sought attention, honors, taking maximum credit, using "indigenous knowledge" as if it were his own, and so much more. Mason so aptly said of IMAOKA: "the most spiritual and egoless person I ever met."

Chapter 13
Seeking a Cosmic Community - Becoming a Cosmic Person[391]

IMAOKA began rebuilding Seisoku Academy immediately after the Pacific War's end. As he had done after the Great Tokyo Earthquake in 1923, he called upon a vast network of acquaintances who gave generously. Seisoku Academy was once again restored, not from rubble but from ashes. One focus for the rest of his life was private education instilled with values that could transform graduates into becoming global citizens – human beings with values of non-sectarian religion that had no boundaries. He led Seisoku Academy as the "Eaton of Japan," the school of future prime ministers. For his 35th year as Seisoku's principal in 1950, he was honored with his first Imperial award, the Order of the Blue Ribbon by Law of Merit. At his 50th anniversary in 1965, he received a second Imperial award, The Fourth Order of Merit with Sacred Treasure. A private ceremony took place at the Imperial Palace, attended just by his family.

Although he had resigned his lectureship at Nihon University in 1936, his accomplishments in academia were recognized in 1955, when he was awarded an honorary membership in the Japanese Academy of Religion. The doctorate that he had missed at Harvard came to him in 1972, as an honorary degree from Meadville/Lombard Theological Seminary in Chicago.

---

391. NOTE ABOUT THIS CHAPTER: Evidence abounds for this period as there were so many witnesses, both Japanese and international. They knew and admired IMAOKA. There are details of IMAOKA's life imbedded in their own histories and memoirs. From 1980 through 1988 I was a witness of IMAOKA's final eight years, adding my own perspective and potential bias. I have made a deliberate choice not to include my encounters with these extraordinary leaders. I mentioned some of them in a talk which became a 1983 booklet, *Liberal Religious Reformation in Japan*. See more concerning this choice in footnotes 373, 407, 416.

IMAOKA's *Yuniterian* Agenda

IMAOKA's pacifism and internationalism had evolved into an even larger vision based on *free religion.* His academic and interreligious work continued to carry the *yuniterian* vision and spirit under a new name: *jiyū shūkyō* (*free religion*), having gone beyond Unitarianism. Even groups that were quite conservative and doctrinaire were encouraged to get involved with the work to help their religious communities find a higher unity. And when religious groups could not work with other religious traditions or were shunned by their own, he helped them start their own organizations. Shinshuren, the New Religious Association, had its beginnings in the 1930s with IMAOKA helping their reorganization in the early 1950s. It brought together newly founded Shinto and Buddhist groups. They had been targeted by the state during the Pacific War because they seemed more concerned about religion than loyalty to the state. Mainstream Shinto and Buddhist traditions did not accept them as authentic in practice and ecclesiastical organization. Konkō-kyō of Izuo (religious or Kyōha Shinto) and Rissho Kosei-kai (new Buddhist and lay led) were discovered by IMAOKA, who recruited them for interfaith cooperation and work for peace. His agenda would be revealed on four levels: personal learning, and action through local, national, and international organizations for study and work for real unity in diversity.

With ANESAKI in declining health, IMAOKA did the organizing for the 1947 Interfaith Conference on Peace. That led to the 1948 Round Table Conference on Religion and Peace. The gatherings brought together religious leaders and scholars from Japan's four traditions (Buddhist, Shinto, Confucian, and Christian). This was a continuation of what Association Concordia had attempted before the war as well as of the national conferences of 1928 and 1931.

Activities prior to the arrival of any American Unitarian

representative after the war demonstrated that IMAOKA had already continued his *yuniterian* vision in the quest for liberating or free religion (*jiyū shūkyō*). (The notion that IMAOKA was awakened by an American initiative is in error to be examined in this chapter.)

The Broken Connection Mended

There is a denominational legend that the American Unitarian Association sent a representative to Japan in 1948 to find Unitarians and Universalists, and he would become the catalyst for their renewal. It was so reported in *The Christian Register.* The reality is much more interesting.

The Rev. John Nicholls Booth, son of a Unitarian minister, had become an accomplished magician before graduating from Meadville Theological School in 1942. He pastored Unitarian churches in Evanston (IL) and Belmont (MA) until 1948. Booth became restless for adventure and travel. According to his account in *Fabulous Destinations* written in 1950,[392] he resigned from his church for a "sabbatical year" in Asia, leaving behind his wife and infant daughter. He anticipated that his adventures would be too strenuous for them. The adventures were indeed daring, dangerous and even foolhardy. He began with Japan, which was under U. S. military occupation. During his visit there, he did a magic show at the Imperial Palace, met with SUZUKI Daisetzu, tried meditation at Enkakuji without learning the abbot's name, climbed Fujiyama, and met with a famous Japanese Christian writer. This book was about his Asian adventures and left out any mention of a Unitarian meeting.

The Unitarian legend is founded on an article compiled and published in *The Christian Register,* which introduced Booth as having had a great success writing Unitarian pamphlets but

---

392. John Nicholls Booth, *Fabulous Destinations* (New York: Macmillan, 1950).

erroneously placed his last ministry in Evanston instead of Belmont.[393] The *Register*'s editor does not even get Booth's departure date from San Francisco correct, implying that it was in September 1942 instead of June. And, this was only one of the many other mistakes that would follow.

On July 6, 1948, Booth appeared late for an historic meeting in the Tokyo home of KAWAMURA Otojiro, president of Kirin Beer. He had arrived 26 years after the last AUA representative had left Japan. Booth had promised reports to the AUA's *Christian Register* and the Chicago *Sun-Times,* using letters from each editor to gain a visa to enter Occupied Japan, which was still barred to most journalists and all tourists. But even as he sailed from San Francisco, his visa was revoked because they learned that he even lacked the credentials of a *cub reporter*. In *Fabulous Destinations,* Booth wrote that he entered Japan on fortuitous mistakes of American officials and remained there just long enough to file several stories.

His report to the *Christian Register* became the centerpiece of Unitarian denominational remembrance for this event.[394] Booth's account of the July meeting is not without problems. Chief among the errors was that Booth thought he was the "catalyst for which [they]

---

393. *The Christian Register* article in the October/November 1948 issue began with a note from the editor:

> Mr. Booth has reached a huge audience with his pamphlets, one of which alone, "Introducing Unitarianism," has had a distribution of more than 100,000. His most recent pamphlets are "The A. B. C.'s of Unitarian Faith," and "The Ministry as a Career." 'After completing six years at the Evanston church, Mr. Booth a few weeks ago left on a year's tour of the Orient. He is sending a series of dispatches to The Register and to the Chicago Sun-Times of which the following, sent from Tokyo, is the first.

One would need access to the UUA's ministerial members-only database to determine why his ministry was listed as Evanston instead of Belmont. This is most likely a mistake as Booth told IMAOKA that he was minister of Belmont.

394. John Nicholls Booth, "Unitarian Advance in the New Japan," *The Christian Register* (October/November, 1948). pp.33-35. (AUA historians might object to the use of the term "denominational" for the association.)

had been waiting" to reestablish the Japan Unitarian Association. In fact, he was attending one of the first discussions in July that would lead to the founding of the Japan Free Religious Association (*Nihon Jiyū Shūkyō Renmei*) in October, a date celebrated every year hence. The Japan Unitarian Association was never reestablished.

Eight liberal religionists – by the old nomenclature all *yuniterian* – met at KAWAMURA's home, and Booth's photograph was taken in KAWAMURA's garden. They were there to discuss IMAOKA's dream, a Japanese version of the American Free Religious Association.[395] Booth's picture and caption was the centerpiece of the *Christian Register* article.

Booth's camera centered him with the eight people at the July 6th meeting.[396] KAWAMURA, the brewer, most likely took the picture

395. A good starting point is Stow Persons, *Free Religion: An American Faith* (Yale University Press, 1947) and continued with a view of 25 years from its 3rd president William J. Potter, *The Free Religious Association: Its Twenty Five Years And Their Meaning* (1892).

396. John Nichells Booth, "Unitarian Advance in the New Japan," *Christian Register* (October/November 1948), p. 33-35.

which shows the religious diversity of the group. The AKASHI's, father and son at the lefthand ends of each row, were becoming Universalists (having been German Liberal Evangelicals before the war). KISHIMOTO Hideo, son of a radical *yuniterian*, was a Congregational church historian and quite a critic of Japanese and American Unitarianism. The others were liberal religionists, some with a long *yuniterian* history. IMAOKA was second from the right in the front row.

This picture was published in the October/November, 1948, *Christian Register* article with the following caption:

The Founding Members of The Japan Unitarian Association: *(Back Row, L. to R.)* Rev. Shigetaro Akashi, *pastor The Free Christian Church of Japan;* Mr. J. C. Orita, B.D., *graduate of Tufts College, Boston;* Rev. John Nicholls Booth; *Professor* Riichiro Hoashi, *Professor of Philosophy, Waseda University, Tokyo;* Dr. Hideo Kishimoto, *Professor of The Science of Religion, Tokyo Imperial University* *(Front Row, L. to R.)* *Professor* Michio Akashi, *Professor of Hebrew, St. John's University, Tokyo;* *Professor* Ichirosuke Aihara, *lecturer at Komazawa Buddhist College;* *Professor* Shinichiro Imaoka, *SeiSoku High School, Tokyo;* Mr. Hiroyuki Aoto, *Director Hibiya Civil Center Co., Ltd.*

Booth correctly learned that the senior AKASHI was formerly pastor of the Togosaka General Evangelical Church. It was the survivor of the German-Swiss Liberal Evangelical Mission. Booth wrote that AKASHI's church was "changing its name immediately to the Free Christian Church (Unitarian) of Japan." This was a mistake as it became Universalist. He also wrote, "It will constitute, in a sense, the first, or mother church of the new association."[397] Booth bragged that "It was my good fortune to preach the first sermon, on July 11th, to the congregation of the newly renamed Free Christian Church of Japan. It required two hours and thirty minutes for [my] sermon to be delivered … [with] translation…"[398]

Booth made a very perceptive observation: "Most of the Unitarian professors seem to have moved toward naturalistic or *cosmic theism*. Their thinking would accord with that of the most advanced trends in American Unitarian circles. The influence of

---

397. *Christian Register, ibid.*, p. 35.

398. *Ibid.* Another mistake as there would never again be a Japanese Unitarian Association.

Buddhism and Confucianism upon them is apparent. They are both appreciative and critical of these two movements."[399]

Booth reported that there were famous Unitarians still living: ABE Isō, member of the Japanese Diet, head of the Socialist Party and now known as the "father of Japanese baseball"; HOSIJIMA J., former minister of Commerce and Industry and then head of the Democratic Liberal Party; MATSUOKA K., chairman of the present Diet and member of the Socialist Party. Booth's article in the *Register* acknowledged help from the Religious and Cultural Resources Division of the American Occupation Army that had found and alerted the AUA concerning Japanese Unitarians. He said that they had facilitated his arrival at the July meeting.[400]

Founding the Japan Free Religious Association

IMAOKA included Booth in the Japanese record of these events, graciously mentioning his presence but not concurring with the account attributed to him. Booth came in the summer of 1948 and left. He facilitated the renewal of Japanese contact with the American Unitarians and Universalists. But, there was no reestablishment of the Japan Unitarian Association as reported or the founding of a "Free Christian Church (Unitarian) of Japan" by Rev. AKASHI Shigetaro. The AKASHIs reestablished Universalism in Japan.[401] IMAOKA's

399. *Ibid.* Emphasis mine.

400. William Parker, who was part of the American intelligence community facilitating in the Occupation, stated that a colleague, Denzel Kerr, also a New England Unitarian, informed the AUA of the existence of Japanese Universalists and Unitarians helping Booth find them. (Personal interview of Parker.)

401. Japanese histories have been written by the AKASHIs. AKASHI Michie, [The 100 Year Mission of the Dojin Universalist Christian Church.] Tokyo: Kyōbunsha, 1990. AKASHI Shigeo, [The Liberal Christian Movement]. Tokyo: Asahi Shorin, 1995. See also William Parker, "The Unitarian Mission in Japan," a 2008 presentation to the Tokyo International Unitarian Fellowship which included both Universalists and the German Mission [manuscript given to author]; and for the earlier period of Japanese Universalism: Carl Seaburg, *Dojin Means All People: The Universalist Mission in Japan, 1890-1942* (Boston: Universalist Historical Society, 1978).

account, as usual, gave everyone else maximum credit.[402] Booth was made a founding member of the Japan Free Religion Association (*Nihon Jiyū Shūkyō Renmei*). However, the JFRA was founded on October 17, 1948, when Booth had already reached China for one of the most dangerous parts of his adventure.[403] IMAOKA wrote: "In this connection, the fact that Rev. John Nicholls Booth, the then Unitarian minister of the First Church in Belmont, Massachusetts, U.S.A., happened to be staying in Japan in those days and became one of the nine co-founders." Prof. KISHIMOTO Hideo was the first president and IMAOKA was chairman of its Board. IMAOKA continued: "The Japan Free Religious Association has thus gone forward beyond liberal Christian movement of the pre-War period. This does not mean, however, that Japan Free Religious Association makes light of liberal Christianity; the only intention being to treat all religious liberals – Christian, Buddhist, Shinto and others – on an equal basis." Within months Seisoku Academy joined the JFRA, as a secular, nonsectarian, private school. And soon afterwards, Tenkō-san's Ittō-en, a lay Buddhist organization, would join. This was the initial membership of the national organization that IMAOKA brought to the international community of liberal religionists.

The Japanese Free Religious Association brought together religious and secular institutions that strove to practice *jiyū shūkyō* (*free religion*) or liberating spirituality in their communities. While *jiyū shūkyō* accurately identified JFRA's connection with Emerson and the American Free Religious Association, IMAOKA's use of two neologisms of the Meiji era, *jiyū* (free) and *shūkyō* (religion), would become both the primary characteristic of his life's work and an enigma that would have major consequences in the years ahead.

402. IMAOKA, *Japan Free Religious Association and two articles on Religious Freedom, "IARF Facts, Prospects"* (n.p., 1964). Handwritten note by Imaoka: "distributed among delegates to the IAFR [*not IARF*] Congress in Hague 1964."

403. Booth's exploits led him to found the Adventurers Club.

Emerson's picture graced the front wall of Unity Hall and was a constant reminder of Free Religion

Founding the Unity Fellowship (Kiitsu Kyōkai)

In November 1948, IMAOKA gathered a small group of *yuniterians* and formed *Kiitsu Kyōkai*. It would be a local gathering for individual cultivation and spiritual practice. This was not re-establishing the Tokyo Unitarian Church just as the JFRA was not a revival of the Japan Unitarian Association. Its distinctive name recalled ANESAKI, NARUSE and SHINOSAWA's Association Concordia, *Kiitsu Kyōkai*. The new *Kiitsu Kyōkai* was pronounced the same as the original organization founded back in 1912 – that had disappeared during the Pacific War.[404] However, the characters with the same pronunciation were carefully chosen to indicate continuity without imitation.

---

404. The Concordia Association was active before WWI but declined in influence afterwards. ANESAKI would die at age 75 on July 24, 1949 of a cerebral hemorrhage, marking its final demise even though organizationally it had died a decade before. See William P. Woodard,, "Interfaith Communication and the Confrontation of Religions in Japan," *Journal of Bible and Religion*, Vol. 32, No. 3 (Jul., 1964), pp. 231-238; KENJO Teiji, "On Religion and Morality: Shibusawa Ei'ichi's Writings in connection with Kiitsu Association ("The Association Concordia")" [http://www.princeton.edu/~collcutt/doc/Kenjo_English.pdf]. For Japanese, see TAKAHASHI Hara, *Tōkyō daigaku shukyōgaku nenpō* [The ideals and fate of Kiitsu kyōkai: Its activity at the beginning of the Shōwa era] 20: 43-54 [reference from Mohr, *ibid.*, p. 289].

IMAOKA's precise use of languages, especially Chinese and Japanese, was signaled by the characters chosen – phonetically the second word was the same but written with different kanji for *kyōkai.* Both written choices referred to a group, one more about a place for discussion and the other a place for learning (sometimes translated "church" as the character was drawn as an ancient temple). The first word, *kiitsu* was the same character for both organizations but the translation was different. For IMAOKA it signified "oneness or unity," rather than "concord or concordia" which was the official English translation of the *Concordia Association.* IMAOKA used an older Chinese character for *kyōkai* rather than its simplified form.[405] He intended it to encompass not only the meanings of *koinonia* in Greek and *gemeinshaft* in German, but also the views of John Haynes Holmes' "community church." And, there was still another influence: *mu-kyōkai* or the "non-church" movement of UCHIMURA. Long ago in Kobe with the radical Congregationalists and the lay Buddhist influence of Tenkō-san, the notion of a non-paid, non-professional ministry without the financial burden of a church building was conveyed in his chosen characters. And linked to this, of course, was *jiyū shūkyō* (*free religion*), which was to be the focus of this fellowship.

IMAOKA wanted Kiitsu Kyōkai to be the "community church" of Holmes' dream, something that united (*kiitsu*) everyone in the common cause of achieving a better, more equitable, more beautiful, more just community (*kyōkai*). That was its local meaning. He had already revealed this vision in his translation of Mason's books on Shinto as a "community church," putting it into Mason's

405. *Kyōkai* 教會 with the second element in the compound the older Chinese radical rather than its simplified form. In his essays IMAOKA had the habit of using older, more difficult *kanji.* See article on *hanzi* and *kanji:* https://en.wikipedia.org/wiki/Chinese_characters.

Bergsonianism.[406] The "community church movement" in Japan, as in America, sought to create a church inclusive of all society, both religious and secular. Now, its multiple dimensions were left for mutual discovery: the national unification of self and others in discussion and meditation (*seiza*), with an international organization both religious and secular, and for the *cosmic* dimension found in free religious experience. It sought to unify persons locally, nationally, and internationally. But placing such a dream of unity upon the reality of two tiny organizations, the Japan Free Religious Association and Kiitsuo Kyōkai, would be as difficult for IMAOKA as it had been for Holmes, who had seen the American Free Religious Association and his Community Church Movement fail.

Home of Kiitsu Kyōkai and JFRA at Seisoku Academy in 1981

IMAOKA's Kyōkai would have no baptism, no lord's supper (communion), no formal ceremony of membership, no "tithes and offerings," no prayer to an absolute deity, no signed covenant of belief and practice, no paid ministry, and hardly even any music. He allowed foreign religionists, especially American Unitarian

406. IMAOKA revealed some of this vision in his 1966 talk, "Re-Examination of Mason's Shinto" (Essay 56 in Imaoka, *Jinsei hyakunen* [Hundred years of a Human Life], Tokyo: Daizō shuppan, 1982.)

Universalists, to call his gathering the "Tokyo Unitarian Church" and call him its minister. However, he did not have this "church" join interfaith, international organizations. That was the role of the Japan Free Religious Association. His local group joined as part of the JFRA. His own yearly "Tentative Statement of Faith" would be so cryptic as to seem almost non-religious (to be pondered at the end of this chapter). He would signal a type of religious experience that was not traditional. It was multidimensional, with a multi-religious identity.

The Oneness or Unity Fellowship, Kiitsuo Kyōkai, was a *gemeinschaft,* a fellowship, that brought together "all" into a real community of care and commitment, to learn about and practice creative liberation, *free religion.* This fellowship was also *ad hoc* in that it did not organize for "institutional survival." It did not incorporate, seek tax exemption, or develop religious business practices. Such a lack of organization and business sense meant that it was not designed to last. Sadly, the *beauty* of art and music that he knew and experienced in Buddhism and Shinto in the Bergsonian vision was neglected in Kiitsuo Kyōkai's simplicity.

IMAOKA spoke once a month even during the last decade of his life – until he was 105. His unpaid assistant was the Rev. KONNO Yoshitsugu, having received training at Starr King School for the Ministry in Berkeley, California, and a teacher at Seisoku Academy.[407]

IMAOKA's Strategy

IMAOKA's winter phase of his life from 1945 to 1988 – 43 years from his 73rd to 106th year – was a torrent of activity on both national and international levels. He had telegraphed his agenda in the precise ways that he named Kiitsu Kyōkai and the Japan Free Religious Association (JFRA) – *Nihon Jiyū Shūkyō Renmei.* Both focused on "free religion" rather than "religious freedom," one locally

407. KONNO Yoshitsugu and Brent Friesmann, *Kurisuchan no tomo e: Yuniterian karano 38shin* (n.p., 1998).

the other nationally. When he brought the JFRA into the International Association of Liberal Christians and Religious Freedom (IALC*RF*) in 1952,[408] he was completing the strategy internationally. World peace required international understanding and cooperation with partners around the globe. But when he joined IALCRF, his translation placed the *kanji* in an order that already made it the International Association of Liberal Christianity and Free Religion (IALC*FR*). It already indicated a commitment to *free religion* in Japanese using *Jiyū Shūkyō* as his translation. His agenda was hidden in plain sight. *Free religion* was his goal from the beginning – personally, locally, nationally, and internationally. The JFRA came into the international association as a non-Christian organization, IALCRF's first non-Christian member even though individuals from the old Japan Unitarian Mission, the Brahmo Samaj (a liberal Hindu reform group), the Ramakrishna Mission and others had attended almost from its beginning in 1900. Yet, none of these liberal groups were accepted as members. IALCRF remained Liberal Christian, exclusive and exclusionary. IMAOKA would change that.

With ANESAKI's death in 1949, it became more and more difficult for IMAOKA to serve without being recognized as the senior leader. And yet, at least in his accounts, his leadership and initiative remained barely visible. He only spoke of helping others. In 1949 when Seisoku Academy joined the Japan Free Religious Association, he credited its Board of Directors with the decision. They had decided that "[e]very activity of school education should be based on Free Religion."[409] He encouraged others to take the leadership roles

408. When it was founded in 1900, its official name was the International Council of Unitarian and Other Liberal Religious Thinkers and Workers. "A decade after its founding what would become known as the IARF was taking shape." That became the International Association for Religious Freedom.

409. In 1950 IMAOKA was receive his first Imperial award: the Order of the Blue Ribbon by Law of Merit.

while he facilitated, organized, and worked as a secretary of each convention, round table or organization.

IMAOKA helped in 1951 with the re-organization of *Shinshuren* (the Association of New Religions, also known as the Federation of New Religious Organizations). These groups were severely persecuted by the state before and during the Pacific War. IMAOKA encouraged the groups to cooperate in serving human needs and society. It would soon include President NIWANO Nikkyo of Rissho Kosei-kai (a lay Buddhist group that later would become very important in IARF). IMAOKA remembered meeting him there in 1951. NIWANO would become the Chair of *Shinshuren* in 1965. Not surprisingly, in an interview by the author, NIWANO did not remember IMAOKA at the gatherings of the *Shinshuren* – illustrating how IMAOKA could blend into the background. He remembered only meeting IMAOKA at the Conference of World Religionists in 1955.[410] Some of the groups and individuals IMAOKA met in *Shishuren* would later join him in the JFRA, and through that, join IARF. Their accounts of their participation in IARF demonstrates the inclusiveness of this interfaith work both at national and international levels.[411]

As the working or chief secretary of two "all faith" conferences in 1955 and 1956, IMAOKA had persons of status provide their names as officers of these meetings, just as ANESAKI had done in the past. This

---

410. Nezu Masuo, "Interreligious Cooperation and Rissho Kosei-kai," (1) *Dharma World* (July/August, 1995, p. 23.

411. Works that have been translated into English include RKK publications in *Dharma World, especially by* NEZU Masuo, "Remembering Dr. Imaoka;" NISHIDA Tenkō's books, *A New Road to Ancient Truth* (1972) and YAMAMOTO Yukitaka's *Kami no Michi* (1988). For those researching this movement, see works by the NIWANOs of Rissho Kosei-kai, the YAMAMOTOs of Tsubaki Grand Shrine, the MIYAKAS of Konkōkyō, the AKASHIS of Japanese Liberal Christianity (Universalists), the NISHIDAs of Ittō-en, Rev. NAKAGAWA of Teppozu Inari Shrine, Rev. YAMAMOTO Genyu of Shosei-ji (Pure Land Buddhist). There were also many individuals, scholars, and lay religionists who knew and worked with IMAOKA sensei. Their accounts are almost completely in Japanese awaiting their own studies.

period after World War II was the moment to champion a commitment to world peace and interfaith cooperation among Japanese faiths. The Conference of World Religionists developed into the Council for Interfaith Cooperation and then into another Round Table of important religious figures, all religious opinion shapers of a Japan rising from its own ashes. IMAOKA was only slightly more visible in the formation of the Japan Religious Cooperative Association.

The renewed connection with the American Unitarian Association gained a bonus. Its Service Committee sent English teachers to instruct at Seisoku Academy in the 1960s. Typically, IMAOKA shared the teachers with Rissho Kosei-kai, where they also taught English in its seminary. The AUA/UUA representatives included the Swains, Greens, Goldthwaits, and Flahertys.[412] Dr. Felix D. Lion, representing Canadian Unitarians, taught in 1970. Not surprisingly, even when American and Canadian witnesses were teaching at Seisoku, they did not learn of the Imperial awards honoring his 50 years as principal of Seisoku Academy and further service to education in Japan. While each made unique contributions, the Flahertys of Stockton, California, would extend their year in Japan to decades. John and Marge Flaherty opened their home in Stockton (CA) to Buddhist and Shinto students as they learned English, attended higher education, and began their mission work in America. One of their sons, Casey, went to Japan and attempted to be the first

412. Robert Traer, *A Brief History of IARF* (n.p, n.d. in a manuscript of 131pp.), p. 118: "Here I want to introduce briefly other emissaries of the UUA to Japan. They were the Rev. Robert Swain, 1964-65; the Rev. Dr. Robert Green and Mrs. Carole Green, 1965-66; the Rev. John Goldthwait and Mrs. Barbara Goldthwait, 1966-67; Mr. John Flaherty and Mrs. Marjorie Flaherty with their two sons [Sean and Casey], 1967-68." Their accounts have never been gathered. The author's connection with the Flaherty family has been extensive.

foreigner to become a seminary trained Shrine Shinto priest.[413] He paved the way for Aikido master, Koichi Barrish, to achieve that goal and to establish a branch shrine of Tsubaki Daijinja at Granite Falls, Washington.[414]

IMAOKA's three-pronged strategy can be discerned in his national and international interfaith activities. They would carry JFRA into resolute action for world peace and interfaith understanding and cooperation. One international organization, IALCRF, would be changed and another, the World Conference on Religion and Peace (WCRP), would be formed.

Renaming IARF for Non-Sectarian Membership

IMAOKA's joining the International Association for Liberal Christianity and Religious Freedom (IALCRF) in 1952 would be of special importance. He joined not as an individual but with a group (the JFRA) of which he was its second president. This was important because it was the first non-Christian group to join IALCRF. JFRA was both religious (Kiitsu Kyōkai and Ittō-en)[415] and secular (Seisoku Academy), becoming both a multi-religious and non-sectarian member. IMAOKA would begin immediately to urge the Liberal Christian organization to go *beyond* both Unitarianism and Liberal Christianity. He saw clearly that the United Nations' Charter had already made "religious freedom" a human right. IALCRF needed to rename and repurpose itself. Although he never directly criticized its illiberality, the implied superiority in IALCRF's name (the LC being

413. Casey Flaherty's experience is one yet to be properly recognized. For some information see my *Liberal Religious Reformation in Japan* (1984), pp. 41-42 and *Shinto* (2005), YAMAMOTO Yukitaka, *Kami no Michi* (1988).

414. See http://www.tsubakishrine.org.

415. Imaoka's non-sectarian fellowship and the lay Buddhist organization founded by Tenkō-san. Japanese Universalists would soon join, followed by Tsubaki Grand Shrine and Teppozu Inari Shrine (both Jinja Shinto), followed by Konko-kyo of Izuo (Religious or Kyōha Shinto), and Shosei-ji Temple of Pure Land Buddhism (Rev. YAMAMOTO Genyu).

Liberal Christianity) bound it to a colonial past of religious superiority and Euro-American *nationalisms*. And even worse, there was evidence of latent racism deeply engrained even in the non-state (liberal) churches of colonial nations. He would begin educating liberal religionists with his proposal for a name change with a Japanese religious presence and vision.

IMAOKA envisioned a liberal, international organization that was inclusive, both in its multi-faith character and its task. By the time IMAOKA traveled to Chicago in 1958 for his first IALCRF Congress, its 16th, this small Japanese – smaller than all the other delegates attending – became a huge presence. The delegates were exclusively liberal Christian, but he wanted them to go *beyond* an exclusive Christian identity. IMAOKA credited a liberal group from the Chicago area with proposing that "Liberal Christian" be deleted from the name.[416] Some members threatened that they would leave IALCRF if "Liberal Christian" was dropped from its official name. Thus, the name change became impossible for three Congresses – Chicago (1958), Davos (1961), and The Hague (1964). Finally in Boston at the 20th World Congress in 1969, liberals agreed to alter the name. They simply dropped "Liberal Christian," becoming IARF, the International Association for Religious Freedom, and welcomed liberal Buddhists, Hindus, Muslims, Jews and others of like spirit during the coming decades.[417]

The 1969 compromise of dropping Liberal Christian from its name had not accomplished IMAOKA's agenda concerning free religion (*jiyū shūkyō*). IMAOKA wanted a commitment to peace, equality,

416. IMAOKA, *Japan Free Religious Association and two articles on Religious Freedom, "IARF Facts, Prospects"* (n.p., 1964). Handwritten note by Imaoka: "distributed among delegates to the IAFR Congress in Hague 1964." Surely, when he wrote this in 1964, he had not forgotten that he had first proposed a name change in 1952!

417. Traer, *ibid*. See also essays on the IARF website by Faber, Traer, Boeke, etc..

equity, freedom, and openness to new or evolving knowledge (science in general; spiritual and physical evolution in particular). Again remember, IMAOKA emphatically stated that when "*yuniterian*" was said in Japanese, it was not the same "Unitarian" as in English. "It is important to go beyond Unitarianism," he loved to say. It was important to go *beyond* liberal religion to *free religion* (*jiyū shūkyō*). Yet, in all the hours of international discussion little study of *free religion* had ever been made.

IMAOKA was able to attend these Congresses because of his wife's business successes beginning in the late 1950s. He would laugh and reflect on how she tried three times in business before she succeeded, and how close he had come to missing out on her success.[418] In 1969 he would visit religious liberals in Israel (Bahá'i), Pakistan (Free Islam - Ahmadhiyya), and India (the Ramakrishna Mission).

Religions for Peace: WCRP

IMAOKA's dream of Japan taking a leading role for world peace emerged again in the 1968 Japan-American Interreligious Consultation on Peace. As president of JFRA, he brought Japanese religious leaders to the consultation with American religious activists. Dana Greeley[419] (1908-96) and Homer Jack[420] (1916-93), the primary AUA leaders, were greatly surprised at how long liberal Japanese religionists had worked for world peace. This consultation resulted in the creation of the World Conference on Religion and Peace (WCRP) in 1969. Its first World Conference was held in Kyoto in 1970.

After the consultation in January 1968, IMAOKA took AUA

418. Her two Imperial awards for her accomplishment in business mark her extraordinary career. She had also been part of the early feminist movement. One of her companies put the first Japanese communications satellite in orbit. Mrs. IMAOKA Utayo died in November, 1978.

419. http://uudb.org/articles/danamcleangreeley.html

420. Homer A. Jack, *Jack's Odyssey: My Quest for Peace and Justice* (1996) and *A Bibliography of the Writings of Homer A. Jack* (1991). http://uudb.org/articles/homeralexanderjack.html

president Dana Greeley to meet RKK's president NIWANO Nikkyo at their headquarters in Tokyo. Greeley and NIWANO made an instant connection, resulting in an invitation for NIWANO to attend the next IALCRF Congress in Chicago in 1969. NIWANO joined IMAOKA and members of the JFRA at the Chicago Congress.

IMAOKA and Shinto Priests YAMAMOTO and NAKAGAWA at IARF in 1969

IMAOKA sought to get NIWANO, co-founder of RKK, to equate Buddhism's central notion of liberation with JFRA's vision of *jiyū shūkyō*. IMAOKA already had a major influence on NIWANO in the early 1960s when RKK was under siege from a rival fundamentalist Nichiren Buddhist group, Soka Gakkai (also known as Nichiren Shoshu). They were in almost daily combat in their newspapers (and even in the secular press) over who was teaching the truth of the Lotus Sutra and who were the real followers of NICHIREN. IMAOKA advised NIWANO indirectly with one of his simple, reflective questions that helped NIWANO decide to take Buddhism's message abroad.[421] NIWANO began a spiritual pilgrimage that would transform him from fundamentalist to progressive, from nationalist to a world citizen. In 1965 he traveled to Rome and met Pope Paul VI and attended Vatican II. He would grow rapidly into one of the world's most important

421. In 1965 NIWANO followed Imaoka's advice and began his international witness of Buddhism. See NIWANO Nikkyo, *Lifetime Beginner,* trans. by Richard Gage (Tokyo: Kosei Publishing, 1978) and NEZU, *op.cit.*

religious figures.[422]

Greeley and NIWANO's instant connection had an unplanned result. Greeley invited NIWANO and RKK to join the newly renamed IARF as a lay Buddhist member group without becoming a member through JFRA. Thus, RKK would avoid the dilemma of joining JFRA, whose name might suggest a *freedom* that was permissive and even immoral. A few Buddhists had led a freedom movement in the early 20th century, but since then liberalism had become anathema for most conservative and traditional Buddhist groups. Joining IMAOKA's *jiyū shūkyō* movement could now be avoided by direct membership in both IARF and WCRP. Ironically, RKK joined organizations of liberals without becoming liberal (*jiyū*). Niwano's leadership in seeking world peace, interreligious cooperation with Western religions, interfaith cooperation among Buddhists and the alleviation of hunger and suffering would lead to the Temple Foundation Prize for Progress in Religion in 1979; numerous other kinds of appreciation recognized his international leadership – many from liberal religious groups.

Celebrating IMAOKA's 100th Birthday

One event in 1981 symbolized Japanese interreligious respect for each other's faith: a birthday celebration. IMAOKA had celebrated others, both living and dead, as often as possible at the International House where he had a lifetime membership. They had commemorated persons and events that looked beyond an island's horizon. In 1966 they remembered J.W.T. Mason on the 25th anniversary of his death.[423] In 1969 IMAOKA organized a centennial commemoration of Svāmī Vivekānanda's birth. The 25th anniversary of the founding of the Japan Free Religious Association in 1973 brought

422. NIWANO, *ibid; A Buddhist Approach to Peace* (1977); see also two films by George Williams, *The Bodhisattva Way of Peace* (1987) and *The Lamp of the Dharma* (1993).

423. IMAOKA, "Revisiting Mason's Shinto," 1966.

a dual remembrance of Emerson and the American Free Religious Association. Despite the fact that he would have been 112 years old, IMAOKA was looking forward to 1993 for the centennial celebration of the 1893 World's Parliament of Religions held in Chicago.

The celebration of his 100th birthday brought together many of the Japanese religious partners in the activities for world peace and interfaith cooperation. He could not have been more astonished by so many friends from academia and the religious community – plus a Shinto priestess dancing ritually in his honor. The real surprise was the publication of a book of his essays: (*Hundred Years of Human Life*). These essays had been published in every kind of journal for over eight decades. The volume contained one essay for every year of his life, plus a few more for good measure. When congratulated for his longevity, he said with his usual chuckle: "I have always been slow, even slow to die."

1981 Celebration of IMAOKA's 100th birthday at the International House

At the 1981 IARF Congress at Noorwijkerhout, Holland, his son, Prof. IMAOKA Ken'ichirō, and daughter-in-law accepted the first

IARF Distinguished Service Award, which was given to him in honor of his interfaith service. IMAOKA at 100 could not attend and said that he was now "too slow for international travel."

Giving IARF a Liberating Purpose

At its 1969 Congress in Boston, IARF had received a new name without setting a new purpose. For IMAOKA, that was a failure. His last chance to give IARF a liberal agenda – the purpose of spiritual liberation – came with the first IARF Congress held in Asia. NIWANO was now president of IARF and welcomed the world's oldest interreligious organization to RKK's Tokyo headquarters. IMAOKA was an honorary president – receiving recognition just as he had honored so many others. He used these circumstances to propose a purposeful name for IARF.

Transforming IARF had been IMAOKA's dream: making it act instead of just talk. It should have a liberating ethical commitment of transforming self, others, and community through commitment to the true, good and beautiful (an echo of Bergson). Liberal religion should be a force for creative evolution. Its ethics (which he taught as Christian literature at Nihon University) should come from a more inclusive *shūkyō*, religion. Religion must go *beyond* religion to *jiyū shūkyō*. For him, *jiyū shūkyō* was more than ordinary or professional religion. It was a free, lay, non-church faith for learning, growing, evolving beyond, striving toward that which is greater and better than the present. It entailed ethical progress toward becoming a *cosmic* being in a local-national-international community. Thus, it would be global – *cosmic.* IMAOKA firmly believed that IARF could bring all religions together in pursuit of liberating religious faith – and help conservative faiths find their liberality. Each particular religion – group, organization or denomination – would share their grasp of what was *liberating* in their tradition. Each religion had as its essence *jiyū shūkyō*, the capacity to *liberate.* Although each tradition approached liberation differently (as liberation from sin, addiction, ignorance, greed, desire, etc.), together in dialogue and through interreligious cooperation a more peaceful and just world, a *cosmic* community, could be created.

A Special Panel about Free Religion

IMAOKA's proposal for the name change of IARF would be presented at the "general business meeting." The governance structure was representative, so "general" had a very contradictory meaning. Only representative delegates from member organizations could vote, and the two largest financial contributors to IARF were the Unitarian Universalist Association and Risshō Kōsei-kai. The old questions about the "gospel of freedom" being a Western license for immorality worried the Board of Directors of RKK. They asked that a special panel be squeezed into an already dense program of the Congress. A slot was found the day before the business meeting to clarify the meaning of *free religion*, especially as understood by American Unitarian Universalists.

Discussing "free religion" honored IMAOKA, the very person most responsible for the IARF Congress being held in Japan. The panel was scheduled immediately after lunch with only an hour for presentations and discussion. Diether Gehrmann, Executive Secretary, asked me to chair the session with George Marshall[424] who would make a presentation on the UUA's understanding of *free religion.* Gehrmann asked me to summarize IMAOKA's usage of it. None of the Executive Committee of IARF could be present because of conflicts. (My account is of course conflicted with the goals for an historian's accuracy and the bias of a participant.)

I met with Marshall over lunch to discuss problems and

[424] The Rev. George Marshall (1915-1993) was in his last year as minister of the Church of the Larger Fellowship. He was a celebrated Unitarian author and speaker, a veteran of WWII and the civil rights movement, and a fiery speaker.

background to IMAOKA's proposal. I sought to discuss the sensitive issues, alerting him to the Japanese Buddhists' fear that "free religion" meant religion without tradition, freedom to do whatever an individual desired, even immorality. I reminded Marshall of the translation process (short sentences, only two or three at a time). Our translator would be NEZU Masuo's daughter, who was fluent in English but not a simultaneous translator like her father, who was famous for his extraordinary ability to listen and translate at the same time. Marshall seemed annoyed with my attempt to shape his presentation. I worried about his speaking style—fast, heavily accented New England-American. Translators at the Congress usually had a manuscript or at least an outline with key terminology to help them. Our ad hoc panel would have only the oral presentations without a script for the translator. The session was crowded into a room for 50. The RKK Board was well represented. The majority in the small room were American Unitarians already supporting the proposal. The very reason for this session was to relieve RKK members of their fear that IMAOKA's free religion (*jiyū shūkyō*) was immoral [*jiyū*, that freedom leads to immorality].

George Williams introducing Dr. George Marshall

Marshall began a presentation on Western heretics, free thinkers, radicals, revolutionaries and martyrs. He identified with them and gloried in retelling their exploits. He spoke faster and louder as he became more excited with his well-rehearsed vignettes. I attempted to limit him to one single sentence at a time, since they were long and complicated. His annoyance with any interruption, especially that of the translator's, was more and more apparent. He had a good Western audience to whom he spoke. But none of the Japanese, not even our translator, could appreciate his command of the centuries of heretics and libertines that he knew so well.

My attempt to let him know the importance of the meeting may have backfired. Marshall asserted his freedom, emphasizing the disregard for medieval morality and belief. There was little wonder that some had to flee their homelands or were burned at the stake. Marshall's presentation confirmed the worst fears of Board of Directors of Risshō Kōsei-kai: "free religion," *jiyū shūkyō*, was an immoral religion and not Japanese. Worse, Marshall talked over and embarrassed our young translator until she broke down in tears and fled the room. Another translator could not be found immediately and time ran out. There was no presentation of IMAOKA's vision and no discussion. The proposal from IMAOKA was dead. It did not even come to a vote in the business meeting.

Two nights later, IMAOKA gave the keynote address before the entire 1984 Congress. It was remarkable in several ways. He chose not to use a translator and spoke in English at 103. The speech that he had carefully written in Japanese was put aside, and he spoke extemporaneously. He received a standing ovation. There had not been a word of disappointment that his final wish had been rejected without a vote.

Because of the bond of friendship between RKK Founder NIWANO and UUA Pres. Dana Greeley, Rissho Kosei-kai would stay in IARF and match UUA contributions until Greeley died. When those matching grants were cut by the UUA and RKK, the future of IARF was dramatically changed.[425] Retrospectively, IARF's history was forever changed at that "free religion" session. The author was told by several high-ranking RKK officials that RKK began to change its focus to the World Conference on Religion and Peace (which evolved into Religion for Peace). Several officials said that continued RKK support past the 1987 Congress was a *goodbye* contribution. The year, 1984, can be seen as the high water mark of IARF (even though the 1987 IARF Congress at Stanford University was quite successful because of the large American attendance).

In 2006 The Executive Committee of the IARF attempted to change the representative association into an agency with the governance structure of a cartel, a self-perpetuating board. They had found Scientology and several similar organizations that would provide financial support. Although the proposal was rejected, IARF would only be saved temporarily by Japanese Shinto groups. The decline of IARF had only been delayed.

Death at 106

After his *Hundred Years of Human Life* was published, IMAOKA was regularly interviewed both by journalists – radio, TV, newspaper – and scholars. His egoless answers provided no further information about his teachings or achievements.

IMAOKA deflected any questions about his specific religious experiences in meditation as implying that his "I" (his ego) had attained something, some goal or insight – possibly even something

425. The Executive Committee of the IARF attempted in 2006 to turn the association into an agency, turning to Scientology and several similar organizations for financial support. That was rejected with IARF having to rely on Japanese Shinto groups for leadership and financial support. The decline of IARF was only temporarily delayed. Currently, it is attempting to forge a future.

that others might characterize as enlightenment. It took many attempts over the years of interviews for him to admit to an experience of "loss of self or ego-consciousness" in meditation. He finally confessed having a sense of merging with the *cosmos*, a term that had special meaning to him and which he thought was an experience of the *free religionist*: that of becoming a *cosmic human being*. Yet, he could not be caught teaching any formula or belief to be achieved or realized. As a teacher, his teachings were *empty*. They gave his listener nothing to copy, nothing to ascribe to him as his true instruction.

There were phenomena about dead friends and ancient figures whom he had experienced that intrigued me. He enjoyed conversing with Plato, Jesus, Emerson, and others. In his alone time, he would engage them about things that they had not left any record of saying or writing. But, then he would add that he hoped he knew them well enough to understand what they would say. He rejected any special knowledge or gift. He also rejected the need to believe in life after death. He did not deny its possibility but found it quite egotistical to think that the *cosmos* needed individual continuity.

When I arrived in Japan in March 1988 to work with RKK on a video project, I learned that I would not be able to speak with IMAOKA. He was comatose. I asked permission from his daughter-in-law (IMAOKA Emi) to visit their new home where she cared for him.[426] I was carrying video equipment with me on the way to RKK headquarters, and Emi-san asked me to take his picture. I started the camera and walked over to the bed beside his blind student, AKIYAMA

[426] IMAOKA's son, Ken'ichirō, died in 1984. IMAOKA wanted to remain in his home near Tokyo Tower with Emi-san taking care of him until he died. His two daughters persuaded him to sell his home and divide the money from the sale three ways. Each could have a private home, "a Japanese mansion." Emi-san began caring for him in their new home in late 1987, where he contracted influenza, then pneumonia and went into a coma.

Kinuko, and began meditating. IMAOKA sensei awoke, took my hand and began talking in English, something unusual. He was speaking without putting in his dentures, something he never did. He had been unconscious for over three months and then spoke for ten or fifteen minutes, holding my hands. Another phenomenon occurred. I became overheated in his very chilly bedroom – down covers keeping him warm. I had to be careful to prevent perspiration falling from my forehead onto him. I begged him to get well, to come to California, to meet my teenage children – all irrationally said, though it seemed natural to voice at that moment. And he promised that he would. When I felt he had become tired, I thanked him for everything that he had done and for what he had taught me – my words coming out inadequate and inarticulate. Almost as soon as he released my hands, he fell asleep. Miss AKIYAMA and I said goodbye to Emi-san and left. Emi-san told me that IMAOKA sensei did not regain consciousness.

About a month later, on April 11th, I was meditating in the outdoor garden of the Chico (CA) Unitarian Fellowship with a group who "demanded three times" that I sit with them. (I am not a meditation teacher. There is a Buddhist custom that, when asked three times, it indicates serious intent. One should help. And, I do love sitting with serious meditators.) Suddenly, I felt IMAOKA's presence and instantly "knew" (quite irrationally) that he had died. By the time I returned home, Rev. YAMAMOTO Yukitaka of Tsubaki Grand Shrine was calling from Japan saying that IMAOKA sensei had indeed died. He arranged a plane ticket for me to fly over immediately for the family funeral. The public funeral would come later.

***

Statement of Faith by a Free Religionist (Tentative)

[distributed to IARF at The Hague, 1966]

1. I Believe in Self

Awakened to the Autonomy, sociality and creativity within me, I find my daily life worth living. Autonomy, sociality and creativity may be called Personality, Divinity and Buddhahood.

2. I Believe in Others

Because of my belief in Self, I can not help but believe in Others as neighbors who have their own Selves.

3. I Believe in Community

Both my Self and other Selves are unique but not absolutely distinct from each other. Hence solidarity, fellowship and Community will be realized.

4. I Believe in the Cosmic Community

Not only Self, Others and Community, but all nature in addition, are one and constitute the Cosmic Community.

5. I Believe in the Church

The Church epitomizes the Cosmic Community and I will be a cosmic man joining the Church.

IMAOKA sensei's translation into English for the 1966 IARF Congress has been clarified with a more precise wording by Prof. Michel Mohr.[427] The phrase, "Cosmic Community," is amplified as "a Cosmic Communal Society." Suddenly, the extent of his concerns about ecology, inequity, social consciousness, world peace and community (local, national and international) are revealed. These were the basic elements of the *yuniterian* movement – from Unity Hall until his death.

This and every faith statement was tentative. From 1966 onwards these elements expressed his integral spirituality, his faith in communal liberation. Although there was no mention of God, Christ or Buddha – technically non-theistic, the divine and sacred had become his life. IMAOKA sensei experienced divinity not in any absolute, only in images or symbols that evoked creative freedom of an evolving humanity – striving for unity in its diversity. Nor was freedom an absolute, as it could only be sought together in community, among seekers of something higher, more beautiful, truer, and better.

Timeline from 1948 to 1988

1947 Interfaith Conference on Peace

1948 Round Table Conference on Religion and Peace

Arrival of Rev. John Nicholls Booth on Asian tour; attended a planning session.

1948 Oct. 17, Japan Free Religious Association (JFRA) founded with AKASHI's (Universalist) and others.

November, founding of Kiitsu Kyōkai, called the "Tokyo Unitarian Church."

1949 Seisoku Academy joined JFRA

1951 IMAOKA helped with the re-organization of *Shishuren* (the Association of New Religions, also known as the Federation of New Religious Organizations)

---

427. IMAOKA Shin'ichirō, "Uchūteki kyōdō shakai o shinzuru: Waga hyakusansai no shinjō" ["I Believe in a Cosmic Communal Society," translated by Michel Mohr], *Rinri* 倫理 (384): 24–31.

1955 Conference of World Religionists
Council for Interfaith Cooperation that developed into the Roundtable.
1956 Chief officer of Japan Religious Cooperative Association
1958-1969 JFRA attended and joined IARF. IMAOKA brought members of JFRA
IMAOKA visited liberal religionists in Israel, Pakistan, India
1964-1969 IMAOKA became a Director on IARF board
1965 IMAOKA received the 4th Order of Merit with Sacred Treasure
1968 Japan-American Interreligious Consultation on Peace resulted in the creation in 1969 of the World Conference on Religion and Peace (WCRP)
1969 Risshō Kōseikai joined IARF but separately from JFRA. Founder NIWANO became a director of IARF.
1970 First World Conference of WCRP held in Kyoto
IMAOKA became director of Japan [chapter of] IARF
1972 IMAOKA received an Honorary Doctorate from Meadville Theological Seminary
1978 Mrs. IMAOKA Utayo died
1979 IMAOKA given World Conference on Religion and Peace Founders Award
1981 IMAOKA received IARF Distinguished Leadership Award
1984 Son, IMAOKA Ken'ichirō, died
IMAOKA was Honorary President of Tokyo IARF World Congress
1988 April 11, IMAOKA sensei died

1984 Tokyo IARF Pre-Congress tour of Japanese member groups

Chapter 14
Epilogue

As I reflect some 30 years after the death of Japan's exemplar of an *integral mysticism,* IMAOKA Shin'ichirō and his spiritual journey have become more relevant than ever. In a dystopian era, his pilgrimage from Buddhist ancestry through multiple Christian conversions – growing in what he called *free religion* ((*jiyū shūkyō*) – distinguishes him as a spiritual role model worthy of remembrance and honor. His conversions were not what William James called *sudden* but were gradual and evolving experiences of growth and learning. They were often linked to life events and existential crises, several quite dramatic, as well as study and contemplation.

Yet, there was more. He experienced both interfaith and intra-faith conversions or transformations in which he retained his identity in each faith. He was a living legend yet a mystery. Buddhists identified him as a *bodhisattva* (a living Buddha) and Shintoists as *kami* (a divine human). Even some Unitarians thought him to be a "saint" (although there has never been a Unitarian saint or a "saint-concept"), and some academics referred to him as the "Emerson of Japan," more for his leadership in the International Association for Religious Freedom and his call for *free religion* than from reading his essays. He has been twice forgotten as he outlived his contemporaries and again after his death. However, there was another reason than "being slow to die." During his century-long life, he dedicated at least seven decades to assisting others, easily forgotten or never known as he remained in their shadows.

The leaders whom he assisted were worthy, as they shaped Meiji Japan's religious, social, political, economic and educational institutions. He willingly disappeared in their deeds and words. As an organizer and enabler, his presence can be found behind the scenes of the most significant socioreligious movements of that era. For five decades he directed the famous Seisoku Academy in Tokyo, overseeing at least 10,000 student graduates, continuing Seisoku's tradition of making national leaders. He was honored for this with two Imperial awards in education – about which few knew outside of his family. For nine decades he practiced a Zen type of meditation each day to free his spirit for creative insight and growth. He practiced an *egolessness* that can be found in Christian and Buddhist ascetic traditions, acknowledging a religious identity in each. He found divinity in the fluid movements of Shinto ritual and in the cool rational ethics of Confucianism. Devotional religion, that could err so easily in dogmatizing beliefs and rules as if they were from God, he found transformative in its gratitude for unmerited gifts, its power to teach humility to inflated egos, and its examples of service and sacrifice. All religions could go beyond their confines to *free religion*, he said.

To question ideologies and absolutes, to examine the causes of inequity, to alleviate forms of exploitation and to build a *cosmic* community that nurtured society and harmonized with nature – these were his life goals as a *free religionist*.

In his understanding, *free religion* (*jiyū shūkyō*) was a universal ideal, yet not an absolute. That which is *beyond* each religion, which goes beyond its highest values and has the power to transform one into an authentic human being – that is *free religion*. It was an image rather than a concept, a metaphor for something beyond conventional belief and religion, beyond theism, liberalism, humanism. This freedom does not conform to any category or "-ism".

Even *rational mysticism* was not for him an attainment, a goal, an experiential realization to be taught or gained. Perhaps, he might have been pleased to think someone would think of him as either *mystical* or *rational*. Since these notions were contradictory enough to cancel out any claim to attainment, one could call him both, if that helped them want to become more human. Yet, his understanding of *humanism* denied its claim of achieving an ideal, but only an aspiration toward a higher possibility.

Religious or Spiritual Experience

Currently in academic circles "religious types" and "religious experience" are said to be obsolete notions, if not anathema.[428] Yet, to grasp the complexity of IMAOKA's spiritual transformations, ancient formulations about religious paths or types and about religious experience can be very useful.

When IMAOKA sensei learned that I had written a book on Svāmī Vivekānanda,[429] he returned to that topic with detailed questions during my many visits. I would eventually learn how IMAOKA had organized a centennial commemoration of Vivekānanda's birth in 1969 and also visited liberal religionists in India that year. Discussions about Vivekānanda clarified why he rejected the notion of spiritual or religious hierarchies.[430] IMAOKA was disappointed to learn that Vivekānanda believed that the spiritual life was one of stages with the goal of attaining enlightenment (*nirvikalpa samādhi*: losing one's identity in the Absolute). However, he was very pleased to learn that Vivekānanda's teacher, Śrī Rāmakrishna, experienced the unity of all spiritual paths meeting at the center, in a union with the

---

428. An excellent introduction to current critique of the category of "religious experience" as meaningful is found in Benjamin Y. Fong's "On Critics and What's Real: Russell McCutcheon on Religious Experience," *Journal of the America Academy of Religion* (Nov. 2018) pp. 1127-1148.

429. Williams, *The Quest for Meaning of Svāmī Vivekānanda* (New Horizons Press, 1974).

430. Later in this chapter and in Appendix B.

Absolute. For Rāmakrishna, there was no hierarchy of paths, as each led to the center. For IMAOKA, Rāmakrishna had seen the relativity of each path and its need to accept the experiential truth found on that path until greater truth was experienced.

Vivekānanda further related his conception of the spiritual life to one's rebirth in this lifetime derived from the consequences of good and bad *karma* of previous lifetimes. One entered the human species with a physical tendency, centered in the senses and needing a path that helped one be righteous as one served as a worker according to the duties and responsibilities of that path (*karma mārga*). Each succeeding lifetime provided a new opportunity to develop spiritually on a new path as one advanced toward mystic union (*samādhi*) with the Absolute (*Brahman*).[431] Rāmakrishna saw all paths leading to the center, the Absolute, and said that he had merged with the Absolute (*nirvikalpa samādhi*) and came back. While Vivekānanda's conception was one of gradual enlightenment requiring many lifetimes, Rāmakrishna saw all paths as one, with the possibility of a *sudden* enlightenment breaking into one's own consciousness as much a gift from the divine (and he identified the divine as Kālī) as the result of one's own striving toward union with the Absolute.

samadhi - enlightenment
raja marga - mystical
jnana marga - cognitional
bhakti marga - devotional
karma marga - actional

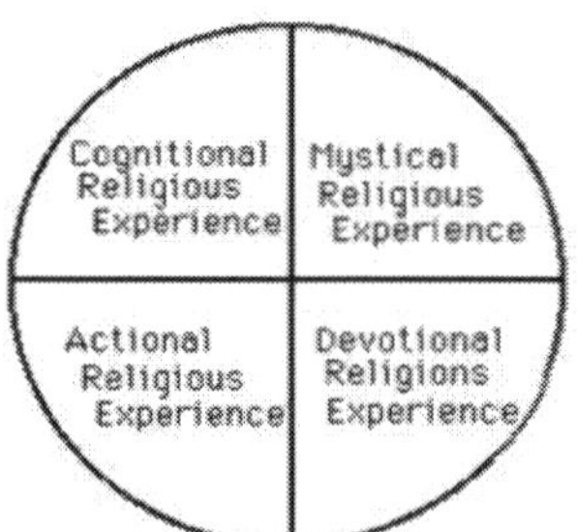

What is fascinating about IMAOKA sensei's spiritual journey are the multiple religious tendencies (*saṁskāras*) or paths (*mārga*s) which he lived: devotional, rational, mystical and actional (or kinesthetic, somatic, sensate: see Appendix B for more

[431] Svāmī Vivekānanda (1868-1901), *Complete Works*. See also, Williams, *Quest for Meaning, ibid.*

information.)[432] These differences in religious perception and practice gave IMAOKA a rich experience of Christianity, Buddhism, Shinto and even Confucianism. His interfaith and intra-faith conversions were processes of growth and maturation, he thought. They were a series of transformations as if toward a center, toward an integral personality that he called a *cosmic human being*. Yet, they were a journey without a destination, a climb without an assent, continuing without arriving. Gratitude was the primal characteristic of every spiritual path or type; mystics just did not anthropomorphize life's gifts.

IMAOKA liked discussing spiritual types up to a point, only taking them as metaphors in the process of becoming and continually growing. Anything else he rejected. But that strength was also a weakness, he would say. Vivekānanda viewed each religious type *hierarchically,* as a step on a ladder leading to a higher spiritual achievement. IMAOKA said that he had not reached any goal nor would he ever claim any *achievement*. For him, there was only the process of becoming free to grow and learn. He delighted in Rāmakrishna's image of the wheel with every spoke leading to the center, to the One, the Divine. That non-hierarchical image of all true paths leading to unity in the center, the *cosmos,* was what IMAOKA had experienced in his own journey. All religious paths potentially led toward *free religion*, yet all the paths were distinct. His experience was unity in diversity – and, potentially, growing in freedom through all negativities. While creative growth and learning required freedom, that freedom did not determine progress or a positive transformation. Freedom meant that one might fail if one's will and effort were not for the good, true and beautiful in life.

---

[432] Asked what is the oldest extant reference to these tendencies, Prof. Arvind Sharma responded in *Textual Studies in Hinduism* (New Horizons Press, 1980) that it would be found in the *Bhagavad Gita*. He later revised the number of *saṁskāras* mentioned there from four to three. I still find four *saṁskāras* in the *Gita*.

Graduation – but No Graduation From Life

IMAOKA's cardinal metaphor of *graduation* meant that he never renounced a previous religious identity, never "burned" any of those "diplomas," which were evidence of a foundation for further growth. Then, he would contradict the metaphor. "There is no graduation from the university of life," he would say so often. He remained Christian, Buddhist, and Shintoist, each having made a distinct and continuing contribution to his life. None was better or higher. Each has its own way of knowing the sacredness of life.[433] He had found that life's journey was multi-religious, growing within and beyond multiple religious identities, all diverse yet united toward something *higher*. And yet, the very use of the terms *higher* or *beyond* was problematic, he thought. It could lead to hubris, the spiritual pride that is a personal cancer. He spoke of having gone *beyond* Christianity and Unitarianism, as did Emerson. However, rejecting Vivekānanda's ladder model of any hierarchy of religious beliefs and practices, *beyond* must be taken as an image (a la Bergson) and a metaphor. There is only process, learning, becoming. It is the paradox of true freedom – free to become but also to fail, to create and also to destroy, to progress and also to regress, to affirm but also to be deceived. Freedom (*jiyū*) required something more to guide one toward the true, good and beautiful – toward becoming *truly human*, that *cosmic being* he sought but never claimed to reach – at least "not yet."

Freedom as Problematic

Freedom (*jiyū*) had come into the Japanese language in a radically transitional time and brought a reputation of immorality and rebellion. *Jiyū* also translated the word "liberal" and was wearing

433. Gregory Bateson formulated multiple epistemologies for modern philosophy in 1970s. Cf., Bateson, G. *Mind and Nature: A Necessary Unity (Advances in Systems Theory, Complexity, and the Human Sciences)*. Hampton Press.(1979).

thin politically in post-World War II Japan. He had loved the word, *jiyū,* and used it in the most inclusive way for his local, national and international visions. However, the negative connotations of *jiyū* led to a rejection of renaming the International Association for Religious Freedom as the International Association of Free Religion in 1958. Imaoka's dream of creating the planet's first international group dedicated to the study and practice of liberating spirituality had failed. But why?

Part of the problem comes from the word "religion" which had been reified as a concept in European languages.[434] Wilford Cantwell Smith suggested using "faith" instead of religion. The very heart of the word "religion" as derived from Latin is *religio*, meaning "to bind." One seeks to bind oneself to God's will and commandments. God's commandments are absolute. His authority is unquestionable. In the sense of *religio*, *free religion* is an oxymoron, not just nonsense but a pernicious misunderstanding of religion's purpose of bringing one into conformity with God's will.

Must one give up freedom to be religious? If so, a religion of obedience to divine commandments or universal precepts (even ones known to be human constructs) seems to be a necessary part of religion. Conservative religion has always championed rule- or law-oriented religion. *Religio* is authoritarian and not to be questioned.

IMAOKA would reject making *shūkyō* a reified concept by wedding it to *jiyū* as a compound and as an image or metaphor. As did Bergson, IMAOKA thought in images. But his meaning seemed to die with him. What had he meant?

IMAOKA would be the first to say that the missionaries, who lived by a rule-oriented religion wedded to fixed beliefs from Divine revelation, had led him to Christianity by the very beauty of their

---

434. Wilford Cantwell Smith, *The Faith of Other Men* and *The Meaning and End of Religion.*

moral and sacrificial lives. They had made sense of a chaotic and imperfect world (sinful, they would say) and chose to live in a devotional perspective – grateful for God's grace that had saved and forgiven them and given them a new life of blessings and hope for eternal salvation.

However, Wilkes and Buxton found rational questioning – the heart of rational religious experience – to be the realm of sin, evil and the devil. Questioning led to doubt and rebellion against God's laws and revelation, they taught – and thus to sin and eternal damnation. Freedom of inquiry was rejected by them as they had no understanding of how reason could function as a religious perspective. For them, it certainly was not a genuine spiritual path for salvation.

In Western religion, the Enlightenment had brought a freedom to revolt against the belief- and rule-oriented religion of orthodoxy – and against all authorianism. The rationals who remained religious struggled with freedom's endless regress of questioning. The certainties of conservative religion were not available for liberal or free religionists as each belief or religious idea was in turn questioned. IMAOKA's pilgrimage from Congregationalist to Unitarian to Free Religionist charts the landscape of rational religion's rugged territory in Japan. Yet, he was never tired of studying life's dilemmas – from multiple religious perspectives – and seeking "the holy" and "sacred" in human relationships and actions.

IMAOKA came to the conclusion that the individualistic freedom coming from the West during the Meiji birth of modern Japan did not lead to the goal of becoming *truly human.* One becomes *human* in community (a la Holmes' *community church* and in progressive Shinto[435] or Buddhism's true *Sangha*). For IMAOKA

435. Williams, *Shinto, op. cit.*, describing Tsubaki Shinto. See also chapter 12 of the visits with Mason.

community had four dimensions, as if legs to a stool, a metaphor for personal, local, national and international. The perspective for all four was a *cosmic* interconnection of all beings, animate and inanimate, with the universe. Community was *kyōkai*, in places of learning – in church, school, art, literature, even politics and economics. One must use one's own freedom in community with others who are also free to transform life toward the good, true and beautiful. Together, through *humanizing* ethics, we evolve toward becoming *cosmic human beings*. Through learning and growth together, in a unifying community, *kiitsu kyōkai* is created as a unity of religious and secular.

Experiential Crises

However, the experiential crises in his own life made him see that the Western (that is the Enlightenment) goal of freedom was individualistic, and consequentially tended to be socially destructive. He knew freedom was needed to create. Just as Bergson and Eucken had done, IMAOKA rejected Darwin's and Spencer's ideas of evolution as mechanistic. Darwin had conceived of evolution without freedom's essence – chaos and choice. Spencer's social evolution linked progress to the certainties of reason. Yet without chaos, there is only a mechanical universe set in motion to evolve as it must. Darwin's mechanistic theory was, to IMAOKA, a crypto-theology with evolution taking the place of a Deistic God, who set everything in motion with a Big Bang and Evolution's scientific laws. Evolution worked its way forward in inanimate matter that evolved into living creatures with evolving consciousness. As had Bergson, IMAOKA rejected any mechanistic notion of evolution while seeing life as creative freedom with no guarantee of progress or positive progression.

IMAOKA had experienced a vision of freedom that he believed allowed him to choose to succeed or fail – to inquire, to learn and study, to construct, and to live a life dedicated to create the good, true and beautiful. He sought to become a *cosmic human being.* He wedded freedom's chaos to a will to be responsible for choices and their consequences personally and socially.[436] Individual freedom with social responsibility meant that he dedicated his life within *free religion*, religion that liberated one for a higher task. He chose his own higher task as a life for others, assisting, sharing, serving. In his century of existence, he was a exemplar of a free religionist, a *cosmic mystic.* This free religion was a liberating faith in community with others, nature, life. This interconnectedness to life was the way of becoming a *cosmic person.*

Non-theistic **Religious Thinking**

IMAOKA's thought evolved toward one concept that was troubling, at least for a theist believing in an Absolute, in a Creator God – which of course includes almost all members of Abrahamic religions. Both mystics and rationals as theologians or philosophers have often been accused of atheism. Even Paul Tillich (1886-1965), the great Lutheran theologian, had questioned traditional theism with his conceptions of "the ground of being" and "God above God." IMAOKA appreciated Tillich's writings but thought that "above" took one back into conceptualizing a "transcendent other," a Creator above or "overhead." He chuckled and said if one used the word God, or *kami*, that was fine. But in his eyes, *cosmic human beings* like Jesus

---

436. IMAOKA anticipated that evolution of the United Nations *Universal Declaration of Human Rights* being linked to duties and responsibilities. See for example, the United Nations' Universal Declaration of Human Rights (1948) and the Declaration of Human Duties and Responsibilities (1998). See also, various countries' charters and declarations. In his own spiritual pilgrimage, and especially with his life crises and failures, he had learned that freedom must be linked to social responsibility. One had to think not only of one's freedom to grow and learn but also the social consequences of personal and group action and behavior. Freedom and responsibility required wisdom – again personal and collective, almost always reflective of past success and failure – to produce a *human being.* For him, becoming *human* was becoming *divine.*

and Buddha were divine enough. He was only expressing his preference of an immanent rather than a transcendent metaphor. He looked for a symbol of divine, holy or sacred that could be experienced. His path required direct experience, and without it, silence. Or, maybe, silence was best anyway. But in this, he privileged meditation (*seiza*).

One could begin to understand a dimension of this problem with a familiar phrase in Evangelical Christianity, "your God is too small." It came from J. B. Phillips, British Biblical scholar.[437] But Phillips was not a mystic. His devotional personification of God demanded a Transcendent Other mighty enough to create everything ex nihilo. Phillips might have tasted the immensity of the sacred in that special prayer experience when one seems to merge into the divine will of the universe in awe, wonder and mystery. Then no concept or belief is large enough to represent such an experience.

However, from the perspective of the cosmos, that cosmic experience of many mystics, this planet and its place in the universe questions theism and the Abrahamic God concept no matter how expansive. It simply is too small. Ninety years of *seiza* gave IMAOKA a personal experience that did not center in any anthropomorphic representation. He just would not use the term God in his annual Affirmation of Faith [See "Statement of Faith by a Free Religionist (Tentative)" distributed to IARF at The Hague in 1966 at the end of chapter 13]. He did not dogmatize his own experience or try to teach it to others. Consistently, he sought no imitators and no disciples.

Spiritual *Non-Theism*

Importantly, IMAOKA's *non-theism* is consistent with a certain type of mysticism rejecting individual ego inflation. Buddhist, Hindu, Jewish, Christian, Sufi and other mystics have lost personal identity

437. J. B. Phillips, *Your God is Too Small* (1953).

and ego in something greater than or beyond themselves, a unity or merging with life, consciousness, or the divine that transported one into a new being. IMAOKA's spiritual or religious *non-theism* also had characteristics of rational thinkers and religionists; for they often developed an ability to handle greater levels of life's uncertainties with cold reason – and affirm some type of a spiritual life. However, there was no "coldness" in his mysticism.

Just as the scientific model of a Polanyi[438] or a Kuhn[439] could embrace relative uncertainty as if it were true until better understanding or more accurate findings replaced it, IMAOKA had grown with "truths" that evolved, ever carrying him *beyond* fixity of absolutes or eternal principles. He had converted from belief- and ritual-centered religion as a devotional Anglican with its mediated "grace-experience" to another type of "grace experience" in Calvinistic Christianity (Congregationalism) modified by a questioning intellect. That mixture of cognitional and devotional spirituality as a Kumi-ai Congregationalist developed further as a Japanese Unitarian, losing much of its devotional features. He could question the Christian Bible's historicity and its construction of Jesus's religion, yet identify as a Christian in the spirit of the Sermon on the Mount – a follower of Jesus' teachings. He remained religiously committed to living a better, nobler, more compassionate existence without having final answers or commandments from an Absolute Being. His years of meditation (*seiza*) granted him another experiential dimension: death of the small self and a paradoxical and metaphoric *birth* of a *cosmic being.* Birth into a *cosmic humanity,* into a *cosmic community* of all beings, animate and inanimate. As said in mystical Buddhism, it is the non-reality of the little self or ego

438. See Michael Polanyi, *Science, Faith and Society* (1946); *Personal Knowledge* (1958); *Personal Knowledge* (1958), etc.

439. Thomas Kuhn, *The Structure of Scientific Revolutions* (1962), especially concerning "paradigm shift."

(*anatman, anatta*) and the inexpressibility of *cosmic being* – *bodhisattva, buddha, nirvāna.*

Freedom and Responsibility

IMAOKA pointed only to *free religion*, a liberating spirituality to be found in any true human activity that sought truth, compassion, beauty and justice. Human freedom can never be complete, he said, and religion (*religio* – Latin, "to bind") tends to conserve the past, not create the new. For IMAOKA, *free* (*jiyū*) and *religion* (*shūkyō*) together meant liberation of one's spirit toward constant growth, renewal and transformation. This *shūkyō* was not the bondage of old dogmas and practices. If *shūkyō* was to be conceived as *religio*, then it must become religionless religion, because it must be free relational, and not binding.[440] Yet, it was responsible to all humanity and to everything in the *cosmos*, human and non-human. With the will to grow in freedom toward the good, true and beautiful, one could become an authentic *human being*, perhaps a *cosmic person.*

Writing without Concepts

When a hundred plus essays were gathered in honor of his 100th birthday in 1981, the enigma of what his teachings meant might been solved. His writing covered many topics that were momentary with much of their context lost. In his last decades he seemed to want only to point to *free religion* and the moments in his spiritual pilgrimage that had helped his evolution.[441]

---

440. "Religionless religion" has been expressed by many Western theologians of dialectical theology like Dietrich Bonhoeffer ("religionless Christianity") and is implicit in much Eastern mystical thought.

441. IMAOKA sensei selected seven essays that represented his thought. He did not distinguish their being better or more mature. He supervised their translation by Bill and Dorothy Parker, although he was particular about precise meanings he wished properly represented. His one hundred essays do not inspire a comparison with Emerson as they were contextual and dated. These seven were chosen not as teachings or wisdom, but as questions to ponder on our own spiritual journeys. For him, the chuckle over the term "Bergsonian" would have turned into a roar of laughter if anyone wished to become a "Imaokan" – and imitate him. He would have said: read and find the strengths and weaknesses in his writings and talks.

He was reluctant to teach any *How-To.* He had been a teacher for seven decades, but he did not want disciples or imitators. Each being's creative freedom had to be used in its own path toward its own becoming. If this seems elusive, even self-contradictory – well, his way was most like a *koan,* to be grasped by intuition, tempered by reason, felt deeply and somatized (made physical or sensate) in actions of compassion deeply felt. All that, in the silence of an egoless and socially active life, was his method of teaching. He chose a few essays that he thought might point one toward a life in *free religion.* Their translation into English follows in Appendix A.

He left no disciples. He left no mark institutionally – no monument, no building. He lived a beautiful, good and compassionate life.

IMAOKA sensei at his desk, 1985 (when he was 104 year old)

APPENDIX A

SELECTED WRITINGS OF IMAOKA SENSEI

- **What Is Free Religion?**
- **My Spiritual Pilgrimage**
- **I Believe In A Universal Cooperative Society**
- **What I Have Learned About Buddhism And Christianity**
- **Meditation Is Source Of Vitality**
- **There Is No Graduation From The University Of Life**
- **Quibbles Of An Old Man**

These English translations are the combined work of William and Dorthy Parker (members of the Tokyo Unitarian Fellowship), AKIYAMA Kinuko (member of Kiitsu Kyōkai) and IMAOKA sensei. IMAOKA sensei felt that English was much too literal a language to express the experiential image of free religion. Yet, he thought these essays might point beyond themselves.

WHAT IS FREE RELIGION?

The reason why representatives of various particular religions and organizations in different countries can come together for dialogue is because they recognize unity in variety. Although every particular religion respects its own characteristic, it recognizes something common among those particular religions, religion behind religions. No particular religion can monopolize religious truth or contain it all. Particular religions contain something more than that which is confined within particular religions. What is that something more? It is universal, super-logical and creative. Is not this what leaders of IARF mean by Free Religion? Rev. A. B. Downing, the chairman of Commission II of IARF, remarked to the point as follows: "A Unitarian is more than a Christian. A member of Rissho

Kosei Kai is something more than a Buddhist. Our awareness of this something more is very important to us in the IARF." Free Religion is neither a new religion ranking among existing religions nor a unification of them. Free Religion is immanent in them, being their essence and goal. All particular religionists become Free Religionists by recognizing the immanence of such super-particular religion within them. Unitarians, Protestants, Catholics, Hindus, Buddhists, Shintoists and Muslims can all become Free Religionists under the said condition.

This reminds me of the fact that the famous British historian Arnold Toynbee wrote on the visitors' album of the Ise Grand Shrine on the occasion of his visit there. "I feel in this holy place the underlying unity of all religions." Although the famous Buddhist poet Saigyo visited the same Shrine, he was not allowed to enter the holy place because he was a Buddhist. But he wrote a poem to the effect, that tears flow down due to devotion to something divine and inexplicable. While Toynbee, a Christian in England, could grasp the unity of religions, i.e., religion behind religions in the Shinto Shrine; Saigyo could feel the essence of religion beyond Buddhism and Shintoism there even though he was prevented from entering the holy place. I understand, therefore, that both Toynbee and Saigyo were typical Free Religionists and Shintoism may be called Free Religion if experienced as Toynbee and Saigyo did.

Free Religion will be discovered not only within particular religions but also within all human activities that are nothing but the realization of human nature, universal, creative, holy and religious. As Professor Tillich put it, religion is man's ultimate concern. In other words, religion aims at none other than becoming a true human being. Zen Buddhism that teaches "Everyday mind is the way" and is therefore Free Religion. Shosan Suzuki, a Zen master, guided his disciple not to practice Zazen (Zen contemplation) but to devote himself to the recitation of Noh songs of which the disciple was very fond. From the standpoint of Free Religion, what is natural and is what matters.

Jesus taught: "Therefore, if thou bring thy gift to the altar, and there rememberest that thy brother hast ought against thee; leave then thy gift before the altar, and go thy way; first be reconciled to thy brother, and then come and offer thy gift."

"For I was hungry, and ye gave me meat. I was thirsty and you gave me drink. I was a stranger, and ye took me in. Naked and ye clothed me. I was sick, and ye visited me: I was in prison, and ye came unto me. Then shall the righteous answer him, saying, Lord, when saw we thee hungry and fed thee? or thirsty, and gave thee drink? When saw we thee a stranger, and took thee in? or naked, and clothed thee? Or when saw we thee sick, or in prison, and came unto thee? And the King shall answer and say unto them, Verily I say unto you, Inasmuch as ye have done it unto one of the least of those my brothers, ye have done it unto me."

Jesus emphasized not religion in the sanctuary but that of daily life. He was a Jew but more than that, a Free Religionist. According to a popular view, the sphere of religion is holy while those of politics, economy, science and art are secular. Free Religionists do not, however, distinguish between holy and secular spheres. Politics, economy, science and art are not mere politics, economy, science and art but realization and development of universal and creative human nature and are therefore sacred, i.e., religious in the broad and true sense of the word. Mr. Kojiro Serizawa wrote : "Literature gives utterance to the silent demand of God: novel writing is a service to God, i.e., a sacred profession." These relevant words apply not only to literature but to all human activities.

Mr. Torajiro Okada who once dominated all Japan by his Seiza (Quiet Sitting), a kind of Zen, said to the effect that all human existence is Seiza, i.e., religion in the broad and true sense of the word, and Seiza is free from even Quiet Sitting because he could guide people to attain the same goal by dance and music. And I think I understand Dr. Felix D. Lion rightly when I say that his views on religion as wholeness is the same as Okada's. The Toshogu (Shinto Shrine) and Rinnoji (Buddhist Temple) for many years engaged in a quarrel which they themselves could not solve religiously but was finally settled by a civil court. Mahatma Gandhi said: "What India needs at present is not missionaries but bread." The former found religion in the law while the latter found it in the economy.

In short, human activities are multifarious but the ultimate goal is to become a true human being. And this is what I mean by Free Religion.

People who are used to associating religion with God, miracles, atonement, Amitabha in the Western Paradise, etc., may not be satisfied with such a dry and commonplace definition. That is the reason why Free Religionists have always been labeled heretics. But times change. I wonder how long hereafter the so-called religions will survive. Although Free Religion is always common like wind and plain like water, Truth is always common and plain. Free Religionists are none other than people who follow such common and plain Truth. They find Free Religion within not only established religions but within politics, economy, science and art, i.e., whole human activities; and they aspire for the realization of an ideal world community, that is nothing else than the Kingdom of God on earth.

I am anxious that IARF should be an organization of Free Religionists. It should be more than an Association for Religious Freedom. The full name of IARF should be changed to International Association for Free Religion as Rev. R. N. West, the former President of UUA, moved at the 1975 Montreal [IARF] Congress.

MY SPIRITUAL PILGRIMAGE

Delivered before the Tokyo Unitarian Fellowship sometime in 1970.

I was born as a farmer's son in the country-side of Shimane Prefecture, Japan in 1881, i.e., 89 years ago. Because my parents were enthusiastic followers of Shin Sect Buddhism, I grew up under Buddhist influence. But my conscious religious life began in my high school days when I happened to come in contact with Rev. B. F. Buxton, an Anglican Church missionary. One day, out of curiosity, I intruded into the premises of Rev. Buxton's mansion that was big and exotic. Even now I remember very well what happened then. Mr. Buxton opened a window and asked me in Japanese in a quiet and subdued tone: "Is it a Japanese manner to intrude into the premises of others?" I was so frightened that I ran away at full speed without saying any excuse. But this was the beginning of my contact with the white man, Western culture and Christianity. Rev. Paget Wilkes, a co-worker of Rev. Buxton, invited us to a class of English conversation and Bible study. I was a very diligent boy to attend the class, being very much interested in English conversation. I had no interest in the Bible at first, but I was attracted to Christianity through the noble characters of the missionaries and was baptized at last at the Matsue Episcopal Church.

In those days (1898) in Japan, Christianity was taken for a religion of devils, and Christians were taken for traitors to the state. The fact that I was baptized, therefore, was a great shock to my parents. My father seriously considered exiling me from the parental roof. My mother was more lenient than my father, but it saddened her more. Recollecting this incident of seventy years ago, I find it became the motive power that made me work later for the solution of inter-faith problems, as the general secretary of the Japan Council for Inter-faith Co-operation.

Soon after I entered college, I began to doubt the historicity of the New Testament story concerning Jesus' life, and the validity of orthodox Christian doctrines. I moved, therefore, to a Congregational Church that was quite liberal in contrast to the Episcopal Church.

After graduating from Tokyo University in 1906, I took a position as minister of a Congregational Church in the city of Kobe. But after three years service, I resigned. The main reason was that I became unable to try to proselytize Buddhists and Shintoists into Christianity. I began to think that the mission of a minister was not proselytizing, but making people more honest believers in their own religions.

While I was working at the Kobe Congressional Church, I happened to know Mr. Tenko Nishida, founder of Ittō-en. Ittō-en is a non-sectarian communal life of penitence and service. According to its principles, man is to live not to become a cause of strife in the society. As such, it is a way of life rather then a religious sect. The centre of its activities located in the suburb of Kyoto consists of 100 families (500 individuals) and has its own kindergarten, primary and high school and junior college.

Tenko is one of a few seniors who influenced me most in my whole life. He practiced the Sermon on the Mount literally. In Tenko's daily life and way of thinking, I found something which I had not found among Christians. That was selflessness or detachment. It seems to be a quite negative way of life superficially, but it is quite positive in reality. It seems to be more Buddhist than Christian. What do you think, however, about the fact that Jesus taught in the Sermon on the Mount and on another occasion as follows: "When you do some act of charity, do not let your left hand know what your right is doing. Your good deeds must be secret."

"If any one wishes to be a follower of mine, he must leave his self behind, he must take up his cross and come with me. Whoever cares for his own safety he is lost, but if a man will let himself be lost for my sake, he will find his true self."

Although Tenko had little regular schooling, he wrote a book, *Life of Penitence*, which has become a best seller. It is now on its 31st edition, sold over 6 million copies since its first edition in 1921. Quite recently its English edition has also been published.

It is a well known fact that he kept putting on tight sleeved dress of a workman even during his term of membership in the Upper House. This reminds me of the fact that Tenko's visit to my house delighted the maid most because whenever Tenko came, he never failed to clean the toilet room and help with the maid's kitchen work.

Tenko was a workman, a servant and a saint at the same time.

Due to Tenko's suggestion, I came in contact with Mr. Torajiro Okada, a master of Seiza, soon after my resignation of the ministry of the Kobe congregational church in 1909. A literal translation of Seiza is Quiet Sitting, a kind of Zen contemplation.

There were several thousand people who practiced Seiza under Mr. Okada's guidance. More than several hundred people, men and women, old and young, businessmen, politicians, teachers, and students gathered at a Buddhist temple just to sit at 6:00 a.m. every day all the year round. Mr. Okada gave no sermon and no lecture. He taught us just to sit aright, to respirate aright and to assume a right posture. Every body, however, who joined the gathering was very much influenced and enlightened by him both physically and spiritually. I was one of those people and kept sitting 7 years until Mr. Okada passed away. I recollect now that it was a true Zen and appreciate Mr. Okada's personality most highly.

From 1932 to 1941, I had a chance to study Shinto with an American friend, J.W.T. Mason, a journalist from New York. He was very much fascinated by Shinto and became a Shintoist himself. When he died in New York in 1942, his ashes were brought to Japan to be buried in the Tama Cemetery in Tokyo, although it was the time when the U.S.A. and Japan were at war with one another.

According to Mason, Shinto is primeval and intuitive truth discovered by the Japanese race and has always been the motive power of self-creative activities of Japan as is shown in her history. Bergson's elan vital is nothing but the French translation of Shinto Spirit.

I will give you an example of Mason's interpretation. When Mason and I visited the Kashiwara Shrine, the chief priest Mr. Uda explained that the door of the sanctuary has been and will be never opened. As soon as the chief priest ended his explanation, Mason cried: "Shinto gods are spiritual! Shinto should keep no image or idol of gods. If any, they should be kept in a museum, not in the sanctuary."

It was in 1948 that we started Japan Free Religious Association consisting of not only liberal Christians, but of liberal Buddhists and liberal Shintoists too and joined I.A.R.F. as a non-Christian member group. In order that I may not speak too long, let me point out only one aspect of the Association that is most important. Many people say that Japan Free Religious Association is an inter-faith cooperation group. There is no doubt about it, but the Association is more than that. Inter-faith cooperation is often nothing but the maintenance of the status quo. The most important aspect in our activities is Freedom. Freedom means autonomy, progress and action.

I cannot omit to refer to Seisoku High School to which I have been related for the past 45 years as a principal and chairman of board of directors. I have always thought: if the school does not have a special character, it is not necessary to exist. Just in the year we started Japan Free Religious Association, the board of directors of Seisoku High School decided to declare to the public that all educational activities in the Seisoku High School should be based on Free Religion, pure and creative. The declaration meant the unity of secular (education) and sacred (religion). In other words, the secular should be as heightened or as deepened as it can be called sacred at the same time. Seisoku High School does not teach religion to students as a regular course, but teachers are urgently required to study and experience religion personally. This sort of religious education does not conflict with the Constitution and can be practiced not only in private schools but in public schools, too. If you ask me, however, whether Seisoku High School has succeeded to make all its every day secular activities themselves so excellent and so splendid that you can not fail to recognize there something divine and holy, I am sorry to confess "Not yet".

I BELIEVE IN A UNIVERSAL COOPERATIVE SOCIETY

MY ARTICLES OF FAITH AT 100 [c.1981]

Sources of Learning and Faith

I was born into a devout Jodo Shinshu (Buddhist) family in Shimane Prefecture and I was not fed until I prayed before the Buddhist altar. I memorized the "Shoshinge" and the "Gobunsho" (sacred texts) without knowing what they meant.

Then I became a Christian when I was in the fourth year of the old style middle school. The fact is, at first, I wanted to learn English conversation and so I attended the school of an English missionary. Later I was baptized when I was attracted by his character and spirituality and had been converted by him. It was in Meiji 30 (1897) that I became a believer in Christianity. This was a time when conversion to Christianity was considered treason and my parents, saying that they were throwing out a Christian from their Shinsu household, just about disinherited me in their fury. Nevertheless, pouring over Uchimura Kanzo's prophetic book, I boiled over with righteous indignation. But as I progressed through the Kumamoto Fifth High School, my doubts about Christianity gradually increased. Did the Virgin Mary give birth to Christ? Was he resurrected after three days having died on the cross? I began to doubt some of the miracles in the Bible. When I was very troubled about this, I met Ebina Danjo and he said that it is all right if you do not believe the miracles in the Bible, Christ is an ordinary man. But you should believe that there is a God. Professor Ebina's thinking was based on the teachings of Free Christian churches as distinct from so-called orthodox Christianity. This teaching saved me.

At the University (Tokyo Imperial University), I chose the philosophy department. Professor Anezaki Masaharu, who was lecturing for the first time on "The Study of Religion," made a great impression on me. The professor's very first lecture was on "Mysticism." He commented broadly on the mystical aspects of various religions in a profoundly interesting manner. Professor

Anezaki was a Buddhist but he had also studied Christianity. I was surprised to hear him express his religious attitude so lucidly, "Because I am a Buddhist, I am a Christian, and because I am a Christian, I am a Buddhist." And so my eyes were once again opened to Buddhism.

It was during my university days that I admired Professor Tsunashima Ryosen. The professor was an exceptional philosopher and a logician. On the occasion of his illness, he achieved a deep religious experience which he announced in the journal, *New Person*, under the title of "An Actual Experience of Seeing God." His was a vivid religious experience of the union of God and himself in the heart of the universe. This can be seen as a broad religious insight transcending Christianity and Buddhism. This article affected me greatly and taught me much.

Lessons from Disqualifying Myself as a Pastor

After graduating from the university, I became the pastor of the Hyogo Christian Church, thanks to Professor Ebina's recommendation. However, my doubts grew about how Christianity should be practiced and I gradually lost confidence in carrying out my duties as pastor. About that time I met Nishida Tenko. It was before he established Ittō-en.

I should comment that the religious people I had met up to that time were all living in another world. They were Buddhist or Zen and some were Christian. They seemed to be practicing literally the teaching of the Sermon on the Mount. "Do not think about tomorrow. Don't worry about life and the economy. Above all, first seek the morality of the Kingdom of God."

Tenko-san taught, "Give up egotism." As a minister I believed that it was my mission as a Christian to teach and lecture, to resent and deplore the corruption of society, to criticize the decline of my superiors and to save sinful society. But in Tenko-san's view, this was no more than egotism. "I indeed am correct. Therefore, I will be saved." Throw away the "I." Then one must become ego-less. He thought that the universe will become one's world if, by first cleaning the detestable toilets of other people, one does away with the self. This teaching of Tenko-san's was shocking. At the same time the vacillation in my way of life was foolish, and I could not make up my mind to leave the ministry. But soon I could not go on.

There are some very exceptional points about Buddhism, so isn't it wrong to convert Buddhists to Christianity? I came to think that the real missionary work to do among Buddhists and Shintoists is rather to convert them to be true Buddhists and true Shintoists. So then I left the ministry after three years, and once more endeavored to redo my research. Since this was in 1910, I was 29 years old.

Arriving at "Free Religion"

Returning to Tokyo, I did meditation with Professor Okada Torajiro. This was recommended by Tenko-san. There was a meditation group every morning from 6 to 7 at the Buddhist temple, Hongyoji, in Nippori. I went there every morning. Professor Okada taught us, "Breathe correctly with correct posture and meditation will make you one with the universe." He also said, "My method of meditation is basically the same as Master Dogen's Zen meditation method." The fact that I was able to take private lessons from Professor Okada during the remaining seven years of his life was a vital force in my life. I continued to practice meditation thereafter, and even now do not neglect it, so that it is my only discipline.

Later, from 1914 through 1915, my esteemed master, Professor Anezaki Masaharu, lectured at Harvard University on the history of Japanese culture, and thanks to the professor's good offices, I accompanied him as an assistant and I was fortunate to be able to study religion and philosophy there.

Upon my return to Japan, I was invited by Nihon University, and for sixteen years I lectured on Christian thought and religious history. Then in 1925, I became principal of Seisoku Academy. I continued to work in that capacity for fifty years, a half century, until I was 92.

During that period, I enjoyed a close relationship with Mr. Mason, an American newspaperman who prided himself on being a Shintoist. Starting in 1932, we conducted Shinto research, and for ten years we prayed at Shinto shrines throughout the nation and visited Shintoists as well. Up until that time, I had thought that Shinto was simply superstition, the residue of a mere primitive religion. But thanks to the stimulation of the foreigner, Mason, my concept of Shinto was uprooted and I came to understand the exceptional ideas that lay behind Shinto and their modern significance.

In this way, in the course of continuing my research, I whose religious awareness started with my becoming a Christian, no longer believed in Christianity exclusively. Nor did I feel that I could profess to be a Buddhist or a Shintoist exclusively. In other words, it seems best to say that at the same time I am a Christian and a Buddhist and a Shintoist. Another way of putting it is that my faith is free religion without any restriction whatsoever.

Human Beings Are Really Gods

The word "religion" infers that one must believe in God. In fact, the relationship between God and man is a definition of religion. However, there are many people in the world who say that they do not know whether there is or is not a God.

As for myself, it used to be that I thought there was a God, but now I cannot imagine that there exists a God in the traditional sense. Rather it is closer to "God has died" (Nietsche). Nowadays I must oppose the idea of God completely, even in its representations. So in my house there is no Buddhist or Shinto altar.

But on the other hand, every human being has religious feeling. I think that so-called religious needs are fundamental and universal elements of humanity. These have taken different forms depending on various environmental factors such as history and climate. There is a certain significance in this, but I think there is only one basis that I want to emphasize.

Putting aside the question of the so-called God, and

considering I am a human being, I attempted to gather together those things that have value which I believe in – in the form of "My Tenets of Faith in Life." These are in five parts.

The first one is "I Believe in Myself." This means that even if one says there is a God somewhere, rather than depend on this, one should first believe in the essence of one's self, and then go on to realize this self. That is, it is the act of establishing one's self. The "self" in this case is not the self that satisfies earthly desires. It is not the self that is a slave to material things and the flesh. It is the self that has the autonomy for becoming one's own hero. Moreover, it is the vigorous self or "creativity" which is constantly trying to progress and improve. It is the self that strives for "unity" and is not isolated from society. The kind of "self" that I believe in makes me feel that life is worth living. To put it in other words, I believe in a sacred quality inside the self. One can think of it as "essential being" or "character" or "divinity" or "Buddhahood." Since it is common in religion to express the idea that man is a child of sin and to reject the self, it may seem that what I am saying is contradictory. But in the present day, when the idea of no god is prevalent, the absence of God in my concept would be exalted. My basic idea is that we should value the human being and believe in the human being. Perhaps we can call this faith in humanism or a religion without God. With this kind of inquiry, I cannot only save myself but also I can respond to the modern tendency of alienation from religion and the various arguments for no religion and against religion.

Universal Cooperative Society

My second tenet of faith in life is "I Believe in Other People." Other people after all represent the autonomy, the creativity and the unitive elements in other people. When I say "other people" I mean that I believe in the "self" that is in my neighbors, assuming that my neighbors possess that "self" also. Putting aside the self and other people, let us believe in true humanity.

Next is my third tenet, "I Believe in a Cooperative Society."

While the self and other people have a certain unique individual character, they are not at all isolated or have a separate existence. By reason of being unique they sprout true mutual reliance, true unity and true love of humanity; thus, they establish a "cooperative society."

One human being does not make humankind. This is so even when we consider an individual's food, clothing and shelter. So the three elements, the self, others and a cooperative society are separate and distinct. Each one has a relationship which actually includes the others. That is to say, these three can be thought of as basically being three-in-one.

Having established this, we come to the fourth tenet, "I Believe in a Universal Cooperative Society." The self, the others, and the cooperative society which are three elements in one are "human society." This alone is not enough. There is something missing. When we think about it, the self, others and a cooperative society all exist because of the universe or nature. Humankind cannot exist apart from nature. That is the basis of our life. I would also like to establish that not only human society but also the heavens, the earth, nature and all the universe are one community (a cooperative society). Animals and plants, the moon and the sun, the air and the water, everything, are in one cooperative society. That is what "Universal Cooperative Society" expresses.

Thus, inevitably, we cannot stop with believing in and embracing all humanity, we must also embrace and make companions of birds and beasts, and plants and trees. There is the biblical proverb, "Behold the lilies of the field...behold the birds in the heavens..." The "Universal Cooperative Society" is composed of the unity of humanity and nature, and the merging of human society with all the universe. I think it is appropriate to think of this as the fourth tenet.

Not the End of Search for Truth

Finally, I add the fifth tenet, "I Believe in the Church." In this case "church" can mean a temple or a shrine or anything of that kind, or a specific denomination or organization or group. All are included in the term of "church." Each possesses certain special characteristics but just as universality does not manifest itself unless some special characteristics are in evidence, some starting point is necessary. So the term "church" is used to refer to these various entities.

Thus, as we comprehend the mystery of a particular church, we can understand the ultimate truth of nature and the universe. A church can be called a microcosm of the universal cooperative society. So people can become universal beings by being members of a church. This is why I have added this tenet.

However, I do not wish to think that these tenets of faith in life are conclusive. I think that they are provisional in the sense that when we reflect further we will see possible revisions. I became 103 on September 16, 1984, but human life has no final point. I believe that there is no graduation from the University of Life. My "Tenets of Faith in Life" are like working principles in the University of Life.

My attitude towards life is to grasp and realize the mystery and the ideals not only of religion but also of all human activity.

From "Rinri" – No. 384, Special Edition "Search for Faith" (Ethics)

WHAT I HAVE LEARNED ABOUT BUDDHISM AND CHRISTIANITY

Because December is the month when Gautama experienced Enlightenment and Jesus was born, I shall speak today of what I have learned about Buddhism and Christianity.

Gautama was said to have experienced Enlightenment, after six years of ascetic practices, under the bodhi tree looking up the morning star on December eighth. The contents of the experience was summarized as the Four Noble Truths, the Eightfold Paths and so on.

Gautama, however, was not satisfied with his private and individual experience and visited five friends who had practiced ascetic discipline with him and some other people. He did not propagate or teach but just reported his experience to ascertain whether his experience was right or not. The dialogue and discussion among them reached a conclusion that religion is not a private matter but a community affair. They found that human existence has two levels, individual and community, and religion is an affair of community. Accordingly, Gautama and friends created a sangha (a church). That was not a mere gathering of individuals but a corporate entity, and Buddhism started as the religion of the sangha. Gautama was not, therefore, the founder of Buddhism.

This fact can be understood by the story of a prodigal son in the St. Luke Gospel. The prodigal son was not saved by his father. The father was very much worried by his son's dissipation. By the repentance and coming back home of the son, not only the son, but the father was also saved. The saviour was not the father but the home.

Jesus is quite different from Gautama in many respects. He was a carpenter, while Gautama was a prince. "The foxes have holes, and the birds of the air have nests, but Son of man (Jesus) has not where to lay his head." (St. Matthew,VIII-20)

Although he blamed the scribes and Pharisees, he had many intimate female friends. Even a woman taken in adultery was not an exception. When he went to Gethsemane, with Peter and two sons of Zebedee, he said "my soul is exceedingly sorrowful even unto death" and prayed "O my father, if this cup may not pass away from you, except I drink it, thy will be done, not as I will." (Matthew XXVI-36) Jesus was thus utterly human, and I am fascinated with his humanity, not divinity. If you wish to keep the word divinity, I will answer to you that divinity in its essence is humanity.

Jesus taught the Golden Rule and Kingdom of Heaven. It is noteworthy that he did not mean Paradise after death by the Kingdom of Heaven. He taught to pray "thy Kingdom come, thy will be done on earth as it is in heaven." (St. Matthew VI-10) The apostle Paul interpreted Jesus' Kingdom of God to be a beloved universal community by saying "there is neither Jew nor Greek, there is neither bond nor free, there is neither male nor female for ye are all one in Christ Jesus." (Galatians III-28) Isn't this what Buddhists mean by the sangha. Both Buddhism and Christianity are not religions of individuals. Both are community activities like language and customs.

In closing, I would like to tell you a story about a conversation between an American missionary and a Japanese Buddhist which took place 70 years ago. The Buddhist asked the missionary, "If I do not believe in Christianity, am I doomed to go to hell?" "It is quite so" answered the missionary. Then the Buddhist asked another question. "My parents were devout Buddhists and had no chance to learn about Christianity. If souls are immortal, where are they now?" The missionary answered:"Of course, they are in Hell because they did not believe in Christ." Then the Buddhist became indignant and said "If what you say is true, I wish to go to hell to see my parents and renew our happy home life even in the hell."

Now I close my talk and wish to listen to your frank criticism of my talk and your response to the American missionary's Christianity.

MEDITATION IS SOURCE OF VITALITY

A new year is here, and having aged one more year, I am now 105 years old. I feel that I would not mind dying any time. To speak of my health, I suffer from failing sight, hearing and, especially, the ability to walk. Several years ago I underwent a prostate operation and because of my age I am not completely cured. So I go to the hospital once a week.

These days I do not exercise or walk very much and I can say that my only good health regimen is that every day without fail since my youth I practice meditation that I learned from Prof. Okada Torajiro (The Okada Method of Meditation). This is Zen meditation simplified and modernized. One sits erect, concentrating one's strength in the stomach and breathing deeply. It is only sitting and not thinking about anything. However, I do not try to prohibit all ideas and thoughts.

I try to do this every day for at least one hour. I can do this anytime, anywhere. When I do to the hospital, I wait my turn for thirty minutes or even an hour, and I do this meditation for that length of time. At first when I do it for 10 or 20 minutes, my arms and legs which had become cold as ice in no time warm up. Blood circulation improves.

However, meditation for me is not just a health practice. You can call it the source of the autonomous creative vitality for both my body and my spirit. Occasionally I can't sleep, but I stay as I am and do the breathing in the correct manner, and I feel all right even if I don't sleep for some time. When I meditate I feel that the heavens and earth are one with the universe.

In my house there is no Buddhist or Shinto altar. Also I do not read the Bible and pray as a daily routine the way I did as a Christian. However, I cannot stop doing meditation. I can say that meditation is the only religious life that I have.

Lively Isolation

After my wife predeceased me in 1978, I led a completely solitary life for some time. The maid who was with us for a long time prepared my meals and took care of me. Soon thereafter, my oldest son and his wife came to live with me. This son also passed away in 1984. Everyone would look at me and say I must be suffering, but to this day I have never been lonely.

In my room I have displayed the photographs of my deceased wife and my three revered masters (Anezaki Seiji, Nishida Tenko and Okada Torajiro). Whenever I remember them, I can call them together; first my wife and then my teachers and friends and I can enjoy all kinds of conversation. Therefore, my room is also full and I am never lonely. In this room is hanging the Irogami of the venerable Matani Roikotsu, the founder of the Chugai Nippo newspaper. When I look at it I can hear his voice full of infectious laughter. In this way

I go on leading a cheerful life.

Now I can't visit my friends any more but they come to talk with me. We exchange letters and keep in touch. Since I became 90 I have made new friends in many parts of Japan and also in foreign countries. I communicate with them by letter. I was surprised to hear in messages from my friends in America and Europe that "My Tenants of Life," which appeared in Issue No. 384 of this journal, has been translated into German and Norwegian.

I am proud not because I have attained the age of 100 but because I have friends who number many hundred times 100. As I accumulate years, I have the strong feeling that people are becoming my brothers and sisters and the world is becoming my home. As I get older, I am gradually becoming more interested in politics, economics and international problems. They are part of the life of my brothers and sisters. Since I am a member of universal cooperative society I have come to embrace a strong interest in and a passion for world movements. I have become concerned about U.S.-Soviet relations, Japan's economic friction with various countries, and the destitute peoples of Africa and India. I don't go to sleep until after I see the last television news at 11 p.m.

History of Past and Present Is Our Own Written Tradition

I feel that when I read the book of someone who has passed away that I can achieve an intimate relationship and understand him or her as well or even better than when they were alive. My vision has greatly deteriorated but thanks to magnifying glasses I can read books somehow, and reading and writing are my favorite daily occupations.

Aside from books by my esteemed masters and friends, the kind I like most are histories and biographies. I read history with the feeling of returning to my youth. The famous English historian, Toynbee, says, "Antiquity, the Middle Ages and recent times are all the present." By which he means that no matter how ancient a thing is we should look at it as if it were happening right in front of us. If we peruse history with such historical insight we will be able to experience an eternity in the present. Within one day an eternity of the past can be comprehended. If this is so, and if I invite the great heroes and the sages and the wise ones of old and of the present, and of the east and of the west, and the nameless common people, they will all come and gather in my study and will come to life before my eyes. I myself as their companion can converse much with them and can understand their feelings. So then my little study becomes a boundless universe, transcending time and space.

In this way, discourse with all the peoples of the east and the west is the greatest delight of my remaining years. When we think about it, the study of history gives us the opportunity to re-live 3,000 years of history. When we try to live in the past with historical figures, we perceive that our own ancestors were one with the ancestors of all humankind. So we then understand that we here today are passing on the history of all humanity. When we read Japanese history and world history as if it were our own written heritage that we are not yet aware of, then our interest is greatly stimulated. In a broad sense, 3,000 years of world history is just like our own biography.

Thereby we not only have a physical and spatial world and universal existence, we can become eternal universal beings unlimited in spirit and by time.

Lengthening One's Life By Looking at the Past

So the study of history is in this sense really interesting. Going back thirty years ago or fifty years ago, or speeding one's thoughts back into the world to 100 years ago or 300 years ago is like making one's self young again in a period that is definitely before one was born. Or to put it another way, I think it is like extending one's life. I say it this way, "I live longer by looking at the past." It is really a kind of longer life. When we speak of getting old, we are usually referring to the future, but isn't it interesting to think of aging from climbing back into the past? That is, we live longer by returning to the past and looking at the past. If this is the case, we can age not just 90 or 100 years, but any number of years that we wish. We can enjoy an ageless long life. From this viewpoint, I think we should reconsider such matters as memorial services to ancestors and ancestor worship or reverence. In Shinto and Buddhism, these customs are prevalent but they now exist in form only. There are many people who worship their ancestors only because it is customary, and there are those who worship them because they fear a curse. However, memorial services to ancestors take on their real meaning when one turns the mind back into the past and returning to the place of one's ancestors, joins them.

The Direct Significance of Memorial Services for Ancestors

To begin with, we call dying "eternal sleep." This is truly an apt expression. If we take a universal viewpoint, death is literally to sleep eternally. It is to return to the bosom, yielding completely.

So, if one went to sleep, then sometime one can awake in some way. Perhaps one cannot awaken in one's original form. For example, according to the Buddhist memorial service, the dead return and are vividly present in the minds of the living. Or even without referring to anything like memorial services, whenever we call the dead person to mind he or she comes back. This act of recall is proof that after all they are not dead. Certainly it may be that the five-foot physical body has disappeared. But the spirit of the person has not died. That is what I think. Therefore, even though we say he or she is dead, it is possible at any time to communicate with their soul.

If I want to live with my departed parents and to see in front of me their souls before they existed as parents, I can do that at any time. Then I can pursue the thread, starting with my parents to their parents, and then to their parents, until I have joined their souls all together and they become one in spirit. I think it would be very meaningful to think of this concept as constituting a memorial service.

We have two parents and they have four parents and they have eight parents, and then these have sixteen parents. And when we go back twenty generations we have over a million parents. If we go back thirty generations, there are one billion. When we consider one billion ancestors as our own flesh and blood, this is the true meaning of memorial services to the dead and ancestor reverence.

Then again, I wonder if it is enough to limit the scope of our ancestors to blood relations. I have natural parents, of course, but I also have spiritual parents without limit. For example, my masters. I cannot forget them. We must add to my masters, their masters, and again their masters. Thinking along these lines, in our respect for ancestors, we cannot limit ourselves to our family's ancestors or to those of Japanese or to those of the east or of the west, but we should include the concept of showing respect to the ancestors of all the world's people.

Theory of Showing Respect for Descendants

I have many grandchildren and great grandchildren. Among the latter there are some in universities, some in high schools and middle schools and some in elementary schools. One day I asked one of them, "How many years difference is there between your grandfather and you?" After thinking awhile, this great grandchild answered, "90 years difference." Hearing this, I was overcome with a feeling of being very old.

I am a 20th Century person who was born near the close of the 19th Century. From the viewpoint that my great grandchildren will be active from now on into the 21st Century, I have the feeling that even I am becoming a 21st Century man.

In this way, with the present as a starting point, we can be back to the distant past and be with our ancestors or we can probe into the future and be with our descendants. So just as we are, in the present, we can create the eternal history of the human race from the past to the present to the future. The Apostle Peter says in the Bible, "In Christ, one day is like 1,000 years, and 1,000 years is like one day." Also the German philosopher, Schleiermacher, said something to the effect that one instant truly fulfilled is an eternity, and that kind of living indeed makes an eternal life. I who am presently in this world intend to live this kind of eternal life one instant at a time.

I think that the world's humankind and the great nature of the universe constitute one great life which must progress and develop from the unlimited past to the unlimited future. Are not we ourselves great living cells of all humanity and of the total universe? While our five-foot bodies are as infinitesimal and transitory as cells, they are one with unlimited eternal life. Although I am actually myself, I am yet not myself. The heaven and the earth and the universe are me. So I think that even when I die, in some form I will go on living an unlimited life. That is to say, I am a universal being so that I think it will be interesting even after I die.

Rinri Kenkyusho, April 1985

THERE IS NO GRADUATION FROM THE UNIVERSITY OF LIFE

Delivered before the National Conference of Free Religionists in Japan held at the Lecture Hall of Seisoku High School on June 3rd, 1979

If not all, at least a vast majority of you attending here are full-fledged members of society taking an active part in various fields of work. You are no longer students. However, I believe, your education has not been completed.

Education should be continued throughout life, even though one has gone out into the world after graduating from school, since lifelong education follows school education. I should like to say that this lifelong education is given by the University of Life.

There are neither school buildings nor definite teachers in the University of Life. Its school building is all of society or the whole universe. While students of ordinary schools, in principle, are depending on their parents, even though they legally become adults, students of the University of Life are independent and self-supporting. Therefore, the University of Life is an adult university.

To become an adult and become free of one's parents means,

first of all, to be able to support oneself or to become economically independent from one's protectors. This means that one doesn't study economics any more, but that one participates in the economy. For that purpose, it is essential to have an occupation.

It is not an easy task to follow the course of practical economy based on engaging in an occupation. It is like a life or death struggle with real swords and quite different from fencing with bamboo swords in a fencing school. In the worst case, one may have to escape in the night, commit burglary or suicide as the result of debts, joblessness or bankruptcy. However, in the education of the University of Life, such a situation is the best training arena. If classroom education contributes to building up human character, such a deadly ordeal in the University of Life is sure to be 100 times as effective as the former. Veterans in the economic world have all been educated and trained in such a university. Consequently, I always cite first of all the practical economy as an important subject in the education of the University of Life.

There was the following episode in the life of Kihachiro Okura, one of the foremost leaders in the industrial field during the Meiji era. When Kamesaburo Yamashita, the founder of the Yamashita Steamship Company, visited Okura to ask him about financing possibilities to tide over financial difficulties his company was confronted with, Okura answered to his request, "All right, I will lend you the money as requested. But, I should like to ask you one question, 'Do you want to be another Kihachiro Okura and give up being Kamesaburo Yamashita?'" At this question, Yamashita was awakened to his own self with a sudden flash. Promptly he left, saying, "I understand what you mean. I withdraw my request for a loan. Thank you." Yamashita discovered himself after considering the words of Okura. He established the Yamashita Steamship Company without Okura's assistance. Thus Okura succeeded in making Yamashita aware of his true self, though Okura was a businessman, not a professional teacher. Some people say with contempt that matters concerning finances or money-making are low-grade earthly affairs, but I am of quite the opposite opinion.

At this juncture, permit me to state my own past experience. Unlike Yamashita's case, I was helped out of financial difficulties by a loan. Many of my acquaintances would think that I have little to do with monetary affairs. However, as a matter of fact, once I thought of throwing myself into the crater of Mihara-yama. The reason why I selected Mihara-yama was that it might conceal my ugly remains from people. However, when I confided my plight to one of my friends, he at once lent me some tens of millions of Yen in cash unconditionally, that is without a bond of debt or interest. Through his friendship and assistance, I was renewed and I owe him my long life – over 90 years by now. I don't believe in the Creator or the Almighty Personal God, but I believe in the Divinity immanent in Humanity. Divinity is nothing but genuine Humanity.

We who have graduated from a school and become full-fledged members of society as adults form first of all a community or a society. To form a community is a political affair, and it is a main subject of the University of Life along with economic matters. Some people might oppose this and say: "While politics forms society, education and religion shape individuals. If individuals become better, society would automatically become better." However, individuals are not independent from society. It is true that an individual may possess their individuality with dignity which cannot be replaced by any other person. But the existence of an individual can be maintained only when he or she is organically integrated into society. In other words, society and the individual are interrelated as one organism. Politics for society is, at the same time, for individuals. Politics aimed at establishing an ideal society is also aimed at bringing up ideal individuals. Therefore, politics should always be combined with education. In this respect, Taisuke Itagaki and Yukio Ozaki, great political leaders during the Meiji era, are good examples. Itagaki remodeled the Japanese people still living under feudal conditions into free men through the movement for democratic rights. Ozaki taught the people that everybody is equal and should have equal rights to vote irrespective of age, property or gender through the universal suffrage movement. Both of them were excellent educators.

Aside from politics and economics, the home is an important classroom in the University of Life. No matter how commonplace or trifling it may be, daily life itself is a subject matter of study in the University of Life. There are many different views on life – mine is "Life is a university," meaning every human experience is material for education. And I wish to go one step further and say, "Education is religion."

Not being a scholar, I can't state a theory of education or religion. The only thing I can do is to state my personal experience. I believe that education consists of building up a human being. It is commonly said that school education is to teach various subjects. It may be true. But, I think it should be more than that. Namely, the school should be the place to make true human beings providing something essential and ultimate in addition to the curriculum. Of course students are already human beings. But even as human as they are, they are not yet true human beings. Human beings become true only when they develop and realize their boundless possibilities under guidance of true educators. In other words, education is to seek and realize the true, the good and the beautiful, which are the ultimate ideals of humankind and nothing but Divinity or Buddhahood. Accordingly, education is, after all, religion. I have reached such a conclusion after many years of religious pilgrimage and teaching experience. Some 50 years ago when I became the principal of Seisoku Academy, I intended to give religious lessons in addition to the then existing curriculum. But, soon I became aware that it was wrong. If realization of human ideals is the ultimate concern of human life, and it is nothing but religion, religion should be found in the curricula. Accordingly, the vital point in practical religious education is not to teach Buddhism, Christianity or Shinto but to bring out the religion immanent in the curriculum itself.

Recently, I was deeply impressed by learning Mr. Ichitaro Kokubu's method of teaching. Mr. Kokubu taught his elementary school pupils the lesson that the three interior angles of a triangle add up to two right angles in the following way. First of all, he told them to draw a triangle at will on a sheet of paper, and then ordered them to cut out three angles from the paper with scissors and put them together. The pupils did as they were told and found that three angles of any triangle formed a straight line. Mr. Kokubu taught them that the straight line means two right angles. A pupil, who was a son of a poor tenant farmer and was deemed to be a slow pupil, was surprised and asked: "My angles also made a straight line. It is the same with everyone?" Mr. Kokubu answered, "You are right. It is the same with a tenant farmer, landowner, teacher or pupil. Even with His Majesty. It is an eternally invariable truth in the universe." It is said that all the pupils were deeply moved, and the arithmetic class seemed to have been converted into a shrine. When a teacher and his pupils are really in earnest, I think, such a scene will be produced in any classroom.

As mentioned before, school education is a little like learning to swim on dry land, while lifelong education in the University of Life is – whether politics, economics or home life – a fight with real swords. I stated previously that Kihachiro Okura was an educator and, at the same time, a businessman. But, from the point of view just mentioned he may be said to have assumed one aspect of the religious human being. In this respect, Eiichi Shibusawa, one of the distinguished business leaders during the Meiji era, is a good example as well. He was a businessman through and through. Because he was a businessman, he could thus be an educator and religionist in my sense. Shibusawa advocated the necessity of harmony of the Analects of Confucius and the abacus, and set up the Association Concordia (Kiitsu Kyokai) which existed for about 30 years. It is said generally that the Association Concordia was established by Masaharu Anesaki, professor of Tokyo University, and Jinzo Naruse, President of Nippon

Women's College. But, this is not correct. Anesaki and Naruse took part in setting up the association as a result of earnest persuasion by Shibusawa. The Association Concordia founded by Shibusawa was, in a sense, the forerunner of our Tokyo Unitarian Church and the liberal religious movement of today.

If Okura and Shibusawa, both being businessmen, were religious men, Itagaki and Ozaki, as I mentioned previously, were also religious men in my sense. Viewed from this point of view, we can understand the reasons why Isoo Abe, Sakusaburo Uchigasaki, and Bunji Suzuki, all of whom were senior leaders in the liberal religious movement in Japan, entered the field of politics. Having a career as pastor of Okayama Church, Professor of Waseda University, Chairman of the Unitarian Association, Abe became a Diet member and founded the Socialist Party of Japan. Uchigasaki also became a Diet member and, later on, Vice Minister of Education, retiring from the posts of Professor of Waseda University and pastor of the Unitarian Church. Suzuki joined the Unitarian Church as the secretary to Dr. MacCauley, representative of the American Unitarian Association, and later, turning to the labor movement, became a Diet member and founded the Labor Federation of today. Because these three leaders left and the Unitarian Church began to decline, somebody criticized their activities as earthly and an apostasy, but in fact they weren't. For them, politics was sacred and the society and the nation were churches. They opened up religion which was confined to the Unity Hall near Shibazono Bridge to the general public; they tried to realize the unity of religion and politics in a new and true sense. Though not called religious, their activities were religious in the sense I have just stated – only it was not especially organized as a religion. It had no need for an organization. I myself call it non-organized religion so as to distinguished it from conventional religions. Non-organized religion is not inferior to ordinary or organized religions as to genuine religiosity. Therefore, in discussing religions, we should never neglect non-organized religion.

The Japan Free Religious Association includes such a non-organized religion. Though the Japan Free Religious Association is the smallest in the world as an organized body, we are firmly convinced that we are having 100 million members – that is virtually the whole population of Japan. Religion in the true and broad sense should not be, as John Dewey thought, bound by a doctrine, religious observance or a religious body. It should be for everybody. In the sense of the Lotus Sutra, commerce and industry are not different from Buddhism.

In conclusion, I should like to say that, if one's whole life-experience is education and religion, there is no graduation from the University of Life. In other words, if the ultimate concern in human life to create true humans or a true society by seeking and realizing truth, good and beauty, which may be called divinity or the Buddha-nature, is religion, then it will never reach an end, i.e., graduation. It should follow its eternal path. If expressed in the sense of Zen Buddhism, we should not cling to a temporary spiritual enlightenment but to continue the study permanently. However, there is an counter argument which asserts that graduation is religion. The assertion is that one is saved or has attained spiritual enlightenment is religion. The achievement of salvation or enlightenment means graduation, it says. In other words, it is asserted that religion should have spiritual attractiveness or something supernatural. However, Jesus Christ, who did not deny but worked many miracles, rejected the request for miracles by the scholars and Pharisees as a claim in that vicious and unjust age. To see religions in the affairs of daily life including politics, economics, etc., is to find sacredness in secular things. It would be religious mystery in the true sense of the word.

At present, politicians and businessmen who became conscious of their own responsibilities are making an endeavor in unanimous cooperation for further development of the United Nations and establishment of the World Federation. If we can realize a truly ideal world community, it would be Heaven or the Land of Buddha.

Politicians, businessman, etc., who strive for realization of the divine land on this earth are more earnest religious men than those who believe in religions that teach them to expect to go to Paradise in the world to come. The establishment of Heaven on this globe is the real attraction. Because the Land of Buddha is not perfectly realized yet, we should devote ourselves to it. It is not a mere endurance race. To be devoted to this, there is boundless hope and inspiration. Gotthold Ephraim Lessing, German poet, playwright and critic, said as follows:

"Suppose that God appears here, with all the truths in the right hand and an eager mind to seek after truth in the left hand, and asks me which I choose. I would in a humble way cling to his left hand and answer that I wish I could have the mind to seek after truth."

At the Lecture Hall of Seisoku High School on June 3rd, 1979

RE-EXAMINATION OF MASON'S SHINTO

Written originally for "Creation" – 1966

This year has been 25 years since that famous newspaperman and Shintoist, J. W. T. Mason, passed away. His Shinto outlook is modern and universal, and is more and more fitting for our country's Shinto culture and for our people in general.

I plan to celebrate the 25th anniversary with a gathering of old friends. It will be nostalgic when we re-read a manuscript published in the *Jinja Shimpo* ("Shrine Bulletin"), to the special delight of the readers of that publication.

His View of Shinto was a Unity Between Heaven and Earth and Man and God as One.

One of the many criticisms of Mason is that the Shinto he advocated was Mason's own brand of Shinto and not Japanese Shinto. It is true that Mason did not study the Japanese language, so that he studied Japan and Shinto through English translations of Japanese articles. But Mason excused this by saying, "Were not Nichiren and Shinran great Buddhists despite the fact that they never studied Sanskrit?" In this, we see evidence of his strength as well as of his weakness. Another criticism of Mason is that the Shinto he advocated is nothing more than a rehash of the philosophy of Bergson. In October, 1939, he did invite 110 Japanese and foreign scholars, educators, and friends to celebrate Bergson's 70th year in Tokyo. Mason considered Bergson a great philosopher.

Mason also asserted that if America accepted Shinto, there would be shrines to Washington and Lincoln, and in the future, shrines to Christ, Sakyamuni, and Confucius are possible. In this also we see Mason's strength and weakness.

I do not agree with Mason's statements without qualification but at the same time that Japan became a defeated nation, I did think that Mason's thoughts were most effective as reference material. I believe that if he were living today, he would play an extremely important role for Japan, for America, and especially for Shinto. I recognize his value now more than ever.

While the 2600th anniversary of the birth of Buddha was being celebrated all over the country, Mason particularly worshipped at Kashiwara Shrine. At that time, Abbot Uda explained to Mason, "The main hall of this shrine is never opened." Mason excitedly said, "This is only natural since the deity of this shrine is formless and is a spiritual being."

When you say that a shrine is never opened, somehow one has the feeling that a mystical statue of a deity is kept there, but Mason did not feel that way at all. I admired him as a man who had the perception to see immediately the connection between "the never opened shrine hall" and "the formless deity".

After his visit to Kashiwara Shrine, Mason prayed at Kamiyama Shrine in Wakayama City. Abbot Adachi guided him and explained that although the shrine and the cemetery existed in almost the same place, not only was the entrance different but the two were treated completely differently. This pleased Mason very much. Somehow he had discovered the same shrine principle in Kamiyama Shrine as in Kashiwara Shrine. He discovered at Kamiyama Shrine the truth that even though the origins of the shrine were temporarily in the cemetery, the shrine was a completely spiritual entity and therefore different from the cemetery by virtue of its being a shrine.

But Mason was not discovering this spirituality for the first time when he prayed at Kashiwara Shrine and Kamiyama Shrine. He had always stated energetically that shrines are spiritual in character and therefore when he prayed at a certain shrine in Izumo and he heard that a statue of Inada-Hime was kept in that shrine, he at once vigorously asserted that this statue was not there as an object of prayer but was an image to be kept in a treasure house or museum.

I journeyed with Mason to shrines all over Japan but of these, I will never be able to forget my impression upon visiting Hinomisaki Shrine in Izumo. This shrine is located on Izumo peninsula which juts out into the Sea of Japan. This is the best place to view the sun setting into the Sea of Japan. After completing our prayer visit through the shrine, we discussed many things with the Abbot Baron Ono. The deities of Hinomisaki Shrine are Amaterasu-omikami and Susuno-wo-no-mikoto. While viewing the beautiful sunset which is the symbol of Amaterasu-omikami, Mason listened quietly to Abbot Ono's commentary:

> Every year from Omisoka (the last day of the year) until Gantan (the first day of the New Year) we conduct a special ceremony at this shrine. This service is conducted only by the abbot and no one else is permitted to participate. It is an extremely important and austere shrine ceremony. It is absolutely forbidden to explain how the ritual is conducted but the theme of the ceremony is to commemorate the presentation of the Murakumo Sword, which he had grasped in the upper reaches Hino River by Susano-wo-no-mikoto to Amaterasu-omikami at Takamagahara.

Mason listened to the abbot's words with great interest. It was fitting that we left on this note about the presentation of the sword. Bathed in the glow of the symbolic sunset, I felt like the abbot's explanation was just like having Susano-wo-no-mikoto explain it in his own words and shake hands with us.

Mason liked Susano-wo-no-mikoto, and so he kept saying that he liked Izumo. At first, I did not completely understand what he meant. But when I thought about Mason's words when we were at the shrine, I understood very well. Susano-wo-no-mikoto was not just a crude, violent deity. The object that he had grasped in his hand was the sacred sword, one of the three divine treasures. This was not the same Susano-wo-no-mikoto who escaped from Takamagahara (Heaven of gods) to Nenokuni (the underworld). It was as if he once again ascended to heaven with the divine sword in his grasp. Susano-wo-no-mikoto's ascent to heaven symbolized the unity of earth and heaven, and the oneness of human and divine. In this, we have the essence of Shinto.

View that Shinto Respects Freedom and Creativity

How would the Shintoists of old feel about the recently promulgated democratic constitution? From the beginning, there have been many people who thought that the democracy itself is not Shinto-like. So many people criticized Mason's Shinto as being too democratic.

Mason pointed to the tale of the meeting of the myraid of deities convoked by Amaterasu-o-mikami and Takami-Musubi-no-Kami and asserted that Amaterasu-o-mikami existed along with deities who themselves made creative things. "Amaterasu-o-mikami was not a dictator but one who governed democratically, emphasizing the responsibility and efforts of each individual. Amaterasu-o-mikami did not neglect those aspects of individual creativity which had as their essence elements closest to his own divine spirit." So, according to Mason's own Shinto, we can consider the new Constitution as being Shinto-like.

It is not generally known but Mason was severely upset by the sudden explosion of the February 26 Incident. He said, "In London's Hyde Park, freedom of thought is permitted. Freedom is proclaimed even in anarchism and communism. There lies the true Shinto also. I feel right now that Shinto has expired somehow. I must leave Japan when one must go on a pilgrimage to a Hyde Park shrine." Shortly after saying this, he actually left Japan. But then after a little while, he came to Japan for a third time. He rejoiced to read the news of Takao Saito's speech questioning the military. Then he visited Mr. Saito to express his appreciation. His comment on Mr. Saito's speech was, "Give me liberty or give me death," paraphrasing Patrick Henry. He believed that this was real Shinto. From this time on, Mason and Saito were extremely close. Accordingly, just as the photo shows the group at the Gakushi Hall, with Mason and his wife in the center, these friends held an evening dinner party, Mason doing the honors, putting Mr. Saito in the middle also and their wives on both sides with the General Araki and Dr. Inoue. When I recall these things and think of what Mason could do for Japan and America if he were still alive, I cannot help grieving that his death was premature. According to Mason, the Japanese quality to apprehend truth directly was revealed in ancient Shinto. It is the quality that consistently made possible their spontaneous creative masterpieces.

In September, 1936, Mason and I were invited by Chief Priest Daiko Furukawa of Kiyomidera at Okitsu to spend the night there. We had a long discussion that night. Furukawa Roshi excited Mason's interest with the following anecdote: "Sesshu went to China to study Buddhism and painting. He stayed for several years but could not find a suitable teacher. When he was about to return to Japan, he painted a landscape of Mt. Fuji, Miho no Matsubara (Miho Pine Grove), and the Kiyomi lagoon. This painting won the admiration of the Chinese, and a great painting authority there honored it with his seal. Whereupon, Sesshu painted another one just like it and had the same expert stamp his seal on it. He left one in China and brought the other painting back to Japan.

However, Sesshu had one problem. In these paintings, he had added a tower outside the main hall of the temple. But it was doubtful whether in fact there was a tower in Kiyomi temple. So when Sesshu returned to Japan, he made a pilgrimage to Kiyomi Temple, and he found that there was no tower to be seen. Sesshu was disappointed. However, he determined, "There will be a tower," and Sesshu underwent great suffering in order to accumulate sufficient funds mainly by his own painting and calligraphy. Finally, a tower existed just like in his paintings, and so he had succeeded. Unfortunately, that tower has not survived. It was destroyed and only the foundation stone remains.

Mason listened in rapt attention to the Roshi's tale. Sesshu had created something from nothing. He had created a tower. Sesshu was a Shintoist as well as a Buddhist.

Written originally for "Creation" – 1966

THOUGHTS ON EMERSON

March, 1981. Lecture to the Kiitsu Kyokai

In my student days, we heard about Emerson and Carlyle together and we read them a great deal. Emerson's writing was introduced to the Tokyo Unitarian Church at that time through a pamphlet entitled, "One Word, One Thousand Gold Pieces" and impressed me so much that I still remember it very well. But I did not read his complete works. Now I have refreshed my memory with a book that I borrowed from Professor Woodroofe to prepare for this talk. In other words, I have only a fragmentary knowledge of Emerson. But the special quality of Emerson is that a fragment is not just a fragment but that everything within the fragment shines forth.

The reason for speaking about Emerson today is that next year will be the centenary of his death in 1882. In America, a committee is planning various observances and Reverend Greeley has asked me to participate. Reverend Greeley is the man who was chairman of the American Unitarian Association and also president of IARF, and he is now a minister in Concord. Concord is famous as the place where Emerson passed away and will always be remembered in association with the "sage of Concord."

Coincidentally, I was born the year before Emerson died in

1882. Also I followed in his footsteps at Harvard, and since he was a Unitarian and my great teacher of free religion, I feel a great responsibility in accepting his spiritual legacy.

Emerson was born in 1803 and after graduating from Harvard University and the Divinity School, he became a Unitarian minister in Boston at the tender age of 30. These were the early days when the Unitarian Association had not yet been formed. Although it was called "Unitarian," it had a deeply conservative tradition and many features which he did not like, such as mass which was derived from "The Last Supper," a ritual which was the same as baptism, and the taking of the wafer and the wine for Christ's flesh and blood. Emerson had doubts about this ritualism and after three years either left or was asked to leave the ministry. Always a poet, a thinker, and a preacher, later he also worked as an author and lecturer. His Divinity School address and his lectures on religion became famous. These are contained in the pamphlet I brought here today. These are the lectures he was asked to deliver before the students who were about to graduate and become ministers. I have just reread these after a long time and find Emerson's writing hard to read. I received a copy of Mr. Kono's complete translation of the *History of Unitarian Thought*. Here also I found many passages I could not understand. In any case, Emerson criticized the mediocrity and the impotence of the church of his time which had become extremely formalized and fossilized. He especially attacked the idea that Christ was the only child of God.

He said that if Christ is the child of God, then we are all children of God, because this universe has a spiritual existence and this divine spirit pervades all sentient beings beginning with humanity. He gave this spirit the name of "oversoul" or great spirit. All humanity possesses this great spirit, that is to say, are children of God. So there are no supernatural, mysterious miracles. If there is such a thing as a miracle, then the universe as it is in its natural state is indeed a miracle.

He preached revolutionary ideas for that time and he was

criticized for his radical opinions. Finally, his preaching was banned not only by Harvard but much more widely. So he went to England and visited Carlyle. Later he went there two more times and they achieved an understanding with each other and became lifelong friends.

Gradually Emerson developed a profound philosophy. His thoughts evolved from the idea of the oversoul. The features that stand out are the dignity and freedom of man, his trust in humanity, and the equality of man. He reasoned that we understand and empathize with the sages of old like Plato and Christ and Shakespeare because we have the same universal oversoul as they did. He thought that each human being is like an encyclopedia and possesses within himself everything in the universe past and present, east and west. That is why all human beings have dignity and are equal. When one realizes this, he must value himself and trust himself. "It is suicidal do imitate others. It is foolish to envy others." I learned these words while I was in high school and they made an indelible impression on me. In imitating others, we abandon ourselves and become like others. Since we kill ourselves, it is suicide. When we envy others, we are forgetting that we ourselves have valuable qualities. In other words, we are being foolish. He taught us to open our eyes to the fact that each of us possesses a part of the oversoul, is a child of God, and has an invaluable treasure inside him, and must do everything we can to trust ourselves to find the way to develop our own individuality and achieve self-realization.

We learn from Plato and Christ but we must not imitate Plato and Christ. We must seek inside and not outside. Reading books and listening to lectures are indirect methods and not the main path for attaining truth. He said that it is only by direct experience, by intuition, by direct observation, and by direct study that we attain truth. In such disciplines as Zen, a master is needed but we must attain Nirvana ourselves, not just through the teachings of the master. Emerson is famous for expressing such thoughts and for the idea of self-reliance.

His sentences are not logically structured prose but take the form of intuitive, poetic essays. So he is a wise man and not a philosopher. Or would you call him a philosophical poet, perhaps? That is why even a fragment is important and also difficult to understand. I must have an attitude of direct observation based on experience in reading his work.

When you say "Unitarian," you think of a very radical, progressive group, but the truth is that in the old days as now there were surprisingly many conservative members. Emerson was treated as a radical by his own associates. So it was that at the age of 40, he opposed the conservative Unitarians and established the Free Religious Association, becoming Deputy Chairman, and thus striving for liberalization of Christianity. Dr. Holmes, the last Chairman, dissolved the association, saying that it had achieved its objectives.

Then, it was ten years ago, that the Unitarian group merged with the Universalist group to form the Unitarian Universalist Association. We think of this as America's Free Religious Association. However, they should not stick forever to the Unitarian Universalist name. Shouldn't they instead return to the spirit of Emerson and, like Japan, make it the Free Religious Association? We are asking the IARF to so the same. It is actually named the International Association for Religious Freedom. Freedom of belief and free religion are two separate ideas and should not be confused with each other. Therefore, I think that they should change the name to the International Association for Free Religion. I have been speaking at every opportunity to the headquarters of the association and to my friends in the very influential American group, but I don't seem to make much progress.

So we in Japan can take pride that we embody the spirit of Emerson more faithfully than the Americans. That is why I would have those who are attending the IARF meeting in the Netherlands understand this idea and seek to bring about its realization.

QUIBBLES OF AN OLD MAN

A Sunday talk before the Tokyo Unitarian Church
by Rev. S. Imaoka, Feb. 13, 1983

Because I shall attain my 102nd year in the coming September, many friends of mine congratulate me on my longevity. But I have neither expected nor striven for longevity throughout my life. I have been a mediocrity, always playing the second fiddle and have fallen behind in dying.

Why are people so anxious to live long? Are they not a little selfish? They seem to have forgotten the teaching of Confucius "If you hear the Way in the morning, you can die happily in the evening." The Marathon race champion can run because he is not conscious of his weight. When one is unconscious of the existence of internal organs, he or she is quite well. If one is troubled with not being able to sleep at night, I advise him or her to lose the desire to sleep. One secret of longevity is not to have a longing for it.

We must lead a busy life. It is a matter of course that a person in the prime of life should be absorbed in one's occupation. But one must not live leisurely even after retirement. They should continue to associate with as many friends as possible. They can write or telephone to friends although they can not make a trip and are obliged to stay at home. They must read books, newspapers and listen to a broadcast, look in on a television. If one finds his or her days tedious, they become a living corpse. I hold that human being is a minor until he or she touches their sixtieth year, and true human life starts thereafter and proceeds without an age limit. From this point of view, Mr. Seisensui's haiku is quite pertinent.

A camphor tree,
although 1000 years old,
comes into bud again this year.

I am not lonesome at all. I am conscious of my individuality and respect it. But self can not exist without others. Of necessity, self and others realize solidarity, fellowship, and community. Apart from community, I cannot exist. I am deeply moved by the fact that I have had so many respected teachers, seniors, and friends due to longevity. I am proud of the fact that I have had almost ten thousand alumni of the Seisoku High School as my dear friends. Moreover, I am finding new respected friends these years. Quite recently a new American friend, Professor George Williams of California University, came to Japan to meet me and delighted me exceedingly.

Because one third of a lifetime is spent by sleeping, I can not help being aware of the positive and important role played by sleeping in human life. While I am sleeping, I am not conscious of myself, but breathing and circulation of blood do not stop. Both are not done by me but without my will. Because breathing and circulation are natural phenomena, I become a part of the Great Nature during sleep. That is the reason why I can work hard the next day, because I was united and invigorated by the Great Nature the preceding night. And I would like to add that Zen contemplation is a kind of sleep. A Zen man sleeps while he is awake. As people become one with Nature by sleeping, so a Zen man becomes one not only with Nature but with Dharma (The ultimate Truth or The Pure, Formless, and Universal Life.) Such remarks, identification of Zen contemplation with sleeping, may be criticized as absurd. But I will be quite satisfied if you will be good enough to understand my lay efforts to find Zen and religion in everyday affairs.

APPENDIX B
VARIETIES OF RELIGIOUS EXPERIENCE

At least twenty centuries ago in India the variety of religious experiences was observed and classified into four broad categories. They were called the four tendencies (Sanskrit: *saṃskāras*), paths (*mārgas*), and practices (*yogas*). The four *saṃskāras* were inclusive of differences in personality, perception, and life purpose (later, the caste system). Spiritual paths (*mārgas*) were more important to them so they saw everything converging into one's spiritual pilgrimage. Then they added some concepts that went beyond the observed evidence with concepts of *karma* (causality) and *saṃsāra* (rebirth). Thus, they constructed a system that saw one's past lives effecting one's present in everything from caste to how one should use one's faculties. These extra beliefs took nearly universal observations about the tendencies we develop emotionally, physically, rationally and intuitively and made them into what is now called Hinduism. However, the observations about the four tendencies would appear in many other ancient systems (astrology, Tarot, indigenous religions.)

Three Indian leaders of the 19th century Hindu Renaissance are responsible for introducing this fourfold paradigm or model of religious experience to the West. They were Rāja Rammohan Roy (1772-1833),[442] Pratap Chundra Mozoomdar (1840-1905),[443] and

[442] Rammohan Roy had shared this concept with none other than Max Mueller. P. C. Mozoomdar (also Majumdar) toured England and American and spoke to much larger audiences. See especially Mozoomdar's 1883 talk to Unitarian ministers, "Protestantism in India."

[443] The first to come to America was the reform Hindu, Pratap Moozumdar [P. C. Majumdar], a member of the Brahmo Samaj – the Society of God. His first trip to the West was in 1873, visiting England and Germany. He visited the U.S. three times, in 1883, 1893, and 1900. He clearly articulates the four *margas* in his "Protestantism in India," delivered in 1883 and published in *Lectures in America &*

Svāmī Vivekānanda (1868-1902).

Svāmī Vivekānanda (1863-1902) used this fourfold classification of personality and the corresponding variety of spiritual paths in his teachings. He was the third Hindu teacher to share this idea with the West, appearing at the World's Parliament of Religions in Chicago in 1893. Many other Indian teachers since Vivekānanda have used the exact English terms which he devised for his presentation of Hindu psychology and spirituality. Vivekānanda taught that the religious tendencies or faculties governed an individual's way of seeing the world, how one organized their response to life, and how and what one would be taught – even concerning the notions of *karma* and rebirth.[444]

Vivekānanda & Mozoomdar

Svāmī Vivekānanda (1863 -1902) used fourfold classification of personality and the corresponding variety of spiritual paths in his teachings. He was the third Hindu teacher to share this idea with the West, appearing at the World's Parliament of Religions in Chicago in 1893. The second was the Brahmo Samaji leader, Pratap Chundra Mozoomdar.

Vivekānanda was a hero for IMAOKA for a multitude of reasons. When IMAOKA learned that I had written a book on Vivekānanda's spiritual journey, he asked precise and different questions on each of my visits. (In fact, his habit of asking for another's knowledge about their interests was a reason why it was so difficult to interview him.) His own interest in Vivekānanda was so deep

Other Papers (Calcutta: Navavidhan Publication Committee, 1955), p.184.

444. Combining *karma* and rebirth (*samsara*) to the empirical observation of the different tendencies unnecessarily links a Hindu solution to the problem of fairness in the universe with the personality types.

that he had organized a centennial celebration in Tokyo in 1963 of Vivekānanda's birth and had visited the Ramakrishna Mission in 1969.

Svāmī Vivekānanda used this classification of personhood and the corresponding variety of spiritual paths in his teachings. Vivekānanda believed in teaching each person according to his/her spiritual tendencies or its corresponding point of view. Each tendency had a path, a practice, a way of knowing, a set of teachings, and a way of experiencing the Absolute governed by one's past *karma*.[445]

> Past lives have moulded our tendencies; give to the taught in accordance with his tendency. Intellectual, mystical, devotional, practical--make one the basis, but teach the others with it. Intellect must be balanced with love, the mystical nature with reason, while practice must form part of every method. Take every one where he stands and push him forward. Religious teaching must always be constructive, not destructive.
>
> Each tendency shows the life-work of the past, the line or radius lead to the centre. Never even attempt to disturb anyone's tendencies; to do that put back both teacher and taught. When you teach Jnana [rational path], you must become a Jnani [rational person] and stand mentally exactly where the taught stands. Similarly in every other Yoga. Develop every faculty as if it were the only one possessed, this is the true secret of so-called harmonious development. That is, get extensity with intensity, but not at its expense. We are infinite. There is no limitation in us, we can be as intense as the most devoted Mohammedan and as broad as the most roaring atheist.[446]

Vivekānanda used the ancient Hindu taxonomy of four religious tendencies in his books on the four paths of spiritual development: *Raja Yoga, Jnana Yoga, Bhakti Yoga,* and *Karma Yoga.* Each *yoga* (discipline, practice) was seen by him as the path (*mārga*) for a different type of spiritual experience, each path leading to a potential experience of the Absolute.

Shri Rāmakrishna (1836-1886), Vivekānanda's *guru* (teacher),

---

445. George Williams, *The Quest for Meaning of Svâmî Vivekânanda* (Chico: New Horizons Press, 1974).

446. Swami Vivekananda, *Complete Works*, VII, 98

taught that any of the four religious tendencies could bring an individual to the Absolute directly. And, he taught that all religions lead to God (the Absolute), since each path is like a spoke of a wheel leading to the hub, the Center or God-consciousness.

Vivekānanda did not agree with his *guru* Rāmakrishna but taught that one climbed a spiritual ladder of disciplines or *yogas*. By changing paths (मार्ग mārga) to disciplines (योग yoga), he created a hierarchy of religious truth. With each step on the path, or climbing up the ladder toward higher truths, an individual obtained more wisdom, one lifetime after another.

IMAOKA was sad when he learned of Vivekānanda's hierarchy of religious experience. He said on numerous occasions: "I have not experienced that. For me, there is only learning, growing, changing."

More Western thinkers became aware of this model for interpreting personality differences at the end of the nineteenth century. Pioneering psychologist Carl Jung (1875-1961) made use of this four-fold system. Jung was no doubt indirectly indebted to Vivekānanda, but this concept had become so popular and watered-down that Jung did not ever acknowledge Vivekānanda as a source for his own theory. This "map" or "paradigm" had become popular and diluted through use in certain circles (liberal religionists, spiritualists, Theosophists, popular culture). Jung may not even have known who to attribute the bringing of this Indian theory to the West and his own attention.[447] There are times that he seems to claim that he discovered his "four psychological types" in the Upanishads. Jung does say that he "rediscovered" the theory in Indian scripture, but also from Chinese alchemy as well as Western alchemical and astrological

[447] I worked on this problem for a book on "Jung and Hinduism" to trace this dependence. At the time I thought Jung had plagiarized from Vivekānanda. I decided to quit the project because I could not find from whom Jung had taken these ideas. Prof. Harold Coward took over as editor and finished the project.

theories.[448]

Jung was seeking support for his resistance to Freud's theory that sex is the fundamental determinant of the self. All of these ancient models of human personality shared a basic fourfold structure, but often with a doubling or tripling factor to handle more elaborate personality differences. Jung called his version of this ancient taxonomy the *Four Personality Types* (publishing a 600 page book on the subject in 1924).[449] His model involved four types of perception: rational, feeling, sensing, and intuiting. He used the doubling factor, proposing that each type was either extrovert or introvert. This again copied the ancient Indian model by replacing *pravritti* (outward progression) and *nirvritti* (inward regression) with his terms of extroversion and introversion.. Jung accepted the ancient notion which Vivekānanda referred to as "harmonious development" by coining the label of the Individuation Process. For some reason, Jung left out a number of features in the ancient spiritual psychologies which suggested structures in the personality which bring about harmony, balance, and epistemological differences.

Vivekānanda's and Jung's classifications of spiritual tendencies and personality functions can be viewed in the following table:

Saṃskāras	**Practice & Path**	**Tendencies (Vivekānanda)**	**Functions or Types (Carl Jung)**
Jñāna - ज्ञान	*yoga & mārga* योग - मार्ग	Intellectual	Rational (thinking type)
Rāja - राज	*yoga & mārga*	Mystical	Intuitional (intuiting type)
Bhakti - भक्ति	*yoga & mārga*	Devotional	Emotional (feeling type)
Karma - कर्म	*yoga & mārga*	Practical	Sensate (sensing type)

In each person, according to Jung and more explicitly in the Neo-

448. Jung "discovered" the theory in translations of the *Upanishands*, a highly mystical text, he wrote.

449. Carl Jung, *Psychological Types* (Princeton: Princeton University Press, 1971).

Jungians, one dominant center of experience becomes the final arbiter of all experience. If this were not so, the person would be divided – confused, indecisive, purposeless, even pathological, schizophrenic, etc. The various ways of interpreting life experiences are individually prioritized so that one can decide more quickly about what one needs and wants. One way of knowing becomes the superior function for each individual's personality or "ego" and contributes to a more purposeful life and a sense of a being a unified self.

Jung's model can be briefly summarized as follows:

1) The *thinking* function - organizes, establishes order, classifies, identifies and makes plans. Its notion of causality is linear--from cause to effect.

2) The *feeling* function - connects the experiencer personally with life. It is the "liking and disliking function." Whatever is happening is given an emotional tag. This function is principally past-oriented as some time is required to become joyful, angry, sensitive to the experiences involved.

3) The *sensing* function - operates directly from the "five" senses: seeing, hearing, touching, tasting, smelling. This is an active and present function; it is the experience of seeing and not the feelings or thoughts about it. Its one time frame is the present.

4) The *intuiting* function - sees the whole from parts. It sees the entire situation from one fragment. Intuition synthesizes the other functions' "data" into a coherent whole or "unitive order." Its time frame is totally different from either the thinking ("linear"), feeling ("past") or sensing ("now") experiences of time. Once a pattern or outline is "seen/intuited" it leaps to the conclusion. It arrives at the "future" as already here and now.

The Triune Brain[450] and the Missing Fourth

Some concurrence with these concepts can be found in early neurophysiology research of the 1970s and 80s. While locating mental and emotional functioning in three physical regions (neocortex, mammalian, and reptilian) was abandoned with further research, searching for a relationship between brain systems and personality has continued. When the cerebral cortex's two lobes or hemispheres were noted, then there were four neurological or brain systems to organize and make sense of all stimuli; these brain systems generally correspond to the four *saṃskāras*--the rational, emotional, actional (or Jung's sensate and Vivekānanda's practical), and intuitive centerings of human experience.[451] As already said, the next generation of research in brain science discarded the "Triune Brain," but the one hundred plus areas of brain functions are beginning to be seen as working together in systems that might influence our personalities and perceptions. Ken Wilber described each of the paths[452] as a stage of the spirit and of the psyche – with corresponding pathologies[453] at each level; seemingly, all traditions have them.[454]

---

450. Paul MacLean and Carl Sagan published extensively on the Triune Brain. "Paul MacLean's Model of the "Triune Brain," *The Tarrytown Letter* (November 1982), pp.4-5. Charles Tart wrote on alternated states of consciousness. Lateralization of the brain led to talk of a Right Brain and a Left (intuitive and rational).

451. For a discussion of Vivekānanda and Jung's use of these categories see George M. Williams, "Methodological Problems in Documenting Religious Change When Change is Denied: Svāmī Vivekānanda's Early Years" in Madhu Sen (ed.), *Studies in Religion and Change* (New Delhi: Books and Books, 1983), pp. 219-230; "Swami Vivekānanda's conception of karma and rebirth," in Ronald Neufeld (ed.) *Karma and Rebirth: Post-classical Developments. New York: SUNY Press, 1986;* "Svāmī Vivekānanda: From the Apostle of Hinduism to Vedanta to the Religion Eternal, the Unity of All Religions" *Religious Traditions* (1990).

452. Ken Wilber, *The Spectrum of Consciousness* (Wheaton:The Theosophical Publishing House, 1977) and *The Atman Project* (Wheaton:The Theosophical House, 1980) plus many others. He credits Da Free John (Master Love Ananda) for pointing out the spiritual stages.

453. Ken Wilber, "A Developmental View of Consciousness," *The Journal of Transpersonal Psychology,* Vol.11, no.1, 1979.

Using the Four Tendencies or Types Heuristically

Heuristic usage is simply taking a classification or organization of data as an aid for understanding. It attempts to simplify something too complex to learn initially. An example in chemistry is the "planetary model" of the atom. It makes graphic the notion of electrons orbiting the nucleus of an atom and helps one visualize how atoms join in molecules. And then, from another perspective, that of the atom as a wave function, one must relativize everything previously learned.

Each of the tendencies (*saṃskāras*) brings together what has been observed as religious experiences into patterns and a model for understanding. Centuries of observations suggest that an individual can *center* in one tendency and its way of perceiving. That becomes a characteristic way or pattern for perceiving "truth" as "spiritual" or "religious." The fourfold model or paradigm of the religious or spiritual experiences has amazing usefulness. It becomes a language with terminology to help articulate in words found in almost every language what humans have taken to be holy, sacred, true, or of ultimate concern.

The perspective of any single tendency can be used to subordinate other spiritual paths or tendencies. Thus, one can remain centered in a devotional faith and practice and find mystical and rational experiences subordinate to it but compatible and supportive. Thus, they are taken as less true than one's own centering. This will become more apparent as each tendency is described in more detail.

Devotional Religious Experience

Devotional religion is a form of human experience gaining

454. For examples, see Ken Wilber, *The Spectrum of Consciousness* (Wheaton: The Theosophical Publishing House, 1977) and *The Atman Project* (Wheaton: The Theosophical Publishing House, 1980) and Heart-Master Da Free John, *The Basket of Tolerance, On the Seven Schools of the One and Great Tradition of God-Talk* (Special Prepublication Edition) and his other writing as in *The Knee of Listening: The Early-Life Ordeal and the "Radical" Spiritual Realization of the Divine World-Teacher and True Heart-Master, Da Avabhasa (the "Bright").*

knowledge of the mystery and meaning of life as personal and relational. It is often described as the way of the heart with love as its most consistent metaphor. When this love inspires awe and wonder, it brings forth gratitude. And characteristically there is a feeling of unworthiness, that one is not owed or entitled to such an unmerited gift. So many devotional traditions call this experience "grace" in a multitude of languages. Devotional religion is distinctive because this gift of love is not impersonal, but from a source that can be personally named, with whom one can have a personal relationship, with whom one can talk or pray, with whom one can commit one's life. And one can respond to the gift of grace by becoming an agent of grace, giving back to others and to life what one has received spiritually – and perhaps materially. In English the generic word, god, is turned into the name for the Personal Other, God the absolute giver of life and eternal salvation.

Almost in every religious tradition worldwide there is a jealousy factor in devotional religion. The personal God is claimed exclusively for one's own group, sect, denomination or tradition. But there are those in all devotional traditions that are universalists, who see God as Isaiah the Hebrew prophet did, as God of all with salvation for all.

Perhaps Martin Buber's conception of the I-Thou relationship captures something to the personal, intimate quality of the God-experience in devotional religion. But those who use Buber usually do not realize that he was searching for an expression of a mystical paradox of an unknown other with whom intimacy appeared. Still, the I-Thou appropriation does describe the devotional experience of many saints.

Devotional religion is necessarily theistic. That is, its personal experience of a personal God is conceived and expressed in language and metaphors of human personhood. Such anthropomorphism must be honestly owed by the devotional religionist as the price of centering in this religious pattern. It can be either monotheistic and polytheistic. In the twentieth century devotional religion is by far the most popular and often described religious type.

The pathologies of devotional religion, with its projection of human personhood upon the cosmos, have been attacked by religious and secular rationals from Confucian scholars to Enlightenment philosophers to founders of modern psychology like Sigmund Freud and to theologians like Frederick Schleiermacher. Yet, for all the pathologies, the experience of divine grace has appeared as transformative for millions of those who follow the devotional path.

Actional Religious Experience

Actional religion is the form of human experience using the senses and movement to gain knowledge of the mystery and meaning of life as energetic and creative. Its very sensate nature makes it observant and realistic, seeing awe and wonder in nature's gifts of beauty and bounty. Its experience of grace is impersonal but no less intense and real. Life gives. Its blessings are adored and celebrated.

Celebration is ritualized, probably first as play, then formally as set aside moments in the chaos of time. Anniversaries remembered great events as holy days and symbolized them in sensate way with song, dance, ritual movements, art, story. The human voice chanted in a myriad ways in the many actional traditions. Sensate (actional) spirituality apprehended a multiplicity in ordinary reality operating under the rule or control of one unifying power, such as Kanagara in Shinto or Mother Nature itself. There is an underlying unity of being and essence to all of Life. Despite this multiplicity and its potential for chaos, there was order and fair rules to be followed. In rituals persons, groups and traditions bonded together in order and unity, with little need to articulate beliefs and theories about the mysteries of life. The groups had found or had been given the very rituals needed to both symbolize a sacred order and reconstruct it in every participant. Practice and participation need only be the assent of observing the community's rituals or taking the role of priest or priestess and leading them in precise ways governed by tradition. Both observer and participant could directly experience the transcending experience of communion as community and order as beauty.

For the actional (sensate) religionist there is no religion at all without beauty. There must be beautiful art, music, movement in dance, voiced in sacred chants. Criticized as the most primitive of religious paths and practices, absence of sensate religious experiences has impoverished traditions that have condemned art and music as sensual and leading to sin and made them guilt-ridden as they confess a longing the sensate's beauty and mystery.

Cognitive Religious Experience

Cognitional religious experience is a form of human experience gaining knowledge of the mystery and meaning of life as rational, principled and ideational. It is centered in human reason's idea of reality as consistent, following the orderliness of the season, stars and mathematics. Finding the principles is thus metaphoric, a quest that seeks order in chaos and constructs natural rules elevated as principles. In China Confucian philosophers were particularly creative in identifying the way (*dao* - 道) of heaven (*tiān* - 天) and the principles or standard of propriety (*li* - 礼) by which heaven ruled. This very function of human reason thrives on a process of questioning, study, learning, and construction. The process can be quite conservative, especially of principles that are deemed holy and sacred, lasting centuries with little apparent change. But the very love of knowledge (*philo+sophia*) was its own transcendent element, a freedom to learn something new and requires a reformative and reconstruction of principles once holding a community together.

Individually, the cognitive (rational) experience of the mysteries of any aspect of life can inspire awe and wonder. It is not unlike solving a problem in math or science that was "unsolvable." Experiencing the power and beauty of mind or consciousness can be a peak experience for one so gifted. And the notion of being gifted with unusual rational capability is crucial to whether the experience is taken as spiritual or not. Does it point human experience beyond the personal self (the small ego, as it were) or does it inflate and create an arrogance of intellectual superiority? Other tendencies see this as the danger of the rational path and its humanism. Religious rationals through the centuries have displayed a remarkable humility, simply because the human intellect can never know enough. There is always something more to explore, to learn, to ponder, to interpret, to construct into a theory or principle. That is the rational's path to awe, wonder and mystery – the good, true and beautiful of life.

Mystical Religious Experience

Mystical religious experience is a form of human experience that find unity in the chaos of a sensed world. It professes a direct knowledge of the oneness of life, of one's own life interconnected to all other beings, animate and inanimate. It is most often found with those who practice types of meditation that silence words or observed one's "chattering money mind" from the viewpoint of an observer – as if observing the "left brain" from the "right brain" (the intuitive). Thus, in the same way, the reasoning, doubting, and questioning faculty is silenced or subordinated to intuition.

Then too, the feeling function with its passions, fears and angers must also be silenced or subordinated. The retreat "away from the world" has been the quiet place for a mystic to have the time and space to master this part of strengthening the intuitive function. And finally, the emotional function's distractions must be stilled. To complete the disturbances of the senses, meditation tends to require the beginning practitioner to use a fixed sitting posture (in *yoga,* an *āsana*) or rhythmic walking or even jogging to quiet sensate stimuli from distracting from meditation.

But meditation is not mystical experience per se. It is only the placing one's self in an opportune state of consciousness and non-distracting activity to be ready for an experience of oneness, unity, merging to something other than the self – the small self, that is, in most traditions that make such distinctions. Conceiving, symbolizing, articulating the mystical experience is problematic. It is an altered state of consciousness, altered by the very process of controlling other ways of confirming reality (rational, sensate, emotional knowing). And one must come out of or down from the mystical experience to talk about it. However, that said, the witness and expressions of mystics are some of humanity's finest literary creations. As early as the Upanishads and throughout the ages in so many religious traditions, there is the awe and wonder of mystical union with the divine, absolute, ultimate, God, Life, Consciousness. These, in their varying metaphors and similes, have inspired a perception of humanity as capable of things better and more beautiful. While gratitude is a primal characteristic of every spiritual path, mystics just do not anthropomorphize life's gifts. The unmerited blessings of life become an intuition of life's interrelatedness.

Critics have attacked mysticism as anti-rational or even pathological, its ecstasies as "divine madness," its retreat as other-worldly and lacking social concern or engagement. Its pathologies are grand deceits and confusions of an inflated ego – illnesses labeled as schizophrenia and megalomania. But these pathologies do not negate the intuitive capacities revealed in the exemplars of this path such as IMAOKA sensei. Its healthy expression is a unity with life itself.

Integral Religious Experience

This stage entails work to complete mastery and direct knowledge of all four spiritual tendencies (sensate, emotional, rational, mystical) and integrate them to be used appropriately, each according to the strength or in a unified way. The individual would function, momentarily or for periods, appropriately in whatever predominate type of functioning was called for. There would be, momentarily or for periods, perfection of being in emotional, rational, intuitive, and sensate situations and a utilization of introverted or extraverted functioning (inner- and outer-directed processing of experience).

Jung never found a living example of psychological integration. However, he refused to go and see if Ramana Maharishi (1879-1950) had reached that level when he visited India in 1937 to receive several honorary doctorates. True saints have been hard to find.

IMAOKA Emi (daughter-in-law), Dr. IMAOKA (104 yrs old), and Prof. George Williams. 1986

Glossary of Key Terms and Figures

[A]

ABE Isō [also, Isoo]. 安部磯雄 (1865-1949) One of Dōshisha Trio, president of Japan Unitarian Association (JUA), professor at Dōshisha and later at Waseda, preacher at Unity Hall, founder to Socialist and Peace parties.

AKASHI Shigetarō. 赤司繁太郎 (1872-1965) Pastor of the Dojin Christian Church (Universalist). One of the founders of the Japan Free Religious Association.

Amaterasu Ōmikami 天照大神・天照大神 – Sun goddess, chief Shinto deity.

ANESAKI Masaharu. 姉崎正治 (1873-1949). KISHIMOTO's protégé, known as the Japanese father of the scientific study of religion, mentor of IMAOKA, studied with HIRAI and then under INOUE Tetsujir at Imperial University becoming a professor of philosophy there, deeply involved in *yunitarian* activities.

Association Concordia 帰一協会 Kiitsu Kyōkai,

[B]

Batchelor, George. (1836-1923) American Unitarian Association (AUA) Secretary from 1894-97, attempted to end Japan Unitarian Mission in 1895 but unable to until 1900.

Bergson, Henri-Louis. (1859-1941) French philosopher, won Nobel Prize in literature in 1927.

Booth, John Nichells. He visited occupied Japan in 1948 as a correspondent and found surviving liberal religionists for the AUA.

Buxton, Barclay Fowell. (n.d.) Anglican (Episcopal) missionary at Matsue important in conversion of IMAOKA to Christianity.

[C]

Cornish, Louis C. (1870-1950). AUA Secretary, mentor of John Day, provides positive narrative for closing mission to Board and in *The Christian Register*.

Cosmos [magazine] 六合雑誌 (*Rikugō Zasshi*)

[D]

Day, John Boynton Wilson. Commissioned by the AUA in 1919, Day was the last director of the Japan Mission and closed it in 1922.

dōjin 同仁 universal benevolence

Dōshisha University 同志社出身; Dōshisha Daigaku 同志社大学

dōtoku 道德・道徳 (morality)

Droppers, Garrett. (1860-1927) One of three professors who went to Keiō to make it a university, arrived in 1889, taught political economics, and stayed until 1898.

[E]

EBINA Danjō 海老名彈正・海老名弾正 (1856–1937). Kumi-ai Congregational leader and early mentor of IMAOKA, debated UEMURA in 1901 liberal developments in Congregational mission.

ekayana. 一乗 An important concept in Buddhism: one way; only one way of Truth; unity of all truths.

Eliot, Charles W. (1834-1926). President of Harvard

Eliot II, Samuel A. (1862-1950). Son of Harvard president Charles W. Eliot, Secretary of AUA 1898-1900, first president when it became the highest officer of AUA, 1900-1927, closed School for Advanced Learning and ended the Japan Mission in 1900, sent MacCauley back to be director of Mission in 1909.

Emerson, Ralph Waldo. (1800-1892). Former Unitarian minister, senior member of American Free Religious Association.

[F]

Fenollosa, Ernest Francisco. (1853-1908). Professor at Tokyo Imperial University (philosophy, art history, political science), a "Harvard man," converted to Buddhism.

free 自由 *jiyû*

Free Religious Association 日本自由宗教連盟 Nihon Jiyū Shūkyō Renmei. Founded in 1948.

Friendly Society 友愛会 founded at Unity Hall by SUZUKI Bunji, second secretary of the JUM.

fuhenteki 普徧的・普遍的 universal, universalism

FUKUDA Utayo (d. 1978) Wife of IMAOKA Shin'ichirō.

FUKUZAWA Yukichi (1834-1901) 福沢諭吉. Statesman, publisher and founder/president of Keiō University, one of the important figures to invite Unitarians to come to Japan, gave them a home at Keiō.

Furness, Caroline. (1869–1936). Professor of astronomy at Vassar, hosted by Mission in 1920-21, IMAOKA was often her translator.

[G]

geza 下座 total humility

great self 大我 *taiga*

[H]

Hawkes, Henry Warburton. (1843-1917) British Unitarian who paid his own way to serve the Unitarian Mission from 1889-1890.

HIRAI Kinza (1859-1916) 平井金三. Attended World's Parliament of Religions, 1893, founded Oriental Hall (Ryuka-juku 劉家塾) as rival to Dōshisha, taught ANESAKI, delegate to 1900 AUA May meeting, New Buddhist Unitarian.

HIROI Tatsutarō (1875-1952) 廣井辰太郎・広井辰太郎. Methodist-Unitarian expelled for heresy, studied under Spinner but felt condescension there, became Unitarian, resigned JUA in January 1910, professor at Chuo University.

Holmes, John Haynes (1879-1964) Influenced IMAOKA concerning concept of "community church."

[I]

IMAOKA Nobuichirō. (1881–1988) 今岡信一良 *See* IMAOKA Shin'ichirō

IMAOKA Shin'ichirō (1881–1988) 今岡信一良 (previously Nobuichirō)

INOUE Enryō (1858–1919) 井上圓了・井上円了. Founded Tetsugakkan (Philosophy Hall).

INOUE Tetsujirō (1855–1944) 井上哲次郎. Philosopher at Tokyo Imperial University.

Institute for Advanced Learning 先進學院・先進学院. Senshin Gakuin (1894-1899/1900). The mission's "graduate school" at Unity Hall, Tokyo.

[J]

James, William (1842-1910). Harvard philosopher and psychologist.

Jung, Carl Gustav (1875-1961). Swiss psychologist who adapted ideas from Indian religion and psychology (the four types, etc.).

Jinsei hyakunen 人生百年 --IMAOKA's book: *A century of human existence*, 1982.

jiyû 自由--free, liberal

Jiyū Shingakkō 自由神學校・自由神学校 School of Liberal Theology, later renamed Senshin Gakuin 先進學院・先進学院 Institute for Advanced Learning

jiyū shūkyō 自由宗教・自由宗教 ---Free Religion

Jōdo Shinshū. 浄土真宗 Devotional branch of Buddhist ("True Pure Land School")

[K]

Kami 神 God, Gods.

KANAMORI Tsūrin (1857–1945) 金森 通倫 One of Kumamoto Band to attend Dōshisha, credited with first Japanese book published in 1891 on liberal Christianity, later known as missionary of thrift and saving.

KANDA Saichirō (1863–1944) 神田佐一郎・神田佐一郎 Returned with first missionary party to become secretary of mission, virtual leader of the Association in 1903, returned to family bank in 1910.

KATAYAMA Sen (1859–1933) 片山 潛・片山 潜. Christian socialist and early leader in *yuniterian* movement.

Keiō Gijuku 慶應義塾・慶応義塾 Keiō College, founded by FUKUZAWA Yukichi in 1858; was given this name in 1868 when it was moved to the center of Tokyo.

Kenkyu-kai. "Group for the Study of Socialism," especially Christian socialism.

Kiitsu Kyōkai 帰一教会. IMAOKA's "Return to the One" fellowship, also referred to as Tokyo Unitarian Church, founded in 1948. [note slight difference in type of association or fellowship].

Kiitsu Kyōkai 帰一協会 ・帰一協会 ・ 歸一協會Association Concordia. Founded in 1913.

KISHIMOTO Hideo 岸本英夫 (1903–64) son of KISHIMOTO Nobuta who married ANESAKI's eldest daughter Miyoko, historian of Japanese Christian history, conservative but joined IMAOKA in the Japan Free Religious Association in 1948.

KISHIMOTO Nobuta 岸本能武太 (1866–1928) Speaker at World's Parliament of Religions in 1893, taught at Dōshisha and then at Waseda, a Christian Socialist, father of Japanese Comparative Religion, editor of Unitarian journal *Shūkyō* then of Cosmos, vice-president of the JUA.

KIYOOKA Eiichi. 清岡 暎一 (1902-) Grandson of FUKUZAWA, historian of Keiō University.

Knapp, Authur May. (1841-1921) First AUA fieldworker to Japan, 1887-90, later returned to Japan as publisher and editor, founder of Tokyo Harvard Club.

KŌTARŌ Sugimura (1872-1945) 杉村 廣太郎 Studied at the Liberal Theology School (renamed School for Advanced Learning), famous journalist and literary critic.

KŌTOKU Shūsui (1871–1911) 幸徳秋水. Radical attendee at Unity Hall, executed for High Treason. Wrote "On the Obliteration of Christ."

Hokke-kai 法華会 (Society of the Lotus Sutra) ANESAKI was a prominent member.

Kokkyō 國教・国教 (National teaching, periodical)

Kumi-ai. Independent church movement within Japanese Congregational Mission.

[L]

Lawrance, William Irvin. (1848-93) Served in Japan from 1891-94, returned to serve in offices at AUA.

Liscomb, William J. (1848-93) Professor of literature, arriving in 1889 with first missionary group to teach at Keiō, stayed until 1893.

[M]

MacCauley, Clay. (1843-1925) Arrived with first group and served in Japan from 1889-1900 and again from 1909-1920. IMAOKA was his last secretary and then would become Day's secretary for a short period.

MURAI Tomoyoshi. 村井知至 (1861-1944). One of the Dōshisha Trio and a major preacher at Unity Hall, delivered "The Synopsis of Socialism" at the first session of the *Kenkyu-kai,* joined all *yuniterian* activities with ABE and KISHIMOTO.

MINAMI Hajime 三並 良 (1865–1940) Major preacher and teacher at Unity Hall, especially of Bergson and Eucken.

MURAI Tomoyoshi 村井知至 (1861–1944) Professor/preacher. Eldest of Doshisha Trio. Presented talk on "The Synopsis of Socialism" at the first session of the Kenkyu-kai (group for the study of socialism)

[N]

NARUSE Jinzō (1858–1919) 成瀬仁蔵 Founder of Tokyo Women's University, one of founders of Association Concordia.

Nihon Jiyū Shūkyō Renmei 日本自由宗教連盟 Free Religious Association. Founded in 1948

Nihon Yuniterian Kyōkai. Japanese Unitarian Association, organized in 1892 with 3 member churches (Mita, Kanda, Shiba). The Mission and the Association would drop Unitarian in its name and be renamed Japan Liberal Christian Mission (Nihon Jiyu Kirisuto Remmai).

NIIJIMA Jō's 新島 襄 (1843–1890) Also known as Joseph Hardy Neesima [also Niisima], founder of Dōshisha which was part of the Congregationalist Mission.

NISHIDA Tenkō 西田天香 (1872–1968) Ittō-en founder.

Nishida Takeshi 西田多戈止 Tenkō's grandson, current head of Ittō-en.

NIWANO Nikkyō 庭野日敬 (1906–1999) Co-founder and President of Rissho Kosei-kai, a lay Buddhist group and prominent member of IARF and WCRP (now Religions for Peace).

[O]

OKADA Torajirō (1872–1920) 岡田虎二郎 . Teacher of *seiza*, involved at Unity Hall.

ŌNISHI Hajime (1864-1899) 大西祝 Co-wrote first book on Liberal Christianity with KANAMORI, became professor of humanities at

Waseda (then called Tōkyō Senmon Gakkō)

OYABE Zen'ichirō. (n.d.) 小谷部全一郎. Hired by Day in 1922 as his secretary, arch-conservative politically, opportunist.

[R]

Rikugō Zasshi 六合雑誌 *Cosmos* periodical.

religion 宗教 *shūkyō*

Risshō Kōseikai (also Risshō Kōsei-kai, RKK) 立正佼成会. Lay Buddhist group, important member of IARF and WCRP (now Religions for Peace).

[S]

Saji Jitsunen 佐治実然 (1856-1920). New Buddhist, president of JUA and main preacher at Unity Hall from 1900-1909, fired by MacCauley in 1909.

seiza 正座 or 正坐 literally "proper sitting"

Senshin Gakuin 先進學院・先進学院--Institute (or School) for Advanced Learning (1894-1899)

Shakaishugi Kenkyu-kai 社会主義研究会 The Research Society of Socialism founded in Oct 1898 by Murai, ABE and KISHIMOTO, and joined by ANESAKI and many other from Unity Hall.

shinga 真我 true self

shōga 小我 small self

small self 小我 *shōga*

soul *tamashii* 魂

shūkyō 宗教 religion

shōga 小我 small self

soul 魂 *tamashii*

Socialism 社会主義 It was Christian socialism and Sermon on the Mount Christianity that was the hallmark of Unity Hall and the *yuniterian* movement.

St. John, Charles E. (n.d.) Secretary of AUA in 1900 when MacCauley puts mission property, especially Unity Hall, as "foreign owner," under his name, and is passed to his widow at his death.

SUZUKI Bunji 鈴木文治 (1885–1946) Second JUM and JUA secretary from 1911-17, founder of Yūaikai in 1912, national fame as lawyer and labor leader.

[T]

taiga 大我 great self

tamashii 魂 soul

Tōdai. See: Tōkyō Teikoku Daigaku. Imperial University of Tokyo.

Toitsu Krisuto Kōdōkai (or Kyōkai) Liberal Christian Association, new name for the Japanese Unitarian Association in 1909.

Tōkyō Teikoku Daigaku. Imperial University of Tokyo, often called Tōdai.

Tokyo Unitarian Church 帰一教会. Kiitsu Kyōkai. IMAOKA's "Return to the One" fellowship or church. Founded in 1948.

TOYOSAKI Zennosuke (1873–n.d.) 豐崎善之介・豊崎善之介 Christian Socialist at Unity Hall, wrote "Gospel of Socialism" (*Shakai shugi no fukuin*).

trikaya three bodies of the Buddha: *dharmakaya* ("doctrinal or essential body"), *sambhogakaya* ("bliss or communal body"), *nirmanakaya* ("transformation body").

true self 真我 *shinga*

Tsubaki Grand Shrine. 椿大神社 Member of JFRA and IARF.

[U]

UCHIGASAKI Sakusaburō 内ケ崎作三郎 (1877-1947). Manchester trained Unitarian minister, professor of English at Waseda. Eventually set up independent Liberal Christian church in Kanda district.

UCHIMURA Kanzō 内村 鑑三 (1861–1930). Leader in the Kumi-ai Christian movement, would not bow to picture of Emperor.

UEMURA Masahisa 植村正久 (1858-1925). Leader in the Kumi-ai Christian movement.

Unity Hall 唯一館 Headquarters of the Unitarian Mission in Tokyo, the building was a gift from Unitarians around the world.

universal 普遍的 *fuhenteki*

[W]

Wendte, Charles W. (1844-1931). He initially opposed the Japan Mission but later headed both AUA foreign affairs and the IARF.

Wigmore, John Henry (1863-1943) Professor of Law at Keiō from 1889-92)

Wilkes, Paget (n.d.). Anglican missionary who converted IMAOKA to Christianity.

Williams, Henry M. (n.d.) AUA Treasurer and lawyer who oversaw selling of Unity Hall in 1923 or later, and returns money to America.

[Y]

YAMAMOTO Yukitaka 山本行隆 (1923–2002) (39th High Priest of Tsubaki Grand Shrine)

YAMAMOTO Yukiteru 山本行輝 (1888–1971) (38th High Priest of Tsubaki Grand Shrine)

YAMAMOTO Yukiyasu 山本行恭 (1952–) (current and 40th High Priest of

Tsubaki Grand Shrine).

YANO Fumio 矢野文雄 [also known as YANO Ryūkei 矢野竜渓] (1850-1931) Japanese journalist who first writes about Unitarianism

YOKOI Tokio 横井時雄 (1857–1928) Former Congregationalist who called for the destruction of old theologies in 1894.

Yūaikai (also Yūai Kai) 友愛会 Friendly Society 友愛會.

Note: I wish to express deep gratitude for the assistance with this Glossary provided by Michel Mohr, Professor of Japanese Religion, Department of Religion, The University of Hawaii.

About the Author

George M. Williams is a Professor Emeritus of religious studies at California State University, Chico. He was awarded a Ph.D. from the University of Iowa in 1972, specializing in religions in modern India. After retirement he held a research chair at the National Institute for Advanced Studies in India, taught twice on Semester At Sea, lectured extensively and published about Asian religions – including, *Handbook of Hindu Mythology* (2002) and *Shinto* (2004). While a Visiting Professor at the University of Hawai'i, Williams has become an archivist for Hawaiian indigenous religion, Kanenuiakea.

Williams was fortunate enough to know personally and work with some of the major religious leaders of 20th century Japan, including Dr. IMAOKA Shin'ichirō, President-Founder NIWANO of Rissho Kosei-kai, and Rev. Dr. YAMAMOTO. For his contributions toward inter-religious understanding and cooperation, the American Chapter of IARF presented Williams a Distinguished Service Award in 1989. His work with liberal and liberating religions of Asia led to the award of *Litterarum Humanorum Doctor* from Starr King School for the Ministry, Berkeley, California in 1994, and *Doctor Honoris Causa* from the United Protestant Theological School of Kolozsvár [Cluj], Romania in 1996.

Currently living in Wai'anae, Hawai'i, Williams was *hanai*-ed (adopted) into the Hawaiian community. He helped the indigenous faith, Kanenuiakea, become a member of the International Association for Religions Freedom (IARF).

Index

Made in the USA
Las Vegas, NV
30 December 2020

15048771R00226